METHODIST
HYMNS OLD & NEW

Compiled by
Revd Peter Bolt
Revd Amos Cresswell
Mrs Tracey Harding
Revd Raymond Short

Acknowledgements

The publishers wish to express their gratitude to the copyright holders who have granted permission to include their material in this book.

Every effort has been made to trace the copyright holders of all the songs in this collection and we hope that no copyright has been infringed. Apology is made and pardon sought if the contrary be the case, and a correction will be made in any reprint of this book.

Important Copyright Information

We would like to remind users of this hymnal that the reproduction of any song texts or music without the permission of the copyright holder is illegal. Details of all copyright holders are clearly indicated under each song.

Many of the song *texts* may be covered either by a Christian Copyright Licensing (CCL) licence or a Calamus licence. If you possess a CCL or Calamus licence, it is essential that you check your instruction manual to ensure that the song you wish to use is covered.

If you are *not* a member of CCL or Calamus, or the song you wish to reproduce is not covered by your licence, you must contact the copyright holder direct for their permission.

Christian Copyright Licensing (Europe) Ltd., have also now introduced a *Music Reproduction Licence*. Again, if you hold such a licence it is essential that you check your instruction manual to ensure that the song you wish to reproduce is covered. The reproduction of any music not covered by your licence is both illegal and immoral.

If you are interested in joining CCL or Calamus they can be contacted at the following addresses:

Christian Copyright Licensing (Europe) Ltd. P.O. Box 1339, Eastbourne, East Sussex. BN 21 1AD.
Tel: 01323 417711, Fax: 01323 417722

Calamus, 30 North Terrace, Mildenhall, Suffolk, IP28 7AB.
Tel: 01638 716579, Fax: 01638 510390.

First published in Great Britain in 2001 by
KEVIN MAYHEW LIMITED
Buxhall, Stowmarket
Suffolk IP14 3BW

Compilation © Kevin Mayhew Ltd 2001

The right of Peter Bolt, Amos Cresswell, Tracey Harding and Raymond Short to be identified as the compilers and editors of this work has been asserted by them in accordance with the Copyright, Designs and Patents Act 1988.

The following editions are available.

Words edition	Catalogue No.1413171	
	ISBN No. 1 84003 674 5	ISMN No. M 57004 810 6
Organ/choir	Catalogue No. 1413174	
	ISBN No. 1 84003 675 3	ISMN No. M 57004 811 3

FOREWORD

The hymns we sing reflect our faith and the characteristics of our faith. This is, perhaps, particularly true of Methodists. The 1934 *Methodist Hymn Book* opened with the words 'Methodism was born in song'. Thus, when we were invited by Kevin Mayhew early in 2000 to help with a book, *Methodist Hymns Old and New*, we felt both the honour and the weight of the task.

Hymns know no denominational barriers. While owing much to the vast treasury of Charles Wesley, whose hymns are a repository of Methodist theology, the hymns which Methodists sing are drawn from many strains and countries. We have remembered the boisterous exuberance enjoyed, particularly perhaps, by the Primitive Methodists; we have respected the German influence which gripped John Wesley; we recall that many Methodist ministers have written verses for particular occasions – and therein is a wealth of hymnody barely known and hardly touched; we were brought up to date with much of the modern generation of hymns by the youngest member of our team.

The 1780 *Wesley's Hymns* has been used as the authoritative text, although some great Wesley hymns were not included in that volume. We have followed John Wesley's strictures on honouring the author's original words as far as possible. Indeed with some hymns we have deliberately left the words used by Wesley, when a more modern word might have been possible, because the original has a firm place in the history and theology of Methodism. 'Inclusive language' is a modern concept and fits modern hymns, but we are satisfied that people understand the generic terms 'man' and 'mankind' and are prepared to sing them in older hymns.

We have recovered some great hymns, such as 'Hark! the Gospel news is sounding', which, sung to *Grace*, was known as 'the marching song of Primitive Methodism', and 'Depth of mercy', Charles Wesley's great penitential hymn.

Most Methodist churches nowadays use a variety of hymn books. We hope that this attempt to gather together the best (with a few looks to the future) will be both an accurate reflection of Methodism and a useful tool for groups, large and small.

PETER BOLT
AMOS CRESSWELL
TRACEY HARDING
RAYMOND SHORT

CONTENTS

CONTENTS

HYMNS AND SONGS

1

Dave Bilbrough
© 1977 Kingsway's Thankyou Music

Abba, Father, let me be
yours and yours alone.
May my will for ever be
more and more your own.
Never let my heart grow cold,
never let me go.
Abba, Father, let me be
yours and yours alone.

2

Henry Francis Lyte (1793-1847)

1. Abide with me,
   fast falls the eventide;
   the darkness deepens;
   Lord, with me abide:
   when other helpers fail,
   and comforts flee,
   help of the helpless,
   O abide with me.

2. Swift to its close
   ebbs out life's little day;
   earth's joys grow dim,
   its glories pass away;
   change and decay
   in all around I see;
   O thou who changest not,
   abide with me.

3. I need thy presence
   ev'ry passing hour;
   what but thy grace can foil
   the tempter's pow'r?
   Who like thyself my guide
   and stay can be?
   Through cloud and sunshine,
   Lord, abide with me.

4. I fear no foe
   with thee at hand to bless;
   ills have no weight,
   and tears no bitterness.
   Where is death's sting?
   Where, grave, thy victory?
   I triumph still,
   if thou abide with me.

5. Hold thou thy cross
   before my closing eyes;
   shine through the gloom,
   and point me to the skies;
   heav'n's morning breaks,
   and earth's vain shadows flee;
   in life, in death, O Lord,
   abide with me.

3

James Montgomery (1771-1854)

1. According to thy gracious word,
   in meek humility,
   this will I do, my dying Lord,
   I will remember thee.

2. Thy body, broken for my sake,
   my bread from heaven shall be;
   thy testamental cup I take,
   and thus remember thee.

3. When to the cross I turn mine eyes,
   and rest on Calvary,
   O Lamb of God, my sacrifice,
   I must remember thee –

4. Remember thee, and all thy pains,
   and all thy love to me;
   yea, while a breath, a pulse remains,
   will I remember thee.

5. And when these failing lips grow dumb,
   and mind and memory flee,
   when thou shalt in thy kingdom come,
   Jesus, remember me.

4

Charles Wesley (1707-1788) alt.

1. A charge to keep I have:
   a God to glorify;
   a never-dying soul to save,
   and fit it for the sky.

2. To serve the present age,
   my calling to fulfil; –
   O may it all my powers engage
   to do my Master's will!

Continued overleaf

3. Arm me with jealous care,
   as in thy sight to live;
   and O thy servant, Lord , prepare
   a strict account to give!

4. Help me to watch and pray,
   and on thyself rely,
   so shall I not my trust betray,
   and so I shall not die.

5 St Germanus (c. 634-c. 734) trans.
John Mason Neale (1818-1866)

1. A great and mighty wonder,
   a full and holy cure!
   The Virgin bears the infant
   with virgin-honour pure:

   Repeat the hymn again!
   'To God on high be glory,
   and peace on earth shall reign.'

2. The Word becomes incarnate,
   and yet remains on high;
   and cherubim sing anthems
   to shepherds from the sky:

3. While thus they sing your monarch,
   those bright angelic bands,
   rejoice, ye vales and mountains,
   ye oceans, clap your hands:

4. Since all he comes to ransom
   by all be he adored,
   the infant born in Bethl'em,
   the Saviour and the Lord:

6 Robert Bridges (1844-1930) from J. Heerman (1585-1647)
alt. based on an 11th century Latin meditation

1. Ah, holy Jesu,
   how hast thou offended,
   that so to judge thee
   mortals have pretended?
   By foes derided,
   by thine own rejected,
   O most afflicted.

2. Who was the guilty?
   Who brought this upon thee?
   Alas, O Lord,
   my treason hath undone thee.
   'Twas I, Lord Jesu,
   I it was denied thee:
   I crucified thee.

3. Lo, the good shepherd
   for the sheep is offered;
   the slave hath sinnèd,
   and the Son hath suffered;
   for our atonement
   Christ himself is pleading,
   still interceding.

4. For me, kind Jesu,
   was thy incarnation,
   thy mortal sorrow,
   and thy life's oblation;
   thy death of anguish
   and thy bitter passion,
   for my salvation.

5. Therefore, kind Jesu,
   since I cannot pay thee,
   I do adore thee,
   and will ever pray thee,
   think on thy pity
   and thy love unswerving,
   not my deserving.

7 Venerable Bede (673-735)
trans. *Lutheran Book of Worship* (1978)

1. A hymn of glory let us sing!
   New hymns throughout the world shall
      ring.
   Alleluia! Alleluia!
   Christ, by a road before untrod,
   ascends unto the throne of God.

   Alleluia! (x5)

2. The holy apostolic band
   upon the Mount of Olives stand.
   Alleluia! Alleluia!
   And with his faithful followers see
   their Lord ascend in majesty.

3. To whom the shining angels cry,
   'Why stand and gaze upon the sky?'
   Alleluia! Alleluia!
   'This is the Saviour!' Thus they say,
   'This is his glorious triumph day!'

4. O risen Christ, ascended Lord,
   all praise to you let earth accord;
   Alleluia! Alleluia!
   You are, while endless ages run,
   with Father and with Spirit one.

8 William Henry Draper (1855-1933) alt.
© J. Curwen & Sons Ltd.

1. All creatures of our God and King,
   lift up your voice and with us sing
   alleluia, alleluia!
   Thou burning sun with golden beam,
   thou silver moon with softer gleam:

   O praise him, O praise him,
   alleluia, alleluia, alleluia!

2. Thou rushing wind that art so strong,
   ye clouds that sail in heav'n along,
   O praise him, alleluia!
   Thou rising morn, in praise rejoice,
   ye lights of evening, find a voice:

3. Thou flowing water, pure and clear,
   make music for thy Lord to hear,
   alleluia, alleluia!
   Thou fire so masterful and bright,
   that givest us both warmth and light:

4. Dear mother earth, who day by day
   unfoldest blessings on our way,
   O praise him, alleluia!
   The flow'rs and fruits that in thee grow,
   let them his glory also show.

5. All you with mercy in your heart,
   forgiving others, take your part,
   O sing ye, alleluia!
   Ye who long pain and sorrow bear,
   praise God and on him cast your care:

6. And thou, most kind and gentle death,
   waiting to hush our latest breath,
   O praise him, alleluia!
   Thou leadest home the child of God,
   and Christ our Lord the way hath trod:

7. Let all things their Creator bless,
   and worship him in humbleness,
   O praise him, alleluia!
   Praise, praise the Father, praise the Son,
   and praise the Spirit, Three in One.

9 vs. 1-4: unknown, vs. 5-7: Damian Lundy (b. 1944-1997)
© Additional words 1996, 1999 Kevin Mayhew Ltd.

1. Alleluia . . .

2. Jesus is Lord . . .

3. And I love him . . .

4. Christ is risen . . .

Additional verses may be composed to suit
the occasion. For example:

5. Send your Spirit . . .

6. Abba, Father . . .

7. Come, Lord Jesus . . .

10 Donald Fishel (b. 1950)
© 1973 Word of God Music. Administered by CopyCare

Alleluia, alleluia,
give thanks to the risen Lord,
alleluia, alleluia, give praise to his name.

1. Jesus is Lord of all the earth.
   He is the King of creation.

2. Spread the good news o'er all the earth.
   Jesus has died and is risen.

3. We have been crucified with Christ.
   Now we shall live for ever.

4. God has proclaimed the just reward:
   'Life for us all, alleluia!'

5. Come, let us praise the living God,
   joyfully sing to our Saviour.

11
Christopher Wordsworth (1807-1885)

1. Alleluia, alleluia,
   hearts to heav'n and voices raise;
   sing to God a hymn of gladness,
   sing to God a hymn of praise:
   he who on the cross a victim
   for the world's salvation bled,
   Jesus Christ, the King of Glory,
   now is risen from the dead.

2. Christ is risen, Christ the first-fruits
   of the holy harvest field,
   which will all its full abundance
   at his second coming yield;
   then the golden ears of harvest
   will their heads before him wave,
   ripened by his glorious sunshine,
   from the furrows of the grave.

3. Christ is risen, we are risen;
   shed upon us heav'nly grace,
   rain, and dew, and gleams of glory
   from the brightness of thy face;
   that we, with our hearts in heaven,
   here on earth may fruitful be,
   and by angel-hands be gathered,
   and be ever, Lord, with thee.

4. Alleluia, alleluia,
   glory be to God on high;
   alleluia to the Saviour,
   who has gained the victory;
   alleluia to the Spirit,
   fount of love and sanctity;
   alleluia, alleluia,
   to the Triune Majesty.

12
Job Hupton (1762-1849), John Mason Neale (1818-1866) alt. © Jubilate Hymns

1. Alleluia! raise the anthem,
   let the skies resound with praise;
   sing to Christ who paid our ransom,
   Ancient of eternal days,
   God eternal, Word incarnate,
   whom the heaven of heaven obeys.

2. Long before he formed the mountains,
   spread the seas or made the sky,
   love eternal, free and boundless,
   moved the Lord of life to die;
   fore-ordained the Prince of princes
   for the throne of Calvary.

3. There for us and our redemption
   see him all his life-blood pour:
   there he wins our full salvation,
   dies that we may die no more –
   then arising lives for ever,
   King of kings whom we adore.

4. Now above the vast creation,
   high in God's all-holy light,
   there he lives and reigns in triumph,
   bears the marks of mortal fight;
   there his own, redeemed for ever,
   sing in wonder day and night.

5. Praise and honour to the Father,
   praise and honour to the Son,
   praise and honour to the Spirit
   ever Three and ever One;
   one in grace and one in glory
   while eternal ages run!

13
William Chatterton Dix (1837-1898) alt.
© This version 1999 Kevin Mayhew Ltd.

1. Alleluia, sing to Jesus,
   his the sceptre, his the throne;
   alleluia, his the triumph,
   his the victory alone:
   hark, the songs of peaceful Sion
   thunder like a mighty flood:
   Jesus, out of ev'ry nation,
   hath redeemed us by his blood.

2. Alleluia, not as orphans
   are we left in sorrow now;
   alleluia, he is near us,
   faith believes, nor questions how;
   though the cloud from sight received him
   when the forty days were o'er,
   shall our hearts forget his promise,
   'I am with you evermore'?

3. Alleluia, bread of angels,
   here on earth our food, our stay;
   alleluia, here the sinful
   come to you from day to day.
   Intercessor, friend of sinners,
   earth's redeemer, plead for me,
   where the songs of all the sinless
   sweep across the crystal sea.

4. Alleluia, King eternal,
   he the Lord of lords we own;
   alleluia, born of Mary,
   earth his footstool, heav'n his throne;
   he within the veil has entered
   robed in flesh, our great High Priest;
   he on earth both priest and victim
   in the Eucharistic Feast.

14 William John Sparrow-Simpson (1859-1952) alt.
© *Novello & Co. Ltd.*

1. All for Jesus! All for Jesus!
   This our song shall ever be;
   for we have no hope nor Saviour
   if we have not hope in thee.

2. All for Jesus! thou wilt give us
   strength to serve thee hour by hour;
   none can move us from thy presence
   while we trust thy love and pow'r.

3. All for Jesus! at thine altar
   thou dost give us sweet content;
   there, dear Saviour, we receive thee
   in thy holy sacrament.

4. All for Jesus! thou hast loved us,
   all for Jesus! thou hast died,
   all for Jesus! thou art with us,
   all for Jesus! glorified!

5. All for Jesus! All for Jesus!
   This the Church's song shall be,
   till at last the flock is gathered
   one in love, and one in thee.

15 St Theodulph of Orleans (d. 821)
trans. John Mason Neale (1818-1866)

All glory, laud and honour,
to thee, Redeemer King,
to whom the lips of children
made sweet hosannas ring.

1. Thou art the King of Israel,
   thou David's royal Son,
   who in the Lord's name comest,
   the King and blessed one.

2. The company of angels
   are praising thee on high,
   and mortals, joined with all things
   created, make reply.

3. The people of the Hebrews
   with palms before thee went:
   our praise and prayer and anthems
   before thee we present.

4. To thee before thy passion
   they sang their hymns of praise:
   to thee now high exalted
   our melody we raise.

5. Thou didst accept their praises,
   accept the prayers we bring,
   who in all good delightest,
   thou good and gracious king.

16 Charles Wesley (1707-1788)

1. All glory to God in the sky,
   and peace upon earth be restored!
   O Jesus, exalted on high,
   appear our omnipotent Lord!
   Who, meanly in Bethlehem born,
   didst stoop to redeem a lost race,
   once more to thy creatures return,
   and reign in thy kingdom of grace.

Continued overleaf

2. When thou in our flesh didst appear,
   all nature acknowledged thy birth;
   arose the acceptable year,
   and heaven was opened on earth;
   receiving its Lord from above,
   the world was united to bless
   the giver of concord and love,
   the prince and the author of peace.

3. O wouldst thou again be made known!
   Again in thy Spirit descend,
   and set up in each of thine own
   a kingdom that never shall end.
   Thou only art able to bless,
   and make the glad nations obey,
   and bid the dire enmity cease,
   and bow the whole world to thy sway.

4. Come then to thy servants again,
   who long thy appearing to know;
   thy quiet and peaceable reign
   in mercy establish below;
   all sorrow before thee shall fly,
   and anger and hatred be o'er,
   and envy and malice shall die,
   and discord afflict us no more.

17 Dave Bilbrough
© 1988 Kingsway's Thankyou Music

All hail the Lamb, enthroned on high;
his praise shall be our battle cry;
he reigns victorious, for ever glorious,
his name is Jesus, he is the Lord.

18 Edward Perronet (1726-1792)
adapted by Michael Forster (b. 1946)
© This version 1999 Kevin Mayhew Ltd.

1. All hail the pow'r of Jesus' name,
   let angels prostrate fall;
   bring forth the royal diadem

   and crown him, crown him, crown him,
   crown him Lord of all.

2. Crown him, all martyrs of your God,
   who from his altar call;
   praise him whose way of pain you trod,
   and crown him . . .

3. O prophets faithful to his word,
   in matters great and small,
   who made his voice of justice heard,
   now crown him . . .

4. All sinners, now redeemed by grace,
   who heard your Saviour's call,
   now robed in light before his face,
   O crown him . . .

5. Let every tribe and every race
   who heard the freedom call,
   in liberation, see Christ's face,
   and crown him . . .

6. Let every people, every tongue
   to him their heart enthral:
   lift high the universal song
   and crown him . . .

19 Tricia Richards
© 1987 Kingsway's Thankyou Music

1. All heav'n declares
   the glory of the risen Lord.
   Who can compare
   with the beauty of the Lord?
   For ever he will be
   the Lamb upon the throne.
   I gladly bow the knee
   and worship him alone.

2. I will proclaim
   the glory of the risen Lord.
   Who once was slain
   to reconcile us all to God.
   For ever you will be
   the Lamb upon the throne.
   I gladly bow the knee
   and worship you alone.

20 Graham Kendrick (b. 1950), based on Philippians 3:8-12
© 1993 Make Way Music

1. All I once held dear, built my life upon,
   all this world reveres, and wars to own,
   all I once thought gain I have
      counted loss;
   spent and worthless now, compared
      to this.

Knowing you, Jesus, knowing you,
there is no greater thing.
You're my all, you're the best,
you're my joy, my righteousness,
and I love you, Lord.

2. Now my heart's desire is to know
     you more,
   to be found in you and known as yours.
   To possess by faith what I could not earn,
   all-surpassing gift of righteousness.

3. Oh, to know the pow'r of your risen life,
   and to know you in your sufferings.
   To become like you in your death,
     my Lord,
   so with you to live and never die.

21 Paul Gerhardt (1607-1676)
Trans Catherine Winkworth (1827-1878)

1. All my heart this night rejoices,
   as I hear,
   far and near,
   sweetest angel voices:
   'Christ is born!' their choirs are singing,
   till the air
   everywhere
   now with joy is ringing.

2. Hark, a voice from yonder manger,
   soft and sweet,
   doth entreat,
   'Flee from woe and danger;
   come, O come; from all doth grieve you
   you are freed,
   all you need
   I will surely give you'.

3. Come then, let us hasten yonder;
   here let all,
   great and small,
   kneel in awe and wonder;
   love him who with love is yearning;
   hail the star
   that from far
   bright with hope is burning!

4. Thee, O Lord, with heed I'll cherish,
   live to thee,
   and with thee
   dying, shall not perish;
   but shall dwell with thee for ever,
   far on high,
   in the joy
   that can alter never.

22 Robert Bridges (1844-1930) alt. based on 'Meine
Hoffnung stehet feste' by Joachim Neander (1650-1680)

1. All my hope on God is founded;
   he doth still my trust renew.
   Me through change and chance
     he guideth,
   only good and only true.
   God unknown, he alone
   calls my heart to be his own.

2. Human pride and earthly glory,
   sword and crown betray his trust;
   what with care and toil he buildeth,
   tow'r and temple, fall to dust.
   But God's pow'r, hour by hour,
   is my temple and my tow'r.

3. God's great goodness aye endureth,
   deep his wisdom, passing thought:
   splendour, light and life attend him,
   beauty springeth out of naught.
   Evermore, from his store,
   new-born worlds rise and adore.

4. Still from earth to God eternal
   sacrifice of praise be done,
   high above all praises praising
   for the gift of Christ his Son.
   Christ doth call one and all:
   ye who follow shall not fall.

23 Roy Turner (b. 1940)
© 1984 Kingsway's Thankyou Music

1. All over the world the Spirit is moving,
   all over the world,
   as the prophets said it would be.
   All over the world there's a mighty
      revelation
   of the glory of the Lord,
   as the waters cover the sea.

2. All over this land the Spirit is
      moving . . .

3. All over the Church the Spirit is
      moving . . .

4. All over us all the Spirit is
      moving . . .

5. Deep down in my heart the Spirit
      is moving . . .

24 Terry Butler
© 1995 Mercy/Vineyard Publishing. Administered by CopyCare

All over the world,
all over the world,
your Spirit is moving
all over the world.

1. Your river is flowing,
   your presence has come,
   your Spirit is moving
   all over the world.
   You're touching the nations,
   you're bringing us love,
   your Spirit is moving
   all over the world.
   You're touching the nations,
   you're bringing us love,
   your Spirit is moving
   all over the world.

2. Your banner is lifted,
   your praises are sung,
   your Spirit is moving
   all over the world.
   Divisions are falling,
   you're making us one,
   your Spirit is moving
   all over the world.
   Divisions are falling,
   you're making us one,
   your Spirit is moving
   all over the world.

25 William Kethe (d. 1594) from Day's Psalter (1560) alt.

1. All people that on earth do dwell,
   sing to the Lord with cheerful voice;
   him serve with fear, his praise forth tell,
   come ye before him and rejoice.

2. The Lord, ye know, is God indeed,
   without our aid he did us make;
   we are his folk, he doth us feed
   and for his sheep he doth us take.

3. O enter then his gates with praise,
   approach with joy his courts unto;
   praise, laud and bless his name always,
   for it is seemly so to do.

4. For why? the Lord our God is good:
   his mercy is for ever sure;
   his truth at all times firmly stood,
   and shall from age to age endure.

5. To Father, Son and Holy Ghost,
   the God whom heav'n and earth adore,
   from us and from the angel-host
   be praise and glory evermore.

26 Charles Wesley (1707-1788)

1. All praise to our redeeming Lord,
   who joins us by his grace,
   and bids us, each to each restored,
   together seek his face.

2. He bids us build each other up;
   and, gathered into one,
   to our high calling's glorious hope
   we hand in hand go on.

3. The gift which he on one bestows,
   we all delight to prove;
   the grace through every vessel flows,
   in purest streams of love.

4. Ev'n now we think and speak the same,
   and cordially agree;
   concentred all, through Jesu's name,
   in perfect harmony.

5. We all partake the joy of one,
   the common peace we feel,
   a peace to sensual minds unknown,
   a joy unspeakable.

6. And if our fellowship below
   in Jesus be so sweet,
   what heights of rapture shall we know
   when round his throne we meet!

27 Cecil Frances Alexander (1818-1895)

All things bright and beautiful,
all creatures great and small,
all things wise and wonderful,
the Lord God made them all.

1. Each little flow'r that opens,
   each little bird that sings,
   he made their glowing colours,
   he made their tiny wings.

2. The purple-headed mountain,
   the river running by,
   the sunset and the morning
   that brightens up the sky.

3. The cold wind in the winter,
   the pleasant summer sun,
   the ripe fruits in the garden,
   he made them every one.

4. The tall trees in the greenwood,
   the meadows for our play,
   the rushes by the water,
   to gather ev'ry day.

5. He gave us eyes to see them,
   and lips that we might tell
   how great is God Almighty,
   who has made all things well.

28 George William Conder (1821-1874)

1. All things praise thee, Lord most high;
   heaven and earth and sea and sky,
   all were for thy glory made,
   that thy greatness thus displayed
   should all worship bring to thee;
   all things praise thee: Lord, may we.

2. All things praise thee; night to night
   sings in silent hymns of light;
   all things praise thee; day to day
   chants thy power, in burning ray;
   time and space are praising thee;
   all things praise thee: Lord, may we.

3. All things praise thee; round her zones
   earth, with her ten thousand tones,
   rolls a ceaseless choral strain;
   roaring wind and deep-voiced main,
   rustling leaf and humming bee,
   all things praise thee: Lord, may we.

4. All things praise thee; high and low,
   rain and dew and seven-hued bow,
   crimson sunset, fleecy cloud,
   rippling stream and tempest loud,
   summer, winter, all to thee
   glory render: Lord, may we.

5. All things praise thee; gracious Lord,
   great Creator, powerful Word,
   omnipresent Spirit, now
   at thy feet we humbly bow,
   lift our hearts in praise to thee;
   all things praise thee: Lord, may we.

29

Charles Wesley (1707-1788) alt.

1. All ye that pass by,
   to Jesus draw nigh:
   to you is it nothing that Jesus
      should die?
   Your ransom and peace
   your surety he is:
   come, see if there ever was sorrow
      like his.

2. He answered for all:
   O come at his call,
   and low at his cross with astonishment
      fall!
   But lift up your eyes
   at Jesus's cries;
   impassive, he suffers; immortal,
      he dies.

3. He dies to atone
   for sins not his own;
   your debt he hath paid, and your
   work he hath done.
   Ye all may receive
   the peace he did leave,
   who made intercession: my Father,
      forgive!

4. For you and for me
   he prayed on the tree:
   the prayer is accepted, the sinner
      is free.
   That sinner am I,
   who on Jesus rely,
   and come for the pardon God
      cannot deny.

5. My pardon I claim;
   for a sinner I am,
   a sinner believing in Jesus's name.
   He purchased the grace
   which now I embrace:
   O Father, thou know'st he hath
   died in my place.

30

John Howard Bertram Masterman (1867-1933) alt.
© Copyright Control

1. Almighty Father, who dost give
   the gift of life to all who live,
   look down on all earth's sin and strife,
   and lift us to a nobler life.

2. Lift up our hearts, O King of kings,
   to brighter hopes and kindlier things,
   to visions eyes can never see,
   and dreams of pure community.

3. Thy world is weary of its pain,
   of selfish greed and fruitless gain,
   of tarnished honour, falsely strong,
   and all its ancient deeds of wrong.

4. Hear thou the prayer thy servants pray,
   uprising from all lands today,
   and o'er the vanquished powers of sin
   O bring thy great salvation in.

31

Christopher Ellis (b. 1949)
© 1999 Kevin Mayhew Ltd.

1. Almighty God, we come to make
      confession,
   for we have sinned in thought and
      word and deed.
   We now repent in honesty and sorrow;
   forgive us, Lord, and meet us in
      our need.

2. Forgiving God, I come to make
      confession
   of all the harm and hurt that
      I have done;
   of bitter words and many selfish
      actions,
   forgive me, Lord, and make me
      like your Son.

3. Forgiving God, I come to make
     confession
   of all that I have failed to do this day;
   of help withheld, concern and
       love restricted,
   forgive me, Lord, and lead me in
       your way.

4. Redeeming God, we come to seek
     forgiveness,
   for Jesus Christ has died to set us free.
   Forgive the past and fill us with
       your Spirit
   that we may live to serve you joyfully.

32 Somerset Corry Lowry (1855-1932)
© Oxford University Press

1. A man there lived in Galilee
   like none who lived before,
   for he alone from first to last
   our flesh unsullied wore;
   a perfect life of perfect deeds
   once to the world was shown,
   that people all might mark his steps
   and in them plant their own.

2. A man there died on Calvary
   above all others brave;
   the human race he saved and blessed,
   himself he scorned to save.
   No thought can gauge the weight
     of woe
   on him, the sinless, laid;
   we only know that with his blood
   our ransom price was paid.

3. A man there reigns in glory now,
   divine, yet human still;
   that human which is all divine
   death sought in vain to kill.
   All pow'r is his; supreme he rules
   the realms of time and space;
   yet still our human cares and needs
   find in his heart a place.

33 vs. 1-4: John Newton (1725-1807) alt.
v. 5: John Rees (1828-1900)

1. Amazing grace! How sweet the sound
   that saved a wretch like me.
   I once was lost, but now I'm found;
   was blind, but now I see.

2. 'Twas grace that taught my heart to fear,
   and grace my fears relieved.
   How precious did that grace appear
   the hour I first believed.

3. Through many dangers, toils and snares
   I have already come.
   'Tis grace that brought me safe thus far,
   and grace will lead me home.

4. The Lord has promised good to me,
   his word my hope secures;
   he will my shield and portion be
   as long as life endures.

5. When we've been there a thousand years,
   bright shining as the sun,
   we've no less days to sing God's praise
   than when we first begun.

34 Charles Wesley (1707-1788)

1. And are we yet alive,
   and see each other's face?
   Glory and praise to Jesus give
   for his redeeming grace!

2. Preserved by power divine
   to full salvation here,
   again in Jesus' praise we join,
   and in his sight appear.

3. What troubles have we seen,
   what conflicts have we passed,
   fightings without, and fears within,
   since we assembled last!

Continued overleaf

4. But out of all the Lord
   hath brought us by his love;
   and still he doth his help afford,
   and hides our life above.

5. Then let us make our boast
   of his redeeming pow'r,
   which saves us to the uttermost,
   till we can sin no more:

6. Let us take up the cross,
   till we the crown obtain;
   and gladly reckon all thing loss,
   so we may Jesus gain.

   Doxology
   Praise ye the Lord, alleluia!
   Praise ye the Lord, alleluia!
   Alleluia, alleluia, alleluia,
   praise ye the Lord!

35 Charles Wesley (1707-1788)

1. And can it be that I should gain
   an int'rest in the Saviour's blood?
   Died he for me, who caused his pain?
   For me, who him to death pursued?
   Amazing love! How can it be
   that thou, my God, shouldst die
     for me?

   *Amazing love! How can it be
   that thou, my God, shouldst die
   for me?*

2. 'Tis myst'ry all! th'Immortal dies:
   who can explore his strange design?
   In vain the first-born seraph tries
   to sound the depths of love divine!
   'Tis mercy all! Let earth adore,
   let angel minds inquire no more.

3. He left his Father's throne above
   so free, so infinite his grace;
   emptied himself of all but love,
   and bled for Adam's helpless race;
   'tis mercy all, immense and free;
   for, O my God, it found out me.

4. Long my imprisoned spirit lay
   fast bound in sin and nature's night;
   thine eye diffused a quick'ning ray,
   I woke, the dungeon flamed with light;
   my chains fell off, my heart was free;
   I rose, went forth, and followed thee.

5. No condemnation now I dread;
   Jesus, and all in him, is mine!
   Alive in him, my living Head,
   and clothed in righteousness divine,
   bold I approach the eternal throne,
   and claim the crown, through Christ
     my own.

36 Jean Ingelow (1820-1897) alt.

1. And didst thou love the race that loved
     not thee?
   And didst thou take to heaven a human
     brow?
   Dost plead with our voice by the
     marvellous sea?
   Art thou our kinsman now?

2. O God, O kinsman, loved, but not
     enough!
   O Man, with eyes majestic after death!
   Whose feet have toiled along our
     pathways rough,
   whose lips drawn human breath!

3. By that one likeness which is ours and
     thine,
   by that one nature which doth hold us
     kin,
   by that high heaven where, sinless, thou
     dost shine,
   to draw us sinners in;

4. By thy last silence in the judgement hall,
   by long foreknowledge of the deadly tree,
   by darkness, by the wormwood and the
     gall,
   I pray thee visit me.

5. Come, lest this heart should, cold and
    cast away,
die e'er the guest adored she entertain –
lest eyes that never saw thine earthly day
should miss thy heavenly reign.

37 William Blake (1757-1827)

1. And did those feet in ancient time
walk upon England's mountains green?
And was the holy Lamb of God
on England's pleasant pastures seen?
And did the countenance divine
shine forth upon our clouded hills?
And was Jerusalem builded here
among those dark satanic mills?

2. Bring me my bow of burning gold!
Bring me my arrows of desire!
Bring me my spear! O clouds unfold!
Bring me my chariot of fire!
I will not cease from mental fight,
nor shall my sword sleep in my hand,
till we have built Jerusalem
in England's green and pleasant land.

38 Graham Kendrick (b. 1950)
© 1991 Make Way Music

And he shall reign for ever,
his throne and crown shall ever endure.
And he shall reign for ever,
and we shall reign with him.

1. What a vision filled my eyes,
one like a Son of man.
Coming with the clouds of heav'n
he approached an awesome throne.

2. He was given sovereign power,
glory and authority.
Every nation, tribe and tongue
worshipped him on bended knee.

3. On the throne for ever,
see the Lamb who once was slain;
wounds of sacrificial love
for ever shall remain.

39 William Bright (1824-1901)

1. And now, O Father, mindful of the love
that bought us, once for all, on Calv'ry's
    tree,
and having with us him that pleads above,
we here present, we here spread forth to
    thee
that only off'ring perfect in thine eyes,
the one true, pure, immortal sacrifice.

2. Look, Father, look on his anointed face,
and only look on us as found in him;
look not on our misusings of thy grace,
our prayer so languid, and our faith so dim:
for lo, between our sins and their reward
we set the Passion of thy Son our Lord.

3. And then for those, our dearest and our
    best,
by this prevailing presence we appeal:
O fold them closer to thy mercy's breast,
O do thine utmost for their souls' true
    weal;
from tainting mischief keep them pure
    and clear,
and crown thy gifts with strength to
    persevere.

4. And so we come: O draw us to thy feet,
most patient Saviour, who canst love us still;
and by this food, so aweful and so sweet,
deliver us from ev'ry touch of ill:
in thine own service make us glad and
    free,
and grant us never more to part with thee.

40 v. 1: unknown, based on John 13:34-35
vs. 2-4: Aniceto Nazareth, based on John 15 and 1 Cor. 13
© 1984, 1999 Kevin Mayhew Ltd.

A new commandment I give unto you:
that you love one another as I have loved you,
that you love one another as I have loved you.

1. By this shall all know
that you are my disciples
if you have love one for another. *(Repeat)*

Continued overleaf

2. You are my friends
   if you do what I command you.
   Without my help you can do nothing.
   (Repeat)

   A new commandment I give unto you:
   that you love one another as I have loved you,
   that you love one another as I have loved you.

3. I am the true vine,
   my Father is the gard'ner.
   Abide in me: I will be with you. *(Repeat)*

4. True love is patient,
   not arrogant nor boastful;
   love bears all things, love is eternal.
   (Repeat)

41 James Montgomery (1771-1854)

1. Angels from the realms of glory,
   wing your flight o'er all the earth;
   ye who sang creation's story
   now proclaim Messiah's birth:

   Come and worship
   Christ, the new-born King;
   come and worship,
   worship Christ, the new-born King.

2. Shepherds, in the field abiding,
   watching o'er your flocks by night,
   God with us is now residing,
   yonder shines the infant Light:

3. Sages, leave your contemplations;
   brighter visions beam afar;
   seek the great Desire of Nations;
   ye have seen his natal star:

4. Saints before the altar bending,
   watching long in hope and fear,
   suddenly the Lord, descending,
   in his temple shall appear:

5. Though an infant now we view him,
   he shall fill his Father's throne,
   gather all the nations to him;
   ev'ry knee shall then bow down:

42 Francis Pott (1832-1909) alt.

1. Angel-voices ever singing
   round thy throne of light,
   angel-harps for ever ringing,
   rest not day nor night;
   thousands only live to bless thee,
   and confess thee Lord of might.

2. Thou who art beyond the farthest
   mortal eye can see,
   can it be that thou regardest
   our poor hymnody?
   Yes, we know that thou art near us
   and wilt hear us constantly.

3. Yea, we know that thou rejoicest
   o'er each work of thine;
   thou didst ears and hands and voices
   for thy praise design;
   craftsman's art and music's measure
   for thy pleasure all combine.

4. In thy house, great God, we offer
   of thine own to thee;
   and for thine acceptance proffer,
   all unworthily,
   hearts and minds and hands and voices
   in our choicest psalmody.

5. Honour, glory, might and merit
   thine shall ever be,
   Father, Son and Holy Spirit,
   blessèd Trinity.
   Of the best that thou hast given
   earth and heaven render thee.

43 Fred Pratt Green (1903-2000)
© 1974 Stainer & Bell Ltd.

1. An upper room did our Lord prepare
   for those he loved until the end:
   and his disciples still gather there,
   to celebrate their risen friend.

2. A lasting gift Jesus gave his own;
   to share his bread, his loving cup.
   Whatever burdens may bow us down,
   he by his cross shall lift us up.

3. And after supper he washed their feet
   for service, too, is sacrament.
   In him our joy shall be made
      complete –
   sent out to serve, as he was sent.

4. No end there is! We depart in peace,
   he loves beyond our uttermost:
   in ev'ry room in our Father's house
   he will be there, as Lord and host.

44 Timothy Dudley-Smith (b. 1926)
   © *Timothy Dudley-Smith*

1. A purple robe, a crown of thorn,
   a reed in his right hand;
   before the soldiers' spite and scorn
   I see my Saviour stand.

2. He bears between the Roman guard
   the weight of all our woe;
   a stumbling figure bowed and scarred
   I see my Saviour go.

3. Fast to the cross's spreading span,
   high in the sunlit air,
   all the unnumbered sins of man
   I see my Saviour bear.

4. He hangs, by whom the world was made,
   beneath the darkened sky;
   the ever-lasting ransom paid,
   I see my Saviour die.

5. He shares on high his Father's throne
   who once in mercy came;
   for all his love to sinners shown
   I sing my Saviour's name.

45 Charles Wesley (1707-1788) alt.

1. Arise, my soul, arise,
   shake off thy guilty fears;
   the bleeding sacrifice
   in my behalf appears:
   before the throne my surety stands;
   my name is written on his hands.

2. He ever lives above,
   for me to intercede,
   his all-redeeming love,
   his precious blood, to plead;
   his blood atoned for all our race,
   and sprinkles now the throne of grace.

3. Five bleeding wounds he bears,
   received on Calvary;
   they pour effectual prayers,
   they strongly speak for me:
   'Forgive him, O forgive!' they cry,
   'nor let that ransomed sinner die!'

4. The Father hears him pray,
   his dear anointed one;
   he cannot turn away
   the presence of his Son:
   his Spirit answers to the blood,
   and tells me I am born of God.

5. My God is reconciled,
   his pardoning voice I hear;
   he owns me for his child
   I can no longer fear.
   With confidence I now draw nigh,
   and 'Father, Abba, Father' cry.

46 Martin Luther (1483-1546)
   Trans Thomas Carlyle (1795-1881)
   v.4 alt. Rupert E. Davies (1909-1994)

1. A safe stronghold our God is still,
   a trusty shield and weapon;
   he'll help us clear from all the ill
   that hath us now o'ertaken.
   The ancient prince of hell
   hath risen with purpose fell;
   strong mail of craft and power
   he weareth in this hour;
   on earth is not his fellow.

Continued overleaf

2. With force of arms we nothing can,
   full soon were we down-ridden;
   but for us fights the proper Man,
   whom God himself hath bidden.
   Ask ye: Who is this same?
   Christ Jesus is his name,
   the Lord Sabaoth's Son;
   he, and no other one,
   shall conquer in the battle.

3. And were this world all devils o'er,
   and watching to devour us,
   we lay it not to heart so sore;
   not they can overpower us.
   And let the prince of ill
   look grim as e'er he will,
   he harms us not a whit;
   for why? His doom is writ;
   a word shall quickly slay him.

4. God's word, for all their craft and force,
   one moment will not linger,
   but, spite of hell, shall have its course;
   'tis written by his finger.
   And though before our eyes
   all that we dearly prize
   they seize beyond recall,
   yet is their profit small:
   God's kingdom ours remaineth.

47 Christopher Idle (b.1938)
© Christopher Idle/Jubilate Hymns

1. Ascended Christ, who gained
   the glory that we sing,
   anointed and ordained,
   our prophet, priest, and king:
   by many tongues
   the church displays
   your power and praise
   in all her songs.

2. No titles, thrones, or powers
   can ever rival yours;
   no passing mood of ours
   can turn aside your laws:
   you reign above
   each other name
   of worth or fame,
   the Lord of love.

3. Now from the Father's side
   you make your people new;
   since for our sins you died
   our lives belong to you:
   from our distress
   you set us free
   for purity
   and holiness.

4. You call us to belong
   within one body here;
   in weakness we are strong
   and all your gifts we share:
   in you alone
   we are complete
   and at your feet
   with joy bow down.

48 Peter West, Mary Lou Locke and Mary Kirkbride
© 1979 Peter West/Integrity's Hosanna! Music/Kingsway's Thankyou Music

Ascribe greatness to our God, the Rock,
his work is perfect and all his ways are
      just.
A God of faithfulness
and without injustice,
good and upright is he.

49 Brian A. Wren (b.1936)
© 1983 Stainer & Bell Ltd.

1. As man and woman we were made,
   that love be found and life begun;
   the likeness of the living God,
   unique, yet called to live as one.
   Through joy or sadness, calm or strife,
   come, praise the love that gives us life.

2. Now Jesus lived and gave his love
   to make our life and loving new;
   so celebrate with him today,
   and drink the joy he offers you
   that makes the simple moment shine
   and changes water into wine.

3. And Jesus died to live again;
   so praise the love that, come what may,
   can bring the dawn and clear the skies,
   and waits to wipe all tears away;
   and let us hope for what shall be,
   believing where we cannot see.

4. Then spread the table, clear the hall,
   and celebrate till day is done;
   let peace go deep between us all,
   and joy be shared by everyone:
   laugh and make merry with your friends,
   and praise the love that never ends!

50 Psalm 42 in 'New Version' (Tate and Brady, 1696)

1. As pants the hart for cooling streams
   when heated in the chase,
   so longs my soul, O God, for thee,
   and thy refreshing grace.

2. For thee, my God, the living God,
   my thirsty soul doth pine:
   O when shall I behold thy face,
   thou majesty divine?

3. Why restless, why cast down, my soul?
   hope still, and thou shalt sing
   the praise of him who is thy God,
   thy health's eternal spring.

4. To Father, Son and Holy Ghost,
   the God whom we adore,
   be glory, as it was, is now,
   and shall be evermore.

51 Robin Mark
© 1996 Daybreak Music Ltd.

1. As sure as gold is precious, and the honey
   sweet,
   so you love this city, and you love these
   streets.
   Ev'ry child out playing by their own front
   door,
   ev'ry baby lying on the bedroom floor.

   I hear that thunder in the distance,
   like a train on the edge of town,
   I can feel the brooding of your Spirit:
   lay your burdens down,
   lay your burdens down.
   Revive us, revive us, revive us with your fire.
   Revive us, revive us, revive us with your fire.

2. From the preacher preaching when the
   well is dry,
   to the lost soul reaching for a higher high.
   From the young man working through
   his hopes and fears,
   to the widow walking through the vale of
   tears.

3. Ev'ry man and woman, ev'ry old and
   young,
   ev'ry father's daughter, ev'ry mother's son;
   I feel it in my spirit, feel it in my bones,
   you're going to send revival, bring them
   all back home.

52 Richard Lewis (b. 1966)
© 1997 Kingsway's Thankyou Music

As the deer pants for the water,
so my soul, it thirsts for you,
for you, O God, for you, O God.
(Repeat)
When can I come before you
and see your face?
My heart and my flesh cry out
for the living God, for the living God.

Continued overleaf

Deep calls to deep
at the thunder of your waterfalls.
Your heart of love
is calling out to me.
By this I know that I am yours
and you are mine.
Your waves of love are breaking over me.
Your waves of love are breaking over me.
Your waves of love are breaking over me.

53 Martin Nystrom, based on Psalm 42:1-2
© 1983 Restoration Music Ltd.
Administered by Sovereign Music UK

1. As the deer pants for the water,
   so my soul longs after you.
   You alone are my heart's desire
   and I long to worship you.

   You alone are my strength, my shield,
   to you alone may my spirit yield.
   You alone are my heart's desire
   and I long to worship you.

2. I want you more than gold or silver,
   only you can satisfy.
   You alone are the real joy-giver
   and the apple of my eye.

3. You're my friend and you are my brother,
   even though you are a king.
   I love you more than any other,
   so much more than anything.

54 John Daniels
© 1979 Word's Spirit of Praise Music
Administered by CopyCare

As we are gathered, Jesus is here;
one with each other, Jesus is here;
joined by the Spirit, washed in the blood,
part of the body, the church of God.
As we are gathered, Jesus is here;
one with each other, Jesus is here.

55 William Chatterton Dix (1837-1898) alt.

1. As with gladness men of old
   did the guiding star behold,
   as with joy they hailed its light,
   leading onward, beaming bright;
   so, most gracious Lord, may we
   evermore be led to thee.

2. As with joyful steps they sped,
   to that lowly manger-bed,
   there to bend the knee before
   him whom heav'n and earth adore,
   so may we with willing feet
   ever seek thy mercy-seat.

3. As their precious gifts they laid,
   at thy manger roughly made,
   so may we with holy joy,
   pure, and free from sin's alloy,
   all our costliest treasures bring,
   Christ, to thee our heav'nly King.

4. Holy Jesu, ev'ry day
   keep us in the narrow way;
   and, when earthly things are past,
   bring our ransomed souls at last
   where they need no star to guide,
   where no clouds thy glory hide.

5. In the heav'nly country bright
   need they no created light,
   thou its light, its joy, its crown,
   thou its sun which goes not down;
   there for ever may we sing
   alleluias to our King.

56 Unknown

1. As your family, Lord, see us here,
   as your family, Lord, see us here,
   as your family, Lord, see us here,
   O Lord, see us here.

2. At your table, Lord, we are fed;
   at your table, Lord, we are fed;
   at your table, Lord, we are fed;
   O Lord, feed us here.

3. Fill our spirits, Lord, with your love,
   fill our spirits, Lord, with your love,
   fill our spirits, Lord, with your love,
   O Lord, give your love.

4. Make us faithful, Lord, to your will,
   make us faithful, Lord, to your will,
   make us faithful, Lord, to your will,
   O Lord, to your will.

5. As your family, Lord, see us here,
   as your family, Lord, see us here,
   as your family, Lord, see us here,
   O Lord, see us here.

57 Henry Twells (1823-1900) alt.

1. At even, ere the sun was set,
   the sick, O Lord, around thee lay;
   O in what divers pains they met!
   O with what joy they went away!

2. Once more 'tis eventide, and we
   oppressed with various ills draw near;
   what if thy form we cannot see?
   We know and feel that thou art here.

3. O Saviour Christ, our woes dispel;
   for some are sick, and some are sad,
   and some have never loved thee well,
   and some have lost the love they had.

4. And some have found the world is vain,
   yet from the world they break not free;
   and some have friends who give them
      pain,
   yet have not sought a friend in thee.

5. And none, O Lord, has perfect rest,
   for none is wholly free from sin;
   and they who fain would serve thee best
   are conscious most of wrong within.

6. O Christ, thou hast been human too,
   thou hast been troubled, tempted, tried;
   thy kind but searching glance can view
   the very wounds that shame would hide.

7. Thy touch has still its ancient pow'r;
   no word from thee can fruitless fall;
   hear, in this solemn evening hour,
   and in thy mercy heal us all.

58 Caroline Maria Noel (1817-1877) alt.

1. At the name of Jesus
   ev'ry knee shall bow,
   ev'ry tongue confess him
   King of glory now;
   'tis the Father's pleasure
   we should call him Lord,
   who, from the beginning,
   was the mighty Word.

2. At his voice creation
   sprang at once to sight,
   all the angels' faces,
   all the hosts of light,
   thrones and dominations,
   stars upon their way,
   all the heav'nly orders
   in their great array.

3. Humbled for a season,
   to receive a name
   from the lips of sinners
   unto whom he came,
   faithfully he bore it,
   spotless to the last,
   brought it back victorious
   when from death he passed.

4. Bore it up triumphant
   with its human light,
   through all ranks of creatures
   to the central height,
   to the throne of Godhead,
   to the Father's breast,
   filled it with the glory
   of that perfect rest.

Continued overleaf

5. In your hearts enthrone him;
   there let him subdue
   all that is not holy,
   all that is not true;
   crown him as your captain
   in temptation's hour;
   let his will enfold you
   in its light and pow'r.

6. Truly, this Lord Jesus
   shall return again,
   with his Father's glory,
   with his angel train;
   for all wreaths of empire
   meet upon his brow,
   and our hearts confess him
   King of glory now.

59 David Mowbray (b.1938)
© David Mowbray/Jubilate Hymns

1. At the supper, Christ the Lord
   gathered friends and said the blessing;
   bread was broken, wine was poured,
   faith in Israel's God expressing:
   signs of the forthcoming passion,
   tokens of a great salvation.

2. After supper, Jesus knelt,
   taking towel and bowl of water;
   washing the disciples' feet,
   servant now as well as master:
   'You,' said he, 'have my example –
   let your way of life be humble!'

3. In the fellowship of faith
   Christ himself with us is present;
   supper of the Lord in truth,
   host and master all-sufficient!
   From this table, gladly sharing,
   send us, Lord, to love and caring.

60 Martin Leckebusch (b.1962)
© 2000 Kevin Mayhew Ltd.

1. At this table we remember
   how and where our faith began:
   in the pain of crucifixion
   suffered by the Son of Man.

2. Looking up in adoration
   faith is conscious - he is here!
   Christ is present with his people,
   his the call that draws us near.

3. Heart and mind we each examine:
   if with honesty we face
   all our doubt, our fear and failure,
   then we can receive his grace.

4. Peace we share with one another:
   as from face to face we turn
   in our brothers and our sisters
   Jesus' body we discern.

5. Bread and wine are set before us;
   as we eat, we look ahead:
   we shall dine with Christ in heaven
   where the Kingdom feast is spread.

6. Nourished by the bread of heaven,
   faith and strength and courage grow –
   so to witness, serve and suffer,
   out into the world we go.

61 Graham Kendrick (b. 1950)
© 1988 Make Way Music

At this time of giving,
gladly now we bring
gifts of goodness and mercy
from a heav'nly King.

1. Earth could not contain the treasures
   heaven holds for you,
   perfect joy and lasting pleasures,
   love so strong and true.

2. May his tender love surround you
   at this Christmastime;
   may you see his smiling face
   that in the darkness shines.

3. But the many gifts he gives
   are all poured out from one;
   come, receive the greatest gift,
   the gift of God's own Son.

Last two choruses and verses:

Lai, lai, lai . . . etc

62 Charles Wesley (1707-1788)

1. Author of faith, eternal Word,
   whose Spirit breathes the active flame;
   faith, like its finisher and Lord,
   today as yesterday the same:

2. To thee our humble hearts aspire,
   and ask the gift unspeakable;
   increase in us the kindled fire,
   in us the work of faith fulfil.

3. By faith we know thee strong to save –
   save us, a present Saviour thou!
   What'er we hope, by faith we have,
   future and past subsisting now.

4. To him that in thy name believes
   eternal life with thee is given;
   into himself he all receives,
   pardon, and holiness, and heaven.

5. The things unknown to feeble sense,
   unseen by reason's glimmering ray,
   with strong, commanding evidence
   their heavenly origin display.

6. Faith lends its realizing light,
   the clouds disperse, the shadows fly;
   the invisible appears in sight,
   and God is seen by mortal eye.

63 Charles Wesley (1707-1788)

1. Author of life divine,
   who hast a table spread,
   furnished with mystic wine
   and everlasting bread,
   preserve the life thyself hast given,
   and feed and train us up for heaven.

2. Our needy souls sustain
   with fresh supplies of love,
   till all thy life we gain,
   and all thy fullness prove,
   and, strengthened by thy perfect grace
   behold without a veil thy face.

64 Geoffrey Anketell Studdert-Kennedy (1883-1929)

1. Awake, awake to love and work,
   the lark is in the sky,
   the fields are wet with diamond dew,
   the worlds awake to cry
   their blessings on the Lord of life,
   as he goes meekly by.

2. Come, let thy voice be one with theirs,
   shout with their shout of praise;
   see how the giant sun soars up,
   great Lord of years and days!
   So let the love of Jesus come,
   and set thy soul ablaze –

3. To give and give and give again
   what God has given thee,
   to spend thyself nor count the cost,
   to serve right gloriously
   the God who gave all worlds that are,
   and all that are to be.

65 Thomas Ken (1637-1711) alt.

1. Awake, my soul, and with the sun
   thy daily stage of duty run;
   shake off dull sloth, and joyful rise
   to pay thy morning sacrifice.

2. Redeem thy mis-spent time that's past,
   and live this day as if thy last;
   improve thy talent with due care;
   for the great day thyself prepare.

3. Let all thy converse be sincere,
   thy conscience as the noon-day clear;
   think how all-seeing God thy ways
   and all thy secret thoughts surveys.

4. Wake, and lift up thyself, my heart,
   and with the angels bear thy part,
   who all night long unwearied sing
   high praise to the eternal King.

Continued overleaf

5. Glory to thee, who safe hast kept
   and hast refreshed me whilst I slept;
   grant, Lord, when I from death shall
      wake,
   I may of endless light partake.

6. Lord, I my vows to thee renew;
   disperse my sins as morning dew;
   guard my first springs of thought
      and will,
   and with thyself my spirit fill.

7. Direct, control, suggest, this day,
   all I design or do or say;
   that all my pow'rs, with all their might,
   in thy sole glory may unite.

This Doxology may be sung after either part:

8. Praise God, from whom all blessings
      flow,
   praise him, all creatures here below,
   praise him above, angelic host,
   praise Father, Son and Holy Ghost.

66 Isaac Watts (1674-1748) based on Isaiah 40:28-31

1. Awake, our souls; away, our fears;
   let every trembling thought be gone;
   awake, and run the heavenly race,
   and put a cheerful courage on.

2. True, 'tis a strait and thorny road,
   and mortal spirits tire and faint;
   but they forget the mighty God
   who feeds the strength of every saint –

3. Thee, mighty God, whose matchless
      power
   is ever new and ever young,
   and firm endures, while endless years
   their everlasting circles run!

4. From thee, the overflowing spring,
   our souls shall drink a fresh supply,
   while such as trust their native strength
   shall faint away, and droop, and die.

5. Swift as an eagle cuts the air,
   we'll mount aloft to thine abode:
   on wings of love our souls shall fly,
   nor tire along the heavenly road.

67 Edward Shillito (1872-1948)
© *Copyright Oxford University Press*

1. Away with gloom, away with doubt!
   With all the morning stars we sing;
   with all the hosts of God we shout
   the praises of a King.
   Alleluia! Alleluia!
   Of our returning King.

2. Away with death, and welcome life;
   in him we died and live again;
   and welcome peace, away with strife!
   For he returns to reign.
   Alleluia! Alleluia!
   The Crucified shall reign.

3. Then welcome beauty, he is fair;
   and welcome youth, for he is young;
   and welcome spring; and everywhere
   let merry songs be sung!
   Alleluia! Alleluia!
   For such a King be sung!

68 Charles Wesley (1707-1788)

1. Away with our fears!
   The glad morning appears
   when an heir of salvation was born!
   From Jehovah I came,
   for his glory I am,
   and to him I with singing return.

2. I sing of thy grace,
   from my earliest days
   ever near to allure and defend;
   hitherto thou hast been
   my preserver from sin,
   and I trust thou wilt save to the end.

3. O the infinite cares,
   and temptations, and snares
   thy hand has conducted me through!
   O the blessings bestowed
   by a bountiful God,
   and the mercies eternally new!

4. What a mercy is this,
   what a heaven of bliss,
   how unspeakably happy am I;
   gathered into the fold,
   with thy people enrolled,
   with thy people to live and to die.

5. All honour and praise
   to the Father of grace,
   to the Spirit, and Son, I return;
   the business pursue
   he has made me to do,
   and rejoice that I ever was born.

6. In a rapture of joy
   my life I employ
   the God of my life to proclaim;
   'tis worth living for, this,
   to administer bliss
   and salvation in Jesus's name.

7. My remnant of days
   I spend in his praise,
   who died the whole world to redeem:
   be they many or few,
   my days are his due,
   and they all are devoted to him.

69 Charles Wesley (1707-1788)

1. Away with our fears,
   our troubles and tears:
   the Spirit is come,
   the witness of Jesus returned to his home.

2. The pledge of our Lord
   to his heaven restored
   is sent from the sky,
   and tells us our Head is exalted on high.

3. Our advocate there
   by his blood and his prayer
   the gift has obtained,
   for us he has prayed, and the Comforter
     gained.

4. Our glorified Head
   his Spirit has shed,
   with his people to stay,
   and never again will he take him away.

5. Our heavenly guide
   with us shall abide,
   his comforts impart,
   and set up his kingdom of love in the heart.

6. The heart that believes
   his kingdom receives,
   his power and his peace,
   his life, and his joy's everlasting increase.

7. Then let us rejoice
   in heart and in voice
   our leader pursue,
   and shout as we travel the wilderness
     through.

8. With the Spirit remove
   to Zion above
   triumphant arise
   and walk with our God till we fly to the
     skies.

70 Darlene Zschech
© 1997 Darlene Zschech/Hillsong Publishing/Kingsway's
Thankyou Music.

Beautiful Lord, wonderful Saviour,
I know for sure all of my days are
held in your hand, crafted into your
     perfect plan.
You gently call me into your presence,
guiding me by your Holy Spirit;
teach me, dear Lord, to live all of my life
through your eyes.
I'm captured by your holy calling,
set me apart, I know you're drawing me
     to yourself;
lead me, Lord, I pray.

Continued overleaf

Take me, mould me,
use me, fill me;
I give my life to the Potter's hand.
Call me, guide me,
Lead me, walk beside me;
I give my life to the Potter's hand.

71 Graham Kendrick (b. 1950)
© 1993 Make Way Music

1. Beauty for brokenness,
   hope for despair,
   Lord, in the suffering,
   this is our prayer.
   Bread for the children,
   justice, joy, peace,
   sunrise to sunset
   your kingdom increase.

2. Shelter for fragile lives,
   cures for their ills,
   work for the craftsmen,
   trade for their skills.
   Land for the dispossessed,
   rights for the weak,
   voices to plead the cause
   of those who can't speak.

   God of the poor,
   friend of the weak,
   give us compassion, we pray,
   melt our cold hearts,
   let tears fall like rain.
   Come, change our love
   from a spark to a flame.

3. Refuge from cruel wars,
   havens from fear,
   cities for sanctu'ry,
   freedoms to share.
   Peace to the killing fields,
   scorched earth to green,
   Christ for the bitterness,
   his cross for the pain.

4. Rest for the ravaged earth,
   oceans and streams,
   plundered and poisoned,
   our future, our dreams.
   Lord, end our madness,
   carelessness, greed;
   make us content with
   the things that we need.

5. Lighten our darkness,
   breathe on this flame,
   until your justice
   burns brightly again;
   until the nations
   learn of your ways,
   seek your salvation
   and bring you their praise.

72 Charles Wesley (1707-1788) alt.

1. Because thou hast said:
   'Do this for my sake',
   the mystical bread
   we gladly partake;
   we thirst for the Spirit
   that flows from above,
   and long to inherit
   thy fullness of love.

2. 'Tis here we look up
   and grasp at thy mind;
   'tis here that we hope
   thine image to find;
   the means of bestowing
   thy gifts we embrace;
   but all things are owing
   to Jesus's grace.

73 Charitie L. Bancroft (1841-1892)

1. Before the throne of God above
   I have a strong, a perfect plea,
   a great High Priest whose name is Love,
   who ever lives and pleads for me.

My name is graven on his hands,
my name is written on his heart;
I know that while in heav'n he stands
no tongue can bid me thence depart,
no tongue can bid me thence depart.

2. When Satan tempts me to despair,
and tells me of the guilt within,
upward I look and see him there
who made an end to all my sin.
Because the sinless Saviour died,
my sinful soul is counted free;
for God the Just is satisfied
to look on him and pardon me,
to look on him and pardon me.

3. Behold him there! The risen Lamb,
my perfect, spotless righteousness;
the great unchangeable I Am,
the King of glory and of grace!
One with himself I cannot die,
my soul is purchased with his blood;
my life is hid with Christ on high,
with Christ, my Saviour and my God,
with Christ, my Saviour and my God.

74 Isaac Watts (1674-1748) alt.

1. Begin, my tongue, some heavenly theme;
awake, my voice, and sing
the mighty works, or mightier name,
of our eternal King.

2. Tell of his wondrous faithfulness,
and sound his power abroad;
sing the sweet promise of his grace,
the quickening word of God.

3. Engraved as in eternal brass,
the mighty promise shines;
nor can the darkest pow'rs erase
those everlasting lines.

4. His every word of grace is strong
as that which built the skies;
the voice that rolls the stars along
speaks all the promises.

5. Now shall my leaping heart rejoice
to know thy favour sure;
I trust the all-creating voice,
and faith desires no more.

75 John Newton (1725-1807)

1. Begone, unbelief;
my Saviour is near,
and for my relief
will surely appear;
by prayer let me wrestle,
and he will perform;
with Christ in the vessel,
I smile at the storm.

2. Though dark be my way,
since he is my guide,
'tis mine to obey,
'tis his to provide;
though cisterns be broken
and creatures all fail,
the word he has spoken
shall surely prevail.

3. His love in time past
forbids me to think
he'll leave me at last
in trouble to sink;
while each Ebenezer
I have in review
confirms his good pleasure
to help me quite through.

4. Why should I complain
of want or distress,
temptation or pain?
He told me no less;
the heirs of salvation,
I know from his word,
through much tribulation
must follow their Lord.

Continued overleaf

5. Since all that I meet
   shall work for my good,
   the bitter is sweet,
   the med'cine is food;
   though painful at present,
   'twill cease before long;
   and then, O how pleasant
   the conqueror's song!

76 Noel Richards and Gerald Coates
   © 1991 Kingsway's Thankyou Music

1. Behold the Lord upon his throne;
   his face is shining like the sun.
   With eyes blazing fire, and feet glowing
      bronze,
   his voice like mighty water roars.
   Holy, holy, Lord God Almighty.
   Holy, holy, we stand in awe of you.

2. The first, the last, the living One,
   laid down his life for all the world.
   Behold, he now lives for evermore,
   and holds the keys of death and hell.
   Holy, holy, Lord God Almighty.
   Holy, holy, we bow before your throne.

3. So let our praises ever ring
   to Jesus Christ, our glorious King.
   All heaven and earth resound as we cry:
   'Worthy is the Son of God!'
   Holy, holy, Lord God Almighty.
   Holy, holy, we fall down at your feet.

77 Scottish Paraphrases (1745 and 1781) alt.
   based on Isaiah 2: 2-5 and Micah 4: 1-5

1. Behold, the mountain of the Lord
   in latter days shall rise
   on mountain-tops, above the hills,
   and draw the wondering eyes.

2. To this the joyful nations round,
   all tribes and tongues, shall flow;
   up to the hill of God, they'll say
   and to his house, we'll go.

3. The beam that shines from Zion's hill
   shall lighten every land;
   the King who reigns in Salem's towers
   shall all the world command.

4. Among the nations he shall judge;
   his judgements truth shall guide;
   his sceptre shall protect the just,
   and quell the sinner's pride.

5. No strife shall vex Messiah's reign
   or mar the peaceful years;
   to ploughshares we shall beat our swords,
   to pruning-hooks our spears.

6. No longer hosts, encountering hosts,
   shall crowds of slain deplore;
   they hang the trumpet in the hall,
   and study war no more.

7. Come then, O come from every land
   to worship at his shrine;
   and, walking in the light of God,
   with holy beauties shine.

78 Samuel Wesley (1662-1735)

1. Behold the Saviour of mankind
   nailed to the shameful tree!
   How vast the love that him inclined
   to bleed and die for thee!

2. Hark, how he groans! while nature shakes,
   and earth's strong pillars bend;
   the temple's veil in sunder breaks,
   the solid marbles rend.

3. 'Tis done! the precious ransom's paid;
   receive my soul! he cries:
   see where he bows his sacred head!
   He bows his head, and dies!

4. But soon he'll break death's envious chain,
   and in full glory shine:
   O Lamb of God, was ever pain,
   was ever love like thine?

79 Charles Wesley (1707-1788)

1. Behold the servant of the Lord!
   I wait thy guiding eye to feel,
   to hear and keep thy every word,
   to prove and do thy perfect will,
   joyful from my own works to cease,
   glad to fulfil all righteousness.

2. Me if thy grace vouchsafe to use,
   meanest of all thy creatures, me,
   the deed, the time, the manner choose;
   let all my fruit be found of thee;
   let all my works in thee be wrought,
   by thee to full perfection brought.

3. My every weak though good design
   o'errule or change, as seems thee meet;
   Jesus, let all my work be thine!
   Thy work, O Lord, is all complete,
   and pleasing in thy Father's sight;
   thou only hast done all things right.

4. Here then to thee thine own I leave;
   mould as thou wilt thy passive clay;
   but let me all thy stamp receive,
   but let me all thy words obey,
   serve with a single heart and eye,
   and to thy glory live and die.

80 John Ellerton (1826-1893)

1. Behold us, Lord, a little space
   from daily tasks set free,
   and met within this holy place
   to rest awhile with thee.

2. Yet these are not the only walls
   wherein thou may'st be sought;
   on homeliest work thy blessing falls,
   in truth and patience wrought.

3. Thine is the loom, the forge, the mart,
   the wealth of land and sea,
   the worlds of science and of art,
   revealed and ruled by thee.

4. Then let us prove our heavenly birth
   in all we do and know,
   and claim the kingdom of the earth
   for thee, and not thy foe.

5. Work shall be prayer, if all be wrought
   as thou wouldst have it done,
   and prayer, by thee inspired and taught,
   itself with work be one.

81 Charles Wesley (1707-1788)

1. Being of beings, God of love,
   to thee our hearts we raise:
   thy all-sustaining power we prove,
   and gladly sing thy praise.

2. Thine, wholly thine, we long to be:
   our sacrifice receive;
   made, and preserved, and saved by thee,
   to thee ourselves we give.

3. Heav'nward our every wish aspires;
   for all thy mercies' store,
   the sole return thy love requires
   is that we ask for more.

4. For more we ask; we open then
   our hearts to embrace thy will;
   turn, and revive us, Lord, again,
   with all thy fullness fill.

5. Come, Holy Ghost, the Saviour's love
   shed in our hearts abroad;
   so shall we ever live, and move,
   and be with Christ in God.

82 Charles Wesley (1707-1788)

1. Be it my only wisdom here
   to serve the Lord with filial fear,
   with loving gratitude;
   superior sense may I display,
   by shunning every evil way,
   and walking in the good.

Continued overleaf

2. O may I still from sin depart!
   A wise and understanding heart,
   Jesus, to me be given;
   and let me through thy Spirit know
   to glorify my God below,
   and find my way to heaven.

83 James Montgomery (1771-1854)

1. Be known to us in breaking bread,
   but do not then depart;
   Saviour, abide with us, and spread
   thy table in our heart.

2. There sup with us in love divine;
   thy body and thy blood,
   that living bread, that heavenly wine,
   be our immortal food.

84 Anne Brontë (1820-1849) alt.

1. Believe not those who say
   the upward path is smooth,
   lest thou shouldst stumble in the way
   and faint before the truth.

2. It is the only road
   unto the realms of joy;
   but those who seek that blest abode
   must all their powers employ.

3. Arm, arm thee for the fight!
   Cast useless loads away;
   watch through the darkest hours of
        night;
   toil through the hottest day.

4. To labour and to love,
   to pardon and endure,
   to lift thy heart to God above,
   and keep thy conscience pure.

5. Be this thy constant aim,
   thy hope, thy chief delight;
   what matter who should whisper blame
   or who should scorn or slight.

6. If but thy God approve,
   and if, within thy breast,
   thou feel the comfort of his love,
   the earnest of his rest?

85 Elizabeth C. Clephane (1830-1869) alt.

1. Beneath the cross of Jesus
   I fain would take my stand,
   the shadow of a mighty rock
   within a weary land;
   a home within a wilderness,
   a rest upon the way,
   from burning heat at noontide and
   the burden of the day.

2. O safe and happy shelter!
   O refuge tried and sweet!
   O trysting place where heaven's love
   and heaven's justice meet!
   As to the holy patriarch
   that wondrous dream was giv'n,
   so seems my Saviour's cross to me
   a ladder up to heav'n.

3. There lies, beneath its shadow,
   but on the farther side,
   the darkness of an awful grave
   that gapes both deep and wide;
   and there between us stands the cross,
   two arms outstretched to save;
   a watchman set to guard the way
   from that eternal grave.

4. Upon that cross of Jesus
   mine eye at times can see
   the very dying form of One
   who suffered there for me;
   and from my stricken heart, with tears,
   two wonders I confess –
   the wonders of redeeming love,
   and my unworthiness.

5. I take, O cross, thy shadow
for my abiding place!
I ask no other sunshine than
the sunshine of his face;
content to let the world go by,
to reckon gain as loss –
my sinful self, my only shame,
my glory all – the cross.

86 Unknown, based on Psalm 46

1. Be still and know that I am God. *(x3)*

2. I am the Lord that healeth thee. *(x3)*

3. In thee, O Lord, I put my trust. *(x3)*

87 David J. Evans (b. 1957)

1. Be still, for the presence of the Lord,
the Holy One, is here.
Come, bow before him now,
with reverence and fear.
In him no sin is found,
we stand on holy ground.
Be still, for the presence of the Lord,
the Holy One, is here.

2. Be still, for the glory of the Lord
is shining all around;
he burns with holy fire,
with splendour he is crowned.
How awesome is the sight,
our radiant King of light!
Be still, for the glory of the Lord
is shining all around.

3. Be still, for the power of the Lord
is moving in this place;
he comes to cleanse and heal,
to minister his grace.
No work too hard for him,
in faith receive from him.
Be still, for the power of the Lord
is moving in this place.

88 Katherina von Schlegel (b. 1697)
trans. Jane L. Borthwick, alt.

1. Be still, my soul: the Lord is at your side;
bear patiently the cross of grief and pain;
leave to your God to order and provide;
in ev'ry change he faithful will remain.
Be still, my soul: your best, your
heav'nly friend,
through thorny ways, leads to a joyful end.

2. Be still, my soul: your God will undertake
to guide the future as he has the past.
Your hope, your confidence let nothing
shake,
all now mysterious shall be clear at last.
Be still, my soul: the tempests still obey
his voice, who ruled them once on Galilee.

3. Be still, my soul: the hour is hastening on
when we shall be for ever with the Lord,
when disappointment, grief and fear
are gone,
sorrow forgotten, love's pure joy restored.
Be still, my soul: when change and tears
are past,
all safe and blessèd we shall meet at last.

89 Irish 8th century, trans. Mary Byrne (1880-1931)
and Eleanor Hull (1860-1935)

1. Be thou my vision, O Lord of my heart,
naught be all else to me save that thou art;
thou my best thought in the day and
the night,
waking or sleeping, thy presence my light.

2. Be thou my wisdom, be thou my
true word,
I ever with thee and thou with me, Lord;
thou my great Father, and I thy true heir;
thou in me dwelling, and I in thy care.

Continued overleaf

3. Be thou my breastplate, my sword for
   the fight,
   be thou my armour, and be thou
   my might,
   thou my soul's shelter, and thou my
   high tow'r,
   raise thou me heav'nward, O Pow'r of
   my pow'r.

4. Riches I need not, nor all the
   world's praise,
   thou mine inheritance through all my days;
   thou, and thou only, the first in my heart,
   high King of heaven, my treasure thou art!

5. High King of heaven, when battle is done,
   grant heaven's joy to me, O bright
   heav'n's sun;
   Christ of my own heart, whatever befall,
   still be my vision, O Ruler of all.

90 Bob Gilman
© 1977 Kingsway's Thankyou Music

Bind us together, Lord,
bind us together with cords
that cannot be broken.
Bind us together, Lord,
bind us together, Lord,
bind us together in love.

1. There is only one God,
   there is only one King.
   There is only one Body,
   that is why we sing:

2. Fit for the glory of God,
   purchased by his precious Blood,
   born with the right to be free:
   Jesus the vict'ry has won.

3. We are the fam'ly of God,
   we are his promise divine,
   we are his chosen desire,
   we are the glorious new wine.

91 Frances Jane van Alstyne (Fanny J. Crosby) (1820-1915)

1. Blessèd assurance, Jesus is mine:
   O what a foretaste of glory divine!
   Heir of salvation, purchase of God;
   born of his Spirit, washed in his blood.

   This is my story, this is my song,
   praising my Saviour all the day long.
   (Repeat)

2. Perfect submission, perfect delight,
   visions of rapture burst on my sight;
   angels descending, bring from above
   echoes of mercy, whispers of love.

3. Perfect submission, all is at rest,
   I in my Saviour am happy and blest;
   watching and waiting, looking above,
   filled with his goodness, lost in his love.

92 Gary Sadler and Jamie Harvill
© 1992 Integrity's Praise! Music/Kingsway's Thankyou Music

Blessing and honour, glory and power
be unto the Ancient of Days;
from every nation, all of creation
bow before the Ancient of Days.

Every tongue in heaven and earth
shall declare your glory,
every knee shall bow at your throne
in worship;
you will be exalted, O God,
and your kingdom shall not pass away,
O Ancient of Days.

Your kingdom shall reign over all the
   earth:
sing unto the Ancient of Days.
For none shall compare to your matchless
   worth:
sing unto the Ancient of Days.

93

vs. 1 and 3: John Keble (1792-1866)
vs. 2 and 4: William John Hall's 'Psalms and Hymns' (1836) alt.

1. Blest are the pure in heart,
   for they shall see our God;
   the secret of the Lord is theirs,
   their soul is Christ's abode.

2. The Lord who left the heav'ns
   our life and peace to bring,
   to dwell in lowliness with us,
   our pattern and our King.

3. Still to the lowly soul
   he doth himself impart,
   and for his dwelling and his throne
   chooseth the pure in heart.

4. Lord, we thy presence seek;
   may ours this blessing be:
   give us a pure and lowly heart,
   a temple meet for thee.

94

Charles Wesley (1707-1788)

1. Blest be the dear uniting love,
   that will not let us part;
   our bodies may far off remove,
   we still are one in heart.

2. Joined in one Spirit to our Head,
   where he appoints we go;
   and still in Jesu's footsteps tread,
   and show his praise below.

3. O may we ever walk in him,
   and nothing know beside,
   nothing desire, nothing esteem,
   but Jesus crucified!

4. Closer and closer let us cleave
   to his belov'd embrace;
   expect his fullness to receive,
   and grace to answer grace.

5. Partakers of the Saviour's grace,
   the same in mind and heart,
   nor joy, nor grief, nor time, nor place,
   nor life, nor death can part.

95

John Fawcett (1740-1817) alt.

1. Blest be the tie that binds
   our hearts in Jesu's love;
   the fellowship of Christian minds
   is like to that above.

2. Before our Father's throne
   we pour our fervent prayers:
   our fears, our hopes, our aims are one,
   our comforts and our cares.

3. When for a while we part,
   one thought shall not be vain,
   that we shall still be joined in heart,
   until we meet again.

4. One glorious hope revives
   our courage by the way:
   that each in expectation lives
   of that tremendous day –

5. When from all toil and pain
   and sin we shall be free,
   and perfect love and friendship reign
   through all eternity.

96

Timothy Dudley-Smith (b.1926)
© Timothy Dudley-Smith

1. Born by the Holy Spirit's breath,
   loosed from the law of sin and death,
   now cleared in Christ from every claim,
   no judgement stands against our name.

2. In us the Spirit makes his home,
   that we in him may overcome;
   Christ's risen life, in all its powers,
   its all-prevailing strength, is ours.

3. Children and heirs of God most high,
   we by his Spirit 'Father' cry;
   that Spirit with our Spirit shares
   to frame and breathe our wordless
   prayers.

Continued overleaf

4. One is his love, his purpose one:
   to form the likeness of his Son
   in all who, called and justified,
   shall reign in glory at his side.

5. Nor death, nor life, nor powers unseen,
   nor height, nor depth, can come
         between;
   we know through peril, pain and sword,
   the love of God in Christ our Lord.

97 Brian R. Hoare (b.1935)
© Brian Hoare/Jubilate Hymns

1. Born in song!
   God's people have always been singing.
   Born in song!
   Hearts and voices raised.
   So today we worship together;
   God alone is worthy to be praised.

2. Praise to God!
   For he is the one who has made us.
   Praise to God!
   We his image bear.
   Heav'n and earth are full of his glory;
   let creation praise him everywhere.

3. Christ is king!
   He left all the glory of heaven.
   Christ is king!
   Born to share in our pain;
   crucified, for sinners atoning,
   risen, exalted, soon to come again.

4. Sing the song!
   God's Spirit is poured out among us.
   Sing the song!
   He has made us anew.
   Ev'ry member part of the Body;
   given his power, his will to seek and do.

5. Tell the world!
   All power to Jesus is given.
   Tell the world!
   He is with us always.
   Spread the word, that all may receive him;
   every tongue confess and sing his praise.

6. Then the end!
   Christ Jesus shall reign in his glory.
   Then the end
   of all earthly days.
   Yet above the song will continue;
   all his people still shall sing his praise.

98 Geoffrey Ainger (b. 1925)
© 1964 Stainer & Bell Ltd.

1. Born in the night, Mary's child,
   a long way from your home;
   coming in need, Mary's child,
   born in a borrowed room.

2. Clear shining light, Mary's child,
   your face lights up our way;
   light of the world, Mary's child,
   dawn on our darkened day.

3. Truth of our life, Mary's child,
   you tell us God is good;
   prove it is true, Mary's child,
   go to your cross of wood.

4. Hope of the world, Mary's child,
   you're coming soon to reign;
   King of the earth, Mary's child,
   walk in our streets again.

99 Reginald Heber (1783-1826)

1. Bread of the world in mercy broken,
   wine of the soul in mercy shed,
   by whom the words of life were spoken,
   and in whose death our sins are dead.

2. Look on the heart by sorrows broken,
   look on the tears by sinners shed;
   and be thy feast to us the token
   that by thy grace our souls are fed.

100
v. 1: Mary Artemisia Lathbury (1841-1913)
vs. 2,3: Alexander Groves (1842-1909)

1. Break thou the bread of life,
   O Lord, to me,
   as thou didst break the loaves
   beside the sea.
   Beyond the sacred page
   I seek thee, Lord;
   my spirit longs for thee,
   O living Word!

2. Thou art the Bread of Life,
   O Lord, to me,
   thy holy word the truth
   that saveth me;
   give me to eat and live
   with thee above;
   teach me to love thy truth,
   for thou art love.

3. O send thy Spirit, Lord,
   now unto me,
   that he may touch my eyes,
   and make me see;
   show me the truth concealed
   within thy word,
   and in thy book revealed
   I see thee, Lord.

101
Edwin Hatch (1835-1889) alt.
© 1999 Kevin Mayhew Ltd.

1. Breathe on me, Breath of God,
   fill me with life anew,
   that as you love, so I may love,
   and do what you would do.

2. Breathe on me, Breath of God,
   until my heart is pure:
   until my will is one with yours
   to do and to endure.

3. Breathe on me, Breath of God,
   fulfil my heart's desire,
   until this earthly part of me
   glows with your heav'nly fire.

4. Breathe on me, Breath of God,
   so shall I never die,
   but live with you the perfect life
   of your eternity.

102
Reginald Heber (1783-1826)

1. Brightest and best
   of the suns of the morning,
   dawn on our darkness
   and lend us thine aid;
   star of the east,
   the horizon adorning,
   guide where our infant
   Redeemer is laid.

2. Cold on his cradle
   the dew-drops are shining;
   low lies his head
   with the beasts of the stall;
   angels adore him
   in slumber reclining,
   Maker and Monarch
   and Saviour of all.

3. Say, shall we yield him,
   in costly devotion,
   odours of Edom,
   and off'rings divine,
   gems of the mountain,
   and pearls of the ocean,
   myrrh from the forest,
   or gold from the mine?

4. Vainly we offer
   each humble oblation,
   vainly with gifts
   would his favour secure:
   richer by far
   is the heart's adoration,
   dearer to God
   are the prayers of the poor.

103
Janet Lunt
© 1978 Sovereign Music UK

Broken for me, broken for you,
the body of Jesus, broken for you.

1. He offered his body, he poured out
   his soul;
   Jesus was broken, that we might
   be whole.

2. Come to my table and with me dine;
   eat of my bread and drink of my wine.

3. This is my body given for you;
   eat it remembering I died for you.

4. This is my blood I shed for you,
   for your forgiveness, making you new.

104
Richard Gillard
© 1977 Scripture in Song, a division of Integrity Music/
Kingsway's Thankyou Music.

1. Brother, sister, let me serve you,
   let me be as Christ to you;
   pray that I may have the grace to
   let you be my servant, too.

2. We are pilgrims on a journey,
   fellow trav'llers on the road;
   we are here to help each other
   walk the mile and bear the load.

3. I will hold the Christlight for you
   in the night-time of your fear;
   I will hold my hand out to you,
   speak the peace you long to hear.

4. I will weep when you are weeping;
   when you laugh, I'll laugh with you.
   I will share your joy and sorrow
   till we've seen this journey through.

5. When we sing to God in heaven,
   we shall find such harmony,
   born of all we've known together
   of Christ's love and agony.

6. Brother, sister, let me serve you,
   let me be as Christ to you;
   pray that I may have the grace to
   let you be my servant, too.

105
George Rawson (1807-1889)

1. By Christ redeemed, in Christ restored,
   we keep the memory adored,
   and show the death of our dear Lord
   until he come.

2. His body, broken in our stead,
   is here in this memorial bread,
   and so our feeble love is fed
   until he come.

3. The drops of his dread agony,
   his life-blood shed for us, we see;
   the wine shall tell the mystery
   until he come.

4. And thus that dark betrayal night
   with the last advent we unite,
   by one blest chain of loving rite,
   until he come.

5. O blessèd hope! With this elate,
   let not our hearts be desolate,
   but, strong in faith, in patience wait
   until he come.

106
Steven Fry
© 1994 Deep Fryed Music/Word Music
Inc./Maranatha! Music/Administered by CopyCare

By his grace we are redeemed,
by his blood we are made clean,
and we now can know him face to face.
By his pow'r we have been raised,
hidden now in Christ by faith,
we will praise the glory of his grace.

107
Elizabeth Cosnett (b.1936)
© Copyright 1980 Elizabeth Cosnett

1. Can we by searching find out God
   or formulate his ways?
   Can numbers measure what he is
   or words contain his praise?

2. Although his being is too bright
   for human eyes to scan,
   his meaning lights our shadowed world
   through Christ, the Son of Man.

3. Our boastfulness is turned to shame,
   our profit counts as loss,
   when earthly values stand beside
   the manger and the cross.

4. We there may recognise his light,
   may kindle in its rays,
   find there the source of penitence,
   the starting-point for praise.

5. There God breaks in upon our search,
   makes birth and death his own:
   he speaks to us in human terms
   to make his glory known.

108 Charles Wesley (1707-1788)

1. Captain of Israel's host, and guide
   of all who seek the land above,
   beneath thy shadow we abide,
   the cloud of thy protecting love;
   our strength thy grace; our rule thy word;
   our end the glory of the Lord.

2. By thine unerring Spirit led,
   we shall not in the desert stray;
   we shall not full direction need,
   nor miss our providential way;
   as far from danger as from fear,
   while love, almighty love, is near.

109 Eddie Espinosa, based on Isaiah 64:8
© 1982 Mercy/Vineyard Publishing
Administered by CopyCare

Change my heart, O God,
make it ever true;
change my heart, O God,
may I be like you. (x2)

You are the potter, I am the clay;
mould me and make me:
this is what I pray.

110 Mary MacDonald (1817-1890)
trans. Lachlan MacBean (1853-1931)
© Copyright control

1. Child in the manger, infant of Mary;
   outcast and stranger, Lord of all;
   child who inherits all our transgressions,
   all our demerits on him fall.

2. Once the most holy child of salvation
   gently and lowly lived below;
   now as our glorious mighty Redeemer,
   see him victorious o'er each foe.

3. Prophets foretold him, infant of wonder;
   angels behold him on his throne;
   worthy our Saviour of all their praises;
   happy for ever are his own.

111 Timothy Dudley-Smith (b.1926)
© Timothy Dudley-Smith

1. Christ be my leader by night as by day;
   safe through the darkness, for he is the
   way.
   Gladly I follow, my future his care,
   darkness is daylight when Jesus is there.

2. Christ be my teacher in age as in youth,
   drifting or doubting, for he is the truth.
   Grant me to trust him; though shifting as
   sand,
   doubt cannot daunt me; in Jesus I stand.

3. Christ be my Saviour in calm as in strife;
   death cannot hold me, for he is the life.
   Nor darkness nor doubting nor sin and
   its stain
   can touch my salvation; with Jesus I
   reign.

112 Charles Wesley (1707-1788)

1. Christ, from whom all blessings flow,
   perfecting the saints below,
   hear us, who thy nature share,
   who thy mystic body are.

Continued overleaf

2. Join us, in one Spirit join,
   let us still receive of thine;
   still for more on thee we call,
   thou who fillest all in all.

3. Closer knit to thee, our Head,
   nourished, Lord, by thee, and fed,
   let us daily growth receive,
   more in Jesus Christ believe.

4. Never from thy service move,
   needful to each other prove,
   use the grace on each bestowed,
   tempered by the art of God.

5. Love, like death, has all destroyed,
   rendered all distinctions void;
   names, and sects, and parties fall:
   thou, O Christ, art all in all.

113 John Byrom (1692-1763) alt.

1. Christians, awake! salute the happy
   morn,
   whereon the Saviour of the world was
   born;
   rise to adore the mystery of love,
   which hosts of angels chanted from
   above:
   with them the joyful tidings first begun
   of God incarnate and the Virgin's Son.

2. Then to the watchful shepherds it was
   told,
   who heard th' angelic herald's voice,
   'Behold,
   I bring good tidings of a Saviour's birth
   to you and all the nations on the earth:
   this day hath God fulfilled his promised
   word,
   this day is born a Saviour, Christ the
   Lord.'

3. He spake; and straightway the celestial
   choir
   in hymns of joy, unknown before,
   conspire;
   the praises of redeeming love they sang,
   and heav'n's whole orb with alleluias
   rang:
   God's highest glory was their anthem still,
   peace on the earth, in ev'ry heart good
   will.

4. To Bethl'em straight th'enlightened
   shepherds ran,
   to see, unfolding, God's eternal plan,
   and found, with Joseph and the blessèd
   maid,
   her Son, the Saviour, in a manger laid:
   then to their flocks, still praising God,
   return,
   and their glad hearts with holy rapture
   burn.

5. O may we keep and ponder in our mind
   God's wondrous love in saving lost
   mankind;
   trace we the babe, who hath retrieved our
   loss,
   from his poor manger to his bitter cross;
   tread in his steps, assisted by his grace,
   till our first heav'nly state again takes place.

6. Then may we hope, th'angelic hosts among,
   to sing, redeemed, a glad triumphal song:
   he that was born upon this joyful day
   around us all his glory shall display;
   saved by his love, incessant we shall sing
   eternal praise to heav'n's almighty King.

114 Brian Wren (b. 1936)
© 1969, 1995 Stainer & Bell Ltd.

1. Christ is alive! Let Christians sing.
   The cross stands empty to the sky.
   Let streets and homes with praises ring.
   Love, drowned in death, shall never die.

2. Christ is alive! No longer bound
   to distant years in Palestine,
   but saving, healing, here and now,
   and touching ev'ry place and time.

3. In ev'ry insult, rift and war,
   where colour, scorn or wealth divide,
   Christ suffers still, yet loves the more,
   and lives, where even hope has died.

4. Women and men, in age and youth,
   can feel the Spirit, hear the call,
   and find the way, the life, the truth,
   revealed in Jesus, freed for all.

5. Christ is alive, and comes to bring
   good news to this and ev'ry age,
   till earth and sky and ocean ring
   with joy, with justice, love and praise.

115 'Urbs beata Jerusalem' (c.7th century)
trans. John Mason Neale, (1818-1866) alt.

1. Christ is made the sure foundation,
   Christ the head and cornerstone,
   chosen of the Lord, and precious,
   binding all the Church in one,
   holy Zion's help for ever,
   and her confidence alone.

2. To this temple, where we call you,
   come, O Lord of hosts, today;
   you have promised loving kindness,
   hear your servants as we pray,
   bless your people now before you,
   turn our darkness into day.

3. Hear the cry of all your people,
   what they ask and hope to gain;
   what they gain from you, for ever
   with your chosen to retain,
   and hereafter in your glory
   evermore with you to reign.

4. Praise and honour to the Father,
   praise and honour to the Son,
   praise and honour to the Spirit,
   ever Three and ever One,
   One in might and One in glory,
   while unending ages run.

116 Latin (pre 9th century)
trans. John Chandler (1806-1876)

1. Christ is our cornerstone,
   on him alone we build;
   with his true saints alone
   the courts of heav'n are filled:
   on his great love our hopes we place
   of present grace and joys above.

2. O then with hymns of praise
   these hallowed courts shall ring;
   our voices we will raise
   the Three in One to sing;
   and thus proclaim in joyful song,
   both loud and long, that glorious name.

3. Here, gracious God, do thou
   for evermore draw nigh;
   accept each faithful vow,
   and mark each suppliant sigh;
   in copious show'r on all who pray
   each holy day thy blessings pour.

4. Here may we gain from heav'n
   the grace which we implore;
   and may that grace, once giv'n,
   be with us evermore,
   until that day when all the blest
   to endless rest are called away.

117 Frank von Christierson (1900-1996)
© *Copyright Control*

1. Christ is risen! Raise your voices
   jubilant with joy and praise.
   Christ is risen! Earth rejoices!
   To the Lord your anthems raise.
   Over sin and death victorious,
   Christ is risen! Hail your King!
   Ever may his praise be glorious;
   let the world his triumph sing!

Continued overleaf

2. Lord of life, our Saviour risen,
   bid the shadows flee away;
   death no more a darkened prison,
   death the door to life's new day.
   This the resurrection chorus,
   lift its music on the air;
   Jesus lives, our Lord victorious,
   tell it! Tell it everywhere.

3. Life eternal! Joy of heaven;
   life abundant – joy of earth;
   life which God in Christ has given
   brings to us new hope, new worth.
   Lift your hearts from sin and sadness,
   trust this joyful sacred word,
   fill the earth with holy gladness:
   Christ is risen! Christ our Lord!

118 Fred Pratt Green (1903-2000)
© 1969 Stainer & Bell Ltd.

1. Christ is the world's Light, he and
       none other;
   born in our darkness, he became
       our Brother;
   if we have seen him, we have seen
       the Father:
   Glory to God on high.

2. Christ is the world's Peace, he and
       none other;
   no-one can serve him and despise
       another;
   who else unites us, one in God the Father?
   Glory to God on high.

3. Christ is the world's Life, he and
       none other;
   sold once for silver, murdered here,
       our Brother –
   he who redeems us, reigns with
       God the Father:
   Glory to God on high.

4. Give God the glory, God and
       none other;
   give God the glory, Spirit, Son
       and Father;
   give God the glory, God in Man
       my brother:
   glory to God on high.

119 Martin Luther (1483-1546)
Trans. Richard Massie (1800-1887)

1. Christ Jesus lay in death's strong bands
   for our offences given;
   but now at God's right hand he stands,
   and brings us life from heaven:
   wherefore let us joyful be,
   and sing to God right thankfully
   loud songs of hallelujah!
   Hallelujah!

2. It was a strange and dreadful strife,
   when life and death contended;
   the victory remained with life,
   the reign of death was ended:
   stripped of power, no more he reigns;
   an empty form alone remains;
   his sting is lost for ever.
   Hallelujah!

3. So let us keep the festival
   whereto the Lord invites us;
   Christ is himself the joy of all,
   the sun that warms and lights us;
   by his grace he doth impart
   eternal sunshine to the heart;
   the night of sin is ended.
   Hallelujah!

4. Then let us feast the Easter day
   on Christ, true Bread of heaven.
   the word of grace hath purged away
   the old and wicked leaven;
   Christ alone our souls will feed,
   he is our meat and drink indeed,
   faith lives upon no other.
   Hallelujah!

120   Patrick Appleford (b.1925)
© 1960 Josef Weinberger Ltd.

1. Christ our King in glory reigning,
   all our strength from you proceeds;
   born of Mary, not disdaining
   work or pain to share our needs;
   you have conquered sin's infection,
   guiltless victim for us killed;
   by your mighty resurrection,
   Christ in us your church rebuild.

2. Lord, look down in your compassion,
   free your people from their sin;
   only by your cross and passion
   may we rise renewed within;
   make us honest in our living,
   with your grace may we be filled;
   by your love and free forgiving,
   Christ in us your church rebuild.

3. Lord, to everyone supplying
   different gifts for all to use;
   give us strength, on you relying,
   all our selfishness to lose;
   may we each in our vocation
   with your Spirit be instilled;
   by your humble incarnation,
   Christ in us your church rebuild.

4. Lord, you call us all to witness
   by our worship and our love;
   Lord, look not on our unfitness,
   send your Spirit from above;
   may he lead us to inherit
   life with you as you have willed;
   by the sending of your Spirit,
   Christ in us your church rebuild.

121   John L. Bell (b. 1949) and Graham Maule (b. 1958)
© 1989 WGRG, Iona Community

1. Christ's is the world in which we move,
   Christ's are the folk we're summoned
      to love,
   Christ's is the voice which calls us to care,
   and Christ is the one who meets us here.

To the lost Christ shows his face;
to the unloved he gives his embrace;
to those who cry in pain or disgrace,
Christ makes with his friends a
   touching place.

2. Feel for the people we most avoid,
   strange or bereaved or never employed;
   feel for the women, and feel for the men
   who fear that their living is all in vain.

3. Feel for the parents who've lost their child,
   feel for the women whom men
      have defiled,
   feel for the baby for whom there's
      no breast,
   and feel for the weary who find no rest.

4. Feel for the lives by life confused,
   riddled with doubt, in loving abused;
   feel for the lonely heart, conscious of sin,
   which longs to be pure but fears to begin.

122   Charles Westley (1707-1788)

1. Christ the Lord is risen today; *Alleluia!*
   Sons of men and angels say:
   raise your joys and triumphs high;
   sing, ye heavens; thou earth, reply:

2. Love's redeeming work is done,
   fought the fight, the battle won;
   vain the stone, the watch, the seal;
   Christ hath burst the gates of hell:

3. Lives again our glorious King;
   where, O death, is now thy sting?
   Once he died our souls to save;
   where's thy victory, boasting grave?

4. Soar we now where Christ hath led,
   following our exalted Head;
   made like him, like him we rise;
   ours the cross, the grace, the skies:

Continued overleaf

5. King of glory! Soul of bliss!
Everlasting life is this,
thee to know, thy power to prove,
thus to sing, and thus to love:

123 Michael Saward (b. 1932)
© Michael Saward/Jubilee Hymns

1. Christ triumphant, ever reigning,
Saviour, Master, King.
Lord of heav'n, our lives sustaining,
hear us as we sing:

Yours the glory and the crown,
the high renown, th'eternal name.

2. Word incarnate, truth revealing,
Son of Man on earth!
Pow'r and majesty concealing
by your humble birth:

3. Suff'ring servant, scorned, ill-treated,
victim crucified!
Death is through the cross defeated,
sinners justified:

4. Priestly King, enthroned for ever
high in heav'n above!
Sin and death and hell shall never
stifle hymns of love:

5. So, our hearts and voices raising
through the ages long,
ceaselessly upon you gazing,
this shall be our song:

124 F. Bland Tucker (1895-1984)
© Church Pension Fund

1. Christ, when for us you were baptised
God's Spirit on you came,
as peaceful as a dove, and yet
as urgent as a flame.

2. God called you his belovèd Son,
called you his servant too;
his kingdom you were called to preach,
his holy will to do.

3. Straightway and steadfast until death
you then obeyed his call,
freely as Son of Man to serve,
and give your life for all.

4. Baptise us with your Spirit, Lord,
your cross on us be signed,
that likewise in God's service we
may perfect freedom find.

125 Charles Wesley (1707-1788)

1. Christ, whose glory fills the skies,
Christ, the true, the only light,
Sun of Righteousness arise,
triumph o'er the shades of night;
Dayspring from on high, be near;
Daystar, in my heart appear.

2. Dark and cheerless is the morn
unaccompanied by thee;
joyless is the day's return,
till thy mercy's beams I see,
till they inward light impart,
glad my eyes, and warm my heart.

3. Visit then this soul of mine,
pierce the gloom of sin and grief;
fill me, radiancy divine,
scatter all my unbelief;
more and more thyself display,
shining to the perfect day.

126 Samuel Johnson (1822-1882) alt.

1. City of God, how broad and far
outspread thy walls sublime!
Thy free and loyal people are
of ev'ry age and clime.

2. One holy Church, one mighty throng,
one steadfast, high intent;
one working band, one harvest-song,
one King omnipotent.

3. How purely hath thy speech come
    down
  from earth's primeval youth!
  How grandly hath thine empire grown
  of freedom, love and truth!

4. How gleam thy watch-fires through
    the night
  with never-fainting ray!
  How rise thy tow'rs, serene and bright,
  to meet the dawning day!

5. In vain the surge's angry shock,
  in vain the drifting sands;
  unharmed upon th'eternal Rock
  th'eternal city stands.

127 Sue McClellan (b. 1951), John Paculabo (b. 1946)
Keith Ryecroft (b. 1949)
© 1974 Kingsway's Thankyou Music

1. Colours of day dawn into the mind,
  the sun has come up, the night is behind.
  Go down in the city, into the street,
  and let's give the message
  to the people we meet.

  So light up the fire and let the flame burn,
  open the door, let Jesus return,
  take seeds of his Spirit, let the fruit grow,
  tell the people of Jesus, let his love show.

2. Go through the park, on into the town;
  the sun still shines on; it never goes down.
  The light of the world is risen again;
  the people of darkness
  are needing our friend.

3. Open your eyes, look into the sky,
  the darkness has come, the sun came to die.
  The evening draws on, the sun disappears,
  but Jesus is living,
  and his Spirit is near.

128 Richard G. Jones (b.1926)
© Richard G. Jones

1. Come, all who look to Christ today,
  stretch out your hands, enlarge your
    mind,
  together share his living way
  where all who humbly seek will find.

2. Come, all who will from every race;
  to lose self-will as Christians should
  then find the Spirit's strong embrace
  which binds us to the common good.

3. Come, young and old from every church,
  bring all your treasuries of prayer,
  join the dynamic Spirit's search
  to press beyond the truths we share.

4. Bring your traditions' richest store,
  your hymns and rites and cherished
    creeds;
  explore our visions, pray for more,
  since God delights to meet fresh needs.

5. Come, trust in Christ and live in peace,
  anticipate that final light
  when strife and bigotry shall cease,
  and faith be lost in praise and sight.

129 Michael Forster (b.1946)
© 1999 Kevin Mayhew Ltd.

1. Come and join the great uprising, life
  begins again,
  springing up triumphant out of tragedy
    and pain,
  death has been defeated and its idol shall
    not reign,
  this is the world's new beginning.

  Rejoice! Rejoice! The captives are released.
  Rejoice! Rejoice! Death's reign of fear has
    ceased.
  Evil is defeated by the Prince of love and
    peace,
  this is the world's new beginning.

Continued overleaf

2. Jesus has defeated all manipulative
      powers,
   proven the futility of fortresses and
      towers;
   victims of oppression share the triumph
      of this hour:
   this is the world's new beginning.

   Rejoice! Rejoice! The captives are released.
   Rejoice! Rejoice! Death's reign of fear has
      ceased.
   Evil is defeated by the Prince of love and
      peace,
   this is the world's new beginning.

3. Life in all its fullness is his gift for us to
      share:
   wholeness and security for people
      everywhere.
   Dare we live his life, to make creation
      just and fair?
   This is the world's new beginning.

4. Share the resurrection hope and put an
      end to fear,
   sorrow turns to joy and life eternal starts
      right here!
   Heav'n and earth unite to give a great
      resounding cheer!
   This is the world's new beginning.

130 Charles Wesley (1707-1788)

1. Come and let us sweetly join
   Christ to praise in hymns divine;
   give we all with one accord
   glory to our common Lord.
   Hands and hearts and voices raise,
   sing as in the ancient days,
   antedate the joys above,
   celebrate the feast of love.

2. Jesu, dear expected guest,
   thou art bidden to the feast;
   for thyself our hearts prepare,
   come, and rest, and banquet there.
   Sanctify us, Lord, and bless,
   breathe thy Spirit, give thy peace;
   thou thyself within us move,
   make our feast a feast of love.

Part 2

3. Let us join – 'tis God commands –
   let us join our hearts and hands;
   help to gain our calling's hope,
   build we each the other up.
   God his blessings shall dispense,
   God shall crown his ordinance,
   here in his appointed ways
   nourish us with social grace.

4. Plead we then for faith alone,
   faith which by our works is shown:
   God it is who justifies;
   only faith the grace applies –
   active faith that lives within,
   conquers earth, and hell, and sin,
   sanctifies and makes us whole,
   forms the Saviour in the soul.

5. Let us for this faith contend;
   sure salvation is its end:
   heav'n already is begun,
   everlasting life is won.
   Only let us persevere,
   till we see our Lord appear:
   never from the Rock remove,
   saved by faith, which works by love.

6. Hence may all our actions flow,
   love the proof that Christ we know;
   mutual love the token be,
   Lord, that we belong to thee.
   Love, thine image, love impart!
   Stamp it on our face and heart!
   Only love to us be given!
   Lord, we ask no other heaven.

131

Graham Kendrick (b. 1950)
© 1989 Make Way Music

1. Come and see, come and see,
   come and see the King of love;
   see the purple robe
   and crown of thorns he wears.
   Soldiers mock, rulers sneer
   as he lifts the cruel cross;
   lone and friendless now,
   he climbs towards the hill.

   We worship at your feet,
   where wrath and mercy meet,
   and a guilty world
   is washed by love's pure stream.
   For us he was made sin –
   oh, help me take it in.
   Deep wounds of love
   cry out 'Father, forgive.'
   I worship, I worship
   the Lamb who was slain.

2. Come and weep, come and mourn
   for your sin that pierced him there;
   so much deeper
   than the wounds of thorn and nail.
   All our pride, all our greed,
   all our fallenness and shame;
   and the Lord has laid
   the punishment on him.

3. Man of heaven, born to earth
   to restore us to your heaven.
   Here we bow in awe
   beneath your searching eyes.
   From your tears comes our joy,
   from your death our life shall spring;
   by your resurrection power
   we shall rise.

132

Charles Wesley (1707-1788)

Come, divine Interpreter,
bring us eyes thy book to read,
ears the mystic words to hear,
words which did from thee proceed,
words that endless bliss impart,
kept in an obedient heart.

1. All who read, or hear, are blessed,
   if thy plain commands we do;
   of thy kingdom here possessed,
   thee we shall in glory view –
   when thou com'st on earth to abide,
   reign triumphant at thy side.

133

'Discendi, amor santo' by Bianco da Siena (d. 1434)
trans. Richard F. Littledale, (1833-1890) alt.

1. Come down, O Love divine,
   seek thou this soul of mine,
   and visit it with thine own ardour glowing;
   O Comforter, draw near,
   within my heart appear,
   and kindle it, thy holy flame bestowing.

2. O let it freely burn,
   till earthly passions turn
   to dust and ashes in its heat consuming;
   and let thy glorious light
   shine ever on my sight,
   and clothe me round, the while my
        path illuming.

3. Let holy charity
   mine outward vesture be,
   and lowliness become mine inner clothing;
   true lowliness of heart,
   which takes the humbler part,
   and o'er its own shortcomings weeps
        with loathing.

4. And so the yearning strong,
   with which the soul will long,
   shall far outpass the pow'r of human telling;
   nor can we guess its grace,
   till we become the place
   wherein the Holy Spirit makes
        his dwelling.

134 Charles Wesley (1707-1788)

1. Come, Holy Ghost, our hearts inspire,
   let us thine influence prove;
   source of the old prophetic fire,
   fountain of life and love.

2. Come, Holy Ghost – for, moved by thee,
   thy prophets wrote and spoke –
   unlock the truth, thyself the key,
   unseal the sacred book.

3. Expand thy wings, celestial Dove,
   brood o'er our nature's night;
   on our disordered spirits move,
   and let there now be light.

4. God, through himself, we then shall
       know,
   if thou within us shine;
   and sound, with all thy saints below,
   the depths of love divine.

135
vs. 1-3, 5: John Cosin (1594-1672)
after Rabanus Maurus (c. 776-856) alt.
v. 4: Michael Forster (b. 1946)
© v.4: 1993 Kevin Mayhew Ltd.

1. Come, Holy Ghost, our souls inspire,
   and lighten with celestial fire;
   thou the anointing Spirit art,
   who dost thy sev'nfold gifts impart.

2. Thy blessèd unction from above
   is comfort, life, and fire of love;
   enable with perpetual light
   the dullness of our blinded sight.

3. Anoint and cheer our soilèd face
   with the abundance of thy grace:
   keep far our foes, give peace at home;
   where thou art guide no ill can come.

4. Show us the Father and the Son,
   in thee and with thee, ever one.
   Then through the ages all along,
   this shall be our unending song.

5. 'Praise to thy eternal merit,
   Father, Son and Holy Spirit.'
   Amen.

136 Charles Wesley (1707-1788)

1. Come, Holy Ghost, thine influence shed,
   and realize the sign;
   thy life infuse into the bread,
   thy power into the wine.

2. Effectual let the tokens prove,
   and made, by heavenly art,
   fit channels to convey thy love
   to every faithful heart.

137
Michael Forster (b. 1946)
based on 1 Corinthians 12: 4-11
© 1992 Kevin Mayhew Ltd.

1. Come, Holy Spirit, come!
   Inflame our souls with love,
   transforming ev'ry heart and home
   with wisdom from above.
   O let us not despise
   the humble path Christ trod,
   but choose, to shame the worldly-wise,
   the foolishness of God.

2. All-knowing Spirit, prove
   the poverty of pride,
   by knowledge of the Father's love
   in Jesus crucified.
   And grant us faith to know
   the glory of that sign,
   and in our very lives to show
   the marks of love divine.

3. Come with the gift to heal
   the wounds of guilt and fear,
   and to oppression's face reveal
   the kingdom drawing near.
   Where chaos longs to reign,
   descend, O holy Dove,
   and free us all to work again
   the miracle of love.

4. Spirit of truth, arise;
   inspire the prophet's voice:
   expose to scorn the tyrant's lies,
   and bid the poor rejoice.
   O Spirit, clear our sight,
   all prejudice remove,
   and help us to discern the right,
   and covet only love.

5. Give us the tongues to speak,
   in ev'ry time and place,
   to rich and poor, to strong and weak,
   the word of love and grace.
   Enable us to hear
   the words that others bring,
   interpreting with open ear
   the special song they sing.

6. Come, Holy Spirit, dance
   within our hearts today,
   our earthbound spirits to entrance,
   our mortal fears allay.
   And teach us to desire,
   all other things above,
   that self-consuming holy fire,
   the perfect gift of love!

138 Isaac Watts (1674-1748)

1. Come, Holy Spirit, heavenly Dove,
   with all thy quickening powers;
   kindle a flame of sacred love
   in these cold hearts of ours.

2. In vain we tune our formal songs,
   in vain we strive to rise,
   hosannas languish on our tongues,
   and our devotion dies.

3. And shall we then for ever live
   at this poor dying rate?
   Our love so faint, so cold to thee
   and thine to us so great!

4. Come, Holy Spirit, heavenly Dove,
   with all thy quickening powers;
   come, shed abroad the Saviour's love,
   and that shall kindle ours.

139 Howard Kingsbury (c. 1850) alt.

1. Come, let us all unite and sing –
   God is love, God is love!
   While heaven and earth their praises
       bring –
   God is love, God is love!
   Let every soul from sin awake,
   in every heart sweet music make,
   and sweetly sing for Jesus' sake –
   God is love, God is love!

2. O tell to earth's remotest bound –
   God is love, God is love!
   In Christ is full redemption found –
   God is love, God is love!
   His blood can cleanse our sins away;
   his Spirit turns our night to day,
   and leads our souls with joy to say –
   God is love, God is love!

3. How happy is our portion here –
   God is love, God is love!
   His promises our spirits cheer –
   God is love, God is love!
   He is our sun and shield by day,
   by night he near our tents will stay,
   he will be with us all the way –
   God is love, God is love!

4. In Zion we shall sing again –
   God is love, God is love!
   Yes, this shall be our highest strain –
   God is love, God is love!
   Whilst endless ages roll along,
   in concert with the heavenly throng,
   this shall be still our sweetest song –
   God is love, God is love!

140 Charles Wesley (1707-1788)

1. Come, let us anew
   our journey pursue,
   roll round with the year,
   and never stand still till the Master
      appear.

2. His adorable will
   let us gladly fulfil,
   and our talents improve,
   by the patience of hope and the labour of
      love.

3. Our life is a dream,
   our time as a stream
   glides swiftly away,
   and the fugitive moment refuses to stay.

4. The arrow is flown,
   the moment is gone,
   the millennial year
   rushes on to our view,
   and eternity's here.

5. O that each in the day
   of his coming may say:
   'I have fought my way through,
   I have finished the work thou didst give
      me to do!'

6. O that each from the Lord
   may receive the glad word:
   'Well and faithfully done;
   enter into my joy, and sit down on my
      throne!'

141 Isaac Watts (1674-1748) alt.

1. Come, let us join our cheerful songs
   with angels round the throne;
   ten thousand thousand are their tongues,
   but all their joys are one.

2. 'Worthy the Lamb that died,' they cry,
   'to be exalted thus.'
   'Worthy the Lamb,' our lips reply,
   'for he was slain for us.'

3. Jesus is worthy to receive
   honour and pow'r divine;
   and blessings, more than we can give,
   be, Lord, for ever thine.

4. Let all creation join in one
   to bless the sacred name
   of him that sits upon the throne,
   and to adore the Lamb.

142 Charles Wesley (1707-1788)

1. Come, let us join our friends above
   that have obtained the prize,
   and on the eagle wings of love
   to joys celestial rise:
   let all the saints terrestrial sing
   with those to glory gone;
   for all the servants of our King,
   in earth and heaven, are one.

2. One family we dwell in him,
   one church, above, beneath,
   though now divided by the stream,
   the narrow stream of death:
   one army of the living God,
   to his command we bow;
   part of his host have crossed the flood,
   and part are crossing now.

3. Ten thousand to their endless home
   this solemn moment fly;
   and we are to the margin come,
   and we expect to die;
   ev'n now by faith we join our hands
   with those that went before,
   and greet the blood-besprinkled bands
   on the eternal shore.

4. Our spirits too shall quickly join,
   like theirs with glory crowned,
   and shout to see our captain's sign,
   to hear his trumpet sound.
   O that we now might grasp our guide!
   O that the word were given!
   Come, Lord of hosts, the waves divide,
   and land us all in heaven.

143 Robert Walmsley (1831-1905)

1. Come, let us sing of a wonderful love,
   tender and true;
   out of the heart of the Father above,
   streaming to me and to you:
   wonderful love
   dwells in the heart of the Father above.

2. Jesus, the Saviour, this gospel to tell,
   joyfully came;
   came with the helpless and hopeless to
       dwell,
   sharing their sorrow and shame;
   seeking the lost,
   saving, redeeming at measureless cost.

3. Jesus is seeking the wanderers yet;
   why do they roam?
   Love only waits to forgive and forget;
   home! weary wanderer, home!
   Wonderful love
   dwells in the heart of the Father above.

4. Come to my heart, O thou wonderful
       love,
   come and abide,
   lifting my life till it rises above
   envy and falsehood and pride;
   seeking to be
   lowly and humble, a learner of thee.

144 John Morison (1750-1798)
as in *Scottish Paraphrases* (1781) based on Hosea 6: 1-4

1. Come, let us to the Lord our God
   with contrite hearts return;
   our God is gracious, nor will leave
   the desolate to mourn.

2. His voice commands the tempest forth,
   and stills the stormy wave;
   and though his arm be strong to smite,
   'tis also strong to save.

3. Long has the night of sorrow reigned;
   the dawn shall bring us light;
   God shall appear, and we shall rise
   with gladness in his sight.

4. Our hearts, if God we seek to know,
   shall know him and rejoice;
   his coming like the morn shall be,
   like morning songs his voice.

5. As dew upon the tender herb,
   diffusing fragrance round;
   as showers that usher in the spring,
   and cheer the thirsty ground:

6. So shall his presence bless our souls,
   and shed a joyful light;
   that hallowed morn shall chase away
   the sorrows of the night.

145 Charles Wesley (1707-1788)

1. Come, let us use the grace divine,
   and all, with one accord,
   in a perpetual cov'nant join
   ourselves to Christ the Lord.

2. Give up ourselves, through Jesu's power,
   his name to glorify;
   and promise, in this sacred hour,
   for God to live and die.

3. The cov'nant we this moment make
   be ever kept in mind:
   we will no more our God forsake,
   or cast his words behind.

Continued overleaf

4. We never will throw off his fear
   who hears our solemn vow;
   and if thou art well pleased to hear,
   come down, and meet us now.

5. To each the cov'nant blood apply,
   which takes our sins away;
   and register our names on high,
   and keep us to that day.

146 Charles Wesley (1707-1788)

1. Come, let us with our Lord arise,
   our Lord, who made both earth and skies:
   who died to save the world he made,
   and rose triumphant from the dead;
   he rose, the Prince of life and peace,
   and stamped the day for ever his.

2. This is the day the Lord has made
   that all may see his love displayed,
   may feel his resurrection's power,
   and rise again, to fall no more,
   in perfect righteousness renewed,
   and filled with all the life of God.

3. Then let us render him his own,
   with solemn prayer approach his throne,
   with meekness hear the gospel word,
   with thanks his dying love record,
   our joyful hearts and voices raise,
   and fill his courts with songs of praise.

4. Honour and praise to Jesus pay
   throughout his consecrated day;
   be all in Jesus' praise employed,
   nor leave a single moment void;
   with utmost care the time improve,
   and only breathe his praise and love.

147 John Newton (1725-1807)

1. Come, my soul, thy suit prepare,
   Jesus loves to answer prayer;
   he himself has bid thee pray,
   therefore will not say thee nay.

2. Thou art coming to a King:
   large petitions with thee bring;
   for his grace and power are such,
   none can ever ask too much.

3. With my burden I begin:
   Lord, remove this load of sin;
   let thy blood, for sinners spilt,
   set my conscience free from guilt.

4. Lord, I come to thee for rest;
   take possession of my breast;
   there thy blood-bought right maintain,
   and without a rival reign.

5. While I am a pilgrim here,
   let thy love my spirit cheer;
   as my guide, my guard, my friend,
   lead me to my journey's end.

148 Patricia Morgan and Dave Bankhead
© 1984 Kingsway's Thankyou Music

Come on and celebrate
his gift of love, we will celebrate
the Son of God who loved us
and gave us life.
We'll shout your praise, O King,
you give us joy nothing else can bring;
we'll give to you our offering
in celebration praise.

Come on and celebrate, celebrate,
celebrate and sing,
celebrate and sing to the King. *(Repeat)*

149 Charles Wesley (1707-1788)

1. Come, O thou all-victorious Lord,
   thy power to us make known;
   strike with the hammer of thy word,
   and break these hearts of stone.

2. Give us ourselves and thee to know,
   in this our gracious day;
   repentance unto life bestow,
   and take our sins away.

3. Conclude us first in unbelief,
   and freely then release;
   fill every soul with sacred grief,
   and then with sacred peace.

4. Impoverish, Lord, and then relieve,
   and then enrich the poor;
   the knowledge of our sickness give,
   the knowledge of our cure.

5. That blessèd sense of guilt impart,
   and then remove the load;
   trouble, and wash the troubled heart
   in the atoning blood.

6. Our desperate state through sin declare,
   and speak our sins forgiven;
   by perfect holiness prepare,
   and take us up to heaven.

150

Charles Wesley (1707-1788)
based on Genesis 32: 26-32

1. Come, O thou traveller unknown,
   whom still I hold, but cannot see!
   My company before is gone,
   and I am left alone with thee;
   with thee all night I mean to stay,
   and wrestle till the break of day.

2. I need not tell thee who I am,
   my misery and sin declare;
   thyself hast called me by my name;
   look on thy hands, and read it there:
   but who, I ask thee, who art thou?
   Tell me thy name, and tell me now.

3. In vain thou strugglest to get free;
   I never will unloose my hold!
   Art thou the Man that died for me?
   The secret of thy love unfold:
   wrestling, I will not let thee go,
   till I thy name, thy nature know.

4. Wilt thou not yet to me reveal
   thy new, unutterable name?
   Tell me, I still beseech thee, tell;
   to know it now resolved I am:
   wrestling, I will not let thee go,
   till I thy name, thy nature know.

5. What though my shrinking flesh
      complain,
   and murmur to contend so long?
   I rise superior to my pain,
   when I am weak, then I am strong;
   and when my all of strength shall fail,
   I shall with the God-Man prevail.

6. Yield to me now; for I am weak,
   but confident in self-despair;
   speak to my heart, in blessings speak,
   be conquered by my instant prayer;
   speak, or thou never hence shalt move,
   and tell me if thy name is Love.

7. 'Tis Love! 'tis Love! Thou diedst for me!
   I hear thy whisper in my heart;
   the morning breaks, the shadows flee,
   pure, universal love thou art;
   to me, to all, thy mercies move:
   thy nature and thy name is Love.

8. My prayer has power with God; the grace
   unspeakable I now receive;
   through faith I see thee face to face,
   I see thee face to face, and live!
   In vain I have not wept and strove:
   thy nature and thy name is Love.

9. I know thee, Saviour, who thou art,
   Jesus, the feeble sinner's friend;
   nor wilt thou with the night depart,
   but stay and love me to the end;
   thy mercies never shall remove:
   thy nature and thy name is Love.

10. The Sun of Righteousness on me
    has risen with healing in his wings;
    withered my nature's strength, from thee
    my soul its life and succour brings;
    my help is all laid up above:
    thy nature and thy name is Love.

11. Contented now upon my thigh
    I halt, till life's short journey end;
    all helplessness, all weakness, I
    on thee alone for strength depend;
    nor have I power from thee to move:
    thy nature and thy name is Love.

Continued overleaf

12. Lame as I am, I take the prey,
hell, earth, and sin with ease o'ercome;
I leap for joy, pursue my way,
and as a bounding hart fly home,
through all eternity to prove
thy nature and thy name is Love.

151 Martin Leckebusch (b.1962)
© 2000 Kevin Mayhew Ltd.

1. Come, see the Lord in his breathtaking
splendour:
gaze at his majesty – bow and adore!
Enter his presence with wonder and
worship –
he is the King and enthroned evermore.

2. He is the Word who was sent by the
Father,
born as a baby, a child of our race:
God here among us, revealed as a servant,
walking the pathway of truth and of grace.

3. He is the Lamb who was slain to redeem
us –
there at the cross his appearance was
marred;
though he emerged from the grave as the
victor,
still from the nails and the spear he is
scarred.

4. He is the Lord who ascended in
triumph –
ever the sound of his praises shall ring!
Hail him the First and the Last, the
Almighty:
Jesus, our Prophet, our Priest and our
King.

5. Come, see the Lord in his breathtaking
splendour:
gaze at his majesty – bow and adore!
Come and acknowledge him Saviour and
Sovereign:
Jesus our King is enthroned evermore.

152 Charles Wesley (1707-1788)

1. Come, sinners, to the gospel feast,
let every soul be Jesu's guest;
you need not one be left behind,
for God has bidden all mankind.

2. Sent by my Lord, on you I call,
the invitation is to all;
come, all the world; come, sinner, thou!
All things in Christ are ready now.

3. Come, all ye souls by sin oppressed,
ye restless wanderers after rest,
ye poor, and maimed, and halt, and
blind,
in Christ a hearty welcome find.

4. His love is mighty to compel;
his conquering love consent to feel;
yield to his love's resistless power,
and fight against your God no more.

5. See him set forth before your eyes;
that precious bleeding sacrifice!
His offered benefits embrace,
and freely now be saved by grace.

6. This is the time; no more delay!
This is the Lord's accepted day;
come in, this moment, at his call,
and live for him who died for all.

153 Charles Wesley (1707-1788)

1. Come, thou everlasting Spirit,
bring to every thankful mind
all the Saviour's dying merit,
all his sufferings for mankind.

2. True recorder of his passion,
now the living faith impart,
now reveal his great salvation,
preach his gospel to our heart.

3. Come, thou witness of his dying;
   come, remembrancer divine,
   let us feel thy power, applying
   Christ to every soul, and mine.

154 Robert Robinson (1735-1790) alt.

1. Come, thou fount of every blessing,
   tune my heart to sing thy grace;
   streams of mercy never ceasing
   call for songs of loudest praise.
   Teach me some melodious measure
   sung by flaming tongues above;
   O the vast, the boundless treasure
   of my Lord's unchanging love!

2. Here I find my greatest treasure:
   'Hither by thy help I've come',
   and I hope, by thy good pleasure,
   safely to arrive at home.
   Jesus sought me when a stranger,
   wandering from the fold of God;
   he, to rescue me from danger,
   interposed his precious blood.

3. O to grace how great a debtor
   daily I'm constrained to be!
   Let that grace, Lord, like a fetter,
   bind my wandering heart to thee.
   Prone to wander, Lord, I feel it,
   prone to leave the God I love;
   take my heart, O take and seal it,
   seal it from thy courts above!

155 Charles Wesley (1707-1788)

1. Come, thou long expected Jesus,
   born to set thy people free;
   from our fears and sins release us;
   let us find our rest in thee.

2. Israel's strength and consolation,
   hope of all the earth thou art;
   dear desire of ev'ry nation,
   joy of ev'ry longing heart.

3. Born thy people to deliver;
   born a child and yet a king;
   born to reign in us for ever;
   now thy gracious kingdom bring.

4. By thine own eternal Spirit,
   rule in all our hearts alone:
   by thine all-sufficient merit,
   raise us to thy glorious throne.

156 David Mowbray (b.1938)
© 1979 Stainer & Bell Ltd .& The Trustees for
Methodist Church Purposes

1. Come to us, creative Spirit,
   in our Father's house,
   every natural talent foster,
   hidden skills arouse,
   that within your earthly temple
   wise and simple
   may rejoice.

2. Poet, painter, music-maker,
   all your treasures bring;
   craftsman, actor, graceful dancer,
   make your offering:
   join your hands in celebration!
   Let creation
   shout and sing!

3. Word from God eternal springing,
   fill our minds, we pray,
   and in all artistic vision
   give integrity.
   May the flame, within us burning,
   kindle yearning
   day by day.

4. In all places and for ever
   glory be expressed
   to the Son with God the Father,
   and the Spirit blest.
   In our worship and our living
   keep us striving
   towards the best.

157

Isaac Watts (1674-1748) alt.

1. Come, we that love the Lord,
   and let our joys be known;
   join in a song with sweet accord,
   and thus surround the throne.

2. The sorrows of the mind
   be banished from the place;
   religion never was designed
   to make our pleasures less.

3. Let those refuse to sing
   that never knew our God;
   but children of the heavenly King
   may speak their joys abroad.

4. We, saved by grace have found
   glory begun below;
   celestial fruits on earthly ground
   from faith and hope may grow.

5. Then let our songs abound,
   and every tear be dry;
   we're marching through Immanuel's
      ground
   to fairer worlds on high.

6. There we shall see his face,
   and never, never sin;
   there, from the rivers of his grace,
   drink endless pleasures in.

158

Martin E. Leckebusch (b. 1962)
© 1999 Kevin Mayhew Ltd.

1. Come, wounded Healer, your
      suff'rings reveal –
   the scars you accepted, our anguish to
      heal.
   Your wounds bring such comfort in
      body and soul
   to all who bear torment and yearn to
      be whole.

2. Come, hated Lover, and gather us near,
   your welcome, your teaching, your
      challenge to hear:
   where scorn and abuse cause rejection
      and pain,
   your loving acceptance makes hope live
      again!

3. Come, broken Victor, condemned to a
      cross –
   how great are the treasures we gain
      from your loss!
   Your willing agreement to share in our
      strife
   transforms our despair into fullness of life.

159

John Mason Neale (1818-1866) and others
based on J. Hupton (1762-1849)

1. Come, ye faithful, raise the anthem,
   cleave the skies with shouts of praise;
   sing to him who found the ransom,
   Ancient of eternal days,
   God of God, the Word incarnate,
   whom the heaven of heaven obeys.

2. Ere he raised the lofty mountains,
   formed the seas, or built the sky,
   love eternal, free, and boundless,
   moved the Lord of life to die,
   fore-ordained the Prince of princes
   for the throne of Calvary.

3. There, for us and our redemption,
   see him all his life-blood pour!
   There he wins our full salvation,
   dies that we may die no more;
   then, arising, lives for ever,
   reigning where he was before.

4. Yet this earth he still remembers,
   still by him the flock are fed;
   yea, he gives them food immortal,
   gives himself, the living Bread;
   leads them where the precious fountain
   from the smitten rock is shed.

5. Trust him, then, ye fearful pilgrims;
who shall pluck you from his hand?
Pledged he stands for your salvation,
leads you to the promised land.
O that we, with all the faithful,
there around his throne may stand!

160
Henry Alford (1810-1871) alt.

1. Come, ye thankful people, come,
raise the song of harvest-home!
All is safely gathered in,
ere the winter storms begin;
God, our maker, doth provide
for our wants to be supplied;
come to God's own temple, come;
raise the song of harvest-home!

2. We ourselves are God's own field,
fruit unto his praise to yield;
wheat and tares together sown,
unto joy or sorrow grown;
first the blade and then the ear,
then the full corn shall appear:
grant, O harvest Lord, that we
wholesome grain and pure may be.

3. For the Lord our God shall come,
and shall take his harvest home,
from his field shall purge away
all that doth offend, that day;
give his angels charge at last
in the fire the tares to cast,
but the fruitful ears to store
in his garner evermore.

4. Then, thou Church triumphant, come,
raise the song of harvest-home;
all be safely gathered in,
free from sorrow, free from sin,
there for ever purified
in God's garner to abide:
come, ten thousand angels, come,
raise the glorious harvest-home!

161
Paul Gerhardt (1607-1676)
Trans. John Wesley (1703-1791)

1. Commit thou all thy griefs
and ways into his hands,
to his sure truth and tender care,
who heaven and earth commands.

2. Who points the clouds their course,
whom winds and seas obey,
he shall direct thy wandering feet.
He shall prepare thy way.

3. Thou on the Lord rely,
so safe shalt thou go on;
fix on his work thy steadfast eye,
so shall thy work be done.

4. No profit canst thou gain
by self-consuming care;
to him commend thy cause; his ear
attends the softest prayer.

5. Thy everlasting truth,
Father, thy ceaseless love,
sees all thy children's wants, and knows
what best for each will prove.

6. Thou everywhere hast sway,
and all things serve thy might;
thy every act pure blessing is,
thy path unsullied light.

Part 2

7. Give to the winds thy fears;
hope, and be undismayed:
God hears thy sighs, and counts thy tears,
God shall lift up thy head.

8. Through waves, and clouds, and storms
he gently clears thy way:
wait thou his time; so shall this night
soon end in joyous day.

9. Still heavy is thy heart?
Still sink thy spirits down?
Cast off the weight, let fear depart,
bid every care be gone.

Continued overleaf

10. What though thou rulest not?
    Yet heav'n, and earth, and hell
    proclaim: God sitteth on the throne,
    and ruleth all things well!

11. Leave to his sovereign sway
    to choose and to command;
    so shalt thou wondering own his way
    how wise, how strong his hand.

12. Far, far above thy thought
    his counsel shall appear,
    when fully he the work hath wrought
    that caused thy needless fear.

13. Thou seest our weakness, Lord;
    our hearts are known to thee:
    O lift thou up the sinking hand,
    confirm the feeble knee!

14. Let us in life, in death,
    thy steadfast truth declare,
    and publish with our latest breath
    thy love and guardian care.

162   George Stringer Rowe (1830-1913)

1. Cradled in a manger, meanly
   laid the Son of Man his head;
   sleeping his first earthly slumber
   where the oxen had been fed.
   Happy were those shepherds listening
   to the holy angel's word;
   happy they within that stable,
   worshipping their infant Lord.

2. Happy all who hear the message
   of his coming from above;
   happier still who hail his coming,
   and with praises greet his love.
   Blessèd Saviour, Christ most holy,
   in a manger thou didst rest;
   canst thou stoop again, yet lower,
   and abide within my breast?

3. Evil things are there before thee;
   in the heart, where they have fed,
   wilt thou pitifully enter,
   Son of Man, and lay thy head?
   Enter, then, O Christ most holy;
   make a Christmas in my heart;
   make a heaven of my manger:
   it is heaven where thou art.

4. And to those who never listened
   to the message of thy birth,
   who have winter, but no Christmas
   bringing them thy peace on earth,
   send to these the joyful tidings;
   by all people, in each home,
   be there heard the Christmas anthem:
   praise to God, the Christ has come!

163   Christ Bowater (b.1947) and Ian Taylor (b.1957)
© 1998 Sovereign Lifestyle Music

1. Creation is awaiting the return of the
   King.
   The trees are poised to clap their hands
   for joy.
   The mountains stand majestic to salute
   their God;
   the desert lies in wait to burst into
   bloom.

   The King is coming,
   The King is coming,
   The King is coming
   to set creation free.
   (Repeat)

2. The church is awaiting the return of the
   King.
   The people joined together in his love.
   Redeemed by his blood, washed in his
   word.
   As a bride longs for her bridegroom,
   the Church looks to God.

The King is coming,
The King is coming,
The King is coming
to receive his bride.
(Repeat)

3. The world is awaiting the return of the
   King.
   The earth is a footstool for his feet.
   Every knee will bow down,
   every tongue confess,
   that Jesus Christ is Lord
   of heaven and earth.

   The King is coming,
   The King is coming,
   The King is coming
   to reign in majesty.
   (Repeat)

164 9th Century
Trans. John Dryden (1631-1700) alt.

1. Creator Spirit, by whose aid
   the world's foundations first were laid,
   come, visit every waiting mind;
   come, pour thy joys on humankind;
   from sin and sorrow set us free,
   and make thy temples worthy thee.

2. O source of uncreated heat,
   the Father's promised Paraclete!
   Thrice holy fount, thrice holy fire,
   our hearts with heavenly love inspire;
   come, and thy sacred unction bring
   to sanctify us while we sing.

3. Plenteous of grace, descend from high,
   rich in thy sevenfold energy;
   make us eternal truths receive,
   and practise all that we believe;
   give us thyself, that we may see
   the Father and the Son by thee.

4. Immortal honour, endless fame,
   attend the almighty Father's name:
   the Saviour Son be glorified,
   who for our souls' redemption died:
   and equal adoration be,
   eternal Paraclete, to thee.

165 Matthew Bridges (1800-1894)

1. Crown him with many crowns,
   the Lamb upon his throne;
   hark, how the heav'nly anthem drowns
   all music but its own:
   awake, my soul, and sing
   of him who died for thee,
   and hail him as thy matchless King
   through all eternity.

2. Crown him the Virgin's Son,
   the God incarnate born,
   whose arm those crimson trophies won
   which now his brow adorn;
   fruit of the mystic Rose,
   as of that Rose the Stem,
   the Root, whence mercy ever flows,
   the Babe of Bethlehem.

3. Crown him the Lord of love;
   behold his hands and side,
   rich wounds, yet visible above,
   in beauty glorified:
   no angel in the sky
   can fully bear that sight,
   but downward bends each burning eye
   at mysteries so bright.

4. Crown him the Lord of peace,
   whose pow'r a sceptre sways
   from pole to pole, that wars may cease,
   absorbed in prayer and praise:
   his reign shall know no end,
   and round his piercèd feet
   fair flow'rs of paradise extend
   their fragrance ever sweet.

Continued overleaf

5. Crown him the Lord of years,
the Potentate of time,
Creator of the rolling spheres,
ineffably sublime.
All hail, Redeemer, hail!
for thou hast died for me;
thy praise shall never, never fail
throughout eternity.

166 John Greenleaf Whittier (1807-1892)

1. Dear Lord and Father of mankind,
forgive our foolish ways!
Re-clothe us in our rightful mind,
in purer lives thy service find,
in deeper rev'rence praise,
in deeper rev'rence praise.

2. In simple trust like theirs who heard,
beside the Syrian sea,
the gracious calling of the Lord,
let us, like them, without a word,
rise up and follow thee,
rise up and follow thee.

3. O Sabbath rest by Galilee!
O calm of hills above,
where Jesus knelt to share with thee
the silence of eternity,
interpreted by love!
Interpreted by love!

4. Drop thy still dews of quietness,
till all our strivings cease;
take from our souls the strain and stress,
and let our ordered lives confess
the beauty of thy peace,
the beauty of thy peace.

5. Breathe through the heats of our desire
thy coolness and thy balm;
let sense be dumb, let flesh retire;
speak through the earthquake,
wind and fire,
O still small voice of calm!
O still small voice of calm!

167 John Hunter (1848-1917)

1. Dear Master, in whose life I see
all that I would, but fail to be,
let thy clear light for ever shine,
to shame and guide this life of mine.

2. Though what I dream and what I do
in my weak days are always two,
help me, oppressed by things undone,
O thou, whose deeds and dreams were one!

168 Charles Wesley (1707 - 1788)

1. Depth of mercy! can there be
mercy still reserved for me?
Can my God his wrath forbear?
Me, the chief of sinners, spare?

2. I have long withstood his grace,
long provoked him to his face,
would not hearken to his calls,
grieved him by a thousands falls.

3. Whence to me this waste of love?
Ask my Advocate above!
See the cause in Jesu's face,
now before the throne of grace.

4. Jesus speaks and pleads his blood
he disarms the wrath of God
now my Father's mercies move,
justice lingers into love.

5. There for me the Saviour stands;
shows his wounds and spreads his hands.
God is love; I know, I feel;
Jesus lives, and loves me still.

6. Jesus, answer from above:
is not all thy nature love?
Wilt thou not the wrong forget?
Suffer me to kiss thy feet?

7. Pity from thine eye let fall;
by a look my soul recall;
now the stone to flesh convert,
cast a look, and break my heart.

169 George Ratcliffe Woodward (1848-1934)
© SPCK

1. Ding dong, merrily on high!
   In heav'n the bells are ringing;
   ding dong, verily the sky
   is riv'n with angels singing.

   Gloria, hosanna in excelsis!
   Gloria, hosanna in excelsis!

2. E'en so here below, below,
   let steeple bells be swungen,
   and io, io, io,
   by priest and people sungen.

3. Pray you, dutifully prime
   your matin chime, ye ringers;
   may you beautifully rhyme
   your evetime song, ye singers.

170 Andy Park
© 1994 Mercy/Vineyard Publishing/Music
Services/CopyCare

1. Down the mountain the river flows,
   and it brings refreshing wherever it goes.
   Through the valleys and over the fields,
   the river is rushing and the river is here.

   The river of God sets our feet a-dancing,
   the river of God fills our hearts with cheer;
   the river of God fills our mouths with
      laughter,
   and we rejoice for the river is here.

2. The river of God is teeming with life,
   and all who touch it can be revived.
   And those who linger on this river's shore
   will come back thirsting for more of the
      Lord.

3. Up to the mountain we love to go
   to find the presence of the Lord.
   Along the banks of the river we run,
   we dance with laughter, giving praise to
      the Son.

171 Graham Kendrick (b. 1950)
© 1994 Make Way Music

1. Earth lies spellbound in darkness,
   sin's oppressive night;
   yet in Bethlehem hope is burning bright.
   Mysteries are unfolding,
   but the only sign is a manger bed
   where a baby cries.

   Wake up, wake up, it's Christmas morning,
   Christ's eternal day is dawning.
   Angels sing in exultation,
   fill the streets with celebration.
   Now to God on high be glory,
   to the earth proclaim the story.
   Ring the bells in jubilation,
   tell the news to every nation:
   Christ has come! Christ has come!

2. Crowding stairways of starlight,
   choirs of angels sing:
   'Glory, glory to God in the highest heav'n.'
   Peace is stilling the violence,
   hope is rising high, God is watching us
      now
   through a baby's eyes.

3. Weakness shatters the pow'rful,
   meekness shames the proud,
   vain imaginings come tumbling down.
   Ancient mercies remembered,
   hungry satisfied, lowly, humble hearts
   are lifted high.

172 Charles Wesley (1707-1788)

1. Earth, rejoice, our Lord is King!
   Sons of men, his praises sing;
   sing ye in triumphant strains,
   Jesus the Messiah reigns!

2. Power is all to Jesus given,
   Lord of hell, and earth, and heaven,
   every knee to him shall bow;
   Satan, hear, and tremble now!

Continued overleaf

3. Angels and archangels join,
   all triumphantly combine,
   all in Jesu's praise agree,
   carrying on his victory.

4. Though the sons of night blaspheme,
   more there are with us than them;
   God with us, we cannot fear;
   fear, ye fiends, for Christ is here!

5. Lo, to faith's enlightened sight,
   all the mountain flames with light!
   Hell is nigh, but God is nigher,
   circling us with host of fire.

6. Christ the Saviour is come down,
   points us to the victor's crown,
   bids us take our seats above,
   more than conquerors in his love.

173 Charles Wesley (1707-1788)

1. Entered the holy place above,
   covered with meritorious scars,
   the tokens of his dying love
   our great high-priest in glory bears;
   he pleads his passion on the tree,
   he shows himself to God for me.

2. Before the throne my Saviour stands,
   my friend and advocate appears;
   my name is graven on his hands,
   and him the Father always hears;
   while low at Jesu's cross I bow,
   he hears the blood of sprinkling now.

3. This instant now I may receive
   the answer of his powerful prayer;
   this instant now by him I live,
   his prevalence with God declare;
   and soon my spirit, in his hands,
   shall stand where my forerunner stands.

174 William Joseph Penn (1875-1956)
© Copyright Control

1. Enthrone thy God within thy heart,
   thy being's inmost shrine;
   he doth to thee the power impart
   to live the life divine.

2. Seek truth in him with Christlike mind;
   with faith his will discern;
   walk on life's way with him, and find
   thy heart within thee burn.

3. With love that overflows thy soul
   love him who first loved thee;
   is not his love thy life, thy goal,
   thy soul's eternity?

4. Serve him in his suffing strength:
   heart, mind, and soul employ;
   and he shall crown thy days at length
   with everlasting joy.

175 John Cennick (1718-1755) alt.

1. Ere I sleep, for every favour
   this day showed
   by my God,
   I will bless my Saviour.

2. O my Lord, what shall I render
   to thy name,
   still the same,
   gracious, good, and tender?

3. Thou hast ordered all my living
   in thy way,
   heard me pray,
   sanctified my giving.

4. Visit me with thy salvation;
   let thy care
   now be near
   round my habitation.

5. Leave me not, but ever love me;
   let thy peace
   be my bliss,
   till thou hence remove me.

6. Thou my rock, my guard, my tower,
safely keep,
while I sleep,
me, with all thy power.

7. So, whene'er in death I slumber,
let me rise
with the wise,
counted in their number.

176 Nicolaus Ludwig von Zinzendorf (1700-1760)
Trans. John Wesley (1703-1791) alt.

1. Eternal depth of love divine,
in Jesus, God with us, displayed;
how bright thy beaming glories shine!
How wide thy healing streams are spread!

2. With whom dost thou delight to dwell?
Sinners, a lost and thankless race;
O God, what tongue aright can tell
how vast thy love, how great thy grace!

3. The dictates of thy sovereign will
with joy our grateful hearts receive;
all thy delight in us fulfil;
lo! all we are to thee we give.

4. To thy sure love, thy tender care,
our flesh, soul, spirit, we resign:
O fix thy sacred presence there,
and seal the abode for ever thine!

5. O King of glory! Thy rich grace
our feeble thought surpasses far;
yea, e'en our sins, though numberless,
less numerous than thy mercies are.

6. Still, Lord, thy saving health display,
and arm our souls with heavenly zeal;
so fearless shall we urge our way
through all the powers of earth and hell.

177 William Whiting (1825-1878) alt.

1. Eternal Father, strong to save,
whose arm doth bind the restless wave,
who bidd'st the mighty ocean deep
its own appointed limits keep:
O hear us when we cry to thee
for those in peril on the sea.

2. O Saviour, whose almighty word
the winds and waves submissive heard,
who walkedst on the foaming deep,
and calm, amid its rage, didst sleep:
O hear us when we cry to thee
for those in peril on the sea.

3. O sacred Spirit, who didst brood
upon the waters dark and rude,
and bid their angry tumult cease,
and give, for wild confusion, peace:
O hear us when we cry to thee
for those in peril on the sea.

4. O Trinity of love and pow'r,
our brethren shield in danger's hour.
From rock and tempest, fire and foe,
protect them whereso'er they go,
and ever let there rise to thee
glad hymns of praise from land and sea.

178 Thomas Binney (1798-1874) alt.

1. Eternal light! Eternal light!
How pure the soul must be,
when, placed within thy searching sight,
it shrinks not, but with calm delight
can live and look on thee.

2. The spirits that surround thy throne
may bear the burning bliss;
but that is surely theirs alone,
since they have never, never known
a fallen world like this.

Continued overleaf

3. O how shall I, whose native sphere
   is dark, whose mind is dim,
   before the Ineffable appear,
   and on my naked spirit bear
   the uncreated beam?

4. There is a way for man to rise
   to that sublime abode:
   an offering and a sacrifice,
   a Holy Spirit's energies,
   an Advocate with God.

5. These, these prepare us for the sight
   of holiness above;
   children of ignorance and night
   may dwell in the eternal light
   through the eternal Love!

179 John White Chadwick (1840-1904) alt.

1. Eternal Ruler of the ceaseless round
   of circling planets singing on their way;
   guide of the nations from the night
     profound
   into the glory of the perfect day;
   rule in our hearts, that we may ever be
   guided and strengthened and upheld
     by thee.

2. We are of thee, the children of thy love,
   by virtue of thy well-belovèd Son;
   descend, O Holy Spirit, like a dove,
   into our hearts, that we may be as one:
   as one with thee, to whom we ever tend;
   as one with him, our Brother and our
     Friend.

3. We would be one in hatred of all wrong,
   one in our love of all things sweet and fair,
   one with the joy that breaketh into song,
   one with the grief that trembles into
     prayer,
   one in the pow'r that makes thy
     children free
   to follow truth, and thus to follow thee.

4. O clothe us with thy heav'nly armour,
     Lord,
   thy trusty shield, thy sword of love
     divine;
   our inspiration be thy constant word;
   we ask no victories that are not thine:
   give or withhold, let pain or pleasure be;
   enough to know that we are
     serving thee.

180 John Wesley (1703-1791)

1. Eternal Son, eternal Love,
   take to thyself thy mighty power;
   let all earth's sons thy mercy prove,
   let all thy saving grace adore.

2. The triumphs of thy love display,
   in every heart reign thou alone,
   till all thy foes confess thy sway,
   and glory ends what grace began.

3. Spirit of grace, and health, and power,
   fountain of light and love below,
   abroad thy healing influence shower,
   o'er all the nations let it flow.

4. Wisdom, and might, and love are thine;
   prostrate before thy face we fall,
   confess thine attributes divine,
   and hail thee sovereign Lord of all.

5. Thee, sovereign Lord, let all confess
   that moves in earth, or air, or sky,
   revere thy power, thy goodness bless,
   tremble before thy piercing eye.

6. Blessing and honour, praise and love,
   co-equal, co-eternal Three,
   in earth below, and heaven above,
   by all thy works be paid to thee!

181
From the German, Lilian Sinclair Stevenson
(1870-1960) © *Oxford University Press*

1. Fairest Lord Jesus,
   Lord of all creation,
   Jesus, of God and man the Son;
   you will I cherish,
   you will I honour,
   you are my soul's delight and crown.

2. Fair are the rivers,
   meadows and forests
   clothed in the fresh
   green robes of spring;
   Jesus is fairer,
   Jesus is purer,
   he makes the saddest heart to sing.

3. Fair is the sunrise,
   starlight and moonlight
   spreading their glory across the sky;
   Jesus shines brighter,
   Jesus shines clearer,
   than all the heavenly host on high.

4. All fairest beauty,
   heavenly and earthly,
   Jesus, my Lord, in you I see;
   none can be nearer,
   fairer or dearer,
   than you, my Saviour, are to me.

182
Dave Bilbrough
© *1995 Kingsway's Thankyou Music*

1. Father God, fill this place
   with your love, with your grace;
   as we call on your name,
   visit us in power again.

2. Spirit come with your peace,
   heal our wounds, bring release;
   Lord, we long for your touch,
   fill our hearts with your love.

   Lord, we worship you.
   Lord, we worship you. (x2)

183
Ian Smale
© *1984 Kingsway's Thankyou Music*

Father God,
I wonder how I managed to exist
without the knowledge of your parenthood
and your loving care.
But now I am your child,
I am adopted in your family
and I can never be alone,
'cause, Father God, you're there beside me.
I will sing your praises,
I will sing your praises,
I will sing your praises,
for evermore.

184
Maria Willis (1824-1908)

1. Father, hear the prayer we offer:
   not for ease that prayer shall be,
   but for strength that we may ever
   live our lives courageously.

2. Not for ever in green pastures
   do we ask our way to be;
   but the steep and rugged pathway
   may we tread rejoicingly.

3. Not for ever by still waters
   would we idly rest and stay;
   but would smite the living fountains
   from the rocks along our way.

4. Be our strength in hours of weakness,
   in our wand'rings be our guide;
   through endeavour, failure, danger,
   Father, be thou at our side.

185
Henry More (1614-1687)
alt. John Wesley (1703-1791)

1. Father, if justly still we claim
   to us and ours the promise made,
   to us be graciously the same,
   and crown with living fire our head.

Continued overleaf

2. Admit our claim, and from above
   of holiness the Spirit shower,
   of wise discernment, humble love,
   and zeal, and unity, and power.

3. The Spirit of convincing speech,
   of power demonstrative, impart,
   such as may every conscience reach,
   and sound the unbelieving heart;

4. The Spirit of refining fire,
   searching the inmost of the mind,
   to purge all fierce and foul desire,
   and kindle life more pure and kind;

5. The Spir't of faith, in this thy day,
   to break the power of cancelled sin,
   tread down its strength, o'erturn its sway,
   and still the conquest more than win.

6. The Spirit breathe of inward life,
   which in our hearts thy laws may write;
   then grief expires, and pain, and strife:
   'tis nature all, and all delight.

186 Bob Fitts
© 1985 Scripture in Song/Integrity Music/Kingsway's
Thankyou Music

Father in heaven, how we love you,
we lift your name in all the earth.
May your kingdom be established in our
    praises
as your people declare your mighty works.
Blessèd be the Lord God Almighty,
who was and is and is to come.
Blessèd be the Lord God Almighty,
who reigns for evermore.

187 George Rawson (1807-1889)

1. Father, in high heaven dwelling,
   may our evening song be telling
   of thy mercy large and free;
   through the day thy love has fed us,
   through the day thy care has led us,
   with divinest charity.

2. Pardon, this day's sins, O Saviour-
   evil thoughts, perverse behaviour,
   envy, pride, and vanity;
   from the world, the flesh, deliver,
   save us now, and save us ever,
   O thou Lamb of Calvary!

3. From enticements of the devil,
   from the might of spirits evil,
   be our shield and panoply;
   let thy power this night defend us,
   and a heavenly peace attend us,
   and angelic company.

4. While the night-dews are distilling,
   Holy Ghost, each heart be filling
   with thine own serenity;
   softly let our eyes be closing,
   loving souls on thee reposing,
   ever-blessèd Trinity.

188 Charles Wesley (1707-1788)

1. Father, in whom we live,
   in whom we are, and move,
   glory, power and praise receive
   of thy creating love.
   Let all the angel throng
   give thanks to God on high;
   while earth repeats the joyful song,
   and echoes to the sky.

2. Incarnate Deity,
   let all the ransomed race
   render in thanks their lives to thee,
   for thy redeeming grace.
   The grace to sinners showed
   ye heavenly choirs proclaim,
   and cry: 'Salvation to our God,
   salvation to the Lamb!'

3. Spirit of holiness,
   let all thy saints adore
   thy sacred energy, and bless
   thy heart-renewing power.
   Not angel tongues can tell
   thy love's ecstatic height,
   the glorious joy unspeakable,
   the beatific sight.

4. Eternal, triune Lord!
   Let all the host above,
   Let all the sons of men, record
   and dwell upon thy love.
   When heaven and earth are fled
   before thy glorious face,
   sing all the saints thy love has made
   thine everlasting praise.

189 Jenny Hewer (b. 1945)
© 1975 Kingsway's Thankyou Music

1. Father, I place into your hands
   the things I cannot do.
   Father, I place into your hands
   the things that I've been through.
   Father, I place into your hands
   the way that I should go,
   for I know I always can trust you.

2. Father, I place into your hands
   my friends and family.
   Father, I place into your hands
   the things that trouble me.
   Father I place into your hands
   the person I would be,
   for I know I always can trust you.

3. Father, we love to see your face,
   we love to hear your voice.
   Father, we love to sing your praise
   and in your name rejoice.
   Father, we love to walk with you
   and in your presence rest,
   for we know we always can trust you.

4. Father, I want to be with you
   and do the things you do.
   Father, I want to speak the words
   that you are speaking too.
   Father, I want to love the ones
   that you will draw to you,
   for I know that I am one with you.

190 John Page Hopps (1834-1911)

1. Father, lead me day by day
   ever in thine own good way;
   teach me to be pure and true,
   show me what I ought to do.

2. When in danger, make me brave;
   make me know that thou canst save;
   keep me safe by thy dear side;
   let me in thy love abide.

3. When I'm tempted to do wrong,
   make me steadfast, wise, and strong;
   and, when all alone I stand,
   shield me with thy mighty hand.

4. When my heart is full of glee,
   help me to remember thee,
   happy most of all to know
   that my Father loves me so.

5. When my work seems hard and dry,
   may I press on cheerily;
   help me patiently to bear
   pain and hardship, toil and care.

6. May I see the good and bright
   when they pass before my sight;
   may I hear the heavenly voice
   when the pure and wise rejoice.

191

Stewart Cross (1928-1989)
© Mrs M. Cross. Used by permission

1. Father, Lord of all creation,
   ground of Being, Life and Love;
   height and depth beyond description
   only life in you can prove:
   you are mortal life's dependence:
   thought, speech, sight are ours by grace;
   yours is ev'ry hour's existence,
   sov'reign Lord of time and space.

2. Jesus Christ, the Man for Others,
   we, your people, make our prayer:
   help us love – as sisters, brothers –
   all whose burdens we can share.
   Where your name binds us together
   you, Lord Christ, will surely be;
   where no selfishness can sever
   there your love the world may see.

3. Holy Spirit, rushing, burning
   wind and flame of Pentecost,
   fire our hearts afresh with yearning
   to regain what we have lost.
   May your love unite our action,
   nevermore to speak alone:
   God, in us abolish faction,
   God, through us your love make known.

192

John Wesley (1703-1791)

1. Father of all, whose powerful voice
   called forth this universal frame,
   whose mercies over all rejoice,
   through endless ages still the same:

2. Inflame our hearts with perfect love,
   in us the work of faith fulfil;
   so heaven's host shall not swifter move
   than we on earth, to do thy will.

3. On thee we cast our care; we live
   through thee, who know'st our every need;
   O feed us with thy grace, and give
   our souls this day the living bread.

4. Eternal, spotless Lamb of God,
   before the world's foundation slain,
   sprinkle us ever with thy blood,
   O cleanse, and keep us ever clean!

5. Giver and Lord of life, whose power
   and guardian care for all are free,
   to thee, in fierce temptation's hour,
   from sin and Satan let us flee.

6. Thine, Lord, we are, and ours thou art;
   in us be all thy goodness showed.
   Renew, enlarge, and fill our heart
   with peace, and joy, and heaven, and God.

7. Thrice holy! Thine the kingdom is,
   the power omnipotent is thine;
   and, when created nature dies,
   thy never-ceasing glories shine.

193

Charles Wesley (1707-1788)

1. Father of everlasting grace,
   thy goodness and thy truth we praise,
   thy goodness and thy truth we prove;
   thou hast, in honour of thy Son,
   the gift unspeakable sent down,
   the Spir't of life, and power, and love.

2. Send us the Spirit of thy Son,
   to make the depths of Godhead known,
   to make us share the life divine;
   send him the sprinkled blood to apply,
   send him our souls to sanctify,
   and show and seal us ever thine.

3. So shall we pray, and never cease,
   so shall we thankfully confess
   thy wisdom, truth, and power, and love,
   with joy unspeakable adore,
   and bless and praise thee evermore,
   and serve thee as thy hosts above.

4. Till, added to that heavenly choir,
we raise our songs of triumph higher,
and praise thee in a bolder strain,
out-soar the first-born seraph's flight,
and sing, with all our friends in light,
thy everlasting love to man.

194 Edward Cooper (1770-1833)

1. Father of heaven, whose love profound
a ransom for our souls has found,
before thy throne we sinners bend;
to us thy pardoning love extend.

2. Almighty Son, incarnate Word,
our Prophet, Priest, Redeemer, Lord,
before thy throne we sinners bend;
to us thy saving grace extend.

3. Eternal Spirit, by whose breath
the soul is raised from sin and death,
before thy throne we sinners bend;
to us thy quickening power extend.

4. Thrice holy-Father, Spirit, Son,
mysterious Godhead, Three in One,
before thy throne we sinners bend;
grace, pardon, life, to us extend.

195 Charles Wesley (1707-1788)

1. Father of Jesus Christ-my Lord,
my Saviour, and my Head –
I trust in thee, whose powerful word
has raised him from the dead.

2. Thou know'st for my offence he died,
and rose again for me,
fully and freely justified
that I might live to thee.

3. Faith in thy power thou seest I have,
for thou this faith hast wrought;
dead souls thou callest from their grave,
and speakest worlds from nought.

4. In hope, against all human hope,
self-desperate, I believe;
thy quickening word shall raise me up,
thou shalt thy Spirit give.

5 Faith, mighty faith, the promise sees,
and looks to that alone,
laughs at impossibilities,
and cries: 'It shall be done!'

6. Obedient faith, that waits on thee,
thou never wilt reprove,
but thou wilt form thy Son in me,
and perfect me in love.

196 Anne Steele (1716-1778)

1. Father of mercies, in thy word
what endless glory shines!
For ever be thy name adored
for these celestial lines.

2. Here may the souls conceived in want
exhaustless riches find;
riches, above what earth can grant,
and lasting as the mind.

3. Here the fair tree of knowledge grows,
and yields a free repast;
sublimer fruits than nature knows
invite the longing taste.

4. Here the Redeemer's welcome voice
spreads heavenly peace around;
and life and everlasting joys
attend the blissful sound.

5. Divine instructor, gracious Lord,
be thou for ever near;
teach me to love thy sacred word,
and view my Saviour there.

197

Charles Wesley (1707-1788)

1. Father, Son, and Holy Ghost,
   One in Three, and Three in One,
   as by the celestial host,
   let thy will on earth be done;
   praise by all to thee be given,
   glorious Lord of earth and heaven.

2. If a sinner such as I
   may to thy great glory live,
   all my actions sanctify,
   all my words and thoughts receive;
   claim me for thy service, claim
   all I have and all I am.

3. Take my soul and body's powers;
   take my memory, mind, and will,
   all my goods, and all my hours,
   all I know, and all I feel,
   all I think, or speak, or do;
   take my heart, but make it new.

4. Now, O God, thine own I am,
   now I give thee back thine own;
   freedom, friends, and health, and fame
   consecrate to thee alone:
   thine I live, thrice happy I;
   happier still if thine I die.

5. Father, Son, and Holy Ghost,
   One in Three, and Three in One,
   as by the celestial host,
   let thy will on earth be done;
   praise by all to thee be given,
   glorious Lord of earth and heaven.

198

Terrye Coelho (b. 1952)
© 1972 Maranatha! Music. Administered by CopyCare

1. Father, we adore you,
   lay our lives before you.
   How we love you!

2. Jesus, we adore you . . .

3. Spirit, we adore you . . .

199

Donna Adkins (b. 1940)
© 1976 Maranatha! Music. Administered by CopyCare

1. Father, we love you,
   we worship and adore you,
   glorify your name in all the earth.
   Glorify your name, glorify your name,
   glorify your name in all the earth.

2. Jesus, we love you . . .

3. Spirit, we love you . . .

200

Percy Dearmer (1867-1936) alt.
© Oxford University Press

1. Father, who on us dost shower
   gifts of plenty from thy dower,
   to thy people give the power
   all thy gifts to use aright.

2. Give pure happiness in leisure,
   temperance in every pleasure,
   wholesome use of earthly treasure,
   bodies clear and spirits bright.

3. Lift from this and every nation
   all that brings us degradation;
   quell the forces of temptation;
   put thine enemies to flight.

4. Be with us, thy strength supplying,
   that, with energy undying,
   ev'ry evil pow'r defying,
   we may rally to the fight.

5. Thou who art our captain ever,
   lead us on to great endeavour;
   may thy church the world deliver:
   give us wisdom, courage, might.

6. Father, who hast sought and found us,
   Son of God, whose love has bound us,
   Holy Spirit, in us, round us-
   hear us, Godhead infinite.

201
Charles Wesley (1707-1788)

1. Father, whose everlasting love
   thy only Son for sinners gave,
   whose grace to all did freely move,
   and sent him down the world to save:

2. Help us thy mercy to extol,
   immense, unfathomed, unconfined;
   to praise the Lamb who died for all,
   the general Saviour of mankind.

3. Thy undistinguishing regard
   was cast on Adam's fallen race;
   for all thou hast in Christ prepared
   sufficient, sovereign, saving grace.

4. The world he suffered to redeem;
   for all he has atonement made;
   for those that will not come to him
   the ransom of his life was paid.

5. Arise, O God, maintain thy cause!
   The fullness of the nations call;
   lift up the standard of thy cross,
   and all shall own thou diedst for all.

202
Godfrey Thring (1823-1903)

1. Fierce raged the tempest o'er the deep,
   watch did thine anxious servants keep;
   but thou wast wrapped in guileless sleep,
   calm and still.

2. 'Save, Lord, we perish!' was their cry,
   'O save us in our agony!'
   Thy word above the storm rose high:
   'Peace! Be still.'

3. The wild winds hushed; the angry deep
   sank, like a little child, to sleep;
   the sullen billows ceased to leap,
   at thy will.

4. So, when our life is clouded o'er,
   and storm-winds drift us from the shore,
   say, lest we sink to rise no more:
   'Peace! Be still.'

203
John Samuel Bewley Monsell (1811-1875) alt.

1. Fight the good fight with all thy might;
   Christ is thy strength, and Christ thy right;
   lay hold on life, and it shall be
   thy joy and crown eternally.

2. Run the straight race through God's
         good grace,
   lift up thine eyes and seek his face;
   life with its way before us lies;
   Christ is the path, and Christ the prize.

3. Cast care aside, lean on thy guide;
   his boundless mercy will provide;
   trust, and thy trusting soul shall prove
   Christ is its life, and Christ its love.

4. Faint not nor fear, his arms are near;
   he changeth not, and thou art dear;
   only believe, and thou shalt see
   that Christ is all in all to thee.

204
John Raphael Peacey (1896-1971)
© The Revd. Mary J. Hancock. Used by permission

1. Filled with the Spirit's pow'r,
   with one accord
   the infant Church
   confessed its risen Lord.
   O Holy Spirit,
   in the Church today
   no less your pow'r
   of fellowship display.

2. Now with the mind of Christ
   set us on fire,
   that unity
   may be our great desire.
   Give joy and peace;
   give faith to hear your call,
   and readiness
   in each to work for all.

Continued overleaf

3. Widen our love, good Spirit,
   to embrace
   in your strong care
   the people of each race.
   Like wind and fire
   with life among us move,
   till we are known as Christ's,
   and Christians prove.

205 Horatius Bonar (1808-1889)

1. Fill thou my life, O Lord my God,
   in every part with praise,
   that my whole being may proclaim
   thy being and thy ways.

2. Not for the lip of praise alone
   nor e'en the praising heart
   I ask, but for a life made up
   of praise in every part:

3. Praise in the common things of life,
   its goings out and in;
   praise in each duty and each deed,
   however small and mean.

4. Fill every part of me with praise;
   let all my being speak
   of thee and of thy love, O Lord,
   poor though I be and weak.

5. So shalt thou, gracious Lord, from me
   receive the glory due;
   and so shall I begin on earth
   the song for ever new.

6. So shall no part of day or night
   from sacredness be free;
   but all my life, in every step,
   be fellowship with thee.

206 Timothy Dudley-Smith (b. 1926)
© Timothy Dudley-Smith

1. Fill your hearts with joy and gladness,
   sing and praise your God and mine!
   Great the Lord in love and wisdom,
   might and majesty divine!
   He who framed the starry heavens
   knows and names them as they shine.

2. Praise the Lord, his people, praise him!
   Wounded souls his comfort know.
   Those who fear him find his mercies,
   peace for pain and joy for woe;
   humble hearts are high exalted,
   human pride and pow'r laid low.

3. Praise the Lord for times and seasons,
   cloud and sunshine, wind and rain;
   spring to melt the snows of winter
   till the waters flow again;
   grass upon the mountain pastures,
   golden valleys thick with grain.

4. Fill your hearts with joy and gladness,
   peace and plenty crown your days!
   Love his laws, declare his judgements,
   walk in all his words and ways;
   he the Lord and we his children,
   praise the Lord, all people, praise!

207 John Henry Newman (1801-1890)

1. Firmly I believe and truly
   God is Three and God is One;
   and I next acknowledge duly
   manhood taken by the Son.

2. And I trust and hope most fully
   in the Saviour crucified;
   and each thought and deed unruly
   do to death as he has died.

3. Simply to his grace and wholly
   light and life and strength belong,
   and I love supremely, solely,
   him the holy, him the strong.

4. And I hold in veneration,
   for the love of him alone,
   holy Church as his creation,
   and her teachings as his own.

5. Adoration ay be given,
   with and through th'angelic host,
   to the God of earth and heaven,
   Father, Son and Holy Ghost.

208 William Walsham How (1823-1897)

1. For all the saints
   who from their labours rest,
   who thee by faith
   before the world confessed,
   thy name, O Jesus,
   be for ever blest.

   Alleluia, alleluia!

2. Thou wast their rock,
   their fortress and their might;
   thou, Lord, their captain
   in the well-fought fight;
   thou in the darkness drear
   their one true light.

3. O may thy soldiers,
   faithful, true and bold,
   fight as the saints
   who nobly fought of old,
   and win, with them,
   the victor's crown of gold.

4. O blest communion!
   fellowship divine!
   We feebly struggle,
   they in glory shine;
   yet all are one in thee,
   for all are thine.

5. And when the strife is fierce,
   the warfare long,
   steals on the ear
   the distant triumph song,
   and hearts are brave again,
   and arms are strong.

6. The golden evening
   brightens in the west;
   soon, soon to faithful
   warriors cometh rest;
   sweet is the calm of
   paradise the blest.

7. But lo! There breaks
   a yet more glorious day;
   the saints triumphant
   rise in bright array:
   the King of glory
   passes on his way.

8. From earth's wide bounds,
   from ocean's farthest coast,
   through gates of pearl
   streams in the countless host,
   singing to Father,
   Son and Holy Ghost.

209
William Walsham How (1823-1897)
Adapted by Michael Forster (b. 1946)
© 2000 Kevin Mayhew Ltd.

1. For all the saints, who from their
      labours rest,
   who thee by faith before the world
      confessed,
   thy name, O Jesus, be for ever blest.
   Alleluia!

2. Thou wast their rock, their refuge and
      their might;
   thou, Lord, the vision ever in their sight;
   thou in the darkness drear their
      one true light.
   Alleluia!

Continued overleaf

3. O may thy servants, faithful, true
    and bold,
   strive for thy kingdom as the saints
    of old,
   and win with them a glorious crown
    of gold.
   Alleluia!

4. O blest communion! fellowship divine!
   We feebly struggle, they in glory shine;
   yet all are one in thee, for all are thine.
   Alleluia!

5. And when the road is steep, the
    journey long,
   steals on the ear the distant welcome song,
   and hope is bright again, and faith
    is strong.
   Alleluia!

6. The golden evening brightens in
    the west;
   soon, soon to faithful pilgrims
    cometh rest;
   sweet is the calm of Paradise the blest.
   Alleluia!

7. But lo! There breaks a yet more
    glorious day;
   the saints triumphant rise in bright array:
   the King of glory passes on his way.
   Alleluia!

8. From earth's wide bounds, from ocean's
    farthest coast,
   through gates of pearl streams in the
    countless host,
   singing to Father, Son and Holy Ghost.
   Alleluia!

210 Rosamond E. Herklots (1905-1987) alt.
© Oxford University Press

1. 'Forgive our sins as we forgive',
   you taught us, Lord, to pray;
   but you alone can grant us grace
   to live the words we say.

2. How can your pardon reach and bless
   the unforgiving heart
   that broods on wrongs, and will not let
   old bitterness depart?

3. In blazing light your Cross reveals
   the truth we dimly knew:
   what trivial debts are owed to us,
   how great our debt to you!

4. Lord, cleanse the depths within our souls,
   and bid resentment cease.
   Then, bound to all in bonds of love,
   our lives will spread your peace.

211 Dave Richards
© 1977 Kingsway's Thankyou Music

For I'm building a people of power
and I'm making a people of praise,
that will move through this land by my
Spirit,
and will glorify my precious name.
Build your church, Lord,
make us strong, Lord,
join our hearts, Lord,
through your Son.
Make us one, Lord, in your body,
in the kingdom of your Son.

212 Folliott Sandforth Pierpoint (1835-1917) alt.

1. For the beauty of the earth,
   for the beauty of the skies,
   for the love which from our birth
   over and around us lies:

   Gracious God, to thee we raise
   this our sacrifice of praise.

2. For the beauty of each hour
   of the day and of the night,
   hill and vale, and tree and flower,
   sun and moon and stars of light:

3. For the joy of ear and eye,
   for the heart and mind's delight,
   for the mystic harmony
   linking sense to sound and sight:

4. For the joy of human love,
   brother, sister, parent, child,
   friends on earth, and friends above,
   pleasures pure and undefiled:

5. For each perfect gift of thine
   to our race so freely given,
   graces human and divine,
   flowers of earth and buds of heaven:

213 Fred Pratt Green (1903-2000)
© 1970 Stainer & Bell Ltd.

1. For the fruits of his creation,
   thanks be to God;
   for his gifts to every nation,
   thanks be to God;
   for the ploughing, sowing, reaping,
   silent growth while we are sleeping,
   future needs in earth's safe-keeping,
   thanks be to God.

2. In the just reward of labour,
   God's will is done;
   in the help we give our neighbour,
   God's will is done;
   in our world-wide task of caring
   for the hungry and despairing,
   in the harvests we are sharing,
   God's will is done.

3. For the harvests of his Spirit,
   thanks be to God;
   for the good we all inherit,
   thanks be to God;
   for the wonders that astound us,
   for the truths that still confound us,
   most of all, that love had found us,
   thanks be to God.

214 Fred Kaan (b.1929)
© 1968 Stainer & Bell Ltd.

1. For the healing of the nations,
   Lord, we pray with one accord;
   for a just and equal sharing
   of the things that earth affords.
   To a life of love in action
   help us rise and pledge our word.

2. Lead us forward, into freedom;
   from despair your world release,
   that, redeemed from war and hatred,
   all may come and go in peace.
   Show us how through care and goodness
   fear will die and hope increase.

3. All that kills abundant living,
   let it from the earth be banned;
   pride of status, race, or schooling,
   dogmas that obscure your plan.
   In our common quest for justice
   may we hallow life's brief span.

4. You, Creator-God, have written
   your great name on humankind;
   for our growing in your likeness
   bring the life of Christ to mind;
   that by our response and service
   earth its destiny may find.

215 Charles Silvester Horne (1865-1914)

1. For the might of thine arm we bless thee,
   our God, our fathers' God;
   thou hast kept thy pilgrim people
   by the strength of thy staff and rod;
   thou hast called us to the journey
   which faithless feet ne'er trod;

   For the might of thine arm we bless thee,
   our God, our fathers' God.

Continued overleaf

2. For the love of Christ constraining,
that bound their hearts as one;
for the faith in truth and freedom
in which their work was done;
for the peace of God's evangel
wherewith their feet were shod;

For the might of thine arm we bless thee,
our God, our fathers' God.

3. We are watchers of a beacon
whose light must never die;
we are guardians of an altar
that shows thee ever nigh;
we are children of thy freemen
who sleep beneath the sod;

4. May the shadow of thy presence
around our camp be spread;
baptise us with the courage
thou gavest to our dead;
O keep us in the pathway
their saintly feet have trod;

216 Shirley Erena Murray (b.1931)
© 1992 Hope Publishing Co. Administered by
CopyCare

1. For the music of creation,
for the song your Spirit sings,
for your sound's divine expression,
burst of joy in living things:
God, our God, the world's composer,
hear us, echoes of your voice:
music is your art, your glory,
let the human heart rejoice!

2. Psalms and symphonies exalt you,
drum and trumpet, string and reed,
simple melodies acclaim you,
tunes that rise from deepest need,
hymns of longing and belonging,
carols from a cheerful throat,
lilt of lullaby and love-song
catching heaven in a note.

3. All the voices of the ages
in transcendent chorus meet,
worship lifting up the senses,
hands that praise and dancing feet;
over discord and division
music speaks your joy and peace,
harmony of earth and heaven,
song of God that cannot cease!

217 Charles Wesley (1707-1788) alt.

1. Forth in thy name, O Lord, I go,
my daily labour to pursue;
thee, only thee, resolved to know,
in all I think or speak or do.

2. The task thy wisdom hath assigned
O let me cheerfully fulfil;
in all my works thy presence find,
and prove thy good and perfect will.

3. Thee may I set at my right hand,
whose eyes my inmost substance see,
and labour on at thy command,
and offer all my works to thee.

4. Give me to bear thy easy yoke,
and ev'ry moment watch and pray,
and still to things eternal look,
and hasten to thy glorious day.

5. For thee delightfully employ
whate'er thy bounteous grace hath giv'n,
and run my course with even joy,
and closely walk with thee to heav'n.

218 Graham Kendrick
© 1985 Kingsway's Thankyou Music

1. For this purpose Christ was revealed
to destroy all the works of the evil one.
Christ in us has overcome,
so with gladness we sing
and welcome his kingdom in.

Over sin he has conquered,
hallelujah, he has conquered.
Over death victorious,
hallelujah, victorious.
Over sickness he has triumphed,
hallelujah, he has triumphed,
Jesus reigns over all!

2. In the name of Jesus we stand,
   by the power of his blood we now claim
     this ground.
   Satan has no authority here,
   powers of darkness must flee,
   for Christ has the victory.

219 George Hunt Smyttan (1822-1870)
adapted by Michael Forster (b. 1946)
© *1999 Kevin Mayhew Ltd.*

1. Forty days and forty nights
   you were fasting in the wild;
   forty days and forty nights,
   tempted still, yet unbeguiled.

2. Sunbeams scorching all the day,
   chilly dew-drops nightly shed,
   prowling beasts about your way,
   stones your pillow, earth your bed.

3. Let us your endurance share,
   and from earthly greed abstain,
   with you vigilant in prayer,
   with you strong to suffer pain.

4. Then if evil on us press,
   flesh or spirit to assail,
   Victor in the wilderness,
   help us not to swerve or fail.

5. So shall peace divine be ours;
   holy gladness, pure and true:
   come to us, angelic powers,
   such as ministered to you.

6. Keep, O keep us, Saviour dear,
   ever constant by your side,
   that with you we may appear
   at th'eternal Eastertide.

220 Ruth Carter (1900-1982) alt.
© *Copyright Control*

1. For your holy book we thank you,
   and for all who served you well,
   writing, guarding and translating,
   that its pages might forth tell
   all your love and tender care
   for your people everywhere.

2. For your holy book we thank you,
   and for those who work today
   that all peoples hear its witness,
   heed, and follow in your way,
   learn your love and tender care
   for your people everywhere.

3. For your holy book we thank you;
   may its message be our guide;
   may we understand its wisdom,
   and the laws it can provide
   in your love and tender care
   for your people everywhere.

4. For your holy book we thank you;
   may its message in our hearts
   lead us now to see in Jesus
   all the grace your word imparts –
   steadfast love and tender care
   for your people everywhere.

221 Isaac Watts (1674-1748) based on Psalm 117

1. From all that dwell below the skies
   let the Creator's praise arise:
   Alleluia!
   Let the Redeemer's name be sung,
   through every land, by every tongue:
   Alleluia!

2. Eternal are thy mercies, Lord;
   eternal truth attends thy word:
   Alleluia!
   Thy praise shall sound from shore to shore,
   till suns shall rise and set no more:
   Alleluia!

222
Martin Luther (1483-1546)
Trans. Catherine Winkworth (1827-1878) alt.

The angel's message:

1. From heaven above to earth I come,
   to bear good news to everyone;
   glad tidings of great joy I bring,
   whereof I now will say and sing:

2. To you this night is born a child
   of Mary, chosen mother mild;
   this new-born babe of lowly birth,
   shall be the joy of all the earth.

3. This is the Christ who far on high
   has heard your sad and bitter cry;
   he will your full salvation be;
   he from all sin will make you free.

The children welcome Christ:

4. Welcome to earth, thou noble guest,
   through whom this sinful world is blest!
   Thou com'st to share our misery;
   what can we render, Lord, to thee?

5. Were earth a thousand times as fair,
   beset with gold and jewels rare,
   she yet were far too poor to be
   a narrow cradle, Lord, for thee.

The congregation's response:

6. Ah, dearest Jesus, holy child,
   make thee a cradle undefiled,
   within my heart, that it may be
   a quiet chamber kept for thee.

7. My heart for very joy doth leap;
   my lips no more can silence keep;
   I too must sing with joyful tongue
   that sweetest ancient cradle song:

8. 'Glory to God in highest heaven,
   who unto us his Son has given!'
   While angels sing with pious mirth
   a glad new year to all the earth.

223
Graham Kendrick (b. 1950)
© 1983 Kingsway's Thankyou Music

1. From heav'n you came, helpless babe,
   entered our world, your glory veiled;
   not to be served but to serve,
   and give your life that we might live.

   This is our God, the Servant King,
   he calls us now to follow him,
   to bring our lives as a daily offering
   of worship to the Servant King.

2. There in the garden of tears,
   my heavy load he chose to bear;
   his heart with sorrow was torn.
   'Yet not my will but yours,' he said.

3. Come see his hands and his feet,
   the scars that speak of sacrifice,
   hands that flung stars into space,
   to cruel nails surrendered.

4. So let us learn how to serve,
   and in our lives enthrone him;
   each other's needs to prefer,
   for it is Christ we're serving.

224
Charles Kingsley (1819-1875) alt.

1. From thee all skill and science flow,
   all pity, care and love,
   all calm and courage, faith and hope;
   O pour them from above!

2. Apportion them, to each and all,
   as each and all shall need,
   to rise like incense, each to thee,
   in noble thought and deed.

3. And hasten, Lord, that perfect day
   when pain and death shall cease;
   and thy just rule shall fill the earth
   with health and light and peace;

4. When ever blue the sky shall gleam,
   and ever green the sod;
   and mortal frailty spoil no more
   the paradise of God.

225
Paul S. Deming
© 1976 Integrity's Hosanna! Music.

1. From the rising of the sun to the going
    down of the same,
   the Lord's name is to be praised. *(x2)*
   Praise ye the Lord,
   praise him all ye servants of the Lord,
    praise the name of the Lord.
   Blessed be the name of the Lord from
    this time forth
   and for evermore.

226
Graham Kendrick (b. 1950)
© 1988 Make Way Music

1. From the sun's rising unto the sun's setting,
   Jesus our Lord, shall be great in the earth;
   and all earth's kingdoms shall be
    his dominion,
   all of creation shall sing of his worth.

   Let ev'ry heart, ev'ry voice,
   ev'ry tongue join with spirits ablaze;
   one in his love, we will circle the world
   with the song of his praise.
   O let all his people rejoice,
   and let all the earth hear his voice.

2. To ev'ry tongue, tribe and nation he
    sends us,
   to make disciples, to teach and baptise.
   For all authority to him is given;
   now, as his witnesses, we shall arise.

3. Come, let us join with the Church from
    all nations,
   cross ev'ry border, throw wide ev'ry door;
   workers with him as he gathers his harvest,
   till earth's far corners our Saviour adore.

227
Traditional

1. Give me joy in my heart, keep me praising,
   give me joy in my heart, I pray.
   Give me joy in my heart, keep my praising,
   keep me praising till the end of day.

Sing hosanna! Sing hosanna!
Sing hosanna to the King of kings!
Sing hosanna! Sing hosanna!
Sing hosanna to the King!

2. Give me peace in my heart,
   keep me resting . . .

3. Give me love in my heart,
   keep me serving . . .

4. Give me oil in my lamp,
   keep me burning . . .

228
Charles Wesley (1707-1788)

1. Give me the faith which can remove
   and sink the mountain to a plain;
   give me the childlike praying love,
   which longs to build thy house again;
   thy love, let it my heart o'erpower;
   and all my simple soul devour.

2. I would the precious time redeem,
   and longer live for this alone:
   to spend, and to be spent, for them
   who have not yet my Saviour known;
   fully on these my mission prove,
   and only breathe, to breathe thy love.

3. My talents, gifts, and graces, Lord,
   into thy blessèd hands receive;
   and let me live to preach thy word,
   and let me to thy glory live;
   my every sacred moment spend
   in publishing the sinners' friend.

4. Enlarge, inflame, and fill my heart
   with boundless charity divine:
   so shall I all my strength exert,
   and love them with a zeal like thine;
   and lead them to thy open side,
   the sheep for whom their Shepherd died.

229
Isaac Watts (1674-1748)

1. Give me the wings of faith to rise
   within the veil, and see
   the saints above how great their joys,
   how bright their glories be.

2. Once they were mourners here below,
   and poured out sighs and tears;
   they wrestled hard, as we do now,
   with sins and doubts and fears.

3. I ask them whence their victory came;
   they, with united breath,
   ascribe their conquest to the Lamb,
   their triumph to his death.

4. They marked the footsteps that he trod,
   (his zeal inspired their breast)
   and, following their incarnate God,
   possess the promised rest.

5. Our glorious leader claims our praise
   for his own pattern given;
   while the long cloud of witnesses
   show the same path to heaven.

230
Henry Smith
© 1978 Integrity's Hosanna! Music.
Administered by Kingsway's Thankyou Music

Give thanks with a grateful heart,
give thanks to the Holy One,
give thanks because he's given
Jesus Christ, his Son. (x2)
And now let the weak say, 'I am strong',
let the poor say, 'I am rich',
because of what the Lord has done for us.
And now let the weak say, 'I am strong',
let the poor say, 'I am rich',
because of what the Lord has done
    for us.

231
Caryl Micklem (b.1925)
© 1975 Caryl Micklem

1. Give to me, Lord, a thankful heart
   and a discerning mind;
   give, as I play the Christian's part,
   the strength to finish what I start
   and act on what I find.

2. When, in the rush of days, my will
   is habit-bound and slow,
   help me to keep in visions, still,
   what love and power and peace can fill
   a life that trusts in you.

3. By your divine and urgent claim,
   and by your human face,
   kindle our sinking hearts to flame,
   and as you teach the world your name
   let it become your place.

4. Jesus, with all your church I long
   to see your kingdom come:
   show me your way of righting wrong
   and turning sorrow into song
   until you bring me home.

232
Isaac Watts (1674-1748) based on Psalm 136, alt.

1. Give to our God immortal praise,
   mercy and truth are all his ways:
   wonders of grace to God belong,
   repeat his mercies in your song.

2. Give to the Lord of lords renown;
   the King of kings with glory crown:
   his mercies ever shall endure,
   when kings and queens are known no
       more.

3. He built the earth, he spread the sky,
   and fixed the starry lights on high:
   wonders of grace to God belong,
   repeat his mercies in your song.

4. He fills the sun with morning light,
   he bids the moon direct the night:
   his mercies ever shall endure,
   when suns and moons shall shine no
        more.

5. He sent his Son with power to save
   from guilt and darkness and the grave:
   wonders of grace to God belong,
   repeat his mercies in your song.

6. Through this brief life he guides our feet,
   and leads us to his heavenly seat:
   his mercies ever shall endure,
   when things of earth shall be no more.

233 John Newton (1725-1807) based on Isaiah 33:20-21, alt.

1. Glorious things of thee are spoken,
   Zion, city of our God;
   he whose word cannot be broken
   formed thee for his own abode.
   On the Rock of Ages founded,
   what can shake thy sure repose?
   With salvation's walls surrounded,
   thou may'st smile at all thy foes.

2. See, the streams of living waters,
   springing from eternal love,
   well supply thy sons and daughters,
   and all fear of want remove.
   Who can faint while such a river
   ever flows their thirst to assuage?
   Grace which, like the Lord, the giver,
   never fails from age to age.

3. Round each habitation hov'ring,
   see the cloud and fire appear
   for a glory and a cov'ring,
   showing that the Lord is near.
   Thus they march, the pillar leading,
   light by night and shade by day;
   daily on the manna feeding
   which he gives them when they pray.

4. Saviour, if of Zion's city
   I through grace a member am,
   let the world deride or pity,
   I will glory in thy name.
   Fading is the worldling's pleasure,
   boasted pomp and empty show;
   solid joys and lasting treasure
   none but Zion's children know.

234 Charles Wesley (1707-1788) alt.

1. Glory be to God on high,
   and peace on earth descend:
   God comes down, he bows the sky,
   and shows himself our friend:
   God the invisible appears:
   God, the blest, the great 'I Am',
   sojourns in this vale of tears,
   and Jesus is his name.

2. Him the angels all adored,
   their Maker and their King;
   tidings of their humbled Lord
   they now to mortals bring.
   Emptied of his majesty,
   of his dazzling glories shorn,
   being's source begins to be,
   and God himself is born!

3. See the eternal Son of God
   a mortal son of man
   dwelling in an earthly clod
   whom heav'n cannot contain!
   Stand amazed, ye heavens, at this!
   see the Lord of earth and skies;
   humbled to the dust he is,
   and in a manger lies.

4. We, earth's children, now rejoice,
   the Prince of Peace proclaim;
   with heaven's host lift up our voice,
   and shout Immanuel's name:
   knees and hearts to him we bow;
   of our flesh and of our bone,
   Jesus is our brother now,
   and God is all our own.

235 Danny Daniels
© 1987 Mercy/Vineyard Publishing. Administered by Copycare

Glory, glory in the highest;
glory to the Almighty;
glory to the Lamb of God,
and glory to the living Word;
glory to the Lamb!
(Repeat)

Men   I give glory,
Women   glory,
Men   glory,
Women   glory,
Men   glory,
All   glory to the Lamb. *(Repeat)*
Last time I give glory to the Lamb.

236 Thomas Ken (1637-1710)

1. Glory to thee, my God, this night
   for all the blessings of the light;
   keep me, O keep me, King of kings,
   beneath thine own almighty wings.

2. Forgive me, Lord, for thy dear Son,
   the ill that I this day have done,
   that with the world, myself and thee,
   I, ere I sleep, at peace may be.

3. Teach me to live, that I may dread
   the grave as little as my bed;
   teach me to die, that so I may
   rise glorious at the aweful day.

4. O may my soul on thee repose,
   and with sweet sleep mine eyelids close;
   sleep that may me more vig'rous make
   to serve my God when I awake.

5. Praise God, from whom all blessings flow;
   praise him, all creatures here below;
   praise him above, ye heav'nly host;
   praise Father, Son and Holy Ghost.

237 Book of Hours (1514)

God be in my head,
and in my understanding;
God be in mine eyes,
and in my looking;
God be in my mouth,
and in my speaking;
God be in my heart,
and in my thinking;
God be at mine end,
and at my departing.

238 Donald Hughes (1911-1967). Based on J.E. Rankin (1828-1904) © *Paul Hughes*

1. God be with you till we meet again;
   may he through the days direct you;
   may he in life's storms protect you;
   God be with you till we meet again.

2. God be with you till we meet again;
   and when doubts and fears oppress you,
   may his holy peace possess you;
   God be with you till we meet again.

3. God be with you till we meet again;
   in distress his grace sustain you;
   in success from pride restrain you;
   God be with you till we meet again.

4. God be with you till we meet again;
   may he go through life beside you,
   and through death in safety guide you;
   God be with you till we meet again.

When Tune 2 is sung, this refrain is used:
Till we meet! Till we meet!
Till we meet at Jesus' feet;
till we meet! Till we meet!
God be with you till we meet again!

239 Carol Owens
© 1972 Bud John Songs/EMI Christian Music Publishing. Administered by CopyCare

1. God forgave my sin in Jesus' name.
   I've been born again in Jesus' name.
   And in Jesus' name I come to you
   to share his love as he told me to.

He said: 'Freely, freely you have received;
freely, freely give.
Go in my name, and because you believe,
others will know that I live.'

2. All pow'r is giv'n in Jesus' name,
   in earth and heav'n in Jesus' name.
   And in Jesus' name I come to you
   to share his pow'r as he told me to.

3. God gives us life in Jesus' name,
   he lives in us in Jesus' name.
   And in Jesus' name I come to you
   to share his peace as he told me to.

240 Charles Coffin (1676-1749)
trans. James Russell Woodford (1820-1885)

1. God from on high has heard;
   let sighs and sorrows cease;
   the skies unfold, and lo!
   descends the gift of peace.

2. Hark! on the midnight air
   celestial voices swell;
   the host of heaven proclaim
   God comes on earth to dwell.

3. Haste with the shepherds; see
   the mystery of grace:
   a manger-bed, a child,
   is all the eye can trace.

4. Is this the eternal Son,
   who on the starry throne
   before the worlds begun
   was with the Father one?

5. Yes, faith can pierce the cloud
   which shrouds his glory now,
   and hail him God and Lord,
   to whom all creatures bow.

6. O child! thy silence speaks,
   and bids us not refuse
   to bear what flesh would shun,
   to spurn what flesh would choose.

7. Fill us with holy love,
   heal thou our earthly pride;
   born in each lowly heart,
   for ever there abide.

241 Maria Matilda Penstone (1859-1910)

1. God has given us a book full of stories,
   which was made for his people of old,
   it begins with the tale of a garden,
   and ends with the city of gold.

2. But the best is the story of Jesus,
   of the babe with the ox in the stall,
   of the song that was sung by the angels,
   the most beautiful story of all.

3. There are stories for parents and children,
   for the old who are ready to rest,
   but for all who can read them or listen,
   the story of Jesus is best.

4. For it tells how he came from the Father,
   his far-away children to call,
   to bring the lost sheep to their Shepherd,
   the most beautiful story of all.

242 George Wallace Briggs (1875-1959) alt.
© 1953, renewal 1981 Hymn Society/Hope Publishing Co.

1. God has spoken – by the prophets,
   spoken the unchanging Word,
   each from age to age proclaiming
   God, the one, the righteous Lord.
   'Mid the world's despair and turmoil
   one firm anchor holding fast:
   God eternal reigns forever,
   God the first, and God the last.

2. God has spoken – by Christ Jesus,
   Christ, the everlasting Son,
   brightness of the Father's glory,
   with the Father ever one;
   spoken by the Word incarnate,
   God of God, ere time was born,
   light of light, to earth descending,
   Christ, as God in human form.

Continued overleaf

3. God is speaking – by the Spirit,
   speaking to our hearts again,
   in the age-long word declaring
   God's own message, now as then.
   Through the rise and fall of nations
   one sure faith yet standing fast;
   God abides, the Word unchanging,
   God the first, and God the last.

243
Fred Pratt Green (1903-2000)
© 1973 Stainer & Bell Ltd.

1. God in his love for us lent us this
      planet,
   gave it a purpose in time and in space:
   small as a spark from the fire of creation,
   cradle of life and the home of our race.

2. Thanks be to God for its bounty and
      beauty,
   life that sustains us in body and mind:
   plenty for all, if we learn how to share it,
   riches undreamed-of to fathom and find.

3. Long have our human wars ruined its
      harvest;
   long has earth bowed to the terror of
      force;
   long have we wasted what others have
      need of,
   poisoned the fountain of life at its source.

4. Earth is the Lord's: it is ours to enjoy it,
   ours, as his stewards, to farm and defend.
   From its pollution, misuse, and
      destruction,
   good Lord, deliver us, world without end!

244
Isaac Watts (1674-1748)

1. God is a name my soul adores,
   almighty Three, eternal One;
   nature and grace with all their powers
   confess the Infinite unknown.

2. Thy voice produced the sea and spheres,
   bade the waves roar, the planets shine;
   but nothing like thyself appears
   through all these spacious works of thine.

3. Still restless nature dies and grows;
   from change to change the creatures run:
   thy being no succession knows,
   and all thy vast designs are one.

4. A glance of thine runs through the globe,
   rules the bright worlds and moves their
      frame;
   of light thou form' st thy dazzling robe,
   thy ministers are living flame.

5. How shall polluted mortals dare
   to sing thy glory or thy grace?
   Beneath thy feet we lie afar,
   and see but shadows of thy face.

6. Who can behold the blazing light?
   Who can approach consuming flame?
   None but thy wisdom knows thy might,
   none but thy word can speak thy name.

245
Fred Pratt Green (1903-2000)
© 1979 Stainer & Bell Ltd.

1. God is here! As we his people
   meet to offer praise and prayer,
   may we find in fuller measure
   what it is in Christ we share.
   Here, as in the world around us,
   all our varied skills and arts
   wait the coming of his Spirit
   into open minds and hearts.

2. Here are symbols to remind us
   of our lifelong need of grace;
   here are table, font and pulpit;
   here the cross has central place.
   Here in honesty of preaching,
   here in silence, as in speech,
   here in newness and renewal,
   God the Spirit comes to each.

3. Here our children find a welcome
   in the Shepherd's flock and fold,
   here as bread and wine are taken,
   Christ sustains us, as of old;
   here the servants of the Servant
   seek in worship to explore
   what it means in daily living
   to believe and to adore.

4. Lord of all, of Church of Kingdom,
   in an age of change and doubt,
   keep us faithful to the gospel,
   help us work your purpose out.
   here, in this day's dedication,
   all we have to give, receive:
   we, who cannot live without you,
   we adore you! We believe!

246 William Tidd Matson (1833-1899)

1. God is in his temple,
   the Almighty Father;
   round his footstool let us gather:
   serve with adoration
   him, the Lord most holy,
   who has mercy on the lowly;
   let us raise
   hymns of praise,
   for his great salvation:
   God is in his temple.

2. Christ comes to his temple:
   we, his word receiving,
   are made happy in believing,
   now from sin delivered;
   he has turned our sadness,
   our deep gloom, to light and gladness;
   let us raise
   hymns of praise,
   for our bonds are severed:
   Christ comes to his temple.

3. Come and claim your temple,
   gracious Holy Spirit,
   in our hearts your home inherit;
   make in us your dwelling,
   your high work fulfilling,
   into ours your will instilling;
   till we raise
   hymns of praise,
   beyond mortal telling,
   in the eternal temple.

247 Percy Dearmer (1867-1936) alt.
© Oxford University Press

1. God is love: his the care,
   tending each, ev'rywhere.
   God is love, all is there!
   Jesus came to show him,
   that we all might know him!

   Sing aloud, loud, loud!
   Sing aloud, loud, loud!
   God is good! God is truth!
   God is beauty! Praise him!

2. None can see God above;
   we can share life and love;
   thus may we Godward move,
   seek him in creation,
   holding ev'ry nation.

3. Jesus lived on the earth,
   hope and life brought to birth
   and affirmed human worth,
   for he came to save us
   by the truth he gave us.

4. To our Lord praise we sing,
   light and life, friend and King,
   coming down, love to bring,
   pattern for our duty,
   showing God in beauty.

248

Timothy Rees (1874-1939) alt.
© Geoffrey Chapman, an imprint of Continuum
International. Used by permission

1. God is love: let heav'n adore him;
   God is love: let earth rejoice;
   let creation sing before him,
   and exalt him with one voice.
   He who laid the earth's foundation,
   he who spread the heav'ns above,
   he who breathes through all creation,
   he is love, eternal Love.

2. God is love: and he enfoldeth
   all the world in one embrace;
   with unfailing grasp he holdeth
   ev'ry child of ev'ry race.
   And when human hearts are breaking
   under sorrow's iron rod,
   then they find that self-same aching
   deep within the heart of God.

3. God is love: and though with blindness
   sin afflicts the human soul,
   God's eternal loving-kindness
   guides and heals and makes us whole.
   Sin and death and hell shall never
   o'er us final triumph gain;
   God is love, so love for ever
   o'er the universe must reign.

249

Richard Bewes, based on Psalm 46
© Richard Bewes/Jubilate Hymns

1. God is our strength and refuge,
   our present help in trouble;
   and we therefore will not fear,
   though the earth should change!
   Though mountains shake and tremble,
   though swirling floods are raging,
   God the Lord of hosts is with us
      evermore!

2. There is a flowing river,
   within God's holy city;
   God is in the midst of her – she shall not
      be moved!
   God's help is swiftly given,
   thrones vanish at his presence –
   God the Lord of hosts is with us evermore!

3. Come, see the works of our maker,
   learn of his deeds all powerful;
   wars will cease across the world when he
      shatters the spear!
   Be still and know your creator,
   uplift him in the nations –
   God the Lord of hosts is with us evermore!

250

Isaac Watts (1674-1748) based on Psalm 46

1. God is the refuge of his saints,
   when storms of sharp distress invade;
   ere we can offer our complaints,
   behold him present with his aid!

2. Let mountains from their seats be hurled
   down to the deep, and buried there,
   convulsions shake the solid world,
   our faith shall never yield to fear.

3. Loud may the troubled ocean roar;
   in sacred peace our souls abide;
   while every nation, every shore,
   trembles, and dreads the swelling tide.

4. There is a stream, whose gentle flow
   makes glad the city of our God,
   life, love, and joy still gliding through,
   and watering our divine abode.

5. This sacred stream, thy vital word,
   thus all our raging fear controls;
   sweet peace thy promises afford,
   and give new strength to fainting souls.

6. Zion enjoys her Monarch's love,
   secure against the threatening hour;
   nor can her firm foundation move,
   built on his faithfulness and power.

251

Arthur Campbell Ainger (1841-1919)
adapted by Michael Forster (b. 1946)
© This version 1996 Kevin Mayhew Ltd.

1. God is working his purpose out
   as year succeeds to year.
   God is working his purpose out,
   and the day is drawing near.
   Nearer and nearer draws the time,
   the time that shall surely be,
   when the earth shall be filled
   with the glory of God
   as the waters cover the sea.

2. From the east to the utmost west
   wherever foot has trod,
   through the mouths of his messengers
   echoes forth the voice of God:
   'Listen to me, ye continents,
   ye islands, give ear to me,
   that the earth shall be filled
   with the glory of God
   as the waters cover the sea.'

3. How can we do the work of God,
   how prosper and increase
   harmony in the human race,
   and the reign of perfect peace?
   What can we do to urge the time,
   the time that shall surely be,
   when the earth shall be filled
   with the glory of God
   as the waters cover the sea?

4. March we forth in the strength of God,
   his banner is unfurled;
   let the light of the gospel shine
   in the darkness of the world:
   strengthen the weary, heal the sick
   and set ev'ry captive free,
   that the earth shall be filled
   with the glory of God
   as the waters cover the sea.

5. All our efforts are nothing worth
   unless God bless the deed;
   vain our hopes for the harvest tide
   till he brings to life the seed.
   Yet ever nearer draws the time,
   the time that shall surely be,
   when the earth shall be filled
   with the glory of God
   as the waters cover the sea.

252 William Cowper (1731-1800)

1. God moves in a mysterious way
   his wonders to perform;
   he plants his footsteps in the sea,
   and rides upon the storm.

2. Deep in unfathomable mines
   of never-failing skill,
   he treasures up his bright designs,
   and works his sov'reign will.

3. Ye fearful saints, fresh courage take;
   the clouds ye so much dread
   are big with mercy, and shall break
   in blessings on your head.

4. Judge not the Lord by feeble sense,
   but trust him for his grace;
   behind a frowning providence
   he hides a shining face.

5. His purposes will ripen fast,
   unfolding ev'ry hour;
   the bud may have a bitter taste,
   but sweet will be the flow'r.

6. Blind unbelief is sure to err,
   and scan his work in vain;
   God is his own interpreter,
   and he will make it plain.

253 Charles Wesley (1707-1788)

1. God of all power, and truth, and grace,
which shall from age to age endure,
whose word, when heaven and earth shall
    pass,
remains and stands for ever sure.

2. That I thy mercy may proclaim,
that all mankind thy truth may see,
hallow thy great and glorious name,
and perfect holiness in me.

3. Thy sanctifying Spirit pour
to quench my thirst and make me clean;
now, Father, let the gracious shower
descend, and make me pure from sin.

4. Give me a new, a perfect heart,
from doubt, and fear, and sorrow free;
the mind which was in Christ impart,
and let my spirit cleave to thee.

5. O that I now, from sin released,
thy word may to the utmost prove,
enter into the promised rest,
the Canaan of thy perfect love!

6. Now let me gain perfection's height,
now let me into nothing fall,
be less then nothing in thy sight,
and feel that Christ is all in all.

254 Charles Wesley (1707-1788)

1. God of all-redeeming grace,
by thy pardoning love compelled,
up to thee our souls we raise,
up to thee our bodies yield:
thou our sacrifice receive,
acceptable through thy Son,
while to thee alone we live,
while we die to thee alone.

2. Meet it is, and just, and right,
that we should be wholly thine,
in thine only will delight,
in thy blessèd service join:
O that every work and word
might proclaim how good thou art,
'Holiness unto the Lord'
still be written on our heart!

255 Charles Wesley (1707-1788)

1. God of almighty love,
by whose sufficient grace
I lift my heart to things above,
and humbly seek thy face:

2. Through Jesus Christ the just
my faint desires receive,
and let me in thy goodness trust,
and to thy glory live.

3. Whate'er I say or do,
thy glory be my aim;
my offerings all be offered through
the ever-blessèd name.

4. Jesus, my single eye
be fixed on thee alone:
thy name be praised on earth, on high,
thy will by all be done.

5. Spirit of faith, inspire
my consecrated heart;
fill me with pure, celestial fire,
with all thou hast and art.

256 Michael Forster (b.1946)
© 1993 Kevin Mayhew Ltd.

1. God of eternal light,
your promises we claim;
as Abram's heirs,
we recognise the honour of your name.
Our sacrifice accept,
our lives of faith inspire,
and ev'ry fearful heart
transform with purifying fire.

2. High on the mountainside
your glory was revealed,
and yet, that great mysterious light
a deeper truth concealed!
What fearful shadows still
those sights and sounds portray:
a dreadful kind of majesty
that words cannot convey!

3. Christ, from the heav'ns descend,
eternal life make known,
and all our mortal bodies change
to copies of your own.
Your great and glorious light
creation then shall see,
when truth and peace are all around,
and justice flowing free!

257 Elizabeth Cosnett (b.1936)
© 1999 Kevin Mayhew Ltd.

1. God of every changing season,
inner worlds and outer space,
still beyond the grasp of reason,
yielding still to love's embrace,
we, your people, make thanksgiving,
bridging culture, language, race,
for the faith that Christ is living,
for two thousand years of grace.

2. When, in savage mock-enthronement,
Jesus died on Calvary,
then was made a real atonement,
rooted deep in history.
Partners now in new creation,
sharing all its joy and pain,
pierced with glad anticipation,
we await his final reign.

3. God, as Holy Spirit working,
help us meanwhile find and clear
all the mines of hatred lurking
in the no-man's-land of fear.
Do not let us worship money,
lost in deserts made by greed,
while your land of milk and honey
waits to satisfy our need.

4. In the world's ongoing story,
now a new page open lies.
Print it, Lord, with grace and glory,
read it with our Saviour's eyes.
Through all trials keep before us
symbols faith will recognise,
cross and crown, to reassure us
God, our source, is God, our prize.

258 Henry Emerson Fosdick (1878-1969)
© Elinor F. Downs

1. God of grace and God of glory,
on thy people pour thy power;
crown thine ancient church's story;
bring her bud to glorious flower.
Grant us wisdom,
grant us courage,
for the facing of this hour.

2. Heal thy children's warring madness;
bend our pride to thy control;
shame our wanton, selfish gladness,
rich in things and poor in soul.
Grant us wisdom,
grant us courage,
lest we miss thy kingdom's goal.

3. Lo, the hosts of evil round us
scorn thy Christ, assail his ways!
Fears and doubts too long have bound us;
free our hearts to work and praise.
Grant us wisdom,
grant us courage,
for the living of these days.

259 Henry Francis Lyte (1793-1847)
based on Psalm 67, alt.

1. God of mercy, God of grace,
show the brightness of thy face;
shine upon us, Saviour, shine,
fill thy Church with light divine;
and thy saving health extend
unto earth's remotest end.

Continued overleaf

2. Let the people praise thee, Lord;
   be by all that live adored;
   let the nations shout and sing
   glory to their Saviour King;
   at thy feet their tribute pay,
   and thy holy will obey.

3. Let the people praise thee, Lord;
   earth shall then her fruits afford;
   God to us his blessing give,
   we to God devoted live;
   all below, and all above,
   one in joy and light and love.

260 Charles Wesley (1707-1788)

1. God of my salvation, hear,
   and help me to believe;
   simply do I now draw near,
   thy blessing to receive:
   full of sin, alas! I am,
   but to thy wounds for refuge flee:

   Friend of sinners, spotless Lamb,
   thy blood was shed for me.

2. Standing now as newly slain,
   to thee I lift mine eye;
   balm of all my grief and pain,
   thy grace is always nigh:
   now as yesterday the same
   thou art, and wilt for ever be:

3. Nothing have I, Lord, to pay,
   nor can thy grace procure;
   empty send me not away,
   for I, thou know'st am poor:
   dust and ashes is my name,
   my all is sin and misery:

4. No good word, or work, or thought
   bring I to gain thy grace;
   pardon I accept unbought,
   thine offer I embrace,
   coming, as at first I came,
   to take, and not bestow on thee:

5. Saviour, from thy wounded side
   I never will depart;
   here will I my spirit hide
   when I am pure in heart:
   till my place above I claim,
   this only shall be all my plea:

261 Peter Trow (b.1956)

Let there be
1. God of the passing centuries,
   of time completed and to come:
   we bring our prayer that you will make
   our longing and our living one.

respect for the earth
peace for its people
2. Give us the wisdom, purpose, strength,
   to cherish all your hand has made,
   that ev'ry nation, ev'ry child,
   may live in peace, be unafraid.

love in our lives
3. We seek, for living fuller lives,
   with stranger, neighbour, loved one,
       friend,
   the love which you intend for all,
   which finds in Christ its source and end.

delight in the good
4. To all that brings delight in life,
   moments of vision, joyful days,
   all that has shaped us: leads us on,
   we say our 'Yes' with thanks and praise.

forgiveness for past wrong
5. God of forgiveness, set us free
   from suffered and inflicted pain,
   heal us from hatred born of fear,
   empower us all for life again.

for a new year
6. That with the turning of the year,
   renewed in hope and glad of heart,
   safe in the knowledge of your grace,
   we may from now, make a new start.

Based on the Millennium Resolution

262 Charles Wesley (1707-1788)

1. God of unexampled grace,
Redeemer of mankind,
matter of eternal praise
we in thy passion find;
still our choicest strains we bring,
still the joyful theme pursue,
thee the friend of sinners sing,
whose love is ever new.

2. Endless scenes of wonder rise
from that mysterious tree,
crucified before our eyes
here we our Maker see;
Jesus, Lord, what hast thou done?
Publish we the death divine,
stop, and gaze, and fall, and own
was never love like thine!

3. Never love nor sorrow was
like that my Saviour showed;
see him stretched on yonder cross,
and crushed beneath our load!
Now discern the Deity,
now his heavenly birth declare;
faith cries out: 'Tis he, 'tis he,
my God, that suffers there!

263 Traditional English

1. God rest you merry, gentlemen,
let nothing you dismay,
remember Christ our Saviour
was born on Christmas day,
to save us all from Satan's pow'r
when we were gone astray:

   O tidings of comfort and joy,
   comfort and joy,
   O tidings of comfort and joy.

2. In Bethlehem, in Jewry,
this blessèd babe was born,
and laid within a manger,
upon this blessèd morn;
the which his mother Mary
did nothing take in scorn:

3. From God, our heav'nly Father,
a blessèd angel came,
and unto certain shepherds,
brought tidings of the same,
how that in Bethlehem was born
the Son of God by name:

4. 'Fear not,' then said the angel,
'let nothing you affright,
this day is born a Saviour
of a pure virgin bright,
to free all those who trust in him
from Satan's power and might:'

5. The shepherds at those tidings,
rejoicèd much in mind,
and left their flocks a-feeding,
in tempest, storm and wind:
and went to Bethlehem straightway,
the Son of God to find:

6. And when they came to Bethlehem,
where our dear Saviour lay,
they found him in a manger,
where oxen feed on hay;
his mother Mary kneeling down,
unto the Lord did pray:

7. Now to the Lord sing praises,
all you within this place,
and with true love and brotherhood
each other now embrace;
this holy tide of Christmas
all others doth deface:

264

Alan Dale and Hubert J. Richards (b. 1921)
© 1982 Kevin Mayhew Ltd.

1. God's Spirit is in my heart.
   He has called me and set me apart.
   This is what I have to do,
   what I have to do.

   He sent me to give
   the Good News to the poor,
   tell pris'ners that they are pris'ners no more,
   tell blind people that they can see,
   and set the down trodden free,
   and go tell ev'ryone the news
   that the kingdom of God has come,
   and go tell ev'ryone the news
   that God's kingdom has come.

2. Just as the Father sent me,
   so I'm sending you out to be
   my witnesses throughout the world,
   the whole of the world.

3. Don't carry a load in your pack,
   you don't need two shirts on your back.
   A workman can earn his own keep,
   can earn his own keep.

4. Don't worry what you have to say,
   don't worry because on that day
   God's Spirit will speak in your heart,
   will speak in your heart.

265

v. 1: Reginald Heber (1783-1826)
v. 2: Richard Whately (1787-1863)

1. God that madest earth and heaven,
   darkness and light;
   who the day for toil hast given,
   for rest the night;
   may thine angel-guards defend us,
   slumber sweet thy mercy send us,
   holy dreams and hopes attend us,
   this live-long night.

2. Guard us waking, guard us sleeping,
   and, when we die,
   may we in thy mighty keeping
   all peaceful lie:
   when the last dread call shall wake us,
   do not thou our God forsake us,
   but to reign in glory take us
   with thee on high.

266

John Arlott (1914-1991)
© The Trustees of the late John Arlott

1. God, whose farm is all creation,
   take the gratitude we give;
   take the finest of our harvest,
   crops we grow that all may live.

2. Take our ploughing, seeding, reaping,
   hopes and fears of sun and rain,
   all our thinking, planning, waiting,
   ripened in this fruit and grain.

3. All our labour, all our watching,
   all our calendar of care,
   in these crops of your creation,
   take, O God: they are our prayer.

267

Fred Kaan (b. 1929)
© 1968, 1996 Stainer & Bell Ltd.

1. God, whose love is all around us,
   who in Jesus sought and found us,
   who to freedom new unbound us,
   keep our hearts with joy aflame.

2. For the sacramental breaking,
   for the honour of partaking,
   for your life our lives remaking,
   young and old, we praise your name.

3. From the service of this table
   lead us to a life more stable,
   for our witness make us able;
   blessings on our work we claim.

4. Through our calling closely knitted,
   daily to your praise committed,
   for a life of service fitted,
   let us now your love proclaim.

268 T. Herbert O'Driscoll (b.1928)
© Herbert O'Driscoll

1. God, you have caused to be written your
   word for our learning;
   grant us that, hearing, our hearts may be
   inwardly burning.
   Give to us grace,
   that in your Son we embrace
   life, all its glory discerning.

2. Now may our God give us joy, and all
   peace in believing
   all things were written in truth for our
   thankful receiving.
   As Christ did preach,
   through all the world love must reach;
   grant us each day love's achieving.

3. Lord, should the powers of the earth and
   the heavens be shaken,
   grant us to see you in all things, our
   vision awaken.
   Help us to see,
   though all the earth cease to be,
   your truth shall never be shaken.

269 J.E. Seddon (1915-1983)
© Mrs. M. Seddon/Jubilate Hymns

1. Go forth and tell! O church of God, awake!
   God's saving news to all the nations take.
   Proclaim Christ Jesus, Saviour, Lord, and
   King,
   that all the world his worthy praise may
   sing.

2. Go forth and tell! God's love embraces all:
   he will in grace respond to all who call.
   How shall they call if they have never heard
   the gracious invitation of his word?

3. Go forth and tell where still the darkness lies
   in wealth or want, the sinner surely dies.
   Give us, O Lord, concern of heart and
   mind,
   a love like yours which cares for all
   mankind.

4. Go forth and tell! The doors are open wide:
   share God's good gifts let no one be
   denied.
   Live out your life as Christ, your Lord,
   shall choose,
   your ransomed powers for his sole glory
   use.

5. Go forth and tell! O Church of God arise!
   Go in the strength which Christ your Lord
   supplies;
   go till all nations his great name adore
   and serve him, Lord and King for evermore.

270 Michael Forster (b. 1946)
© 1999 Kevin Mayhew Ltd.

1. Going home, moving on,
   through God's open door;
   hush, my soul, have no fear,
   Christ has gone before.
   Parting hurts, love protests,
   pain is not denied;
   yet, in Christ, life and hope
   span the great divide.
   Going home, moving on,
   through God's open door;
   hush, my soul, have no fear,
   Christ has gone before,
   Christ has gone before.

2. No more guilt, no more fear,
   all the past is healed:
   broken dreams now restored,
   perfect grace revealed.
   Christ has died, Christ is ris'n,
   Christ will come again:
   death destroyed, life restored,
   love alone shall reign.
   Going home, moving on,
   through God's open door;
   hush, my soul, have no fear,
   Christ has gone before,
   Christ has gone before.

271
John Mason Neale (1818-1866) alt.

1. Good Christians, all, rejoice
with heart and soul and voice!
Give ye heed to what we say:
News! News! Jesus Christ is born today;
ox and ass before him bow,
and he is in the manger now:
Christ is born today, Christ is born today!

2. Good Christians all, rejoice
with heart and soul and voice!
Now ye hear of endless bliss:
Joy! Joy! Jesus Christ was born for this.
He hath opened heaven's door,
and we are blest for evermore:
Christ was born for this,
Christ was born for this.

3. Good Christians all, rejoice
with heart and soul and voice!
Now ye need not fear the grave:
Peace! Peace! Jesus Christ was born to save;
calls you one, and calls you all,
to gain his everlasting hall:
Christ was born to save,
Christ was born to save.

272
Cyril Argentine Alington (1872-1955) alt.
© Hymns Ancient & Modern

1. Good Christians all, rejoice and sing.
Now is the triumph of our King.
To all the world glad news we bring:
Alleluia!

2. The Lord of Life is ris'n for ay:
bring flow'rs of song to strew his way;
let all mankind rejoice and say:
Alleluia!

3. Praise we in songs of victory
that Love, that Life, which cannot die,
and sing with hearts uplifted high:
Alleluia!

4. Thy name we bless, O risen Lord,
and sing today with one accord
the life laid down, the life restored:
Alleluia!

273
John Mason Neale (1818-1866) alt.

1. Good King Wenceslas looked out
on the feast of Stephen,
when the snow lay round about,
deep, and crisp, and even;
brightly shone the moon that night,
though the frost was cruel,
when a poor man came in sight,
gath'ring winter fuel.

2. 'Hither, page, and stand by me,
if thou know'st it, telling,
yonder peasant, who is he,
where and what his dwelling?'
'Sire, he lives a good league hence,
underneath the mountain,
right against the forest fence,
by Saint Agnes' fountain.'

3. 'Bring me flesh, and bring me wine,
bring me pine logs hither:
thou and I will see him dine,
when we bring them thither.'
Page and monarch, forth they went,
forth they went together;
through the rude wind's wild lament,
and the bitter weather.

4. 'Sire, the night is darker now,
and the wind blows stronger;
fails my heart, I know not how;
I can go no longer.'
'Mark my footsteps good, my page;
tread thou in them boldly:
thou shalt find the winter's rage
freeze thy blood less coldly.'

5. In his master's steps he trod,
   where the snow lay dinted;
   heat was in the very sod
   which the Saint had printed.
   Therefore, Christians all, be sure,
   wealth or rank possessing,
   ye who now will bless the poor,
   shall yourselves find blessing.

274 Traditional

Go, tell it on the mountain,
over the hills and ev'rywhere.
Go, tell it on the mountain
that Jesus Christ is born.

1. While shepherds kept their watching
   o'er wand'ring flocks by night,
   behold, from out of heaven,
   there shone a holy light.

2. And lo, when they had seen it,
   they all bowed down and prayed;
   they travelled on together
   to where the babe was laid.

3. When I was a seeker,
   I sought both night and day:
   I asked my Lord to help me
   and he showed me the way.

4. He made me a watchman
   upon the city wall,
   and, if I am a Christian,
   I am the least of all.

275 Thomas Toke Lynch (1818-1871)

1. Gracious Spirit, dwell with me;
   I myself would gracious be,
   and with words that help and heal
   would thy life in mine reveal,
   and with actions bold and meek
   would for Christ my Saviour speak.

2. Truthful Spirit, dwell with me;
   I myself would truthful be,
   and with wisdom kind and clear
   let thy life in mine appear,
   and with actions neighbourly
   speak my Lord's sincerity.

3. Silent Spirit, dwell with me;
   I myself would quiet be,
   quiet as the growing blade
   which through earth its way has made;
   silently, like morning light,
   putting mists and chills to flight.

4. Mighty Spirit, dwell with me;
   I myself would mighty be,
   mighty so as to prevail
   where unaided I must fail;
   ever by a mighty hope
   pressing on and bearing up.

5. Holy Spirit, dwell with me;
   I myself would holy be;
   separate from sin, I would
   choose and cherish all things good,
   and, whatever I can be,
   give to him who gave me thee.

276 Christopher Wordsworth (1807-1885)

1. Gracious Spirit, Holy Ghost,
   taught by thee, we covet most
   of thy gifts at Pentecost,
   holy, heav'nly love.

2. Love is kind, and suffers long,
   love is meek, and thinks no wrong,
   love than death itself more strong;
   therefore give us love.

3. Prophecy will fade away,
   melting in the light of day;
   love will ever with us stay;
   therefore give us love.

Continued overleaf

4. Faith will vanish into sight;
hope be emptied in delight;
love in heav'n will shine more bright;
therefore give us love.

5. Faith and hope and love we see
joining hand in hand agree;
but the greatest of the three,
and the best, is love.

6. From the overshadowing
of thy gold and silver wing
shed on us, who to thee sing,
holy, heav'nly love.

277 Charles Wesley (1707-1788)

1. Granted is the Saviour's prayer,
sent the gracious Comforter;
promise of our parting Lord,
Jesus now to heaven restored.

2. Christ who, now gone up on high,
captive leads captivity;
while his foes from him receive
grace that God with man may live.

3. God, the everlasting God,
makes with mortals his abode;
whom the heav'ns cannot contain,
he vouchsafes to dwell in man.

4. Never will he thence depart,
inmate of a humble heart;
carrying on his work within,
striving till he casts out sin.

5 Come, divine and peaceful Guest,
enter our devoted breast;
Holy Ghost, our hearts inspire,
kindle there the Gospel-fire.

6 Now descend, and shake the earth;
wake us into second birth;
life divine in us renew,
thou the gift and giver too!

278 Samuel Davis (1723-1761) alt.

1. Great God of wonders! All thy ways
display the glory all divine;
but countless acts of pardoning grace
beyond thine other wonders shine:

Who is a pardoning God like thee?
Or who has grace so rich and free?

2. In wonder lost, with trembling joy
we take the pardon of our God –
pardon for crimes of deepest dye,
a pardon bought with Jesus' blood.

3. Pardon – from an offended God!
Pardon – for sins of deepest dye!
Pardon – bestowed through Jesus' blood!
Pardon – that brings the rebel nigh!

4. O may this strange, this matchless grace,
this God-like miracle of love,
fill the wide earth with grateful praise,
as now it fills the choirs above!

279 Charles Wesley (1707-1788) based on Psalm 48

1. Great is our redeeming Lord
in power, and truth, and grace;
him, by highest heaven adored,
his church on earth doth praise.
In the city of our God,
in his holy mount below,
publish, spread his name abroad,
and all his greatness show.

2. For thy loving-kindness, Lord,
we in thy temple stay;
here thy faithful love record,
thy saving power display.
With thy name thy praise is known,
glorious thy perfections shine;
earth's remotest bounds shall own
thy works are all divine.

3. See the gospel church secure,
   and founded on a rock;
   all her promises are sure;
   her bulwarks who can shock?
   Count her every precious shrine;
   tell, to after-ages tell:
   fortified by power divine,
   the church can never fail.

4. Zion's God is all our own,
   who on his love rely;
   we his pardoning love have known,
   and live to Christ, and die.
   To the new Jerusalem
   he our faithful guide shall be:
   him we claim, and rest in him,
   through all eternity.

280 Thomas Obadiah Chisholm (1866-1960)
© 1951 Hope Publishing Co.

1. Great is thy faithfulness,
   O God, my Father,
   there is no shadow
   of turning with thee;
   thou changest not,
   thy compassions, they fail not;
   as thou hast been
   thou for ever wilt be.

   Great is thy faithfulness!
   Great is thy faithfulness!
   Morning by morning
   new mercies I see;
   all I have needed
   thy hand hath provided,
   great is thy faithfulness,
   Lord, unto me!

2. Summer and winter,
   and springtime and harvest,
   sun, moon and stars
   in their courses above,
   join with all nature
   in manifold witness
   to thy great faithfulness,
   mercy and love.

3. Pardon for sin
   and a peace that endureth,
   thine own dear presence
   to cheer and to guide;
   strength for today
   and bright hope for tomorrow,
   blessings all mine,
   with ten thousand beside!

281 William Williams (1717-1791)
trans. Peter Williams (1727-1796) and others

1. Guide me, O thou great Jehovah,
   pilgrim through this barren land;
   I am weak, but thou art mighty,
   hold me with thy pow'rful hand:
   Bread of Heaven, Bread of Heaven,
   feed me now and evermore,
   feed me now and evermore.

2. Open now the crystal fountain,
   whence the healing stream doth flow;
   let the fire and cloudy pillar
   lead me all my journey through;
   strong deliv'rer, strong deliv'rer,
   be thou still my strength and shield,
   be thou still my strength and shield.

3. When I tread the verge of Jordan,
   bid my anxious fears subside;
   death of death, and hell's destruction,
   land me safe on Canaan's side;
   songs of praises, songs of praises,
   I will ever give to thee,
   I will ever give to thee.

282 Greek (3rd century or earlier)
trans. John Keble (1792-1866)

1. Hail, gladdening Light,
   of his pure glory poured
   from th' immortal Father,
   heav'nly, blest,
   holiest of holies,
   Jesus Christ our Lord.

Continued overleaf

2. Now we are come
   to the sun's hour of rest,
   the lights of evening
   round us shine,
   we hymn the Father,
   Son and Holy Spirit divine.

3. Worthiest art thou at all times
   to be sung with undefilèd tongue,
   Son of our God,
   giver of life, alone:
   therefore in all the world thy glories,
   Lord, they own.

283 Charles Wesley (1707-1788)

1. Hail! Holy, holy, holy, Lord!
   Whom One in Three we know;
   by all thy heavenly host adored,
   by all thy Church below.

2. One undivided Trinity
   with triumph we proclaim;
   thy universe is full of thee,
   and speaks thy glorious name.

3. Thee, holy Father, we confess,
   thee, holy Son, adore,
   thee, Spir't of truth and holiness,
   we worship evermore.

4. Three Persons equally divine
   we magnify and love;
   and both the choirs ere long shall join
   to sing thy praise above:

5. Hail! Holy, holy, holy, Lord,
   our heavenly song shall be,
   supreme, essential One, adored
   in co-eternal Three.

284 Charles Wesley (1707-1788)
Thomas Cotterill (1779-1823) and others, alt.

1. Hail the day that sees him rise, *alleluia!*
   to his throne above the skies; *alleluia!*
   Christ the Lamb, for sinners giv'n, *alleluia!*
   enters now the highest heav'n! *alleluia!*

2. There for him high triumph waits;
   lift your heads, eternal gates!
   He hath conquered death and sin;
   take the King of Glory in!

3. Circled round with angel-pow'rs,
   their triumphant Lord and ours;
   wide unfold the radiant scene,
   take the King of Glory in!

4. Lo, the heav'n its Lord receives,
   yet he loves the earth he leaves;
   though returning to his throne,
   calls the human race his own.

5. See, he lifts his hands above;
   see, he shows the prints of love;
   hark, his gracious lips bestow
   blessings on his Church below.

6. Still for us he intercedes,
   his prevailing death he pleads;
   near himself prepares our place,
   he the first-fruits of our race.

7. Lord, though parted from our sight,
   far above the starry height,
   grant our hearts may thither rise,
   seeking thee above the skies.

8. Ever upward let us move,
   wafted on the wings of love;
   looking when our Lord shall come,
   longing, sighing after home.

285 John Bakewell (1721-1819) and others

1. Hail, thou once despisèd Jesus,
   hail, thou Galilean King!
   Thou didst suffer to release us,
   thou didst free salvation bring.
   Hail, thou agonising Saviour,
   bearer of our sin and shame;
   by thy merits we find favour;
   life is given through thy name!

2. Paschal Lamb by God appointed,
all our sins on thee were laid;
by almighty love anointed,
thou hast full atonement made:
all thy people are forgiven
through the virtue of thy blood;
opened is the gate of heaven;
mortals are at peace with God.

3. Jesus, hail! enthroned in glory,
there for ever to abide;
all the heavenly host adore thee,
seated at thy Father's side:
there for sinners thou art pleading,
there thou dost our place prepare,
ever for us interceding,
till in glory we appear.

4. Worship, honour, power, and blessing,
thou art worthy to receive;
loudest praises without ceasing,
meet it is for us to give.
Help, ye bright angelic spirits,
bring your sweetest, noblest lays;
help to sing our Saviour's merits,
help to chant Immanuel's praise!

286 Paraphrase of Psalm 72 by James Montgomery (1771-1854)

1. Hail to the Lord's anointed,
great David's greater son!
Hail, in the time appointed,
his reign on earth begun!
He comes to break oppression,
to set the captive free;
to take away transgression,
and rule in equity.

2. He comes with succour speedy
to those who suffer wrong;
to help the poor and needy,
and bid the weak be strong;
to give them songs for sighing,
their darkness turn to light,
whose souls, condemned and dying,
were precious in his sight.

3. He shall come down like showers
upon the fruitful earth,
and love, joy, hope, like flowers,
spring in his path to birth:
before him on the mountains
shall peace the herald go;
and righteousness in fountains
from hill to valley flow.

4. Kings shall fall down before him,
and gold and incense bring;
all nations shall adore him,
his praise all people sing;
to him shall prayer unceasing
and daily vows ascend;
his kingdom still increasing,
a kingdom without end.

5. O'er ev'ry foe victorious,
he on his throne shall rest,
from age to age more glorious,
all-blessing and all-blest;
the tide of time shall never
his covenant remove;
his name shall stand for ever;
that name to us is love.

287 Tim Cullen, alt.
© 1975 Celebration/Kingsway's Thankyou Music

Hallelujah, my Father,
for giving us your Son;
sending him into the world
to be given up for all,
knowing we would bruise him
and smite him from the earth!
Hallelujah, my Father,
in his death is my birth.
Hallelujah, my Father,
in his life is my life.

288

Robert Bridges (1844-1930)
based on 'O quam juvat',
Charles Coffin (1676-1749) alt.

1. Happy are they, they that love God,
   whose hearts have Christ confessed,
   who by his cross have found their life,
   and 'neath his yoke their rest.

2. Glad is the praise, sweet are the songs,
   when they together sing;
   and strong the prayers that bow the ear
   of heav'n's eternal King.

3. Christ to their homes giveth his peace
   and makes their loves his own:
   but ah, what tares the evil one
   hath in his garden sown!

4. Sad were our lot, evil this earth,
   did not its sorrows prove
   the path whereby the sheep may find
   the fold of Jesus' love.

5. Then shall they know, they that love him,
   how hope is wrought through pain;
   their fellowship, through death itself,
   unbroken will remain.

289

Karl Johann Philipp Spitta (1801-1859)
Trans. Honor Mary Thwaites (1914- 1993)
© Mr Michael R. Thwaites

1. Happy the home that welcomes you,
   Lord Jesus,
   truest of friends, most honoured guest of
   all,
   where hearts and eyes are bright with joy
   to greet you,
   your lightest wishes eager to fulfil.

2. Happy the home where man and wife
   together
   are of one mind believing in your love;
   through love and pain, prosperity and
   hardship,
   through good and evil days your care
   they prove.

3. Happy the home, O loving friend of
   children,
   where they are giv'n to you with hands of
   prayer,
   where at your feet they early learn to listen
   to your own words, and thank you for
   your care.

4. Happy the home where work is done to
   please you,
   in tasks both great and small, that you
   may see
   your servants doing all as you would
   wish them
   as members of your household, glad and
   free.

5. Happy the home that knows your
   healing comfort,
   where, unforgotten, every joy you share,
   until they all, their work on earth
   completed,
   come to your Father's house to meet you
   there.

290

Charles Wesley (1707-1788)

1. Happy the man that finds the grace,
   the blessing of God's chosen race,
   the wisdom coming from above,
   the faith that sweetly works by love.

2. Happy beyond description he
   who knows 'The Saviour died for me'
   the gift unspeakable obtains,
   and heav'nly understanding gains.

3. Wisdom divine! Who tells the price
   of wisdom's costly merchandise?
   Wisdom to silver we prefer,
   and gold is dross compared to her.

4. Her hands are filled with length of days,
   true riches, and immortal praise,
   riches of Christ, on all bestowed,
   and honour that descends from God.

5. To purest joys she all invites,
   chaste, holy, spiritual delights;
   her ways are ways of pleasantness,
   and all her flowery paths are peace.

6. Happy the man who wisdom gains,
   thrice happy who his guest retains;
   he owns, and shall for ever own,
   wisdom, and Christ, and heaven are one.

291 William Cowper (1731-1800) based on John 21:16

1. Hark, my soul, it is the Lord;
   'tis thy Saviour, hear his word;
   Jesus speaks, and speaks to thee,
   'Say, poor sinner, lov'st thou me?

2. 'I delivered thee when bound,
   and, when wounded, healed thy wound;
   sought thee wand'ring, set thee right,
   turned thy darkness into light.

3. 'Can a woman's tender care
   cease towards the child she bare?
   Yes, she may forgetful be,
   yet will I remember thee.

4. 'Mine is an unchanging love,
   higher than the heights above,
   deeper than the depths beneath,
   free and faithful, strong as death.

5. 'Thou shalt see my glory soon,
   when the work of grace is done;
   partner of my throne shalt be:
   say, poor sinner, lov'st thou me?'

6. Lord, it is my chief complaint
   that my love is weak and faint;
   yet I love thee, and adore;
   O for grace to love thee more!

292 Philip Doddridge (1702-1751) based on Luke 4:18-19

1. Hark the glad sound! the Saviour comes,
   the Saviour promised long:
   let ev'ry heart prepare a throne,
   and ev'ry voice a song.

2. He comes, the pris'ners to release
   in Satan's bondage held;
   the gates of brass before him burst,
   the iron fetters yield.

3. He comes, the broken heart to bind,
   the bleeding soul to cure,
   and with the treasures of his grace
   to bless the humble poor.

4. Our glad hosannas, Prince of Peace,
   thy welcome shall proclaim;
   and heav'n's eternal arches ring
   with thy belovèd name.

293 William Sanders (1799-1882)

1. Hark! the gospel news is sounding:
   Christ hath suffered on the tree;
   streams of mercy are abounding;
   grace for all is rich and free.
   Now, poor sinner,
   look to him who died for thee.

2. Grace is flowing like a river;
   millions there have been supplied;
   still it flows as fresh as ever
   from the Saviour's wounded side:
   none need perish;
   all may live, for Christ hath died.

3. Christ alone shall be our portion;
   soon we hope to meet above,
   then we'll bathe in the full ocean
   of the great Redeemer's love;
   all his fullness,
   we shall then for ever prove.

294 Charles Wesley (1707-1788), George Whitefield (1714-1770), Martin Madan (1726-1790) and others, alt.

1. Hark, the herald-angels sing
glory to the new-born King;
peace on earth and mercy mild,
God and sinners reconciled:
joyful, all ye nations rise,
join the triumph of the skies,
with th'angelic host proclaim,
'Christ is born in Bethlehem.'

Hark, the herald-angels sing
glory to the new-born King.

2. Christ, by highest heav'n adored,
Christ, the everlasting Lord,
late in time behold him come,
offspring of a virgin's womb!
Veiled in flesh the Godhead see,
hail, th'incarnate Deity!
Pleased as man with us to dwell,
Jesus, our Emmanuel.

3. Hail, the heav'n-born Prince of Peace!
Hail, the Sun of Righteousness!
Light and life to all he brings,
ris'n with healing in his wings;
mild he lays his glory by,
born that we no more may die,
born to raise us from the earth,
born to give us second birth.

295 Frederic W. H. Myers (1843-1901) alt.

1. Hark what a sound, and too divine for
hearing,
stirs on the earth and trembles in the air!
Is it the thunder of the Lord's appearing?
Is it the music of his people's prayer?

2. Surely he cometh, and a thousand voices
shout to the strains of trumpet and of
drum;
surely he cometh, and the earth rejoices,
glad in his coming who hath sworn: I
come!

3. This hath he done, and shall we not
adore him?
This shall he do, and can we still despair?
Come, let us quickly fling ourselves
before him,
cast at his feet the burden of our care.

4. Through life and death, through sorrow
and through sinning,
he shall suffice me, for he hath sufficed:
Christ is the end, for Christ was the
beginning,
Christ the beginning, for the end is
Christ.

296 Bryn Rees (1911-1983)
© Alexander Scott

1. Have faith in God, my heart,
trust and be unafraid;
God will fulfil in every part
each promise he has made.

2. Have faith in God, my mind,
though oft your light burns low;
God's mercy holds a wiser plan
than you can fully know.

3. Have faith in God, my soul;
his cross for ever stands;
and neither life nor death can pluck
his children from his hands.

4. Lord Jesus, make me whole;
grant me no resting place,
until I rest, heart, mind, and soul,
the captive of your grace.

297
Charles Wesley (1707-1788)

1. Head of thy Church, whose Spirit fills
   and flows through every faithful soul,
   unites in mystic love, and seals
   them one, and sanctifies the whole:

2. 'Come, Lord!' thy glorious Spirit cries;
   and souls beneath the altar groan;
   'Come, Lord,' the bride on earth replies,
   'and perfect all our souls in one!

3. Pour out the promised gift on all,
   answer the universal 'Come!'
   The fullness of the Gentiles call,
   and take thine ancient people home.

4. To thee let all the nations flow,
   let all obey the gospel word;
   let all their suffering Saviour know,
   filled with the glory of the Lord.

5. O for thy truth and mercy's sake
   the purchase of thy passion claim;
   thine heritage, the nations, take,
   and cause the world to know thy name!

298
William Henry Gill (1839-1923)

1. Hear us, O Lord, from heaven, thy
      dwelling-place:
   like them of old, in vain we toil all night,
   unless with us thou go, who art the light;
   come then, O Lord, that we may see thy
      face.

2. Thou, Lord, dost rule the raging of the
      sea,
   when loud the storm and furious is the
      gale;
   strong is thine arm; our little barques are
      frail:
   send us thy help; remember Galilee.

3. We thank thee, Lord, for sunshine, dew,
      and rain,
   broadcast from heaven by thine almighty
      hand –
   source of all life, unnumbered as the
      sand –
   bird, beast and fish, herb, fruit, and
      golden grain.

4. O Bread of Life, thou in thy word hast
      said:
   'Who feeds in faith on me shall never
      die'.
   In mercy hear thy hungry children's cry:
   'Father, give us this day our daily bread!'

5. Sow in our hearts the seeds of thy dear
      love,
   that we may reap contentment, joy, and
      peace;
   and when at last our earthly labours
      cease,
   grant us to join thy harvest home above.

299
William Charter Piggott (1872-1943) alt.
© Oxford University Press

1. Heavenly Father, may your blessing
   rest upon your children now,
   when in praise your name we hallow,
   when in prayer to you we bow;
   in the wondrous story reading
   of the Lord of truth and grace,
   may we see your love reflected
   in the light of his dear face.

2. May we learn from this great story
   all the arts of friendliness;
   truthful speech and honest action,
   courage, patience, steadfastness;
   how to master self and temper,
   how to make our conduct fair;
   when to speak and when be silent,
   when to do and when forbear.

Continued overleaf

3. May your Spirit wise and holy
   with his gifts our spirits bless,
   make us loving, joyous, peaceful,
   rich in goodness, gentleness,
   strong in self-control, and faithful,
   kind in thought and deed; for he
   teaches, 'What you do for others
   you are doing unto me.'

300
John L. Bell (b. 1949) and Graham Maule (b. 1958)
© 1987 WGRG, Iona Community

1. Heav'n shall not wait
   for the poor to lose their patience,
   the scorned to smile,
   the despised to find a friend:
   Jesus is Lord,
   he has championed the unwanted;
   in him injustice
   confronts its timely end.

2. Heav'n shall not wait
   for the rich to share their fortunes,
   the proud to fall,
   the élite to tend the least:
   Jesus is Lord;
   he has shown the master's privilege –
   to kneel and wash
   servants' feet before they feast.

3. Heav'n shall not wait
   for the dawn of great ideas,
   thoughts of compassion
   divorced from cries of pain:
   Jesus is Lord;
   he has married word and action;
   his cross and company
   make his purpose plain.

4. Heav'n shall not wait
   for our legalised obedience,
   defined by statute,
   to strict conventions bound:
   Jesus is Lord;
   he has hallmarked true allegiance –
   goodness appears
   where his grace is sought and found.

5. Heav'n shall not wait
   for triumphant hallelujahs,
   when earth has passed
   and we reach another shore:
   Jesus is Lord
   in our present imperfection;
   his pow'r and love
   are for now and then for evermore.

301
Traditional

1. He brings us in to his banqueting table,
   his banner over me is love; *(x3)*
   his banner over me is love.

2. The one way to peace
   is the power of the cross ...

3. He builds his Church
   on a firm foundation ...

4. In him we find a new creation ...

5. He lifts us up to heavenly places ...

302
Twila Paris
© 1985 Straightway/Mountain Spring/EMI Christian
Music Publishing

He is exalted,
the King is exalted on high;
I will praise him.
He is exalted,
for ever exalted
and I will praise his name!
He is the Lord;
for ever his truth shall reign.
Heaven and earth rejoice
in his holy name.
He is exalted,
the King is exalted on high.

303
Unknown

1. He is Lord, he is Lord.
   He is risen from the dead and he is Lord.
   Ev'ry knee shall bow, ev'ry tongue confess
   that Jesus Christ is Lord.

2. He is King, he is King,
   He is risen from the dead and he is King.
   Ev'ry knee shall bow, ev'ry tongue confess
   that Jesus Christ is King.

3. He is love, he is love.
   He is risen from the dead and he is love.
   Ev'ry knee shall bow, ev'ry tongue confess
   that Jesus Christ is love.

304

William Watkins Reid (b.1923) alt.
© 1959, renewal 1987 by the Hymn Society/Hope
Publishing Co.

1. Help us, O Lord, to learn
   the truths your word imparts,
   to study that your laws may be
   inscribed upon our hearts.

2. Help us, O Lord, to live
   that faith which we proclaim,
   that all our thoughts and words and
   deeds
   may glorify your name.

3. Help us, O Lord, to teach
   the beauty of your ways,
   that all who seek may find the Christ,
   and make a life of praise.

305

Charles Wesley (1707-1788)

1. Help us to help each other, Lord,
   each other's cross to bear,
   let each his friendly aid afford,
   and feel his brother's care.

2. Help us to build each other up,
   our little stock improve;
   increase our faith, confirm our hope,
   and perfect us in love.

3. Up into thee, our living Head,
   let us in all things grow,
   till thou hast made us free indeed,
   and spotless here below.

4. Then, when the mighty work is wrought,
   receive thy ready bride;
   give us in heaven a happy lot
   with all the sanctified.

306

Chris Bowater
© 1981 Sovereign Lifestyle Music Ltd.

Here I am, wholly available.
As for me, I will serve the Lord.
Here I am, wholly available.
As for me, I will serve the Lord.

1. The fields are white unto harvest,
   but O, the labourers are so few,
   so, Lord, I give myself to help the
   reaping,
   to gather precious souls unto you.

2. The time is right in the nation
   for works of power and authority;
   God's looking for a people who are
   willing
   to be counted in his glorious victory.

3. As salt are we ready to savour,
   in darkness are we ready to be light?
   God's seeking out a very special people
   to manifest his truth and his might.

307

Graham Kendrick (b. 1950)
© 1992 Make Way Music

1. Here is bread, here is wine,
   Christ is with us, he is with us.
   Break the bread, taste the wine,
   Christ is with us here.

   In this bread there is healing,
   in this cup is life for ever.
   In this moment, by the Spirit,
   Christ is with us here.

2. Here is grace, here is peace.
   Christ is with us, he is with us;
   know his grace, find his peace,
   feast on Jesus here.

Continued overleaf

3. Here we are, joined in one,
   Christ is with us, he is with us;
   we'll proclaim, till he comes,
   Jesus crucified.

308 William Rees (1802-1883)

1. Here is love vast as the ocean,
   loving kindness as the flood.
   When the Prince of Life, our ransom,
   shed for us his precious blood.
   Who his love will not remember?
   Who can cease to sing his praise?
   He can never be forgotten,
   throughout heav'n's eternal days.

2. On the mount of crucifixion
   fountains opened deep and wide;
   through the floodgates of God's mercy
   flowed a vast and gracious tide.
   Grace and love, like mighty rivers,
   poured incessant from above,
   and heaven's peace and perfect justice
   kissed a guilty world in love.

309 Charles Venn Pilcher (1879-1961)
© Mrs I.E.V. Pilcher

1. Here, Lord, we take the broken bread
   and drink the wine, believing
   that by your life our souls are fed,
   your parting gifts receiving.

2. As you have giv'n, so we would give
   ourselves for others' healing;
   as you have lived, so we would live,
   the Father's love revealing.

310 Horatius Bonar (1808-1889)

1. Here, O my Lord, I see thee face to face;
   here would I touch and handle things
       unseen,
   here grasp with firmer hand the eternal
       grace,
   and all my weariness upon thee lean.

2. Here would I feed upon the bread of
       God,
   here drink with thee the royal wine of
       heaven;
   here would I lay aside each earthly load,
   here taste afresh the calm of sin forgiven.

3. Mine is the sin, but thine the
       righteousness;
   mine is the guilt, but thine the cleansing
       blood;
   here is my robe, my refuge, and my
       peace –
   thy blood, thy righteousness, O Lord, my
       God.

4. Too soon we rise; the symbols disappear;
   the feast, though not the love, is past and
       gone;
   the bread and wine remove, but thou art
       here,
   nearer then ever, still our shield and sun.

5. Feast after feast thus comes and passes by,
   yet, passing, points to the glad feast
       above,
   giving sweet foretaste of the festal joy,
   the Lamb's great bridal feast of bliss and
       love.

311 John Bunyan (1628-1688)

1 He that is down needs fear no fall,
   he that is low, no pride;
   he that is humble ever shall
   have God to be his guide.

2. I am content with what I have,
   little be it or much;
   and, Lord, contentment still I crave,
   because thou savest such.

3. Fullness to such a burden is
   that go on pilgrimage;
   here little, and hereafter bliss,
   is best from age to age.

Alternative verse 1.

1. *They that are down need fear no fall,*
   they that are low, no pride;
   they that are humble ever shall
   have God to be their guide.

312 Unknown

Higher, higher, higher, higher, higher,
higher, higher, lift up Jesus higher.
Higher, higher, higher, higher, higher,
higher, higher, lift up Jesus higher.

Lower, lower, lower, lower, lower,
lower, lower, lower Satan lower.
Lower, lower, lower, lower, lower,
lower, lower, lower Satan lower.

Cast your burdens onto Jesus,
he cares for you.
Cast your burdens onto Jesus,
he cares for you.

313 Isaac Watts (1674-1748) alt. based on Psalm 36: 5-9

1. High in the heavens, eternal God,
   thy goodness in full glory shines;
   thy truth shall break through every cloud
   that veils and darkens thy designs.

2. For ever firm thy justice stands,
   as mountains their foundations keep;
   wise are the wonders of thy hands;
   thy judgements are a mighty deep.

3. Thy providence is kind and large,
   all living things thy bounty share;
   the whole creation is thy charge,
   but saints are thy peculiar care.

4. My God, how excellent thy grace,
   whence all our hope and comfort springs!
   The race of Adam in distress
   flies to the shadow of thy wings.

5. Life, like a fountain rich and free,
   springs from the presence of the Lord;
   and in thy light our souls shall see
   the glories promised in thy word.

314 Charles Edward Oakley (1832-1865), adapted

1. Hills of the north, rejoice,
   echoing songs arise,
   hail with united voice
   him who made earth and skies:
   he comes in righteousness and love,
   he brings salvation from above.

2. Isles of the southern seas
   sing to the list'ning earth,
   carry on ev'ry breeze
   hope of a world's new birth:
   in Christ shall all be made anew,
   his word is sure, his promise true.

3. Lands of the east, arise,
   he is your brightest morn,
   greet him with joyous eyes,
   praise shall his path adorn:
   the God whom you have longed to know
   in Christ draws near, and calls you now.

4. Shores of the utmost west,
   lands of the setting sun,
   welcome the heav'nly guest
   in whom the dawn has come:
   he brings a never-ending light
   who triumphed o'er our darkest night.

5. Shout, as you journey on,
   songs be in ev'ry mouth,
   lo, from the north they come,
   from east and west and south:
   in Jesus all shall find their rest,
   in him the longing earth be blest.

315
Unknown

1. Holy, holy, holy is the Lord,
   holy is the Lord God almighty.
   Holy, holy, holy is the Lord,
   holy is the Lord God almighty:
   who was, and is, and is to come;
   holy, holy, holy is the Lord.

2. Jesus, Jesus, Jesus is the Lord,
   Jesus is the Lord God almighty: *(Repeat)*
   who was, and is, and is to come;
   Jesus, Jesus, Jesus is the Lord.

3. Worthy, worthy, worthy is the Lord,
   worthy is the Lord God almighty: *(Repeat)*
   who was, and is and is to come;
   worthy, worthy, worthy is the Lord.

4. Glory, glory, glory to the Lord,
   glory to the Lord God almighty: *(Repeat)*
   who was, and is, and is to come;
   glory, glory, glory to the Lord.

316
Reginald Heber (1783-1826) alt.

1. Holy, holy, holy!
   Lord God almighty!
   Early in the morning
   our song shall rise to thee;
   holy, holy, holy!
   Merciful and mighty!
   God in three persons,
   blessèd Trinity!

2.* Holy, holy, holy!
   All the saints adore thee,
   casting down their golden crowns
   around the glassy sea;
   cherubim and seraphim
   falling down before thee,
   which wert, and art,
   and evermore shall be.

3. Holy, holy, holy!
   Though the darkness hide thee,
   though the sinful human eye
   thy glory may not see,
   only thou art holy,
   there is none beside thee,
   perfect in pow'r,
   in love, and purity.

4. Holy, holy, holy!
   Lord God almighty!
   All thy works shall praise thy name,
   in earth and sky and sea;
   holy, holy, holy!
   Merciful and mighty!
   God in three persons,
   blessèd Trinity!
   * *May be omitted*

317
William John Sparrow-Simpson (1859-1952)
© Novello & Co. Ltd.

1. Holy Jesu, by thy passion,
   by the woes which none can share,
   borne in more than kingly fashion,
   by thy love beyond compare:

   Crucified, I turn to thee,
   Son of Mary, plead for me.

2. By the treachery and trial,
   by the blows and sore distress,
   by desertion and denial,
   by thine awful loneliness:

3. By thy look so sweet and lowly,
   while they smote thee on the face,
   by thy patience, calm and holy,
   in the midst of keen disgrace:

4. By the hour of condemnation,
   by the blood which trickled down,
   when, for us and our salvation,
   thou didst wear the robe and crown:

5. By the path of sorrows dreary,
   by the cross, thy dreadful load,
   by the pain, when, faint and weary,
   thou didst sink upon the road:

6. By the Spirit which could render
   love for hate and good for ill,
   by the mercy, sweet and tender,
   poured upon thy murd'rers still:

318
Brian Foley (b.1919)
© Copyright 1971 Faber Music Ltd.

1. Holy Spirit, come, confirm us
   in the truth that Christ makes known;
   we have faith and understanding
   through your helping gifts alone.

2. Holy Spirit, come, console us,
   come as Advocate to plead;
   loving Spirit from the Father,
   grant in Christ the help we need.

3. Holy Spirit, come, renew us,
   come yourself to make us live:
   holy through your loving presence,
   holy through the gifts you give.

4. Holy Spirit, come, possess us,
   you the love of Three in One,
   Holy Spirit of the Father,
   Holy Spirit of the Son.

319
William Henry Parker (1845-1929)

1. Holy Spirit, hear us;
   help us while we sing;
   breathe into the music
   of the praise we bring.

2. Holy Spirit, prompt us
   when we kneel to pray;
   nearer come, and teach us
   what we ought to say.

3. Holy Spirit, shine thou
   on the book we read;
   gild its holy pages
   with the light we need.

4. Holy Spirit, give us
   each a lowly mind;
   make us more like Jesus,
   gentle, pure, and kind.

5. Holy Spirit, help us
   daily by thy might,
   what is wrong to conquer,
   and to choose the right.

320
Samuel Longfellow (1819-1892)

1. Holy Spirit, truth divine,
   dawn upon this soul of mine;
   Word of God, and inward light,
   wake my spirit, clear my sight.

2. Holy Spirit, love divine,
   glow within this heart of mine,
   kindle every high desire,
   perish self in thy pure fire.

3. Holy Spirit, power divine,
   fill and nerve this will of mine;
   by thee may I strongly live,
   bravely bear, and nobly strive.

4. Holy Spirit, right divine,
   King within my conscience reign;
   be my law, and I shall be
   firmly bound, for ever free.

5. Holy Spirit, peace divine,
   still this restless heart of mine,
   speak to calm this tossing sea,
   stayed in thy tranquillity.

6. Holy Spirit, joy divine,
   gladden thou this heart of mine;
   in the desert ways I sing:
   'Spring, O Well, for ever spring!'

321

Carl Tuttle
© 1985 Mercy/Vineyard Publishing
Administered by CopyCare

1. Hosanna, hosanna,
hosanna in the highest! *(Repeat)*

Lord, we lift up your name,
with hearts full of praise;
be exalted, O Lord, my God!
Hosanna in the highest!

2. Glory, glory, glory
to the King of kings! *(Repeat)*

322

Charles Wesley (1707-1788)

1. How can we sinners know
our sins on earth forgiven?
How can our gracious Saviour show
our names inscribed in heaven?

2. We who in Christ believe
that he for us hath died,
we all his unknown peace receive,
and feel his blood applied.

3. His love, surpassing far
the love of all beneath,
we find within our hearts, and dare
the pointless darts of death.

4. Stronger than death and hell
the mystic power we prove;
and, conquerors of the world, we dwell
in heaven, who dwell in love.

5. The meek and lowly heart
that in our Saviour was,
to us his Spirit doth impart,
and signs us with his cross.

6. Our nature's turned, our mind
transformed in all its powers;
and both the witnesses are joined,
the Spir't of God with ours.

7. His glory our design,
we live our God to please;
and rise with filial fear divine,
to perfect holiness.

323

Charles Wesley (1707-1788)

1. How do thy mercies close me round!
For ever be thy name adored!
I blush in all things to abound;
the servant is above his Lord!

2. Inured to poverty and pain,
a suffering life my Master led;
the Son of God, the Son of Man,
he had not where to lay his head.

3. But, lo, a place he hath prepared
for me, whom watchful angels keep;
yea, he himself becomes my guard,
he smoothes my bed, and gives me sleep.

4. Jesus protects; my fears, begone!
What can the Rock of Ages move?
Safe in thy arms I lay me down,
thy everlasting arms of love.

5. While thou art intimately nigh,
who, who shall violate my rest?
Sin, earth, and hell I now defy;
I lean upon my Saviour's breast.

6. I rest beneath the Almighty's shade,
my griefs expire, my troubles cease:
thou, Lord, on whom my soul is stayed,
wilt keep me still in perfect peace.

7. Me for thine own thou lov'st to take,
in time and in eternity;
thou never, never wilt forsake
a helpless soul that trusts in thee.

324

Isacc Watts (1674-1748) alt.

1. How gracious are their feet
who stand on Zion's hill,
who bring salvation on their tongues,
and words of peace reveal!

2. How cheering is their voice,
   how sweet their tidings are:
   'Zion, behold thy Saviour-King!
   He reigns and triumphs here'.

3. How happy are our ears
   that hear this joyful sound,
   which kings and prophets waited for,
   and sought, but never found!

4. How blessèd are our eyes
   that see this heavenly light!
   Prophets and monarchs sought it long,
   but died without the sight.

5. The sentries join their voice,
   and tuneful notes employ;
   Jerusalem breaks forth in songs,
   and deserts learn the joy.

6. The Lord makes bare his arm
   through all the earth abroad;
   let all the nations now behold
   their Saviour and their God.

325 Charles Wesley (1707-1788)

1. How happy are thy servants, Lord,
   who thus remember thee!
   What tongue can tell our sweet accord,
   our perfect harmony?

2. Who thy mysterious supper share,
   here at thy table fed,
   many, and yet but one we are,
   one undivided bread.

3. One with the living bread divine
   which now by faith we eat,
   our hearts and minds and spirits join,
   and all in Jesus meet.

4. So dear the tie where souls agree
   in Jesus' dying love;
   then only can it closer be
   when all are joined above.

326 v. 1: Leonard E. Smith Jnr. (b. 1942)
based on Isaiah 52, 53; vs 2-4: unknown.
© 1974 Kingsway's Thankyou Music

1. How lovely on the mountains
   are the feet of him
   who brings good news, good news,
   announcing peace,
   proclaiming news of happiness:
   our God reigns, our God reigns.

Our God reigns. (x4)

2. You watchmen, lift your voices
   joyfully as one,
   shout for your King, your King!
   See eye to eye,
   the Lord restoring Zion:
   our God reigns, our God reigns.

3. Wasteplaces of Jerusalem,
   break forth with joy!
   We are redeemed, redeemed.
   The Lord has saved
   and comforted his people:
   our God reigns, our God reigns.

4. Ends of the earth, see
   the salvation of our God!
   Jesus is Lord, is Lord!
   Before the nations,
   he has bared his holy arm:
   our God reigns, our God reigns.

327 John Mason (c. 1645-1694)

1. How shall I sing that majesty
   which angels do admire?
   Let dust in dust and silence lie;
   sing, sing, ye heavenly choir.
   Thousands of thousands stand around
   thy throne, O God most high;
   ten thousand times ten thousand sound
   thy praise; but who am I?

Continued overleaf

2. Thy brightness unto them appears,
   whilst I thy footsteps trace;
   a sound of God comes to my ears,
   but they behold thy face.
   They sing because thou art their Sun;
   Lord, send a beam on me;
   for where heav'n is but once begun
   there alleluias be.

3. How great a being, Lord, is thine,
   which doth all beings keep!
   Thy knowledge is the only line
   to sound so vast a deep.
   Thou art a sea without a shore,
   a sun without a sphere;
   thy time is now and evermore,
   thy place is ev'rywhere.

328 John Newton (1725-1807)

1. How sweet the name of Jesus sounds
   in a believer's ear!
   It soothes our sorrows, heals our
       wounds,
   and drives away our fear.

2. It makes the wounded spirit whole,
   and calms the troubled breast;
   'tis manna to the hungry soul,
   and to the weary rest.

3. Dear name! the rock on which I build,
   my shield and hiding-place,
   my never-failing treas'ry filled
   with boundless stores of grace.

4. Jesus! my shepherd, brother, friend,
   my prophet, priest, and king,
   my Lord, my life, my way, my end,
   accept the praise I bring.

5. Weak is the effort of my heart,
   and cold my warmest thought;
   but when I see thee as thou art,
   I'll praise thee as I ought.

6. Till then I would thy love proclaim
   with ev'ry fleeting breath;
   and may the music of thy name
   refresh my soul in death.

329 Dave Bilbrough
© 1983 Kingsway's Thankyou Music

I am a new creation,
no more in condemnation,
here in the grace of God I stand.
My heart is overflowing,
my love just keeps on growing,
here in the grace of God I stand.
And I will praise you, Lord,
yes, I will praise you, Lord,
and I will sing of all that you have done.
A joy that knows no limit,
a lightness in my spirit,
here in the grace of God I stand.

330 Dora Greenwell (1821-1882)

1. I am not skilled to understand
   what God has willed, what God had
       planned;
   I only know at his right hand
   stands one who is my Saviour.

2. I take God at his word and deed:
   Christ died to save me, this I read;
   and in my heart I find a need
   of him to be my Saviour.

3. And was there then no other way
   for God to take? I cannot say;
   I only bless him, day by day,
   who saved me through my Saviour.

4. That he should leave his place on high
   and come for sinners once to die,
   you count it strange? So do not I,
   since I have known my Saviour.

5. And O that he fulfilled may see
   the travail of his soul in me,
   and with his work contented be,
   as I with my dear Saviour!

6. Yea, living, dying, let me bring
   my strength, my solace, from this spring,
   that he who lives to be my King
   once died to be my Saviour.

331 Suzanne Toolan (b. 1927)
© 1966 GIA Publications Inc.

1. I am the bread of life.
   You who come to me shall not hunger;
   and who believe in me shall not thirst.
   No one can come to me
   unless the Father beckons.

   And I will raise you up,
   and I will raise you up,
   and I will raise you up on the last day.

2. The bread that I will give
   is my flesh for the life of the world,
   and if you eat of this bread,
   you shall live for ever,
   you shall live for ever.

3. Unless you eat
   of the flesh of the Son of Man,
   and drink of his blood,
   and drink of his blood,
   you shall not have life within you.

4. I am the resurrection,
   I am the life.
   If you believe in me,
   even though you die,
   you shall live for ever.

5. Yes, Lord, I believe
   that you are the Christ,
   the Son of God,
   who has come
   into the world.

332 Frances Ridley Havergal (1836-1879)

1. I am trusting thee, Lord Jesus,
   trusting only thee;
   trusting thee for full salvation,
   great and free.

2. I am trusting thee for pardon,
   at thy feet I bow;
   for thy grace and tender mercy,
   trusting now.

3. I am trusting thee for cleansing
   in the crimson flood;
   trusting thee to make me holy
   by thy blood.

4. I am trusting thee to guide me;
   thou alone shalt lead,
   every day and hour supplying
   all my need.

5. I am trusting thee for power,
   thine can never fail;
   words which thou thyself shalt give me
   must prevail.

6. I am trusting thee, Lord Jesus;
   never let me fall;
   I am trusting thee for ever,
   and for all.

333 Marc Nelson
© 1987 Mercy/Vineyard Publishing
Administered by CopyCare

1. I believe in Jesus;
   I believe he is the Son of God.
   I believe he died and rose again.
   I believe he paid for us all.
   And I believe he's here now
   standing in our midst;
   here with the power to heal now,
   and the grace to forgive.

Continued overleaf

2. I believe in you, Lord;
   I believe you are the Son of God.
   I believe you died and rose again.
   I believe you paid for us all.
   And I believe you're here now
   standing in our midst;
   here with the power to heal now,
   and the grace to forgive.

334
William Young Fullerton (1857-1932) alt.
© Copyright control

1. I cannot tell
   how he whom angels worship
   should stoop to love
   the peoples of the earth,
   or why as shepherd
   he should seek the wand'rer
   with his mysterious promise
   of new birth.
   But this I know,
   that he was born of Mary,
   when Bethl'em's manger
   was his only home,
   and that he lived at
   Nazareth and laboured,
   and so the Saviour,
   Saviour of the world, is come.

2. I cannot tell
   how silently he suffered,
   as with his peace
   he graced this place of tears,
   or how his heart
   upon the cross was broken,
   the crown of pain
   to three and thirty years.
   But this I know,
   he heals the broken-hearted,
   and stays our sin,
   and calms our lurking fear,
   and lifts the burden
   from the heavy laden,
   for yet the Saviour,
   Saviour of the world, is here.

3. I cannot tell
   how he will win the nations,
   how he will claim
   his earthly heritage,
   how satisfy
   the needs and aspirations
   of east and west,
   of sinner and of sage.
   But this I know,
   all flesh shall see his glory,
   and he shall reap
   the harvest he has sown,
   and some glad day
   his sun shall shine in splendour
   when he the Saviour,
   Saviour of the world, is known.

4. I cannot tell
   how all the lands shall worship,
   when, at his bidding,
   ev'ry storm is stilled,
   or who can say
   how great the jubilation
   when ev'ry heart
   with perfect love is filled.
   But this I know,
   the skies will thrill with rapture,
   and myriad, myriad
   human voices sing,
   and earth to heav'n,
   and heav'n to earth, will answer:
   'At last the Saviour,
   Saviour of the world, is King!'

335
Brian A. Wren (b. 1936)
© 1971, 1995 Stainer & Bell Ltd.

1. I come with joy, a child of God,
   forgiven, loved and free,
   the life of Jesus to recall,
   in love laid down for me.

2. I come with Christians far and near
   to find, as all are fed,
   the new community of love
   in Christ's communion bread.

3. As Christ breaks bread, and bids us share,
each proud division ends.
The love that made us, makes us one,
and strangers now are friends.

4. The Spirit of the risen Christ,
unseen, but ever near,
is in such friendship better known,
alive among us here.

5. Together met, together bound
by all that God has done,
we'll go with joy, to give the world
the love that makes us one.

336

Sydney Carter (b. 1915)
© 1963 Stainer & Bell Ltd.

1. I danced in the morning
when the world was begun,
and I danced in the moon
and the stars and the sun,
and I came down from heaven
and I danced on the earth,
at Bethlehem I had my birth.

Dance then, wherever you may be,
I am the Lord of the Dance, said he,
and I'll lead you all, wherever you may be,
and I'll lead you all in the dance, said he.

2. I danced for the scribe
and the Pharisee,
but they would not dance
and they wouldn't follow me.
I danced for the fishermen,
for James and John –
they came with me
and the dance went on.

3. I danced on the Sabbath
and I cured the lame;
the holy people,
they said it was a shame.
They whipped and they stripped
and they hung me on high,
and they left me there
on a cross to die.

4. I danced on a Friday
when the sky turned black –
it's hard to dance
with the devil on your back.
They buried my body,
and they thought I'd gone,
but I am the Dance,
and I still go on.

5. They cut me down
and I leapt up high;
I am the life
that'll never, never die;
I'll live in you
if you'll live in me –
I am the Lord
of the Dance, said he.

337

Carl Tuttle
© 1982 Mercy/Vineyard Publishing
Administered by CopyCare

1. I give you all the honour
and praise that's due your name,
for you are the King of Glory,
the Creator of all things.

And I worship you,
I give my life to you,
I fall down on my knees.
Yes, I worship you,
I give my life to you,
I fall down on my knees.

2. As your Spirit moves upon me now,
you meet my deepest need,
and I lift my hands up to your throne,
your mercy I've received.

3. You have broken chains that bound me,
you've set this captive free,
I will lift my voice to praise your name
for all eternity.

338 Horatius Bonar (1808-1889)

1. I heard the voice of Jesus say,
   'Come unto me and rest;
   lay down, thou weary one, lay down
   thy head upon my breast.'
   I came to Jesus as I was,
   so weary, worn and sad;
   I found in him a resting-place,
   and he has made me glad.

2. I heard the voice of Jesus say,
   'Behold, I freely give
   the living water, thirsty one;
   stoop down and drink and live.'
   I came to Jesus, and I drank
   of that life-giving stream;
   my thirst was quenched, my soul revived,
   and now I live in him.

3. I heard the voice of Jesus say,
   'I am this dark world's light;
   look unto me, thy morn shall rise,
   and all thy day be bright.'
   I looked to Jesus, and I found
   in him my star, my sun;
   and in that light of life I'll walk
   till trav'lling days are done.

339 Lewis Hartsough (1828-1919) alt.

1. I hear thy welcome voice
   that calls me, Lord, to thee,
   for cleansing in thy precious blood
   that flowed on Calvary.

   I am coming, Lord,
   coming now to thee:
   wash me, cleanse me, by the blood
   that flowed on Calvary.

2. Though weak I come to thee,
   thou dost my strength assure;
   thou dost my spirit fully cleanse,
   till spotless all and pure.

3. 'Tis Jesus calls me on
   to perfect faith and love,
   to perfect hope, and peace, and trust,
   for earth and heaven above.

4. 'Tis Jesus who confirms
   the blessèd work within,
   by adding grace to welcomed grace,
   where reigned the power of sin.

5. All hail, atoning blood!
   All hail, redeeming grace!
   All hail, the gift of Christ our Lord,
   our strength and righteousness!

340 John Samuel Bewley Monsell (1815-1875)

1. I hunger and I thirst;
   Jesus, my manna be:
   ye living waters, burst
   out of the rock for me.

2. Thou bruised and broken Bread,
   my life-long wants supply;
   as living souls are fed,
   O feed me, or I die.

3. Thou true life-giving Vine,
   let me thy sweetness prove;
   renew my life with thine,
   refresh my soul with love.

4. Rough paths my feet have trod
   since first their course began;
   feed me, thou Bread of God;
   help me, thou Son of Man.

5. For still the desert lies
   my thirsting soul before;
   O living water, rise
   within me evermore.

341 Charles Wesley (1707-1788)

1. I know that my Redeemer lives,
   and ever prays for me;
   a token of his love he gives,
   a pledge of liberty.

2. I find him lifting up my head,
   he brings salvation near,
   his presence makes me free indeed,
   and he will soon appear.

3. He wills that I should holy be;
   what can withstand his will?
   The counsel of his grace in me
   he surely shall fulfil.

4. Jesus, I hang upon thy word;
   I steadfastly believe
   thou wilt return and claim me, Lord,
   and to thyself receive.

5. Thy love I soon expect to find
   in all its depth and height,
   to comprehend the eternal mind,
   and grasp the Infinite.

6. When God is mine, and I am his,
   of paradise possessed,
   I taste unutterable bliss
   and everlasting rest.

342 Samuel Medley (1738-1799)

1. I know that my Redeemer lives –
   what joy the blest assurance gives!
   He lives, he lives, who once was dead;
   he lives, my everlasting Head.

2. He lives, to bless me with his love;
   he lives, to plead for me above;
   he lives, my hungry soul to feed;
   he lives, to help in time of need.

3. He lives, and grants me daily breath;
   he lives, and I shall conquer death;
   he lives, my mansion to prepare;
   he lives, to lead me safely there.

4. He lives, all glory to his name;
   he lives, my Saviour, still the same;
   what joy the blest assurance gives,
   I know that my Redeemer lives!

343 Amos Cresswell, based on a hymn by Jochen Klepper (1903-1942)
© Amos Cresswell

1. I lay me down in your safe hands
   to sleep the sleep of heaven,
   that child who in your keeping stands
   the truest rest is given.

2. Alone you stand awake, my Lord,
   to guard, to help, to calm me,
   when darkest fears sound sombre chords
   and shadows press to harm me.

3. Your strong right arm is reaching far
   to save me from all evil
   while I sleep, safely, freed from care
   protected from the devil.

4. You close my eyes with touch so light
   I sleep at peace till dawning,
   for he who leads me into night
   will lead me through to morning.

344 Isaac Watts (1674-1748) alt. based on Psalm 146

1. I'll praise my Maker while I've breath;
   and when my voice is lost in death,
   praise shall employ my nobler powers:
   my days of praise shall ne'er be past,
   while life and thought and being last,
   or immortality endures.

2. Happy are they whose hopes rely
   on Israel's God! He made the sky,
   and earth and sea, with all their train:
   his truth for ever stands secure;
   he heals the sick, he feeds the poor,
   and none shall find his promise vain.

3. The Lord pours eyesight on the blind;
   the Lord supports the fainting mind;
   he sends the labouring conscience peace;
   he helps the stranger in distress,
   the widow and the fatherless,
   and grants the prisoner sweet release.

Continued overleaf

4. I'll praise him while he lends me breath;
and when my voice is lost in death,
praise shall employ my nobler powers:
my days of praise shall ne'er be past,
while life and thought and being last,
or immortality endures.

345 Laurie Klein
© 1978 Maranatha! Music. Administered by CopyCare

I love you, Lord,
and I lift my voice to worship you,
O my soul rejoice.
Take joy, my King, in what you hear.
May it be a sweet, sweet sound in your ear.

346 Rob Hayward
© 1985 Kingsway's Thankyou Music

I'm accepted, I'm forgiven,
I am fathered by the true and living God.
I'm accepted, no condemnation,
I am loved by the true and living God.
There's no guilt or fear as I draw near
to the Saviour and Creator of the world.
There is joy and peace as I release
my worship to you, O Lord.

347 Graham Kendrick (b. 1950)
© 1988 Make Way Music

Immanuel, O Immanuel,
bowed in awe I worship at your feet,
and sing Immanuel,
God is with us,
sharing my humanness, my shame,
feeling my weaknesses, my pain,
taking the punishment, the blame,
Immanuel.
And now my words cannot explain,
all that my heart cannot contain,
how great are the glories of your name,
Immanuel.

Immanuel, O Immanuel,
bowed in awe I worship at your feet,
and sing Immanuel . . .

348 Walter Chalmers Smith (1824-1908)
based on 1 Timothy 1:17

1. Immortal, invisible,
God only wise,
in light inaccessible hid
from our eyes,
most blessèd, most glorious,
the Ancient of Days,
almighty, victorious,
thy great name we praise.

2. Unresting, unhasting,
and silent as light,
nor wanting, nor wasting,
thou rulest in might;
thy justice like mountains
high soaring above
thy clouds which are fountains
of goodness and love.

3. To all life thou givest,
to both great and small;
in all life thou livest,
the true life of all;
we blossom and flourish
as leaves on the tree,
and wither and perish;
but naught changeth thee.

4. Great Father of glory,
pure Father of light,
thine angels adore thee,
all veiling their sight;
all laud we would render,
O help us to see
'tis only the splendour
of light hideth thee.

349 John Greenleaf Whittier (1807-1892)

1. Immortal Love, forever full,
forever flowing free,
forever shared, forever whole,
a never-ebbing sea!

2. Our outward lips confess the name
   all other names above;
   Love only knoweth whence it came,
   and comprehendeth love.

3. We may not climb the heavenly steeps
   to bring the Lord Christ down;
   in vain we search the lowest deeps,
   for him no depths can drown.

4. And not for signs in heaven above
   or earth below they look,
   who know with John his smile of love,
   with Peter his rebuke.

5. But warm, sweet, tender, even yet
   a present help is he;
   and faith has still its Olivet,
   and love its Galilee.

6. Through him the first fond prayers are
      said
   our lips of childhood frame;
   the last low whispers of our dead
   are burdened with his name.

7. Alone, O Love ineffable,
   thy saving name is given!
   To turn aside from thee is hell,
   to walk with thee is heaven!

350 Isaac Watts (1674-1748) alt. based on 2 Timothy 1:12

1. I'm not ashamed to own my Lord,
   or to defend his cause,
   maintain the honour of his word,
   the glory of his cross.

2. Jesus, my God, I know his name,
   his name is all my trust;
   nor will he put my soul to shame,
   nor let my hope be lost.

3. Firm as his throne his promise stands,
   and he can well secure
   what I've committed to his hands
   till the decisive hour.

4. Then will he own my humble name
   before his Father's face,
   and in the new Jerusalem
   appoint my soul a place.

351 Isaac Watts (1674-1748) based on Psalm 139

1. In all my vast concerns with thee,
   in vain my soul would try
   to shun thy presence, Lord, or flee
   the notice of thine eye.

2. Thy all-surrounding sight surveys
   my rising and my rest,
   my public walks, my private ways,
   the secrets of my breast.

3. My thoughts lie open to thee, Lord,
   before they're formed within;
   and, ere my lips pronounce the word,
   thou know'st the sense I mean.

4. O wondrous knowledge, deep and high;
   where can a creature hide?
   Within thy circling arms I lie,
   beset on every side.

5. So let thy grace surround me still,
   and like a bulwark prove,
   to guard my soul from every ill,
   secured by sovereign love.

352 Martin E. Leckebusch (b. 1962)
© 1999 Kevin Mayhew Ltd.

1. In an age of twisted values
   we have lost the truth we need;
   in sophisticated language
   we have justified our greed;
   by our struggle for possessions
   we have robbed the poor and weak –
   hear our cry and heal our nation:
   your forgiveness, Lord, we seek.

Continued overleaf

2. We have built discrimination
   on our prejudice and fear;
   hatred swiftly turns to cruelty
   if we hold resentments dear.
   For communities divided
   by the walls of class and race
   hear our cry and heal our nation:
   show us, Lord, your love and grace.

3. When our families are broken;
   when our homes are full of strife;
   when our children are bewildered,
   when they lose their way in life;
   when we fail to give the aged
   all the care we know we should –
   hear our cry and heal our nation
   with your tender fatherhood.

4. We who hear your word so often
   choose so rarely to obey;
   turn us from our wilful blindness,
   give us truth to light our way.
   In the power of your Spirit
   come to cleanse us, make us new:
   hear our cry and heal our nation
   till our nation honours you.

353 John Oxenham (1852-1941) alt.
© Desmond Dunkerley

1. In Christ there is no east or west,
   in him no south or north,
   but one great fellowship of love
   throughout the whole wide earth.

2. In him shall true hearts ev'rywhere
   their high communion find;
   his service is the golden cord,
   close binding humankind.

3. Join hands, united in the faith,
   whate'er your race may be;
   who serve my Father as their own
   are surely kin to me.

4. In Christ now meet both east and west,
   in him meet south and north;
   all Christlike souls are one in him,
   throughout the whole wide earth.

354 Annie Sherwood Hawks (1835-1918)

1. I need thee ev'ry hour,
   most gracious Lord;
   no tender voice like thine
   can peace afford.

   I need thee, O I need thee!
   ev'ry hour I need thee;
   O bless me now,
   my Saviour! I come to thee.

2. I need thee ev'ry hour;
   stay thou near by;
   temptations lose their pow'r
   when thou art nigh.

3. I need thee ev'ry hour,
   in joy or pain;
   come quickly and abide,
   or life is vain.

4. I need thee ev'ry hour;
   teach me thy will,
   and thy rich promises
   in me fulfil.

5. I need thee ev'ry hour,
   most Holy One;
   O make me thine indeed,
   thou blessèd Son!

355 Trans. from the Polish by Edith Margaret Gellibrand
Reed (1885-1933). © *Copyright control*

1. Infant holy, infant lowly,
   for his bed a cattle stall;
   oxen lowing, little knowing
   Christ the babe is Lord of all.
   Swift are winging angels singing,
   nowells ringing, tidings bringing,
   Christ the babe is Lord of all,
   Christ the babe is Lord of all.

2. Flocks were sleeping, shepherds keeping
vigil till the morning new;
saw the glory, heard the story,
tidings of a gospel true.
Thus rejoicing, free from sorrow,
praises voicing, greet the morrow,
Christ the babe was born for you,
Christ the babe was born for you.

356 Anna Laetitia Waring (1820-1910) based on Psalm 23

1. In heav'nly love abiding,
no change my heart shall fear;
and safe is such confiding,
for nothing changes here.
The storm may roar without me,
my heart may low be laid,
but God is round about me,
and can I be dismayed?

2. Wherever he may guide me,
no want shall turn me back;
my Shepherd is beside me,
and nothing shall I lack.
His wisdom ever waketh,
his sight is never dim,
he knows the way he taketh,
and I will walk with him.

3. Green pastures are before me,
which yet I have not seen;
bright skies will soon be o'er me,
where the dark clouds have been.
My hope I cannot measure,
my path to life is free,
my Saviour has my treasure,
and he will walk with me.

357 Charles Wesley (1707-1788)

1. In Jesus we live, in Jesus we rest,
and thankful receive his dying bequest;
the cup of salvation his mercy bestows
and all his passion, our happiness
flows.

2. With mystical wine he comforts us here,
and gladly we join, till Jesus appear,
with hearty thanksgiving his death to
record;
the living, the living should sing of their
Lord.

3. He hallowed the cup which now we
receive,
the pledge of our hope with Jesus to live,
(where sorrow and sadness shall never be
found)
with glory and gladness eternally crowned.

4. The fruit of the vine (the joy it implies)
again we shall join to drink in the skies,
exult in his favour, our triumph renew;
and I, saith the Saviour, will drink it with
you.

358 Christina Georgina Rossetti (1830-1894)

1. In the bleak mid-winter
frosty wind made moan,
earth stood hard as iron,
water like a stone;
snow had fallen, snow on snow,
snow on snow,
in the bleak mid-winter, long ago.

2. Our God, heav'n cannot hold him
nor earth sustain;
heav'n and earth shall flee away
when he comes to reign.
In the bleak mid-winter
a stable-place sufficed
the Lord God almighty, Jesus Christ.

3. Enough for him, whom cherubim
worship night and day,
a breastful of milk,
and a mangerful of hay:
enough for him, whom angels
fall down before,
the ox and ass and camel which adore.

Continued overleaf

4. Angels and archangels
   may have gathered there,
   cherubim and seraphim
   thronged the air;
   but only his mother
   in her maiden bliss
   worshipped the belovèd with a kiss.

5. What can I give him,
   poor as I am?
   If I were a shepherd
   I would bring a lamb;
   if I were a wise man
   I would do my part,
   yet what I can I give him:
   give my heart.

359 John Bowring (1792-1872)

1. In the cross of Christ I glory:
   towering o'er the wrecks of time,
   all the light of sacred story
   gathers round its head sublime.

2. When the woes of life o'ertake me,
   hopes deceive and fears annoy,
   never shall the cross forsake me,
   lo, it glows with peace and joy.

3. When the sun of bliss is beaming
   light and love upon my way,
   from the cross the radiance streaming
   adds more lustre to the day.

4. Bane and blessing, pain and pleasure,
   by the cross are sanctified;
   peace is there that knows no measure,
   joys that through all time abide.

5. In the cross of Christ I glory:
   towering o'er the wrecks of time,
   all the light of sacred story
   gathers round its head sublime.

360 Isaac Watts (1674-1748)

1. I sing the almighty power of God,
   that made the mountains rise,
   that spread the flowing seas abroad,
   and built the lofty skies.

2. I sing the wisdom that ordained
   the sun to rule the day;
   the moon shines full at his command,
   and all the stars obey.

3. I sing the goodness of the Lord,
   that filled the earth with food;
   he formed the creatures with his word,
   and then pronounced them good.

4. Lord, how thy wonders are displayed
   where'er I turn mine eye,
   if I survey the ground I tread,
   or gaze upon the sky!

5. God's hand is my perpetual guard,
   he guides me with his eye;
   why should I then forget the Lord,
   whose love is ever nigh?

361 Edmund Hamilton Sears (1810-1876) alt.

1. It came upon the midnight clear,
   that glorious song of old,
   from angels bending near the earth
   to touch their harps of gold:
   'Peace on the earth, goodwill to all,
   from heav'ns all gracious King!'
   The world in solemn stillness lay
   to hear the angels sing.

2. Still through the cloven skies they come,
   with peaceful wings unfurled;
   and still their heav'nly music floats
   o'er all the weary world:
   above its sad and lowly plains
   they bend on hov'ring wing;
   and ever o'er its Babel-sounds
   the blessèd angels sing.

3. Yet with the woes of sin and strife
   the world has suffered long;
   beneath the angel-strain have rolled
   two thousand years of wrong;
   and warring humankind hears not
   the love-song which they bring;
   O hush the noise of mortal strife,
   and hear the angels sing!

4. And ye, beneath life's crushing load,
   whose forms are bending low,
   who toil along the climbing way
   with painful steps and slow:
   look now! for glad and golden hours
   come swiftly on the wing;
   O rest beside the weary road,
   and hear the angels sing.

5. For lo, the days are hast'ning on,
   by prophets seen of old,
   when with the ever-circling years
   comes round the age of gold;
   when peace shall over all the earth
   its ancient splendours fling,
   and all the world give back the song
   which now the angels sing.

362 Dan Schutte, based on Isaiah 6
© 1981 Daniel L. Schutte and New Dawn Music

1. I, the Lord of sea and sky,
   I have heard my people cry.
   All who dwell in dark and sin
   my hand will save.
   I who made the stars of night,
   I will make their darkness bright.
   Who will bear my light to them?
   Whom shall I send?

   Here I am, Lord. Is it I, Lord?
   I have heard you calling in the night.
   I will go, Lord, if you lead me.
   I will hold your people in my heart.

2. I, the Lord of snow and rain,
   I have borne my people's pain.
   I have wept for love of them.
   They turn away.
   I will break their hearts of stone,
   give them hearts for love alone.
   I will speak my word to them.
   Whom shall I send?

3. I, the Lord of wind and flame,
   I will tend the poor and lame.
   I will set a feast for them.
   My hand will save.
   Finest bread I will provide
   till their hearts be satisfied.
   I will give my life to them.
   Whom shall I send?

363 William Walsham How (1823-1897)

1. It is a thing most wonderful,
   almost too wonderful to be,
   that God's own Son should come from
      heav'n,
   and die to save a child like me.

2. And yet I know that it is true:
   he chose a poor and humble lot,
   and wept and toiled, and mourned and
      died,
   for love of those who loved him not.

3. I cannot tell how he could love
   a child so weak and full of sin;
   his love must be most wonderful,
   if he could die my love to win.

4. I sometimes think about the cross,
   and shut my eyes, and try to see
   the cruel nails and crown of thorns,
   and Jesus crucified for me.

5. But even could I see him die,
   I could but see a little part
   of that great love which, like a fire,
   is always burning in his heart.

Continued overleaf

6. It is most wonderful to know
   his love for me so free and sure;
   but 'tis more wonderful to see
   my love for him so faint and poor.

7. And yet I want to love thee, Lord;
   O light the flame within my heart,
   and I will love thee more and more,
   until I see thee as thou art.

364
Fred Pratt Green (1903-2000)
© 1977 Stainer & Bell Ltd.

1. It is God who hold the nations
   in the hollow of his hand;
   it is God whose light is shining
   in the darkness of the land;
   it is God who builds his city
   on the rock and not on sand:
   may the living God be praised!

2. It is God whose purpose summons
   us to use the present hour;
   who recalls us to our senses
   when a nation's life turns sour;
   in the discipline of freedom
   we shall know his saving power:
   may the living God be praised!

3. When a thankful nation, looking back,
   has cause to celebrate
   those who win our admiration
   by their service to the state;
   when self-giving is a measure
   of the greatness of the great:
   may the living God be praised!

4. He reminds us every sunrise
   that the world is ours on lease –
   for the sake of life tomorrow,
   may our love for it increase;
   may all races live together,
   share its riches, be at peace:
   may the living God be praised!

365
Psalm 121
Scottish Psalter (1650)

1. I to the hills will lift mine eyes;
   from whence doth come mine aid?
   My safety cometh from the Lord,
   who heaven and earth hath made.

2. Thy foot he'll not let slide, nor will
   he slumber that thee keeps;
   behold, he that keeps Israel,
   he slumbers not, nor sleeps.

3. The Lord thee keeps; the Lord thy shade
   on thy right hand doth stay;
   the moon by night thee shall not smite,
   nor yet the sun by day.

4. The Lord shall keep thy soul; he shall
   preserve thee from all ill,
   henceforth thy going out and in
   God keep for ever will.

366
Mary Shekleton (1827-1883)

1. It passeth knowledge, that dear love of thine,
   my Saviour, Jesus! Yet this soul of mine
   would of thy love, in all its breadth and length,
   its height and depth, and everlasting strength,
   know more and more.

2. It passeth telling, that dear love of thine,
   my Saviour, Jesus! Yet these lips of mine
   would fain proclaim to sinners far and near
   a love which can remove all guilty fear,
   and love beget.

3. It passeth praises, that dear love of thine,
   my Saviour, Jesus! Yet this heart of mine
   would sing that love, so full, so rich, so free,
   which brings a rebel sinner, such as me,
   nigh unto God.

4. O fill me, Saviour Jesus, with thy love!
Lead, lead me to the living fount above;
thither may I, in simple faith, draw nigh,
and never to another fountain fly,
but unto thee.

5. And then, when Jesus face to face I see,
when at his lofty throne I bow the knee,
then of his love, in all its breadth and
    length,
its height and depth, its everlasting
    strength,
my soul shall sing.

367   James Grindlay Small (1817-1888)

1. I've found a friend; O such a friend!
He loved me ere I knew him;
he drew me with the cords of love,
and thus he bound me to him;
and round my heart still closely twine
those ties which nought can sever;
for I am his, and he is mine,
for ever and for ever.

2. I've found a friend; O such a friend!
He bled, he died to save me;
and not alone the gift of life,
but his own self he gave me.
Nought that I have mine own I call,
I hold it for the giver:
my heart, my strength, my life, my all
are his, and his for ever.

3. I've found a friend; O such a friend!
All power to him is given,
to guard me on my onward course
and bring me safe to heaven.
Eternal glories gleam afar,
to nerve my faint endeavour;
so now to watch, to work, to war,
and then to rest for ever.

4. I've found a friend; O such a friend!
So kind, and true, and tender!
So wise a counsellor and guide,
so mighty a defender!
From him who loves me now so well
what power my soul shall sever?
Shall life or death? Shall earth or hell?
No! I am his for ever.

368   Mark Altrogge
© 1982 PDI Music/CopyCare

1. I want to serve the purpose of God
in my generation.
I want to serve the purpose of God
while I am alive.
I want to give my life for something
that'll last for ever,
oh, I delight, I delight to do your will.

What is on your heart?
Show me what to do.
Let me know your will
and I will follow you.
(Repeat)

2. I want to build with silver and gold
in my generation . . .

3. I want to see the kingdom of God
in my generation . . .

4. I want to see the Lord come again
in my generation . . .

369   Graham Kendrick (b.1950)
© 1988 Make Way Music

Men	I will build my church
Women	I will build my church
Men	and the gates of hell
Women	and the gates of hell
Men	shall not prevail
Women	shall not prevail
All	against it.

(Repeat)

Continued overleaf

So you pow'rs in the heavens above,
bow down!
And you pow'rs on the earth below,
bow down!
And acknowledge that Jesus, Jesus,
Jesus is Lord, is Lord.

370 Leona von Brethorst
© 1976 Maranatha! Music/CopyCare

I will enter his gates
with thanksgiving in my heart,
I will enter his courts with praise,
I will say this is the day
that the Lord has made,
I will rejoice for he has made me glad.
He has made me glad, he has made me glad,
I will rejoice for he has made me glad.
He has made me glad, he has made me glad,
I will rejoice for he has made me glad.

371 Matt Redman
© 1994 Kingsway's Thankyou Music

1. I will offer up my life
in spirit and truth,
pouring out the oil of love
as my worship to you.
In surrender I must give
my every part;
Lord, receive the sacrifice
of a broken heart.

Jesus, what can I give,
what can I bring
to so faithful a friend,
to so loving a King?
Saviour, what can be said,
what can be sung
as a praise of your name
for the things you have done?
O my words could not tell,
not even in part,
of the debt of love that is owed
by this thankful heart.

2. You deserve my every breath
for you've paid the great cost;
giving up your life to death,
even death on a cross.
You took all my shame away,
there defeated my sin,
opened up the gates of heav'n,
and have beckoned me in.

372 Francis Harold Rawley (1854-1952)
© HarperCollins Religious/CopyCare

1. I will sing the wondrous story
of the Christ who died for me,
how he left the realms of glory
for the cross on Calvary.
Yes, I'll sing the wondrous story
of the Christ who died for me –
sing it with his saints in glory,
gathered by the crystal sea.

2. I was lost but Jesus found me,
found the sheep that went astray,
raised me up and gently led me
back into the narrow way.
Days of darkness still may meet me,
sorrow's path I oft may tread;
but his presence still is with me,
by his guiding hand I'm led.

3. He will keep me till the river
rolls its waters at my feet:
then he'll bear me safely over,
made by grace for glory meet.
Yes, I'll sing the wondrous story
of the Christ who died for me –
sing it with his saints in glory,
gathered by the crystal sea.

373

Sondra Corbett
© 1983 Integrity's Hosanna! Music/Kingsway's
Thankyou Music

I worship you, Almighty God,
there is none like you.
I worship you, O Prince of Peace,
that is what I love to do.
I give you praise,
for you are my righteousness.
I worship you, Almighty God,
there is none like you.

374

T.S. Colvin (b.1925) based on a song from
North Ghana
© 1969 Hope Publishing

Jesu, Jesu,
fill us with your love,
show us how to serve
the neighbours we have from you.

1. Kneels at the feet of his friends,
   silently washes their feet,
   Master who acts as a slave to them.
   Jesu, Jesu ......

2. Neighbours are wealthy and poor,
   varied in colour and race,
   neighbours are near us and far away.
   Jesu, Jesu ....

3. These are the ones we should serve,
   these are the ones we should love,
   all these are neighbours to us and you.
   Jesu, Jesu ....

4. Loving puts us on our knees,
   silently washing their feet,
   this is the way we should live with you.
   Jesu, Jesu ....

375

Charles Wesley (1707-1788) alt.

1. Jesu, lover of my soul,
   let me to thy bosom fly,
   while the gath'ring waters roll,
   while the tempest still is high:
   hide me, O my Saviour, hide,
   till the storm of life is past;
   safe into the haven guide,
   O receive my soul at last.

2. Other refuge have I none,
   hangs my helpless soul on thee;
   leave, ah, leave me not alone,
   still support and comfort me.
   All my trust on thee is stayed,
   all my help from thee I bring;
   cover my defenceless head
   with the shadow of thy wing.

3. Plenteous grace with thee is found,
   grace to cleanse from ev'ry sin;
   let the healing streams abound,
   make and keep me pure within.
   Thou of life the fountain art,
   freely let me take of thee,
   spring thou up within my heart,
   rise to all eternity.

376

Henry Collins (1827-1919)

1. Jesu, my Lord, my God, my all,
   hear me, blest Saviour, when I call;
   hear me, and from thy dwelling-place
   pour down the riches of thy grace:

   Jesu, my Lord, I thee adore;
   O make me love thee more and more.

2. Jesu, too late I thee have sought;
   how can I love thee as I ought?
   And how extol thy matchless fame,
   the glorious beauty of thy name?

Continued overleaf

3. Jesu, what didst thou find in me,
   that thou hast dealt so lovingly?
   How great the joy that thou hast brought,
   so far exceeding hope or thought?

   Jesu, my Lord, I thee adore;
   O make me love thee more and more.

4. Jesu, of thee shall be my song;
   to thee my heart and soul belong;
   all that I have or am is thine,
   and thou, blest Saviour, thou art mine:

377   Johann Franck (1618-1677) alt.

1. Jesu, priceless treasure,
   source of purest pleasure,
   truest friend to me;
   ah, how long I've panted,
   and my heart hath fainted,
   thirsting, Lord, for thee!
   Thine I am, O spotless Lamb,
   I will let no other hide thee,
   naught I ask beside thee.

2. Hence, all fears and sadness,
   for the Lord of gladness,
   Jesus, enters in;
   they who love the Father,
   though the storms may gather,
   still have peace within;
   yea, whate'er I here must bear,
   still in thee lies purest pleasure,
   Jesu, priceless treasure.

378   Cecil Frances Alexander (1818-1895)

1. Jesus calls us: o'er the tumult
   of our life's wild, restless sea;
   day by day his sweet voice soundeth,
   saying, 'Christian, follow me.'

2. As of old Saint Andrew heard it
   by the Galilean lake,
   turned from home and toil and kindred,
   leaving all for his dear sake.

3. Jesus calls us from the worship
   of the vain world's golden store,
   from each idol that would keep us,
   saying, 'Christian, love me more.'

4. In our joys and in our sorrows,
   days of toil and hours of ease,
   still he calls, in cares and pleasures,
   that we love him more than these.

5. Jesus call us: by thy mercies,
   Saviour, make us hear thy call,
   give our hearts to thine obedience,
   serve and love thee best of all.

379   Matt Redman
© 1995 Kingsway's Thankyou Music

1. Jesus Christ, I think upon your sacrifice;
   you became nothing, poured out to
      death.
   Many times I've wondered at your gift of
      life,
   and I'm in that place once again,
   I'm in that place once again.

   And once again I look upon
   the cross where you died,
   I'm humbled by your mercy
   and I'm broken inside.
   Once again I thank you,
   once again I pour out my life.

2. Now you are exalted to the highest place,
   King of the heavens, where one day I'll
      bow.
   But for now I marvel at this saving grace,
   and I'm full of praise once again,
   I'm full of praise once again.

   Thank you for the cross, thank you for
      the cross,
   thank you for the cross, my friend.
   Thank you for the cross, thank you for
      the cross,
   thank you for the cross, my friend.

380

Anonymous: *Lyra Davidica* (1708)
Trans. from 14th century manuscript

1. Jesus Christ is risen to-day,
   Alleluia!
   Our triumphant holy day,
   Alleluia!
   Who did once upon the cross,
   Alleluia!
   Suffer to redeem our loss,
   Alleluia!

2. Hymns of praises let us sing,
   unto Christ our heavenly King,
   who endured the cross and grave,
   sinners to redeem and save:

3. But the pain, which he endured,
   our salvation hath procured;
   now above the sky he's King,
   where the angels ever sing:

4. Sing we to our God above,
   praise eternal as his love,
   praise him, all ye heavenly host,
   Father, Son, and Holy Ghost!

381

John L. Bell (b. 1949) and Graham Maule (b. 1958)
© 1988 WGRG Iona Community, from the 'Enemy of
Apathy' collection, Wild Goose Publications, 1988

1. Jesus Christ is waiting,
   waiting in the streets:
   no one is his neighbour,
   all alone he eats.
   Listen, Lord Jesus,
   I am lonely too;
   make me, friend or stranger,
   fit to wait on you.

2. Jesus Christ is raging,
   raging in the streets
   where injustice spirals
   and all hope retreats.
   Listen, Lord Jesus,
   I am angry too;
   in the kingdom's causes
   let me rage with you.

3. Jesus Christ is healing,
   healing in the streets
   curing those who suffer,
   touching those he greets.
   Listen, Lord Jesus,
   I have pity too;
   let my care be active,
   healing just like you.

4. Jesus Christ is dancing,
   dancing in the streets,
   where each sign of hatred
   his strong love defeats.
   Listen, Lord Jesus,
   I feel triumph too;
   on suspicion's graveyard,
   let me dance with you.

5. Jesus Christ is calling,
   calling in the streets,
   'Come and walk faith's tightrope,
   I will guide your feet.'
   Listen, Lord Jesus,
   let my fears be few;
   walk one step before me,
   I will follow you.

382

Charles Wesley (1707-1788)

1. Jesus comes with all his grace,
   comes to save a fallen race:
   object of our glorious hope,
   Jesus comes to lift us up.
   Alleluia!

2. Let the living stones cry out;
   let the seed of Abram shout;
   praise we all our lowly King,
   give him thanks, rejoice, and sing.
   Alleluia!

3. He has our salvation wrought,
   he our captive souls has bought,
   he has reconciled to God,
   he has washed us in his blood.
   Alleluia!

Continued overleaf

4. We are now his lawful right,
   walk as children of the light;
   we shall soon obtain the grace,
   pure in heart, to see his face.
   Alleluia!

5. We shall gain our calling's prize;
   after God we all shall rise,
   filled with joy, and love, and peace,
   perfected in holiness.
   Alleluia!

383 Geoff Bullock
© 1995 Word /Maranatha! Music. Administered by
Copycare

1. Jesus, God's righteousness revealed,
   the Son of Man, the Son of God,
   his kingdom comes.
   Jesus, redemption's sacrifice,
   now glorified, now justified,
   his kingdom comes.

   And his kingdom will know no end,
   and its glory shall know no bounds,
   for the majesty and power
   of this kingdom's King has come,
   and this kingdom's reign,
   and this kingdom's rule,
   and this kingdom's power and authority,
   Jesus, God's righteousness revealed.

2. Jesus, the expression of God's love,
   the grace of God, the word of God,
   revealed to us;
   Jesus, God's holiness displayed,
   now glorified, now justified,
   his kingdom comes.

384 Percy Dearmer (1867-1936)
after John Mason Neale (1818-1866) alt.
© Oxford University Press

1. Jesus, good above all other,
   gentle child of gentle mother,
   in a stable born our brother,
   give us grace to persevere.

2. Jesus, cradled in a manger,
   for us facing ev'ry danger,
   living as a homeless stranger,
   make we thee our King most dear.

3. Jesus, for thy people dying,
   risen Master, death defying,
   Lord in heav'n thy grace supplying,
   keep us to thy presence near.

4. Jesus, who our sorrows bearest,
   all our thoughts and hopes thou sharest,
   thou to us the truth declarest;
   help us all thy truth to hear.

5. Lord, in all our doings guide us;
   pride and hate shall ne'er divide us;
   we'll go on with thee beside us,
   and with joy we'll persevere.

385 Charles Wesley (1707-1788)

1. Jesus has died that I might live,
   might live to God alone,
   in him eternal life receive,
   and be in spirit one.

2. Saviour, I thank thee for the grace,
   the gift unspeakable!
   And wait with arms of faith to embrace,
   and all thy love to feel.

3. My soul breaks out in strong desire
   the perfect bliss to prove;
   my longing heart is all on fire
   to be dissolved in love.

4. Give me thyself – from every boast,
   from every wish set free,
   let all I am in thee be lost;
   but give thyself to me.

5. Thy gifts, alone, cannot suffice
   unless thyself be given;
   thy presence makes my paradise,
   and where thou art is heaven.

386
Dave Bolton
© 1975 Kingsway's Thankyou Music

Jesus, how lovely you are,
you are so gentle, so pure and kind.
You shine as the morning star,
Jesus, how lovely you are.

1. Hallelujah, Jesus is my Lord and King;
   hallelujah, Jesus is my everything.

2. Hallelujah, Jesus died and rose again;
   hallelujah, Jesus forgave all my sin.

3. Hallelujah, Jesus is meek and lowly;
   hallelujah, Jesus is pure and holy.

387
Charles Wesley (1707-1788)

1. Jesus, I fain would find
   thy zeal for God in me,
   thy yearning pity for mankind,
   thy burning charity.

2. In me thy Spirit dwell;
   in me thy mercies move:
   so shall the fervour of my zeal
   be thy pure flame of love.

388
Charles Wesley (1707-1788)

1. Jesus, if still the same thou art,
   if all thy promises are sure,
   set up thy kingdom in my heart,
   and make me rich, for I am poor;
   to me be all thy treasures given,
   the kingdom of an inward heaven.

2. Thou hast pronounced the mourners blest;
   and lo, for thee I ever mourn:
   I cannot – no, I will not rest,
   till thou, my only rest, return;
   till thou, the Prince of Peace, appear,
   and I receive the Comforter.

3. Where is the blessedness bestowed
   on all that hunger after thee?
   I hunger now, I thirst for God;
   see the poor fainting sinner, see,
   and satisfy with endless peace,
   and fill me with thy righteousness.

4. Shine on thy work, disperse the gloom,
   light in thy light I then shall see;
   say to my soul: 'Thy light is come,
   glory divine is risen on thee,
   thy warfare's past, thy mourning's o'er;
   look up, for thou shalt weep no more!'

389
Basil E. Bridge (b.1927)
© 1999 Kevin Mayhew Ltd.

1. Jesus, in your life we see you
   making God's compassion known,
   'Surely you have borne our sorrows,
   surely made our pain your own!'
   See your touch bring hope and healing,
   see your word set captives free,
   see you suffer, mocked, rejected,
   dying on the shameful tree.

2. Risen Lord, you reign in glory;
   but your wounded hands still show
   you can share the outcast's torment,
   sound the depths of human woe,
   know where greed exploits the helpless,
   hear the addict's lonely cry,
   grieve at so much waste and heartbreak,
   feel for all who question 'why?'

3. Risen Lord, you bear their sorrow,
   know how much they need your peace;
   as you once healed broken bodies,
   offered captive souls release,
   take us, use us in your service;
   we would follow where you lead;
   only your divine compassion
   meets the depths of human need.

390

Wendy Churchill
© 1982 Springtide/Word Music/CopyCare

1. Jesus is King and I will extol him,
    give him the glory and honour his name.
    He reigns on high, enthroned in the
        heavens,
    Word of the Father, exalted for us.

2. We have a hope that is steadfast and
        certain,
    gone through the curtain and touching
        the throne.
    We have a Priest who is there interceding,
    pouring his grace on our lives day by day.

3. We come to him, our Priest and Apostle,
    clothed in his glory and bearing his
        name,
    laying our lives with gladness before him;
    filled with his Spirit we worship the
        King.

4. O holy One, our hearts do adore you;
    thrilled with your goodness we give you
        our praise.
    Angels in light with worship surround
        him,
    Jesus, our Saviour, for ever the same.

391

David J. Mansell
© 1982 Word's Spirit of Praise Music
Administered by CopyCare

1. Jesus is Lord!
    Creation's voice proclaims it,
    for by his pow'r each tree and flow'r
    was planned and made.
    Jesus is Lord! The universe declares it;
    sun, moon and stars in heaven cry:
    Jesus is Lord!

    Jesus is Lord! Jesus is Lord!
    Praise him with alleluias
    for Jesus is Lord!

2. Jesus is Lord!
    Yet from his throne eternal
    in flesh he came to die in pain
    on Calv'ry's tree.
    Jesus is Lord! From him all life proceeding,
    yet gave his life as ransom
    thus setting us free.

3. Jesus is Lord!
    O'er sin the mighty conqu'ror,
    from death he rose and all his foes
    shall own his name.
    Jesus is Lord! God sends his Holy Spirit
    to show by works of power
    that Jesus is Lord.

392

Philip Lawson Johnston
© 1991 Kingsway's Thankyou Music

1. Jesus is the name we honour;
    Jesus is the name we praise.
    Majestic Name above all other names,
    the highest heav'n and earth proclaim
    that Jesus is our God.

    We will glorify,
    we will lift him high,
    we will give him honour and praise.
    We will glorify,
    we will lift him high,
    we will give him honour and praise.

2. Jesus is the name we worship;
    Jesus is the name we trust.
    He is the King above all other kings,
    let all creation stand and sing
    that Jesus is our God.

3. Jesus is the Father's splendour;
    Jesus is the Father's joy.
    He will return to reign in majesty,
    and every eye at last will see
    that Jesus is our God.

393

John Barnett
© 1980 Mercy/Vineyard Publishing/CopyCare

Jesus, Jesus,
holy and anointed One, Jesus.
Jesus, Jesus,
risen and exalted One, Jesus.

Your name is like honey on my lips,
your Spirit like water to my soul.
Your word is a lamp unto my feet.
Jesus, I love you, I love you.

394

Frances Jane van Alstyne (Fanny J. Crosby)
(1820-1915)

1. Jesus, keep me near the Cross;
   there a precious fountain,
   free to all, a healing stream,
   flows from Calvary's mountain.

   In the Cross, in the Cross,
   be my glory ever;
   till my raptured soul shall find
   rest beyond the river.

2. Near the Cross, a trembling soul,
   love and mercy found me;
   there the bright and morning star
   shed its beams around me.

3. Near the Cross: O Lamb of God,
   bring its scenes before me;
   help me walk from day to day,
   with its shadow o'er me.

4. Near the Cross I'll watch and wait,
   hoping, trusting ever,
   till I reach the golden strand,
   just beyond the river.

395

Christian Fürchtegott Gellert (1715-1769)
trans. Frances Elizabeth Cox (1812-1897) alt.

1. Jesus lives! thy terrors now
   can no more, O death, appal us;
   Jesus lives! by this we know
   thou, O grave, canst not enthral us.
   Alleluia.

2. Jesus lives! henceforth is death
   but the gate of life immortal:
   this shall calm our trembling breath,
   when we pass its gloomy portal.
   Alleluia.

3. Jesus lives! for us he died;
   then, alone to Jesus living,
   pure in heart may we abide,
   glory to our Saviour giving.
   Alleluia.

4. Jesus lives! our hearts know well
   naught from us his love shall sever;
   life nor death nor pow'rs of hell
   tear us from his keeping ever.
   Alleluia.

5. Jesus lives! to him the throne
   over all the world is given:
   may we go where he is gone,
   rest and reign with him in heaven.
   Alleluia.

396

Charles Wesley (1707-1788)

1. Jesus, Lord, we look to thee,
   let us in thy name agree;
   show thyself the Prince of Peace;
   bid our jarring conflicts cease.

2. By thy reconciling love,
   every stumbling-block remove;
   each to each unite, endear;
   come, and spread thy banner here.

3. Make us of one heart and mind,
   courteous, pitiful, and kind,
   lowly, meek in thought and word,
   altogether like our Lord.

4. Let us for each other care,
   each the other's burden bear,
   to thy church the pattern give,
   show how true believers live.

Continued overleaf

5. Free from anger and from pride,
   let us thus in God abide;
   all the depth of love express,
   all the height of holiness.

397
Charles Wesley (1707-1788)

1. Jesus, my strength, my hope,
   on thee I cast my care,
   with humble confidence look up,
   and know thou hear'st my prayer.
   Give me on thee to wait,
   till I can all things do,
   on thee, almighty to create,
   almighty to renew.

2. I want a godly fear,
   a quick-discerning eye
   that looks to thee when sin is near,
   and sees the tempter fly:
   a spirit still prepared,
   and armed with jealous care,
   for ever standing on its guard
   and watching unto prayer.

3. I want a true regard,
   a single, steady aim,
   unmoved by threatening or reward,
   to thee and thy great name;
   a jealous, just concern
   for thine immortal praise;
   a pure desire that all may learn
   and glorify thy grace.

4. I want with all my heart
   thy pleasure to fulfil,
   to know thyself, and what thou art,
   and what thy perfect will –
   this blessing over all,
   always to pray, I want,
   out of the deep on thee to call,
   and never, never faint.

5. I rest upon thy word;
   the promise is for me;
   my succour and salvation, Lord,
   shall surely come from thee:
   but let me still abide,
   nor from my hope remove,
   till thou my patient spirit guide
   into thy perfect love.

398
Charles Wesley (1707-1788)

1. Jesus, my Truth, my Way,
   my sure, unerring Light,
   on thee my feeble steps I stay,
   which thou wilt lead aright.

2. My Wisdom and my Guide,
   my Counsellor, thou art;
   O never let me leave thy side,
   or from thy paths depart!

3. Teach me the happy art
   in all things to depend
   on thee; O never, Lord, depart,
   but love me to the end!

4. Through fire and water bring
   into the wealthy place;
   and teach me the new song to sing,
   when perfected in grace.

5. O make me all like thee,
   before I hence remove!
   Settle, confirm, and stablish me,
   and build me up in love.

6. Let me thy witness live,
   when sin is all destroyed;
   and then my spotless soul receive,
   and take me home to God.

399
Nadia Hearn (b. 1944)
© 1974 Scripture in Song, a division of Integrity Music
Administered by Kingsway's Thankyou Music

Jesus, Name above all names,
beautiful Saviour, glorious Lord,
Emmanuel, God is with us,
blessèd Redeemer, living Word.

400

Timothy Dudley-Smith (b. 1926)
© Timothy Dudley-Smith

1. Jesus, Prince and Saviour,
Lord of life who died;
Christ, the friend of sinners,
mocked and crucified;
for a world's salvation,
he his body gave,
lay at last death's victim,
lifeless in the grave.

Lord of life triumphant,
risen now to reign!
King of endless ages,
Jesus lives again!

2. In his pow'r and Godhead
ev'ry vict'ry won;
pain and passion ended,
all his purpose done.
Christ the Lord is risen!
sighs and sorrows past,
death's dark night is over,
morning comes at last!

3. Resurrection morning!
sinners' bondage freed;
Christ the Lord is risen –
he is ris'n indeed!
Jesus, Prince and Saviour,
Lord of Life who died,
Christ the King of Glory
now is glorified!

401

Graham Kendrick (b. 1950)
© 1992 Make Way Music

1. Jesus, restore to us again
the gospel of your holy name,
that comes with pow'r, not words alone,
owned, signed and sealed from heaven's
    throne.
Spirit and word in one agree;
the promise to the power wed.

The word is near,
here in our mouths
and in our hearts,
the word of faith;
proclaim it on the Spirit's breath:
Jesus.

2. Your word, O Lord, eternal stands,
fixed and unchanging in the heav'ns.
The Word made flesh, to earth came down
to heal our world with nail-pierced hands.
Among us here you lived and breathed,
you are the message we received.

3. Spirit of truth, lead us, we pray,
into all truth as we obey.
And as God's will we gladly choose,
your ancient pow'r again will prove
Christ's teaching truly comes from God,
he is indeed the living Word.

4. Upon the heights of this dark land
with Moses and Elijah stand.
Reveal your glory once again,
show us your face, declare your name.
Prophets and law, in you, complete
where promises and power meet.

5. Grant us in this decisive hour
to know the Scriptures and the pow'r;
the knowledge in experience proved,
the pow'r that moves and works by love.
May words and works join hands as one,
the word go forth, the Spirit come.

402

Isaac Watts (1674-1748) based on Psalm 72: 5-19

1. Jesus shall reign where'er the sun
doth his successive journeys run;
his kingdom stretch from shore to shore,
till moons shall wax and wane no more.

2. For him shall endless prayer be made,
and praises throng to crown his head;
his name like sweet perfume shall rise
with every morning sacrifice;

3. People and realms of every tongue
   dwell on his love with sweetest song;
   and infant voices shall proclaim
   their early blessings on his name.

4. Blessings abound where'er he reigns;
   the prisoners leap to lose their chains;
   the weary find eternal rest,
   and all the humble poor are blest.

5. Let every creature rise and bring
   peculiar honours to our King;
   angels descend with songs again,
   and earth repeat the loud amen.

403 Chris Bowater
© 1988 Sovereign Lifestyle Music Ltd.

Jesus shall take the highest honour,
Jesus shall take the highest praise;
let all earth join heav'n in exalting
the Name which is above all other names.
Let's bow the knee in humble adoration,
for at his name ev'ry knee must bow.
Let ev'ry tongue confess
he is Christ, God's only Son,
Sov'reign Lord, we give you glory now.

For all honour and blessing and power
belongs to you, belongs to you.
All honour and blessing and power
belongs to you, belongs to you,
Lord Jesus Christ, Son of the living God.

404 Graham Kendrick (b. 1950)
© 1977 Kingsway's Thankyou Music

1. Jesus, stand among us
   at the meeting of our lives,
   be our sweet agreement
   at the meeting of our eyes.

   O Jesus, we love you,
   so we gather here,
   join our hearts in unity
   and take away our fear.

2. So to you we're gath'ring
   out of each and ev'ry land,
   Christ the love between us
   at the joining of our hands.

   Optional verse for Communion

3. Jesus stand among us
   at the breaking of the bread;
   join us as one body
   as we worship you, our Head.

405 William Pennefather (1816-1873)

1. Jesus, stand among us
   in thy risen pow'r;
   let this time of worship
   be a hallowed hour.

2. Breathe the Holy Spirit
   into ev'ry heart;
   bid the fears and sorrows
   from each soul depart.

3. Thus with quickened footsteps
   we'll pursue our way,
   watching for the dawning
   of eternal day.

406 Horatuis Bonar (1808-1889)

1. Jesus, sun and shield art thou,
   sun and shield for ever!
   Never canst thou cease to shine,
   cease to guard us, never.
   Cheer our steps as on we go,
   come between us and the foe.

2. Jesus, peace and joy art thou,
   joy and peace for ever!
   Joy that fades not, changes not,
   peace that leaves us never.
   Joy and peace we have in thee,
   now and through eternity.

3. Jesus, song and strength art thou,
   strength and song for ever!
   Strength that never can decay,
   song that ceaseth never.
   Still to us this strength and song
   through eternal days prolong.

4. Jesus, bread and wine art thou,
   wine and bread for ever!
   Never canst thou cease to feed,
   or refresh us, never.
   Feed we still on bread divine,
   drink we still of heavenly wine.

407 Charles Wesley (1707-1788)

1. Jesus, the Conqueror, reigns,
   in glorious strength arrayed,
   his kingdom over all maintains,
   and bids the earth be glad.
   Ye peoples all, rejoice
   in Jesus' mighty love;
   lift up your heart, lift up your voice,
   to him who rules above.

2. Extol his kingly power,
   kiss the exalted Son,
   who died; and lives, to die no more,
   high on his Father's throne:
   our Advocate with God,
   he undertakes our cause,
   and spreads through all the earth abroad
   the vict'ry of his cross.

3. 'Courage!' your Captain cries,
   who all your toil foreknew;
   'Toil ye shall have; yet all despise,
   I have o'ercome for you.'
   This is the victory!
   Before our faith they fall;
   Jesus has died for you and me;
   believe, and conquer all!

408 Charles Wesley (1707-1788)

1. Jesus, the First and Last,
   on thee my soul is cast:
   thou didst thy work begin
   by blotting out my sin;
   thou wilt the root remove,
   and perfect me in love.

2. Yet when the work is done,
   the work is but begun:
   partaker of thy grace,
   I long to see thy face;
   the first I prove below,
   the last I die to know.

409 Charles Wesley (1707-1788) based on Psalm 23

1. Jesus the good Shepherd is,
   Jesus died the sheep to save;
   he is mine and I am his,
   all I want in him I have:
   life, and health, and rest, and food,
   all the plenitude of God.

2. Jesus loves and guards his own;
   me in verdant pastures feeds,
   makes me quietly lie down,
   by the streams of comfort leads:
   following him where'er he goes,
   silent joy my heart o'erflows.

3. He in sickness makes me whole,
   guides into the paths of peace;
   he revives my fainting soul,
   'stablishes in righteousness;
   who for me vouchsafed to die,
   loves me still – I know not why!

4. Love divine shall still embrace,
   love shall keep me to the end;
   surely all my happy days
   I shall in thy temple spend,
   till I to thy house remove,
   thy eternal house above!

410

Unknown. Trans. Dermott Monahan (1906-1957)
© *The Trustees for Methodist Church Purposes*

1. Jesus the Lord said: 'I am the Bread,
   the Bread of Life for mankind am I.
   The Bread of Life for mankind am I,
   the Bread of Life for mankind am I.'
   Jesus the Lord said: 'I am the Bread,
   The Bread of Life for mankind am I.'

2. Jesus the Lord said: 'I am the Door,
   the Way and the Door for the poor am I.'
   The Way and the Door for the poor
       am I,
   the Way and the Door for the poor am I.'
   Jesus the Lord said: 'I am the Door,
   the Way and the Door for the poor am I.'

3. Jesus the Lord said: 'I am the Light,
   the one true Light of the world am I.
   The one true Light of the world am I,
   the one true Light of the world am I.'
   Jesus the Lord said: 'I am the Light,
   the one true Light of the world am I.'

4. Jesus the Lord said: 'I am the
       Shepherd,
   the one good Shepherd of the sheep
       am I.'
   The one good Shepherd of the sheep
       am I,
   the one good Shepherd of the sheep
       am I.'
   Jesus the Lord said: 'I am the
       Shepherd,
   the one good Shepherd of the sheep
       am I.'

5. Jesus the Lord said: 'I am the Life,
   the Resurrection and the Life am I.
   The Resurrection and the Life am I,
   the Resurrection and the Life am I.'
   Jesus the Lord said: 'I am the Life,
   the Resurrection and the Life am I'.

411

Charles Wesley (1707-1788)

1. Jesus, the name high over all,
   in hell, or earth, or sky:
   angels and mortals prostrate fall,
   and devils fear and fly.

2. Jesus, the name to sinners dear,
   the name to sinners giv'n;
   it scatters all their guilty fear,
   it turns their hell to heav'n.

3. Jesus, the pris'ner's fetters breaks,
   and bruises Satan's head;
   pow'r into strengthless souls he speaks,
   and life into the dead,

4. O, that the world might taste and see
   the riches of his grace!
   The arms of love that compass me,
   hold all the human race.

5. His only righteousness I show,
   his saving grace proclaim:
   'tis all my business here below
   to cry: 'Behold the Lamb!'

6. Happy, if with my latest breath
   I may but gasp his name:
   preach him to all, and cry in death:
   'Behold, behold the Lamb!'

412

Charles Wesley (1707-1788)

1. Jesus, the word bestow,
   the true immortal seed;
   thy gospel then shall greatly grow,
   and all our land o'erspread;

2. Through earth extended wide
   shall mightily prevail,
   destroy the works of self and pride,
   and shake the gates of hell.

3. Its energy exert
   in the believing soul;
   diffuse thy grace through every part,
   and sanctify the whole;

4. Its utmost virtue show
   in pure consummate love,
   and fill with all thy life below,
   and give us thrones above.

413 Charles Wesley (1707-1788)

1. Jesus, thou soul of all our joys,
   for whom we now lift up our voice
   and all our strength exert,
   vouchsafe the grace we humbly claim,
   compose into a thankful frame,
   and tune thy people's heart.

2. The secret pride, the subtle sin,
   O let it never more steal in,
   to offend thy glorious eyes,
   to desecrate our hallowed strain,
   and make our solemn service vain,
   and mar our sacrifice.

3. Thee let us praise, our common Lord,
   and sweetly join with one accord
   thy goodness to proclaim;
   Jesus, thyself in us reveal,
   and all our faculties shall feel
   thy harmonising name.

4. With calmly reverential joy,
   O let us all our lives employ
   in setting forth thy love;
   and raise in death our triumph higher,
   and sing with all the heavenly choir
   that endless song above!

414 Nicolaus Ludwig von Zinzendorf (1700-1760)
Trans. John Wesley (1703-1791)

1. Jesus, thy blood and righteousness
   my beauty are, my glorious dress;
   midst flaming worlds, in these arrayed,
   with joy shall I lift up my head.

2. Bold shall I stand in thy great day;
   for to my charge who aught shall lay?
   Fully absolved through these I am,
   from sin and fear, from guilt and shame.

3. That holy, meek, unspotted Lamb,
   who from the Father's bosom came,
   who suffered for me to atone,
   now for my Lord and God I own.

4. Lord, I believe thy precious blood,
   which at the mercy-seat of God
   for ever doth for sinners plead,
   for me, e'en for my soul, was shed.

5. When from the dust of death I rise
   to claim my mansion in the skies,
   e'en then this shall be all my plea –
   Jesus hath lived, hath died for me!

415 Paul Gerhardt (1607-1676)
Trans. John Wesley (1703-1791)

1. Jesus, thy boundless love to me
   no thought can reach, no tongue declare;
   O knit my thankful heart to thee,
   and reign without a rival there:
   thine wholly, thine alone, I am;
   be thou alone my constant flame.

2. From all eternity, with love
   unchangeable thou hast me viewed;
   ere knew this beating heart to move,
   thy tender mercies me pursued:
   ever with me thy love abide,
   and close me in on every side.

3. O grant that nothing in my soul
   may dwell, but thy pure love alone;
   O may thy love possess me whole,
   my joy, my treasure, and my crown:
   strange fires far from my heart remove;
   my every act, word, thought, be love.

Continued overleaf

4. Still let thy love point out my way;
   how wondrous things thy love has
      wrought!
   still lead me, lest I go astray;
   direct my word, inspire my thought;
   and if I fall, soon may I hear
   thy voice, and know that love is near.

5. In suffering be thy love my peace,
   in weakness my almighty power;
   and when the storms of life shall cease,
   Jesus, in that important hour,
   in death as life be thou my guide,
   and save me, who for me hast died.

416 Charles Wesley (1707-1788)

1. Jesus, thy far-extended fame
   my drooping soul exults to hear;
   thy name, thy all-restoring name,
   is music in a sinner's ear.

2. Sinners of old thou didst receive
   with comfortable words and kind,
   their sorrows cheer, their wants relieve,
   heal the diseased, and cure the blind.

3. And art thou not the Saviour still,
   in every place and age the same?
   Hast thou forgot thy gracious skill,
   or lost the virtue of thy name?

4. Faith in thy changeless name I have;
   the good, the kind physician, thou
   art able now our souls to save,
   art willing to restore them now.

5. Wouldst thou the body's health restore;
   and not regard the sin-sick soul?
   The soul thou lovest yet the more,
   and surely thou shalt make it whole.

6. My soul's disease, my every sin,
   to thee, O Jesus, I confess;
   in pardon, Lord, my cure begin,
   and perfect it in holiness.

417 Charles Wesley (1707-1788)

1. Jesus, thy wandering sheep behold!
   See, Lord, with tenderest pity see
   the sheep that cannot find the fold,
   till sought and gathered in by thee.

2. Lost are they now, and scattered wide,
   in pain, and weariness, and want;
   with no kind shepherd near to guide
   the sick, and spiritless, and faint.

3. Thou, only thou, the kind and good
   and sheep-redeeming Shepherd art:
   collect thy flock, and give them food,
   and pastors after thine own heart.

4. Give the pure word of general grace,
   and great shall be the preachers' crowd;
   preachers, who all the sinful race
   point to the all-atoning blood.

5. Open their mouth, and utterance give;
   give them a trumpet-voice, to call
   on all the world to turn and live,
   through faith in him who died for all.

6. Thy only glory let them seek;
   O let their hearts with love o'erflow!
   Let them believe, and therefore speak,
   and spread thy mercy's praise below.

7. Mercy for all be all their song,
   mercy which every soul may claim,
   mercy which doth to all belong,
   mercy for all in Jesu's name.

418 Charles Wesley (1707-1788)

1. Jesus, united by thy grace
   and each to each endeared,
   with confidence we seek thy face,
   and know our prayer is heard.

2. Still let us own our common Lord,
   and bear thine easy yoke,
   a band of love, a threefold cord,
   which never can be broke.

3. O make us of one spirit drink;
   baptise into thy name;
   and let us always kindly think
   and sweetly speak the same.

4. Touched by the lodestone of thy love,
   let all our hearts agree,
   and ever t'ward each other move,
   and ever move t'ward thee.

5. To thee, inseparably joined,
   let all our spirits cleave;
   O may we all the loving mind
   that was in thee receive.

6. This is the bond of perfectness,
   thy spotless charity;
   O let us (still we pray) possess
   the mind that was in thee.

419 Patrick Matsikenyiri
© Copyright Control

Jesus, we are here;
Jesus, we are here;
Jesus, we are here:
we are here for you.

Jesu tawa pano;
Jesu tawa pano;
Jesu tawa pano
tawa pano mu zita renyu.
(except last time) Mambo Jesu.

420 Paul Kyle
© 1980 Kingsway's Thankyou Music

Jesus, we enthrone you,
we proclaim you our King,
standing here in the midst of us,
we raise you up with our praise.
And as we worship, build a throne,
and as we worship, build a throne,
and as we worship, build a throne;
come, Lord Jesus, and take your place.

421 Charles Wesley (1707-1788)

1. Jesus, we look to thee,
   thy promised presence claim;
   thou in the midst of us shalt be,
   assembled in thy name.

2. Thy name salvation is,
   which here we come to prove;
   thy name is life and health and peace
   and everlasting love.

3. We meet, the grace to take
   which thou hast freely given;
   we meet on earth for thy dear sake,
   that we may meet in heaven.

4. Present we know thou art,
   but O thyself reveal!
   Now, Lord, let every bounding heart
   the mighty comfort feel.

5. O may thy quickening voice
   the death of sin remove;
   and bid our inmost souls rejoice
   in hope of perfect love!

422 Charles Wesley (1707-1788)

1. Jesus, we thus obey
   thy last and kindest word;
   here, in thine own appointed way,
   we come to meet thee, Lord.

2. Our hearts we open wide
   to make the Saviour room;
   and lo! the Lamb, the Crucified,
   the sinners' friend, is come!

3. His presence makes the feast;
   and now our spirits feel
   the glory not to be expressed,
   the joy unspeakable.

Continued overleaf

4. With pure celestial bliss
he doth our spirits cheer;
his house of banqueting is this,
and he hath brought us here.

5. He bids us drink and eat
imperishable food;
he gives his flesh to be our meat,
and bids us drink his blood.

6. Whate'er the Almighty can
to pardoned sinners give,
the fullness of our God made man
we here with Christ receive.

423 Tanya Riches
© 1995 Tanya Riches/Hillsong Publishing.
Administered by Kingsway's Thankyou Music

1. Jesus, what a beautiful name.
Son of God, Son of Man,
Lamb that was slain.
Joy and peace, strength and hope,
grace that blows all fear away.
Jesus, what a beautiful name.

2. Jesus, what a beautiful name.
Truth revealed, my future sealed,
healed my pain.
Love and freedom, life and warmth,
grace that blows all fear away.
Jesus, what a beautiful name.

3. Jesus, what a beautiful name.
Rescued my soul, my stronghold,
lifts me from shame.
Forgiveness, security, power and love,
grace that blows all fear away.
Jesus, what a beautiful name.

424 William Cowper (1731-1800)

1. Jesus, where'er thy people meet,
there they behold thy mercy seat;
where'er they seek thee thou art found,
and ev'ry place is hallowed ground.

2. For thou, within no walls confined,
inhabitest the humble mind;
such ever bring thee when they come,
and, going, take thee to their home.

3. Dear Shepherd of thy chosen few,
thy former mercies here renew;
here to our waiting hearts proclaim
the sweetness of thy saving name.

4. Here may we prove the pow'r of prayer
to strengthen faith and sweeten care,
to teach our faint desires to rise,
and bring all heav'n before our eyes.

5. Lord, we are few, but thou art near;
nor short thine arm, nor deaf thine ear;
O rend the heav'ns, come quickly down,
and make a thousand hearts thine own.

425 St Bernard of Clairvaux (1091-1153)
trans. Edward Caswall (1814-1878) alt.

1. Jesu, the very thought of thee
with sweetness fills the breast;
but sweeter far thy face to see,
and in thy presence rest.

2. No voice can sing, no heart can frame,
nor can the mem'ry find,
a sweeter sound than Jesu's name,
the Saviour of mankind.

3. O hope of ev'ry contrite heart,
O joy of all the meek,
to those who ask how kind thou art,
how good to those who seek!

4. But what to those who find? Ah, this
nor tongue nor pen can show;
the love of Jesus, what it is
his true disciples know.

5. Jesu, our only joy be thou,
as thou our prize wilt be;
in thee be all our glory now,
and through eternity.

426

12th century. Trans. Ray Palmer (1808-1887)

1. Jesu, thou joy of loving hearts,
   thou fount of life, thou perfect grace;
   from the best bliss that earth imparts
   we turn unfilled to seek thy face.

2. Thy truth unchanged hath ever stood;
   thou savest those that on thee call;
   to them that seek thee thou art good,
   to them that find thee, all in all.

3. We taste thee, O thou living bread,
   and long to feast upon thee still;
   we drink of thee, the fountain head,
   and thirst our souls from thee to fill.

4. Our restless spirits yearn for thee,
   where'er our changeful lot is cast;
   glad when thy gracious smile we see,
   blest when our faith can hold thee fast.

5. O Jesus, ever with us stay;
   make all our moments calm and bright;
   chase the dark night of sin away;
   shed o'er the world thy holy light.

427

Isaac Watts (1674-1748)

1. Join all the glorious names
   of wisdom, love, and power,
   that ever mortals knew,
   that angels ever bore:
   all are too mean to speak his worth,
   too mean to set my *Saviour* forth.

2. But O what gentle terms,
   what condescending ways
   doth our *Redeemer* use
   to teach his heavenly grace!
   Mine eyes with joy and wonder see
   what forms of love he bears for me.

3. Great *Prophet* of my God,
   my tongue would bless thy name;
   by thee the joyful news
   of our salvation came:
   the joyful news of sins forgiven,
   of hell subdued and peace with heaven.

4. Jesus my great *High-priest*
   offered his blood and died;
   my guilty conscience seeks
   no sacrifice besides:
   his powerful blood did once atone,
   and now it pleads before the throne.

5. My dear almighty *Lord*,
   my *Conqueror* and my *King*,
   thy sceptre and thy sword,
   thy reign of grace, I sing;
   thine is the power: behold I sit
   in willing bonds before thy feet.

6. Now let my soul arise,
   and tread the tempter down;
   my *Captain* leads me forth
   to conquest and a crown.
   A feeble saint shall win the day,
   though death and hell obstruct the way.

7. Should all the hosts of death,
   and powers of hell unknown,
   put their most dreadful forms
   of rage and mischief on,
   I shall be safe, for *Christ* displays
   superior power, and guardian grace.

428

Henry Van Dyke (1852-1933) alt.
© *Copyright Control.*

1. Joyful, joyful, we adore thee, God of
      glory, Lord of love;
   hearts unfold like flowers before thee,
      opening to the sun above.
   Melt the clouds of sin and sadness; drive
      the dark of doubt away.
   Giver of immortal gladness, fill us with
      the light of day!

Continued overleaf

2. All thy works with joy surround thee,
    earth and heaven reflect thy rays,
    stars and angels sing around thee, centre
        of unbroken praise.
    Field and forest, vale and mountain,
        flowery meadow, flashing sea,
    chanting bird and flowing fountain, call
        us to rejoice in thee.

3. Thou art giving and forgiving, ever
        blessing, ever blest,
    well-spring of the joy of living, ocean
        depth of happy rest!
    Thou our Father, Christ our brother, all
        who live in love are thine;
    teach us how to love each other, lift us to
        the joy divine.

4. Mortals, join the mighty chorus which
        the morning stars began;
    love divine is reigning o'er us, binding all
        within its span.
    Ever singing, march we onward, victors
        in the midst of strife;
    joyful music leads us sunward, in the
        triumph-song of life.

429 Isaac Watts (1674-1748), based on Psalm 98, alt.

1. Joy to the world! The Lord is come;
    let earth receive her King;
    let ev'ry heart prepare him room,
    and heav'n and nature sing,
    and heav'n and nature sing,
    and heav'n and heav'n and nature sing.

2. Joy to the earth! The Saviour reigns;
    let us our songs employ;
    while fields and floods, rocks,
        hills and plains
    repeat the sounding joy,
    repeat the sounding joy,
    repeat, repeat the sounding joy.

3. He rules the world with truth and grace,
    and makes the nations prove
    the glories of his righteousness,
    and wonders of his love,
    and wonders of his love,
    and wonders, and wonders of his love.

430 Fred Dunn (1907-1979)
© 1977 Kingsway's Thankyou Music

Jubilate, ev'rybody,
serve the Lord in all your ways and
come before his presence singing;
enter now his courts with praise.
For the Lord our God is gracious,
and his mercy everlasting.
Jubilate, jubilate, jubilate Deo!

431 Henry Scott Holland (1847-1918) alt.

1. Judge eternal, throned in splendour,
    Lord of lords and King of kings,
    with thy living fire of judgement
    purge this realm of bitter things:
    solace all its wide dominion
    with the healing of thy wings.

2. Still the weary folk are pining
    for the hour that brings release:
    and the city's crowded clangour
    cries aloud for sin to cease;
    and the homesteads and the woodlands
    plead in silence for their peace.

3. Crown, O God, thine own endeavour;
    cleave our darkness with thy sword;
    feed thy people's hungry spirits
    with the richness of thy word:
    cleanse the body of this nation
    through the glory of the Lord.

432 Charlotte Elliott (1789-1871)

1. Just as I am, without one plea
   but that thy blood was shed for me,
   and that thou bidst me come to thee,
   O Lamb of God, I come.

2. Just as I am, though tossed about
   with many a conflict, many a doubt,
   fightings and fears within, without,
   O Lamb of God, I come.

3. Just as I am, poor, wretched, blind;
   sight, riches, healing of the mind,
   yea, all I need, in thee to find,
   O Lamb of God, I come.

4. Just as I am, thou wilt receive,
   wilt welcome, pardon, cleanse, relieve:
   because thy promise I believe,
   O Lamb of God, I come.

5. Just as I am, thy love unknown
   has broken ev'ry barrier down,
   now to be thine, yea, thine alone,
   O Lamb of God, I come.

6. Just as I am, of that free love
   the breadth, length, depth and height
      to prove,
   here for a season, then above,
   O Lamb of God, I come.

433 George Herbert (1593-1633)

1. King of glory, King of peace,
   I will love thee;
   and, that love may never cease,
   I will move thee.
   Thou hast granted my appeal,
   thou hast heard me;
   thou didst note my ardent zeal,
   thou hast spared me.

2. Wherefore with my utmost art,
   I will sing thee,
   and the cream of all my heart
   I will bring thee.
   Though my sins against me cried,
   thou didst clear me,
   and alone, when they replied,
   thou didst hear me.

3. Sev'n whole days, not one in sev'n,
   I will praise thee;
   in my heart, though not in heav'n,
   I can raise thee.
   Small it is, in this poor sort
   to enrol thee:
   e'en eternity's too short
   to extol thee.

434 Charles Wesley (1707-88)

1. Lamb of God, whose dying love
   we now recall to mind,
   send the answer from above,
   and let us mercy find;
   think on us, who think on thee;
   and every struggling soul release:
   O remember Calvary,
   and bid us go in peace!

2. By thine agonising pain
   and sweat of blood, we pray,
   by thy dying love to man,
   take all our sins away;
   burst our bonds, and set us free;
   from all iniquity release:
   O remember Calvary,
   and bid us go in peace!

3. Lord, we would not hence depart
   till thou our wants relieve,
   write forgiveness on our heart,
   and all thine image give.
   Still our souls shall cry to thee,
   till perfected in holiness:
   O remember Calvary,
   and bid us go in peace!

435 Charles Wesley (1707-88)

1. Leader of faithful souls, and guide
   of all that travel to the sky,
   come and with us, ev'n us, abide,
   who would on thee alone rely,
   on thee alone our spirits stay,
   while held in life's uneven way.

2. We've no abiding city here,
   but seek a city out of sight;
   thither our steady course we steer,
   aspiring to the plains of light,
   Jerusalem, the saints' abode,
   whose founder is the living God.

3. Through thee, who all our sins hast
       borne,
   freely and graciously forgiven,
   with songs to Zion we return,
   contending for our native heaven;
   that palace of our glorious King,
   we find it nearer while we sing.

4. Raised by the breath of love divine,
   we urge our way with strength renewed;
   the church of the first-born to join,
   we travel to the mount of God,
   with joy upon our heads arise,
   and meet our Captain in the skies.

436 John Henry Newman (1801-1890)

1. Lead, kindly light,
   amid th'encircling gloom,
   lead thou me on;
   the night is dark,
   and I am far from home;
   lead thou me on.
   Keep thou my feet;
   I do not ask to see
   the distant scene;
   one step enough for me.

2. I was not ever thus,
   nor prayed that thou
   shouldst lead me on;
   I loved to choose
   and see my path; but now
   lead thou me on.
   I loved the garish day,
   and, spite of fears,
   pride ruled my will:
   remember not past years.

3. So long thy pow'r
   hath blest me, sure it still
   will lead me on,
   o'er moor and fen,
   o'er crag and torrent, till
   the night is gone;
   and with the morn
   those angel faces smile,
   which I have loved long since,
   and lost awhile.

437 Samuel Sebastian Wesley (1810-1876)

Lead me, Lord,
lead me in your righteousness,
make your way plain before my face. *(x2)*
For it is you, Lord,
you, Lord, only
that makes me to dwell in safety. *(x2)*

438 James Edmeston (1791-1867)

1. Lead us, heav'nly Father, lead us
   o'er the world's tempestuous sea;
   guard us, guide us, keep us, feed us,
   for we have no help but thee;
   yet possessing ev'ry blessing
   if our God our Father be.

2. Saviour, breathe forgiveness o'er us,
all our weakness thou dost know,
thou didst tread this earth before us,
thou didst feel its keenest woe;
lone and dreary, faint and weary,
through the desert thou didst go.

3. Spirit of our God, descending,
fill our hearts with heav'nly joy,
love with ev'ry passion blending,
pleasure that can never cloy;
thus provided, pardoned, guided,
nothing can our peace destroy.

439
Michael Forster (b.1946)
© 1993 Kevin Mayhew Ltd.

1. Lead, us, O God, on the journey of
faithfulness,
call us to trust in your promise of grace.
Teach us to travel together in harmony,
singing of hope for the whole human
race.

2. Christ, who as Word of salvation we
recognise,
lead us in faith on the road to the cross,
speaking of hope at the heart of adversity,
finding true life at the moment of loss.

3. You who have suffered injustice and
treachery,
false accusation and undeserved pain,
help us to live in compassionate
hopefulness,
firm in the promise that justice shall
reign.

440
Graham Kendrick (b. 1950)
© 1983 Kingsway's Thankyou Music

1. Led like a lamb to the slaughter,
in silence and shame,
there on your back you carried a world
of violence and pain.
Bleeding, dying, bleeding, dying.

You're alive, you're alive,
you have risen!
Alleluia! And the pow'r
and the glory is given,
alleluia! Jesus to you.

2. At break of dawn, poor Mary,
still weeping she came,
when through her grief she heard your
voice
now speaking her name.
Mary, Master, Mary, Master.

3. At the right hand of the Father
now seated on high
you have begun your eternal reign
of justice and joy.
Glory, glory, glory, glory.

441
Liturgy of St James, trans. G. Moultrie (1829-1885)

1. Let all mortal flesh keep silence
and with fear and trembling stand;
ponder nothing earthly-minded,
for with blessing in his hand
Christ our God on earth descendeth,
our full homage to demand.

2. King of kings, yet born of Mary,
as of old on earth he stood,
Lord of lords, in human vesture,
in the body and the blood.
He will give to all the faithful
his own self for heav'nly food.

3. Rank on rank the host of heaven
spreads its vanguard on the way,
as the Light of light descendeth
from the realms of endless day,
that the pow'rs of hell may vanish
as the darkness clears away.

4. At his feet the six-winged seraph;
cherubim, with sleepless eye,
veil their faces to the Presence,
as with ceaseless voice they cry,
alleluia, alleluia,
alleluia, Lord most high.

442 George Herbert (1593-1633)

1. Let all the world in ev'ry corner sing,
   my God and King!
   The heav'ns are not too high,
   his praise may thither fly;
   the earth is not too low,
   his praises there may grow.
   Let all the world in ev'ry corner sing,
   my God and King!

2. Let all the world in ev'ry corner sing,
   my God and King!
   The Church with psalms must shout,
   no door can keep them out;
   but, above all, the heart
   must bear the longest part.
   Let all the world in ev'ry corner sing,
   my God and King!

443 Charles Wesley (1707-1788)

1. Let earth and heaven agree,
   angels and men be joined,
   to celebrate with me
   the Saviour of mankind;
   to adore the all-atoning Lamb,
   and bless the sound of Jesu's name.

2. Jesus, transporting sound!
   The joy of earth and heaven;
   no other help is found,
   no other name is given,
   by which we can salvation have;
   but Jesus came the world to save.

3. Jesus, harmonious name!
   It charms the hosts above;
   they evermore proclaim
   and wonder at his love;
   'tis all their happiness to gaze,
   'tis heaven to see our Jesu's face.

4. His name the sinner hears,
   and is from sin set free;
   'tis music in his ears,
   'tis life and victory;
   new songs do now his lips employ,
   and dances his glad heart for joy.

5. Stung by the scorpion sin,
   my poor expiring soul
   the healing sound drinks in,
   and is at once made whole:
   see there my Lord upon the tree!
   I hear, I feel, he died for me.

6. O unexampled love,
   O all-redeeming grace!
   How swiftly didst thou move
   to save a fallen race!
   What shall I do to make it known
   what thou for all mankind hast done?

7. O for a trumpet voice
   on all the world to call,
   to bid their hearts rejoice
   in him who died for all!
   For all my Lord was crucified,
   for all, for all my Saviour died.

444 Charles Wesley (1707-1788)

1. Let earth and heaven combine,
   angels and men agree,
   to praise in songs divine
   th' incarnate Deity,
   our God contracted to a span,
   incomprehensibly made man.

2. He laid his glory by,
   he wrapped him in our clay;
   unmarked by human eye,
   the latent Godhead lay;
   infant of days he here became,
   and bore the mild Immanuel's name.

3. Unsearchable the love
   that has the Saviour brought;
   the grace is far above
   or men or angels' thought:
   suffice for us that God, we know,
   our God, is manifest below.

4. He deigns in flesh to appear,
   widest extremes to join;
   to bring our vileness near,
   and make us all divine:
   and we the life of God shall know,
   for God is manifest below.

5. Made perfect first in love,
   and sanctified by grace,
   we shall from earth remove,
   and see his glorious face:
   his love shall then be fully showed,
   and man shall all be lost in God.

445   Fred Pratt Green (1903-2000)
© 1971 Stainer & Bell Ltd.

1. Let every Christian pray,
   this day, and every day,
   come, Holy Spirit, come!
   Was not the Church we love
   commissioned from above?
   Come, Holy Spirit, come!

2. The Spirit brought to birth
   the church of Christ on earth
   to seek and save the lost:
   never has he withdrawn,
   since that tremendous dawn,
   his gifts at Pentecost.

3. Age after age, he strove
   to teach her how to love:
   come, Holy Spirit, come!
   Age after age, anew,
   she proved the gospel true:
   come, Holy Spirit, come!

4. Only the Spirit's power
   can fit us for this hour:
   come, Holy Spirit, come!
   Instruct, inspire, unite;
   And make us see the light:
   come, Holy Spirit, come!

446   Charles Wesley (1707-1788)

1. Let him to whom we now belong
   his sovereign right assert,
   and take up every thankful song
   and every loving heart.

2. He justly claims us for his own,
   who brought us with a price;
   the Christian lives to Christ alone,
   to Christ alone he dies.

3. Jesus, thine own at last receive,
   fulfil our hearts' desire,
   and let us to thy glory live,
   and in thy cause expire.

4. Our souls and bodies we resign;
   with joy we render thee
   our all, no longer ours, but thine
   to all eternity.

447   Graham Kendrick (b.1950)
© 1988 Make Way Music

Let it be to me according to your word.
Let it be to me according to your word.
I am your servant,
no rights shall I demand.
Let it be to me,
let it be to me,
let it be to me according to your word.

448 Michael Forster (b. 1946)
© 1995 Kevin Mayhew Ltd.

1. Let love be real, in giving and receiving,
   without the need to manage and to own;
   a haven free from posing and pretending,
   where ev'ry weakness may be safely known.
   Give me your hand,
   along the desert pathway,
   give me your love
   wherever we may go.

   As God loves us,
   so let us love each other:
   with no demands,
   just open hands and space to grow.

2. Let love be real, not grasping or confining,
   that strange embrace that holds yet sets
     us free;
   that helps us face the risk of truly living,
   and makes us brave to be what we
     might be.
   Give me your strength
   when all my words are weakness;
   give me your love
   in spite of all you know.

3. Let love be real, with no manipulation,
   no secret wish to harness or control;
   let us accept each other's incompleteness,
   and share the joy of learning to be whole.
   Give me your hope
   through dreams and disappointments;
   give me your trust
   when all my failings show.

449 Michael Forster (b.1946)
© 1998 Kevin Mayhew Ltd.

1. Let the heav'nly pow'rs rejoice and holy
     angels sing,
   all creation gather round to glorify the
     King,
   celebrate salvation, let the joyful trumpet
     swing!
   Jesus is risen for ever!

He lives! He lives! Let all the poor rejoice!
He lives! He lives! The voiceless find a
  voice!
Death is overcome, let life and freedom
  be our choice,
Jesus is risen for ever!

2. Let the whole creation in eternal
     splendour shine,
   sharing in the brightness of the majesty
     divine,
   Christ with glory fills us, love alone shall
     be our sign,
   Jesus is risen for ever!

3. Let the Mother Church her songs of
     exultation raise,
   Christ the risen Saviour shines with love
     and hope ablaze!
   Let this place resound with joy and echo
     perfect praise,
   Jesus is risen for ever!

450 Dave Bilbrough
© 1979 Kingsway's Thankyou Music

Let there be love shared among us,
let there be love in our eyes.
May now your love sweep this nation;
cause us, O Lord, to arise.
Give us a fresh understanding,
brotherly love that is real.
Let there be love shared among us,
let there be love.

451 Unknown
© 1996 Kevin Mayhew Ltd.

1. Let us break bread together with the Lord;
   let us break bread together with the Lord:

   When I fall on my knees,
   with my face to the rising sun,
   O Lord, have mercy on me.

2. Let us drink wine together with the Lord;
   let us drink wine together with the Lord:

3. Let us praise God together in the Lord;
   let us praise God together in the Lord:

452 John Milton (1608-1674), based on Psalm 136

1. Let us, with a gladsome mind,
   praise the Lord, for he is kind;

   for his mercies ay endure,
   ever faithful, ever sure.

2. Let us blaze his name abroad,
   for of gods he is the God;

3, He, with all-commanding might,
   filled the new-made world with light;

4. He the golden-tressèd sun
   caused all day his course to run;

5. And the moon to shine at night,
   'mid her starry sisters bright;

6. All things living he doth feed,
   his full hand supplies their need;

7. Let us, with a gladsome mind,
   praise the Lord, for he is kind;

453 Charles Edward Mudie (1818-1890)

1. Life and light and joy are found
   in the presence of the Lord:
   life with richest blessing crowned,
   light from many fountains poured –
   life and light and holy joy,
   none can darken or destroy.

2. Bring to him life's brightest hours,
   he will make them still more bright;
   give to him your noblest powers,
   he will hallow all your might;
   come to him with eager quest,
   you shall hear his high behest.

3. All your questions large and deep,
   all the open thoughts of youth,
   bring to him, and you shall reap
   all the harvest of his truth;
   you shall find in that great store
   largest love and wisest lore.

4. Then when comes life's wider sphere
   and its busier enterprise,
   you shall find him ever near,
   looking, with approving eyes,
   on all honest work and true
   his dear servants' hands can do.

454 Michael Robert Newbolt (1874-1956) based on George William Kitchin (1827-1912) © Hymns Ancient and Modern/Canterbury Press Ltd.

Lift high the Cross, the love of Christ
   proclaim
till all the world adore his sacred name!

1. Follow the path on which our Captain
   trod,
   our King victorious, Christ the Son of
   God:

2. Each new-born soldier of the Crucified
   bears on his brow the seal of him who
   died:

3. Led on their way by this triumphant sign,
   the hosts of God in conquering ranks
   combine:

4. From farthest regions let them homage
   bring,
   and on his cross adore their Saviour
   King:

5. O Lord, once lifted on the glorious tree,
   as thou hast promised, draw men unto
   thee:

6. Set up thy throne, that earth's despair
   may cease
   beneath the shadow of its healing peace:

455

Georg Weissel (1590-1635)
Trans Catherine Winkworth (1827-1878)

1. Lift up your heads, ye mighty gates,
   behold the King of glory waits!
   The King of kings is drawing near,
   the Saviour of the world is here;
   life and salvation doth he bring,
   wherefore rejoice and gladly sing.
   We praise thee, Father, now,
   Creator, wise art thou!

2. The Lord is just, a helper tried,
   mercy is ever at his side;
   his kingly crown is holiness;
   his sceptre, pity in distress;
   the end of all our woe he brings,
   wherefore the earth is glad and sings.
   We praise thee, Saviour, now,
   mighty in deed art thou!

3. O blest the land, the city blest,
   where Christ the ruler is confest!
   O happy hearts and happy homes,
   to whom this King in triumph comes!
   The cloudless Sun of joy he is,
   who bringeth pure delight and bliss.
   O Comforter Divine,
   what boundless grace is thine!

4. Fling wide the portals of your heart,
   make it a temple set apart
   from earthly use, for heaven's employ,
   adorned with prayer, and love, and joy;
   so shall your Sovereign enter in,
   and new and nobler life begin.
   To thee, O God, be praise,
   for word and deed and grace.

5. Redeemer, come, we open wide
   our heart to thee; here, Lord, abide!
   Thine inner presence let us feel,
   thy grace and love in us reveal,
   thy Holy Spirit guide us on,
   until the glorious goal is won.
   Eternal praise and fame
   we offer to thy name.

456

Henry Montagu Butler (1833-1918) alt.

1. 'Lift up your hearts!'
   We lift them, Lord, to thee;
   here at thy feet
   none other may we see:
   'Lift up your hearts!'
   E'en so, with one accord,
   we lift them up,
   we lift them to the Lord.

2. Above the swamps
   of subterfuge and shame,
   the deeds, the thoughts,
   that honour may not name,
   the halting tongue
   that dares not tell the whole,
   O Lord of truth,
   lift ev'ry human soul.

3. Lift ev'ry gift
   that thou thyself hast giv'n:
   low lies the best
   till lifted up to heav'n;
   low lie the pounding heart,
   the teeming brain,
   till, sent from God,
   they mount to God again.

4. Then, as the trumpet-call,
   in after years,
   'Lift up your hearts!'
   rings pealing in our ears,
   still shall those hearts respond,
   with full accord,
   'We lift them up,
   we lift them to the Lord.'

457

Charles Wesley (1707-1788)

1. Lift up your hearts to things above,
   ye followers of the Lamb,
   and join with us to praise his love
   and glorify his name.

2. To Jesus's name give thanks and sing,
   whose mercies never end:
   rejoice! rejoice! the Lord is King;
   the King is now our Friend!

3. We, for his sake, count all things loss;
   on earthly good look down;
   and joyfully sustain the cross,
   till we receive the crown.

4. O let us stir each other up,
   our faith by works to approve,
   by holy, purifying hope,
   and the sweet task of love.

5. You on our minds we ever bear,
   whoe'er to Jesus bow;
   stretch out the arms of faith and prayer,
   and lo, we reach you now.

6. The blessings all on you be shed,
   which God in Christ imparts;
   we pray the Spirit of our Head
   into your faithful hearts.

7. Live till the Lord in glory come,
   and wait his heaven to share;
   our Saviour now prepares our home:
   go on; we'll meet you there.

458 Charles Wesley (1707-1788)

1. Light of the world, thy beams I bless;
   on thee, bright Sun of Righteousness,
   my faith has fixed its eye;
   guided by thee, through all I go,
   nor fear the ruin spread below,
   for thou art always nigh.

2. Not all the powers of hell can fright
   a soul that walks with Christ in light;
   he walks, and cannot fall:
   clearly he sees, and wins his way,
   shining unto the perfect day,
   and more than conquers all.

3. I rest in thine almighty power;
   the name of Jesus is a tower
   that hides my life above;
   thou canst, thou wilt my helper be;
   my confidence is all in thee,
   the faithful God of love.

4. Wherefore, in never-ceasing prayer,
   my soul to thy continual care
   I faithfully commend;
   assured that thou through life shalt save,
   and show thyself beyond the grave
   my everlasting friend.

459 Graham Kendrick (b. 1950)
© Copyright 1988 Make Way Music

1. Like a candle flame,
   flick'ring small
   in our darkness,
   uncreated light
   shines through infant eyes.

   God is with us,
   alleluia,
   come to save us,
   alleluia,
   alleluia!

2. Stars and angels sing,
   yet the earth
   sleeps in shadows;
   can this tiny spark
   set a world on fire?

3. Yet his light shall shine
   from our lives,
   spirit blazing,
   as we touch the flame
   of his holy fire.

460 Charles Wesley (1707-1788), John Cennick
(1718-1755) and Martin Madan (1728-1790) alt.

1. Lo, he comes with clouds descending,
   once for mortal sinners slain;
   thousand thousand saints attending
   swell the triumph of his train.
   Alleluia! Alleluia! Alleluia!
   Christ appears on earth to reign.

Continued overleaf

2. Ev'ry eye shall now behold him
   robed in dreadful majesty;
   we who set at naught and sold him,
   pierced and nailed him to the tree,
   deeply grieving, deeply grieving,
      deeply grieving,
   shall the true Messiah see.

3. Those dear tokens of his passion
   still his dazzling body bears,
   cause of endless exultation
   to his ransomed worshippers:
   with what rapture, with what rapture,
      with what rapture
   gaze we on those glorious scars!

4. Yea, amen, let all adore thee,
   high on thine eternal throne;
   Saviour, take the pow'r and glory,
   claim the kingdom for thine own.
   Alleluia! Alleluia! Alleluia!
   Thou shalt reign, and thou alone.

461 Fred Pratt Green (1903-2000)
© 1971 Stainer & Bell Ltd.

1. Long ago, prophets knew
   Christ would come, born a Jew,
   come to make all things new,
   bear his people's burden,
   freely love and pardon.

   Ring, bells, ring, ring, ring!
   Sing, choirs, sing, sing, sing!
   When he comes, when he comes,
   who will make him welcome?

2. God in time, God in man,
   this is God's timeless plan:
   he will come, as a man,
   born himself of woman,
   God divinely human.

3. Mary, hail! Though afraid,
   she believed, she obeyed.
   In her womb, God is laid:
   till the time expected,
   nurtured and protected'.

4. Journey ends! Where afar
   Bethlem shines, like a star,
   stable door stands ajar.
   Unborn Son of Mary,
   Saviour, do not tarry!

462 Thomas Kelly (1769-1855)

1. Look, ye saints, the sight is glorious;
   see the Man of Sorrows now
   from the fight returned victorious;
   every knee to him shall bow:
   Crown him! Crown him!
   Crowns become the Victor's brow.

2. Crown the Saviour, angels, crown him;
   rich the trophies Jesus brings;
   in the seat of power enthrone him,
   while the vault of heaven rings:
   Crown him! Crown him!
   Crown the Saviour, King of kings!

3. Sinners in derision crowned him,
   mocking thus the Saviour's claim;
   Saints and angels throng around him,
   own his title praise his name:
   Crown him! Crown him!
   Spread abroad the Victor's fame.

4. Hark, those bursts of acclamation;
   hark, those loud triumphant chords;
   Jesus takes the highest station:
   O what joy the sight affords!
   Crown him! Crown him!
   King of kings, and Lord of lords!

463 Timothy Dudley-Smith (b. 1926)
© Timothy Dudley-Smith

1. Lord, for the years
   your love has kept and guided,
   urged and inspired us,
   cheered us on our way,
   sought us and saved us,
   pardoned and provided,
   Lord of the years,
   we bring our thanks today.

2. Lord, for that word,
   the word of life which fires us,
   speaks to our hearts
   and sets our souls ablaze,
   teaches and trains,
   rebukes us and inspires us,
   Lord of the word,
   receive your people's praise.

3. Lord, for our land,
   in this our generation,
   spirits oppressed by pleasure,
   wealth and care;
   for young and old,
   for commonwealth and nation,
   Lord of our land,
   be pleased to hear our prayer.

4. Lord, for our world;
   when we disown and doubt you,
   loveless in strength,
   and comfortless in pain;
   hungry and helpless,
   lost indeed without you:
   Lord of the world,
   we pray that Christ may reign.

5. Lord for ourselves;
   in living power remake us –
   self on the cross
   and Christ upon the throne,
   past put behind us,
   for the future take us:
   Lord of our lives,
   to live for Christ alone.

464 Thomas Hornblower Gill (1819-1906)

1. Lord God, by whom all change is wrought,
   by whom new things to birth are
       brought,
   in whom no change is known;
   whate'er thou dost, whate'er thou art,
   thy people still in thee have part;
   still, still thou art our own.

2. Ancient of Days, we dwell in thee;
   out of thine own eternity
   our peace and joy are wrought;
   we rest in our eternal God,
   and make secure and sweet abode
   with thee, who changest not.

3. Spirit, who makest all things new,
   thou leadest onward; we pursue
   the heavenly march sublime.
   'Neath thy renewing fire we glow,
   and still from strength to strength we go,
   from height to height we climb.

4. Darkness and dread we leave behind;
   new light, new glory still we find,
   new realms divine possess;
   new births of grace new raptures bring;
   triumphant, the new song we sing,
   the great Renewer bless.

5. To thee we rise, in thee we rest;
   we stay at home, we go in quest,
   still thou art our abode.
   The rapture swells, the wonder grows,
   as full on us new life still flows
   from our unchanging God.

465 Fred Pratt Green (1903-2000)
© Copyright 1980 Stainer & Bell Ltd.

1. Lord God, in whom all worlds,
   all life, all work began;
   give us the faith to know
   we serve your master plan.
   How happy they who thus have found
   contentment in the daily round.

2. But when good work receives
   no adequate reward;
   when meaningless routines
   leave willing workers bored;
   when time is spent in needless strife:
   make us ashamed, O Lord of life.

Continued overleaf

3. And if, in leaner years,
   what we had gained is lost;
   if progress must be bought
   at someone else's cost:
   make us, one nation, swift to share
   the hardships others have to bear.

4. So, for tomorrow's sake,
   teach us new skills today,
   to do your perfect will
   in our imperfect way,
   and live as those whom you have called
   to be your work-force in the world.

466 James Montgomery (1771-1854)

1. Lord God the Holy Ghost,
   in this accepted hour,
   as on the day of Pentecost,
   descend in all thy power.

2. We meet with one accord
   in our appointed place,
   and wait the promise of our Lord,
   the Spirit of all grace.

3. Like mighty rushing wind
   upon the waves beneath,
   move with one impulse every mind,
   one soul, one feeling breathe.

4. The young, the old, inspire
   with wisdom from above;
   and give us hearts and tongues of fire,
   to pray and praise and love.

5. Spirit of light, explore
   and chase our gloom away,
   with lustre shining more and more
   unto the perfect day.

6. Spirit of truth, be thou
   in life and death our guide;
   O Spirit of adoption, now
   may we be sanctified.

467 From Ghana, traditional

1. Lord, have mercy.
   Lord, have mercy.
   Lord, have mercy.
   Lord, have mercy on us.

   Kyrie eleison.
   Kyrie eleison.
   Kyrie eleison.
   Kyrie eleison.

468 From Russia, traditional

1. Lord, have mercy.
   Lord, have mercy.
   Lord, have mercy.

   Kyrie eleison.
   Kyrie eleison.
   Kyrie eleison.

469

Geoff Bullock

1. Lord, I come to you,
   let my heart be changed, renewed,
   flowing from the grace
   that I found in you.
   And, Lord, I've come to know
   the weaknesses I see in me
   will be stripped away
   by the power of your love.

   Hold me close,
   let your love surround me,
   bring me near,
   draw me to your side;
   and as I wait,
   I'll rise up like an eagle,
   and I will soar with you;
   your Spirit leads me on
   in the power of your love.

2. Lord, unveil my eyes,
   let me see you face to face,
   the knowledge of your love
   as you live in me.
   Lord, renew my mind
   as your will unfolds in my life,
   in living every day
   in the power of your love.

470 Charles Wesley (1707-1788)

1. Lord, if at thy command
   the word of life we sow,
   watered by thy almighty hand,
   the seed shall surely grow.

2. The virtue of thy grace
   a large increase shall give,
   and multiply the faithful race
   who to thy glory live.

3. Now then the ceaseless shower
   of gospel blessings send,
   and let the soul-converting power
   thy ministers attend.

4. On multitudes confer
   the heart-renewing love,
   and by the joy of grace prepare
   for fuller joys above.

471 Charles Wesley (1707-1788)

1. Lord, in strength of grace,
   with a glad heart and free,
   myself, my residue of days,
   I consecrate to thee.

2. Thy ransomed servant, I
   restore to thee thine own;
   and, from this moment, live or die
   to serve my God alone.

472 Richard Baxter (1615-1691)

1. Lord, it belongs not to my care
   whether I die or live;
   to love and serve thee is my share,
   and this thy grace must give.

2. If life be long, I will be glad
   that I may long obey;
   if short, yet why should I be sad
   to soar to endless day?

3. Christ leads me through no darker rooms
   than he went through before;
   he that into God's kingdom comes
   must enter by this door.

4. Come, Lord, when grace has made me
      meet
   thy blessèd face to see;
   for if thy work on earth be sweet,
   what will thy glory be!

5. My knowledge of that life is small,
   the eye of faith is dim;
   but 'tis enough that Christ knows all,
   and I shall be with him.

473 William Tidd Matson (1833-1899)

1. Lord, I was blind! I could not see
   in thy marred visage any grace;
   but now the beauty of thy face
   in radiant vision dawns on me.

2. Lord, I was deaf! I could not hear
   the thrilling music of thy voice;
   but now I hear thee and rejoice,
   and all thine uttered words are dear.

3. Lord, I was dumb! I could not speak
   the grace and glory of thy name;
   but now, as touched with living flame,
   my lips thine eager praises wake.

Continued overleaf

4. Lord, I was dead! I could not stir
   my lifeless soul to come to thee;
   but now, since thou hast quickened me,
   I rise from sin's dark sepulchre.

5. For thou hast made the blind to see,
   the deaf to hear, the dumb to speak,
   the dead to live; and lo, I break
   the chains of my captivity!

474 Patrick Appleford (b. 1925)
© 1960 Josef Weinberger Ltd.

1. Lord Jesus Christ, you have come to us,
   you are one with us, Mary's Son.
   Cleansing our souls from all their sin,
   pouring your love and goodness in,
   Jesus, our love for you we sing,
   living Lord.

2. Lord Jesus Christ, now and ev'ry day
   teach us how to pray, Son of God.
   You have commanded us to do
   this in remembrance, Lord, of you.
   Into our lives your power breaks through,
   living Lord.

3. Lord Jesus Christ, you have come to us,
   born as one of us, Mary's Son.
   Led out to die on Calvary,
   risen from death to set us free,
   living Lord Jesus, help us see
   you are Lord.

4. Lord Jesus Christ, I would come to you,
   live my life for you, Son of God.
   All your commands I know are true,
   your many gifts will make me new,
   into my life your power breaks through,
   living Lord.

475 James Ashcroft Noble (1844-1896)

1. Lord Jesus, in the days of old
   two walked with thee in waning light;
   and love's blind instinct made them bold
   to crave thy presence through the night.
   As night descends, we too would pray:
   O leave us not at close of day!

2. Did not their hearts within them burn?
   And, though their Lord they failed to
      know,
   did not their spirits inly yearn?
   They could not let the Stranger go.
   Much more must we who know thee pray:
   O leave us not at close of day!

3. Perchance we have not always wist
   who has been with us by the way;
   amid day's uproar we have missed
   some word that thou hast had to say.
   In silent night, O Saviour dear,
   we would not fail thy voice to hear.

4. Day is far spent, and night is nigh;
   stay with us, Saviour, through the night;
   talk with us, touch us tenderly,
   lead us to peace, to rest, to light;
   dispel our darkness with thy face,
   radiant with resurrection grace.

5. Nor this night only, blessèd Lord,
   we, every day and every hour,
   would walk with thee Emmaus-ward
   to hear thy voice of love and power;
   and every night would by thy side
   look, listen, and be satisfied.

476 Fred Pratt Green (1903-2000)
© Copyright 1971 Stainer & Bell Ltd.

1. Lord Jesus, once a child,
   Saviour of young and old,
   receive *this little child of ours (these*
      little ones)
   into your flock and fold.

2. You drank the cup of life,
   its bitterness and bliss,
   and loved us to the uttermost
   for *such a child as this. (children such as
      these)*

3. So help us, Lord, to trust,
   through this baptismal rite,
   not in our own imperfect love,
   but in your saving might.

4. Lord Jesus, for *his* sake, *(her, their)*
   lend us your constant aid,
   that he, when older, may rejoice *(she, they)*
   we kept the vows we made.

477 Bishop Synesius (375-430)
trans. Allen William Chatfield (1808-1896)

1. Lord Jesus, think on me,
   and purge away my sin;
   from earth-born passions set me free,
   and make me pure within.

2. Lord Jesus, think on me,
   with care and woe opprest;
   let me thy loving servant be,
   and taste thy promised rest.

3. Lord Jesus, think on me
   amid the battle's strife;
   in all my pain and misery
   be thou my health and life.

4. Lord Jesus, think on me,
   nor let me go astray;
   through darkness and perplexity
   point thou the heav'nly way.

5. Lord Jesus, think on me,
   when flows the tempest high:
   when on doth rush the enemy,
   O Saviour, be thou nigh.

6. Lord Jesus, think on me,
   that, when the flood is past,
   I may th'eternal brightness see,
   and share thy joy at last.

478 Derek Robert Farrow (b.1925)
© *The Trustees for Methodist Church Purposes.*

1. Lord, look upon this helpless child *(each)*
   before he knows you're there; *(she knows,
      they know)*
   surround him with protective love, *(her,
      them)*
   enfold *him* in your care. *(her, them)*

2. Your church on earth, O Lord, affirms
   by clear baptismal sign
   what you from heaven made manifest
   by merciful design.

3. By merciful design and love
   through Saviour Jesus' birth,
   you succour every one that's born
   to serve you here on earth.

4. These joyful parents strengthen, Lord,
   and help them to provide
   a Christian home, where faithfulness
   and patient love abide.

5. Thus may all children brought to you
   be nurtured in your way,
   and so in goodness and in truth
   your Spirit's fruit display.

479 Oliver Wendell Holmes (1809-1894)

1. Lord of all being, throned afar,
   thy glory flames from sun and star;
   centre and soul of every sphere,
   yet to each loving heart how near.

2. Sun of our life, thy quickening ray
   sheds on our path the glow of day;
   star of our hope, thy softened light
   cheers the long watches of the night.

3. Our midnight is thy smile withdrawn,
   our noontide is thy gracious dawn.
   Our rainbow arch thy mercy's sign;
   all, save the clouds of sin, are thine.

Continued overleaf

4. Lord of all life, below, above,
   whose light is truth, whose warmth is love,
   before thy ever-blazing throne
   we ask no lustre of our own.

5. Grant us thy truth to make us free,
   and kindling hearts that burn for thee,
   till all thy living altars claim
   one holy light, one heavenly flame.

480 Jan Struther (1901-1953)
© Oxford University Press

1. Lord of all hopefulness,
   Lord of all joy,
   whose trust, ever childlike,
   no cares could destroy,
   be there at our waking,
   and give us, we pray,
   your bliss in our hearts, Lord,
   at the break of the day.

2. Lord of all eagerness,
   Lord of all faith,
   whose strong hands were skilled
   at the plane and the lathe,
   be there at our labours,
   and give us, we pray,
   your strength in our hearts, Lord,
   at the noon of the day.

3. Lord of all kindliness,
   Lord of all grace,
   your hands swift to welcome,
   your arms to embrace,
   be there at our homing,
   and give us, we pray,
   your love in our hearts, Lord,
   at the eve of the day.

4. Lord of all gentleness,
   Lord of all calm,
   whose voice is contentment,
   whose presence is balm,
   be there at our sleeping,
   and give us, we pray,
   your peace in our hearts, Lord,
   at the end of the day.

481 Timothy Dudley-Smith (b. 1926)
© Timothy Dudley-Smith

1. Lord of all life and power
   at whose creative word
   in nature's first primeval hour
   our formless being stirred,
   you made the light to shine,
   O shine on us, we pray,
   renew with light and life divine
   your church in this our day.

2. Lord of the fertile earth
   who caused the world to be,
   whose life alone can bring to birth
   the fruits of land and sea,
   teach us to use aright
   and share the gifts you give,
   to tend the earth as in your sight
   that all the world may live.

3. Lord of the cross and grave
   who died and lives again,
   who came in love to seek and save
   and then to rise and reign,
   we share, as once you shared,
   in mortal birth and breath,
   and ours the risen life that dared
   to vanquish sin and death.

4. Lord of the wind and flame,
   the promised Spirit's sign,
   possess our hearts in Jesus' name,
   come down, O Love divine!
   Help us in Christ to grow,
   from sin and self to cease,
   and daily in our lives to show
   your love and joy and peace.

5. Lord of the passing years
   whose changeless purpose stands,
   our lives and loves, our hopes and fears,
   we place within your hands;
   we bring you but your own,
   forgiven, loved and free,
   to follow Christ, and Christ alone,
   through all the days to be.

482

Jack Winslow (1882-1974) alt.
© Copyright Control

1. Lord of creation, to you be all praise!
   Most mighty your working, most
     wondrous your ways!
   Your glory and might are beyond us to
     tell,
   and yet in the heart of the humble you
     dwell.

2. Lord of all power, I give you my will,
   in joyful obedience your tasks to fulfil.
   Your bondage is freedom; your service is
     song;
   and, held in your keeping, my weakness
     is strong.

3. Lord of all wisdom, I give you my mind,
   rich truth that surpasses my knowledge
     to find;
   what eye has not seen and what ear has
     not heard
   is taught by your Spirit and shines from
     your word.

4. Lord of all bounty, I give you my heart;
   I praise and adore you for all you impart,
   your love to inspire me, your counsel to
     guide,
   your presence to shield me, whatever
     betide.

5. Lord of all being, I give you my all;
   if e'er I disown you, I stumble and fall;
   but, led in your service your word to
     obey,
   I'll walk in your freedom to the end of
     the way.

483

Frances Ridley Havergal (1836-1879)

1. Lord, speak to me, that I may speak
   in living echoes of thy tone;
   as thou hast sought, so let me seek
   thy erring children lost and lone.

2, O lead me, Lord, that I may lead
   the wandering and the wavering feet;
   O feed me, Lord, that I may feed
   thy hungering ones with manna sweet.

3. O strengthen me, that, while I stand
   firm on the rock, and strong in thee,
   I may stretch out a loving hand
   to wrestlers with the troubled sea.

4. O teach me, Lord, that I may teach
   the precious things thou dost impart;
   and wing my words, that they may reach
   the hidden depths of many a heart.

5. O give thine own sweet rest to me,
   that I may speak with soothing power
   a word in season, as from thee,
   to weary ones in needful hour.

6. O use me, Lord, use even me,
   just as thou wilt, and when, and where,
   until thy blessèd face I see,
   thy rest, thy joy, thy glory share.

484

James Montgomery (1771-1854) alt.

1. Lord, teach us how to pray aright
   with rev'rence and with fear;
   though fallen sinners in thy sight,
   we may, we must, draw near.

2. Our spirits fail through lack of prayer:
   O grant us pow'r to pray;
   and, when to meet thee we prepare,
   Lord, meet us by the way.

3. God of all grace, we bring to thee
   a broken, contrite heart;
   give what thine eye delights to see,
   truth in the inward part;

4. Faith in the only sacrifice
   that can for sin atone,
   to cast our hopes, to fix our eyes,
   on Christ, on Christ alone.

Continued overleaf

5. Patience to watch and wait and weep,
   though mercy long delay;
   courage our fainting souls to keep,
   and trust in thee alway.

6. Give these, and then thy will be done;
   thus, strengthened with all might,
   we, through thy Spirit and thy Son,
   shall pray, and pray aright.

485   Charles Wesley (1707-1788)

1. Lord, that I may learn of thee,
   give me true simplicity;
   wean my soul, and keep it low,
   willing thee alone to know.

2. Let me cast myself aside,
   all that feeds my knowing pride;
   not to man, but God submit,
   lay my reasonings at thy feet;

3. Of my boasted wisdom spoiled,
   docile, helpless, as a child,
   only seeing in thy light,
   only walking in thy might.

4. Then infuse the teaching grace,
   Spir't of truth and righteousness;
   knowledge, love divine, impart,
   life eternal, to my heart.

486   Graham Kendrick (b. 1950)
© 1987 Make Way Music

1. Lord, the light of your love is shining,
   in the midst of the darkness, shining;
   Jesus, Light of the World, shine upon us,
   set us free by the truth you now bring us.
   Shine on me, shine on me.

   Shine, Jesus, shine,
   fill this land with the Father's glory;
   blaze, Spirit, blaze,
   set our hearts on fire.

Flow, river, flow,
flood the nations with grace and mercy;
send forth your word, Lord,
and let there be light.

2. Lord, I come to your awesome presence,
   from the shadows into your radiance;
   by the blood I may enter your brightness,
   search me, try me, consume all
      my darkness.
   Shine on me, shine on me.

3. As we gaze on your kingly brightness,
   so our faces display your likeness,
   ever changing from glory to glory;
   mirrored here may our lives tell your story.
   Shine on me, shine on me.

487   Hugh Sherlock (b.1905) alt.
© The Trustees for Methodist Church Purposes

1. Lord, thy church on earth is seeking
   thy renewal from above;
   teach us all the art of speaking
   with the accent of thy love.
   We would heed thy great commission:
   go ye into every place –
   preach, baptise, fulfil my mission,
   serve with love and share my grace.

2. Freedom give to those in bondage,
   lift the burdens caused by sin.
   Give new hope, new strength and courage,
   grant release from fears within:
   light for darkness; joy for sorrow;
   love for hatred; peace for strife.
   These and countless blessings follow
   as the Spirit gives new life.

3. In the streets of every city
   where the bruised and lonely dwell,
   let us show the Saviour's pity,
   let us of his mercy tell.
   In all lands and with all races
   let us serve, and seek to bring
   all the world to render praises,
   Christ to thee, Redeemer, King.

488 Henry Williams Baker (1821-1877)

1. Lord, thy word abideth,
   and our footsteps guideth;
   who its truth believeth
   light and joy receiveth.

2. When our foes are near us,
   then thy word doth cheer us,
   word of consolation,
   message of salvation.

3. When the storms are o'er us,
   and dark clouds before us,
   then its light directeth,
   and our way protecteth.

4. Who can tell the pleasure,
   who recount the treasure,
   by thy word imparted
   to the simple-hearted?

5. Word of mercy, giving
   succour to the living;
   word of life, supplying
   comfort to the dying.

6. O that we, discerning
   its most holy learning,
   Lord, may love and fear thee,
   evermore be near thee.

489 Charles Wesley (1707-1788)

1. Lord, we believe to us and ours
   the apostolic promise given;
   we wait the pentecostal powers,
   the Holy Ghost sent down from heaven.

2. To every one whom God shall call
   the promise is securely made;
   to you far off – he calls you all;
   believe the word which Christ hath said:

3. 'The Holy Ghost, if I depart,
   the Comforter, shall surely come,
   shall make the contrite sinner's heart
   his loved, his everlasting home.'

4. Assembled here with one accord,
   calmly we wait the promised grace,
   the purchase of our dying Lord:
   come, Holy Ghost, and fill the place.

5. If every one that asks may find,
   if still thou dost on sinners fall,
   come as a mighty rushing wind;
   great grace be now upon us all.

6. Behold, to thee our souls aspire,
   and languish thy descent to meet;
   kindle in each thy living fire,
   and fix in every heart thy seat.

490 Fred Pratt Green (1903-2000)
© Copyright 1979 Stainer & Bell Ltd.

1. Lord, we have come at your own
      invitation,
   chosen by you, to be counted your friends;
   yours is the strength that sustains
      dedication,
   ours a commitment we know never ends.

2. Here, at your table, confirm our
      intention,
   give it your seal of forgiveness and grace;
   teach us to serve, without pride or
      pretension,
   Lord, in your kingdom, whatever our
      place.

3. When, at your table, each time of
      returning,
   vows are renewed and our courage
      restored,
   may we increasingly glory in learning
   all that it means to accept you as Lord.

4. So, in the world, where each duty
      assigned us
   gives us the chance to create or destroy,
   help us to make those decisions that bind
      us,
   Lord, to yourself, in obedience and joy.

491

Martin E. Leckebusch (b. 1962)
© 1999 Kevin Mayhew Ltd.

1. Lord, we thank you for the promise
   seen in ev'ry human birth:
   you have planned each new beginning –
   who could hope for greater worth?
   Hear our prayer for those we cherish;
   claim our children as your own:
   in the fertile ground of childhood
   may eternal seed be sown.

2. Lord, we thank you for the vigour
   burning in the years of youth:
   strength to face tomorrow's challenge,
   zest for life and zeal for truth.
   In the choice of friends and partners,
   when ideas and values form,
   may the message of your kingdom
   be the guide, the goal, the norm.

3. Lord, we thank you for the harvest
   of the settled, middle years:
   times when work and home can prosper,
   when life's richest fruit appears;
   but when illness, stress and hardship
   fill so many days with dread,
   may your love renew the vision
   of a clearer road ahead.

4. Lord, we thank you for the beauty
   of a heart at last mature:
   crowned with peace and rich in wisdom,
   well-respected and secure;
   but to those who face the twilight
   frail, bewildered, lacking friends,
   Lord, confirm your gracious offer:
   perfect life which never ends.

492

Martin Smith
© 1992 Kingsway's Thankyou Music

Lord, you have my heart,
and I will search for yours;
Jesus, take my life and lead me on.
Lord, you have my heart,
and I will search for yours;
let me be to you a sacrifice.

And I will praise you, Lord
(I will praise you, Lord).
And I will sing of love come down
(I will sing of love come down).
And as you show your face
(show your face),
we'll see your glory here.

493

Christina Georgina Rossetti (1830-1894)

1. Love came down at Christmas,
   Love all lovely, Love divine;
   Love was born at Christmas,
   star and angels gave the sign.

2. Worship we the Godhead,
   Love incarnate, Love divine;
   worship we our Jesus:
   but wherewith for sacred sign?

3. Love shall be our token,
   love be yours and love be mine,
   love to God and all men,
   love for plea and gift and sign.

494

Charles Wesley (1707-1788) alt.

1. Love divine, all loves excelling,
   joy of heav'n, to earth come down,
   fix in us thy humble dwelling,
   all thy faithful mercies crown.

2. Jesu, thou art all compassion,
   pure unbounded love thou art;
   visit us with thy salvation,
   enter ev'ry trembling heart.

3. Breathe, O breathe thy loving Spirit
   into ev'ry troubled breast;
   let us all in thee inherit,
   let us find thy promised rest.

4. Take away the love of sinning,
   Alpha and Omega be;
   end of faith, as its beginning,
   set our hearts at liberty.

5. Come, almighty to deliver,
let us all thy grace receive;
suddenly return, and never,
nevermore thy temples leave.

6. Thee we would be always blessing,
serve thee as thy hosts above;
pray, and praise thee without ceasing,
glory in thy perfect love.

7. Finish then thy new creation,
pure and spotless let us be;
let us see thy great salvation
perfectly restored in thee.

8. Changed from glory into glory,
till in heav'n we take our place,
till we cast our crowns before thee,
lost in wonder, love, and praise.

495 Luke Connaughton (1917-1979) alt.
© McCrimmon Publishing Co. Ltd.

1. Love is his word, love is his way,
feasting with all, fasting alone,
living and dying, rising again,
love only love, is his way.

Richer than gold is the love of my Lord:
better than splendour and wealth.

2. Love is his way, love is his mark,
sharing his last Passover feast,
Christ at the table, host to the twelve,
love, only love, is his mark.

3. Love is his mark, love is his sign,
bread for our strength, wine for our joy,
'This is my body, this is my blood.'
Love, only love, is his sign.

4. Love is his sign, love is his news,
'Do this,' he said, 'lest you forget
all my deep sorrow, all my dear blood.'
Love, only love, is his news.

5. Love is his news, love is his name,
we are his own, chosen and called,
family, brethren, cousins and kin.
Love, only love, is his name.

6. Love is his name, love is his law,
hear his command, all who are his,
'Love one another, I have loved you.'
Love, only love, is his law.

7. Love is his law, love is his word,
love of the Lord, Father and Word,
love of the Spirit, God ever one,
love, only love, is his word.

496 Charles Wesley (1707-1788)

1. Loving Jesus, gentle Lamb,
in thy gracious hands I am;
make me, Saviour, what thou art;
like thyself within my heart.

2. Fain I would to thee be brought;
gracious Lord, forbid it not;
in the kingdom of thy grace
give a little child a place.

3. Fain I would be as thou art;
give me thy obedient heart;
thou art pitiful and kind;
let me have thy loving mind.

4. Let me above all fulfil
God my heavenly Father's will;
never his good Spirit grieve,
only to his glory live.

5. I shall then show forth thy praise,
serve thee all my happy days;
then the world shall always see
Christ, the holy child, in me.

497 Robert Lowry (1826-1899)

1. Low in the grave he lay,
Jesus, my Saviour;
waiting the coming day,
Jesus, my Lord.

Continued overleaf

Up from the grave he arose,
with a mighty triumph o'er his foes;
he arose a victor
from the dark domain,
and he lives for ever
with his saints to reign.
He arose! He arose!
Hallelujah! Christ arose!

2. Vainly they watch his bed,
Jesus, my Saviour;
vainly they seal the dead,
Jesus, my Lord.

3. Death cannot keep its prey,
Jesus, my Saviour;
he tore the bars away,
Jesus, my Lord.

498 Jack W. Hayford (b. 1934)
© Rocksmith Music Inc./Leosong Copyright Service Ltd.

Majesty, worship his majesty;
unto Jesus be glory, honour and praise.
Majesty, kingdom authority
flow from his throne unto his own:
his anthem raise.
So exalt, lift up on high the name of Jesus;
magnify, come glorify Christ Jesus the King.
Majesty, worship his majesty,
Jesus who died, now glorified,
King of all kings.

499 George Matheson (1842-1906)

1. Make me a captive, Lord,
and then I shall be free;
force me to render up my sword,
and I shall conqueror be.
I sink in life's alarms
when by myself I stand;
imprison me within thine arms,
and strong shall be my hand.

2. My power is faint and low
till I have learned to serve;
it wants the needed fire to glow,
it wants the breeze to nerve;
it cannot freely move,
till thou hast wrought its chain;
enslave it with thy matchless love,
and deathless it shall reign.

3. My will is not my own
till thou hast made it thine;
if it would reach a monarch's throne
it must its crown resign;
it only stands unbent,
amid the clashing strife,
when on thy bosom it has leant
and found in thee its life.

500 Sebastian Temple (1928-1997)
based on the Prayer of St Francis
© 1967 OCP Publications

1. Make me a channel of your peace.
Where there is hatred, let me bring
your love.
Where there is injury, your pardon, Lord;
and where there's doubt, true faith in you.

O, Master, grant that I may never seek
so much to be consoled as to console,
to be understood as to understand,
to be loved as to love with all my soul.

2. Make me a channel of your peace.
Where there's despair in life, let me
bring hope.
Where there is darkness, only light,
and where there's sadness, ever joy.

3. Make me a channel of your peace.
It is in pardoning that we are pardoned,
in giving of ourselves that we receive,
and in dying that we're born to eternal life.

501

Graham Kendrick (b. 1950)
© 1986 Kingsway's Thankyou Music

1. Make way, make way, for Christ the King
   in splendour arrives;
   fling wide the gates and welcome him
   into your lives.

   Make way (make way), make way (make way),
   for the King of kings (for the King of kings);
   make way (make way), make way (make way),
   and let his kingdom in!

2. He comes the broken hearts to heal,
   the pris'ners to free;
   the deaf shall hear, the lame shall dance,
   the blind shall see.

3. And those who mourn with heavy hearts,
   who weep and sigh,
   with laughter, joy and royal crown
   he'll beautify.

4. We call you now to worship him
   as Lord of all,
   to have no gods before him,
   their thrones must fall.

502

Philipp Bliss (1838-1876) alt.

1. Man of sorrows! What a name
   for the Son of God who came
   ruined sinners to reclaim!
   Alleluia! What a Saviour!

2. Bearing shame and scoffing rude,
   in my place condemned he stood;
   sealed my pardon with his blood;
   Alleluia! What a Saviour!

3. Guilty, vile and helpless we;
   spotless Lamb of God was he:
   full atonement – can it be?
   Alleluia! What a Saviour!

4. Lifted up was he to die:
   'It is finished!' was his cry;
   now in heav'n exalted high;
   Alleluia! What a Saviour!

5. When he comes, our glorious King,
   all his ransomed home to bring,
   then anew this song we'll sing:
   Alleluia! what a Saviour!

503

Michael Forster (b. 1946)
© 1996 Kevin Mayhew Ltd.

1. Mary, blessèd teenage mother,
   with what holy joy you sing!
   Humble, yet above all other,
   from your womb shall healing spring.
   Out of wedlock pregnant found,
   full of grace with blessing crowned.

2. Mother of the homeless stranger
   only outcasts recognise,
   point us to the modern manger;
   not a sight for gentle eyes!
   Oh the joyful news we tell:
   'Even here, Immanuel!'

3. Now, throughout the townships ringing,
   hear the black madonna cry,
   songs of hope and freedom singing,
   poor and humble lifted high.
   Here the Spirit finds a womb
   for the breaker of the tomb!

4. Holy mother, for the nations
   bring to birth the child divine:
   Israel's strength and consolation,
   and the hope of Palestine!
   All creation reconciled
   in the crying of a child!

504

Frances Ridley Havergal (1836-1879)

1. Master, speak! Thy servant heareth,
   waiting for thy gracious word,
   longing for thy voice that cheereth;
   Master, let it now be heard.
   I am listening, Lord, for thee;
   what hast thou to say to me?

Continued overleaf

2. Speak to me by name, O Master,
let me know it is to me;
speak, that I may follow faster,
with a step more firm and free,
where the Shepherd leads the flock
in the shadow of the rock.

3. Master, speak! Though least and lowest,
let me not unheard depart;
Master, speak! For O thou knowest
all the yearning of my heart,
knowest all its truest need;
speak, and make me blest indeed.

4. Master, speak: and make me ready,
when thy voice is truly heard,
with obedience glad and steady
still to follow every word.
I am listening, Lord, for thee;
Master, speak! O speak to me!

505 Kate Barclay Wilkinson (1859-1928)

1. May the mind of Christ my Saviour
live in me from day to day,
by his love and power controlling
all I do and say.

2. May the word of God dwell richly
in my heart from hour to hour,
so that I may triumph only
in his saving power.

3. May the peace of God my Father
rule my life in everything,
that I may be calm to comfort
sick and sorrowing.

4. May the love of Jesus fill me,
as the waters fill the sea;
him exalting, self abasing,
this is victory.

5. May I run the race before me,
strong and brave to face the foe,
looking only unto Jesus,
as I onward go.

506 Graham Kendrick (b. 1950)
© 1986 Kingsway's Thankyou Music

1. Meekness and majesty,
manhood and deity,
in perfect harmony, the Man who is God.
Lord of eternity dwells in humanity,
kneels in humility and washes our feet.

O what a mystery, meekness and majesty.
Bow down and worship for this is your God,
this is your God.

2. Father's pure radiance,
perfect in innocence,
yet learns obedience to death on a cross.
Suffering to give us life,
    conquering through sacrifice,
and as they crucify prays: 'Father forgive.'

3. Wisdom unsearchable,
God the invisible,
love indestructible in frailty appears.
Lord of infinity, stooping so tenderly,
lifts our humanity to the heights of
    his throne.

507 Charles Wesley (1707-1788)

1. Meet and right it is to sing,
in every time and place,
glory to our heavenly King,
the God of truth and grace:
join we then with sweet accord,
all in one thanksgiving join;
holy, holy, holy Lord,
eternal praise be thine.

2. Thee the first-born sons of light,
in choral symphonies,
praise by day, day without night,
and never, never cease;
angels and archangels all
praise and mystic Three in One,
sing, and stop, and gaze, and fall
o'erwhelmed before thy throne.

3. Vying with that happy choir,
   who chant thy praise above,
   we on eagles' wings aspire,
   the wings of faith and love:
   thee they sing with glory crowned,
   we extol the slaughtered Lamb;
   lower if our voices sound,
   our subject is the same.

4. Father, God, thy love we praise,
   which gave thy Son to die;
   Jesus, full of truth and grace,
   alike we glorify;
   Spirit, Comforter divine,
   praise by all to thee be given;
   till we in full chorus join,
   and earth is turned to heaven.

Adaptation of Te Deum by St Ambrose (340-397)
ascribed to Ignaz Franz (1719-1790)
trans. Amos Cresswell © Amos Cresswell

508

1. Mighty God, we praise your name,
   strong your arms below and round us;
   all creation knows your fame,
   all your powers and works astound us;
   you were there when time began,
   you remain when all is done.

2. Hosts of angels own your praise,
   songs and service never ending;
   you, the Lord of endless days,
   always to your children bending;
   all in heaven and earth and sea,
   all give homage, Lord, to thee.

3. All with knowledge of your love
   join the saints to sing your glory;
   all the martyr hosts above
   join to tell the Easter story;
   wondrous gift to us is given,
   Jesus is our way to heaven.

4. Now we seek your mercy, Lord,
   give us all your great salvation;
   lead us, trusting on your word;
   make us one, your holy nation;
   Father, Spirit, Risen Son,
   share your triumph, dearly won.

Julia Ward Howe (1819-1910) alt.
© 1992, 1994 Kevin Mayhew Ltd.

509

1. Mine eyes have seen the glory
   of the coming of the Lord.
   He is tramping out the vintage
   where the grapes of wrath are stored.
   He has loosed the fateful lightning
   of his terrible swift sword.
   His truth is marching on.

   Glory, glory hallelujah!
   Glory, glory hallelujah!
   Glory, glory hallelujah!
   His truth is marching on.

2. I have seen him in the watchfires
   of a hundred circling camps.
   They have gilded him an altar
   in the evening dews and damps.
   I can read his righteous sentence
   by the dim and flaring lamps.
   His day is marching on.

3. He has sounded forth the trumpet
   that shall never sound retreat.
   He is sifting out all human hearts
   before his judgement seat.
   O, be swift my soul to answer him,
   be jubilant my feet!
   Our God is marching on.

4. In the beauty of the lilies
   Christ was born across the sea,
   with a glory in his bosom
   that transfigures you and me.
   As he died to make us holy,
   let us live that all be free,
   whilst God is marching on.

510

Eleanor Farjeon (1881-1965)
© David Higham Associates. Used by permission from
'The Children's Bells' published by Oxford University Press

1. Morning has broken like the first morning,
   blackbird has spoken like the first bird.
   Praise for the singing!
       Praise for the morning!
   Praise for them, springing
       fresh from the Word!

2. Sweet the rain's new fall, sunlit from heaven,
   like the first dew-fall on the first grass.
   Praise for the sweetness of the wet garden,
   sprung in completeness where his feet pass.

3. Mine is the sunlight! Mine is the morning
   born of the one light Eden saw play!
   Praise with elation, praise ev'ry morning,
   God's re-creation of the new day!

511

Estelle White (b. 1925)
© McCrimmon Publishing Co. Ltd.

1. 'Moses, I know you're the man,'
   the Lord said.
   'You're going to work out my plan,'
   the Lord said.
   'Lead all the Israelites out of slavery,
   and I shall make them a wandering race
   called the people of God.'

   So ev'ry day we're on our way,
   for we're a travelling, wandering race
   called the people of God.

2. 'Don't get too set in your ways,'
   the Lord said.
   'Each step is only a phase,'
   the Lord said.
   'I'll go before you and I shall be a sign
   to guide my travelling, wandering race.
   You're the people of God.'

3. 'No matter what you may do,'
   the Lord said,
   'I shall be faithful and true,'
   the Lord said.
   'My love will strengthen you as you go along,
   for you're my travelling, wandering race.
   You're the people of God.'

4. 'Look at the birds in the air,'
   the Lord said.
   'They fly unhampered by care,'
   the Lord said.
   'You will move easier if you're trav'lling
       light,
   for you're a wandering, vagabond race.'
   You're the people of God.'

5. 'Foxes have places to go,'
   the Lord said,
   'but I've no home here below,'
   the Lord said.
   'So if you want to be with me all
       your days,
   keep up the moving and travelling on.
   You're the people of God.'

512

Ray Palmer (1808-1887)

1. My faith looks up to thee,
   thou Lamb of Calvary,
   Saviour divine!
   Now hear me while I pray,
   take all my guilt away,
   O let me from this day
   be wholly thine.

2. May thy rich grace impart
   strength to my fainting heart,
   my zeal inspire.
   As thou hast died for me,
   O may my love to thee
   pure, warm and changeless be,
   a living fire.

3. While life's dark maze I tread,
   and griefs around me spread,
   be thou my guide;
   bid darkness turn to day,
   wipe sorrow's tears away,
   nor let me ever stray
   from thee aside.

4. When ends life's transient dream,
   when death's cold sullen stream
   shall o'er me roll,
   blest Saviour, then in love,
   fear and distrust remove;
   O bear me safe above,
   a ransomed soul.

513 Frederick William Faber (1814-1863) alt.
© *Jubilate Hymns*

1. My God, how wonderful you are,
   your majesty how bright;
   how beautiful your mercy-seat
   in depths of burning light!

2. Creator from eternal years
   and everlasting Lord,
   by holy angels day and night
   unceasingly adored!

3. How wonderful, how beautiful
   the sight of you must be –
   your endless wisdom, boundless power,
   and awesome purity!

4. O how I fear you, living God,
   with deepest, tenderest fears,
   and worship you with trembling hope
   and penitential tears!

5. But I may love you too, O Lord,
   though you are all-divine,
   for you have stooped to ask of me
   this feeble love of mine.

6. Father of Jesus, love's reward,
   great King upon your throne,
   what joy to see you as you are
   and know as I am known!

514 Charles Wesley (1707-1788)

1. My God, I am thine;
   what a comfort divine,
   what a blessing to know that my Jesus is
      mine!
   In the heavenly Lamb
   thrice happy I am,
   and my heart it doth dance at the sound
   of his name.

2. True pleasures abound
   in the rapturous sound;
   and whoever hath found it hath paradise
      found.
   My Jesus to know,
   and feel his blood flow,
   'tis life everlasting, 'tis heaven below.

3. Yet onward I haste
   to heavenly feast:
   that, that is the fullness; but this is the
      taste;
   and this I shall prove,
   till with joy I remove
   to the heaven of heavens in Jesus's love.

515 Charles Wesley (1707-1788)

1. My God! I know, I feel thee mine,
   and will not quit my claim,
   till all I have is lost in thine
   and all renewed I am.

2. I hold thee with a trembling hand,
   but will not let thee go,
   till steadfastly by faith I stand
   and all thy goodness know.

3. When shall I see the welcome hour
   that plants my God in me –
   Spirit of health, and life, and power,
   and perfect liberty?

Continued overleaf

4. Jesus, thine all-victorious love
   shed in my heart abroad;
   then shall my feet no longer rove,
   rooted and fixed in God.

5. O that in me the sacred fire
   might now begin to glow,
   burn up the dross of base desire,
   and make the mountains flow!

6. O that it now from heaven might fall,
   and all my sins consume!
   Come, Holy Ghost, for thee I call,
   Spirit of burning, come!

7. Refining fire, go through my heart,
   illuminate my soul;
   scatter thy life through every part,
   and sanctify the whole.

516 Latin (17th century)
trans. Edward Caswall (1814-1878)

1. My God, I love thee; not because
   I hope for heav'n thereby,
   nor yet because who love thee not
   are lost eternally.

2. Thou, O my Jesus, thou didst me
   upon the cross embrace;
   for me didst bear the nails and spear,
   and manifold disgrace.

3. And griefs and torments numberless,
   and sweat of agony;
   yea death itself – and all for me
   who was thine enemy.

4. Then why, O blessèd Jesu Christ,
   should I not love thee well?
   Not for the sake of winning heav'n,
   nor of escaping hell.

5. Not from the hope of gaining aught,
   not seeking a reward;
   but as thyself hast lovèd me,
   O ever-loving Lord.

6. So would I love thee, dearest Lord,
   and in thy praise will sing;
   solely because thou art my God,
   and my most loving King.

517 Adelaide Anne Procter (1825-1864)

1. My God, I thank thee, who hast made
   the earth so bright,
   so full of splendour and of joy,
   beauty and light;
   so many glorious things are here,
   noble and right.

2. I thank thee, Lord, that thou hast made
   joy to abound,
   so many gentle thoughts and deeds
   circling us round,
   that in the darkest spot of earth
   some love is found.

3. I thank thee too that often joy
   is touched with pain,
   that shadows fall on brightest hours,
   that thorns remain,
   so that earth's bliss may be our guide,
   and not our chain.

4. I thank thee, Lord, that thou hast kept
   the best in store;
   we have enough, yet not too much
   to long for more –
   a yearning for a deeper peace
   not known before.

5. I thank thee, Lord, that here our lives,
   though amply blest,
   can never find, although they seek,
   a perfect rest,
   nor ever shall, until we lean
   on Jesu's breast.

518

Benjamin Rhodes (1743-1815)

1. My heart and voice I raise,
   to spread Messiah's praise;
   Messiah's praise let all repeat:
   the universal Lord,
   by whose almighty word
   creation rose in form complete.

2. A servant's form he wore,
   and in his body bore
   our dreadful curse on Calvary:
   he like a victim stood,
   and poured his sacred blood,
   to set the guilty captives free.

3. But soon the victor rose
   triumphant o'er his foes,
   and led the vanquished host in chains:
   he threw their empire down,
   his foes compelled to own
   o'er all the great Messiah reigns.

4. With mercy's mildest grace,
   he governs all our race
   in wisdom, righteousness, and love:
   who to Messiah fly
   shall find redemption nigh,
   and all his great salvation prove.

5. Hail, Saviour, Prince of Peace!
   Thy kingdom shall increase,
   till all the world thy glory see,
   and righteousness abound
   as the great deep profound,
   and fill the earth with purity.

519

Charles Wesley (1707-1788)

1. My heart is full of Christ, and longs
   its glorious matter to declare!
   Of him I make my loftier songs,
   I cannot from his praise forbear;
   my ready tongue makes haste to sing
   the glories of my heavenly king.

2. Fairer than all the earth-born race,
   perfect in comeliness thou art;
   replenished are thy lips with grace,
   and full of love thy tender heart:
   God ever blest! We bow the knee,
   and own all fullness dwells in thee.

3. Gird on thy thigh the Spirit's sword,
   and take to thee thy power divine;
   stir up thy strength, almighty Lord,
   all power and majesty are thine:
   assert thy worship and renown;
   O all-redeeming God, come down!

4. Come, and maintain thy righteous cause,
   and let thy glorious toil succeed;
   dispread the victory of thy cross,
   ride on and prosper in thy deed;
   through earth triumphantly ride on,
   and reign in every heart alone.

520

William R. Featherstone (1846-1873)

1. My Jesus, I love thee, I know thou art
      mine,
   for thee all the pleasures of sin I resign;
   my gracious Redeemer, my Saviour art
      thou,
   if ever I loved thee, my Jesus, 'tis now.

2. I love thee because thou hast first lovèd
      me,
   and purchased my pardon on Calvary's
      tree;
   I love thee for wearing the thorns on thy
      brow,
   if ever I loved thee, my Jesus, 'tis now.

3. I'll love thee in life, I'll love thee in death,
   and praise thee as long as thou lendest
      me breath;
   and say, when the death-dew lies cold on
      my brow,
   if ever I loved thee, my Jesus, 'tis now.

Continued overleaf

4. In mansions of glory and endless delight,
   I'll ever adore thee and dwell in thy sight;
   I'll sing with the glittering crown on my
      brow,
   if ever I loved thee, my Jesus, 'tis now.

521 Darlene Zschech

My Jesus, my Saviour,
Lord, there is none like you.
All of my days I want to praise
the wonders of your mighty love.
My comfort, my shelter,
tower of refuge and strength,
let ev'ry breath, all that I am,
never cease to worship you.

Shout to the Lord,
all the earth, let us sing
power and majesty,
praise to the King.
Mountains bow down
and the seas will roar
at the sound of your name.
I sing for joy
at the work of your hands.
For ever I'll love you,
for ever I'll stand.
Nothing compares to the promise
I have in you.

522 Graham Kendrick (b. 1950)

1. My Lord, what love is this,
   that pays so dearly,
   that I, the guilty one,
   may go free!

   Amazing love, O what sacrifice,
   the Son of God, given for me.
   My debt he pays, and my death he dies,
   that I might live,
   that I might live.

2. And so they watched him die,
   despised, rejected;
   but O, the blood he shed
   flowed for me!

3. And now this love of Christ
   shall flow like rivers;
   come, wash your guilt away,
   live again!

523 Paulus Gerhardt (1607-1676). Trans. John Wesley
(1703-1791)

1. My Saviour! how shall I proclaim,
   how pay the mighty debt I owe?
   Let all I have, and all I am,
   ceaseless to all thy glory show.

2. Too much to thee I cannot give;
   too much I cannot do for thee;
   let all thy love, and all thy grief,
   graven on my heart for ever be.

524 Samuel Crossman (c. 1624-1684) alt.

1. My song is love unknown,
   my Saviour's love to me,
   love to the loveless shown,
   that they might lovely be.
   O who am I, that for my sake,
   my Lord should take frail flesh and die?

2. He came from his blest throne,
   salvation to bestow;
   but men refused, and none
   the longed-for Christ would know.
   But O, my friend, my friend indeed,
   who at my need his life did spend!

3. Sometimes they strew his way,
   and his sweet praises sing;
   resounding all the day
   hosannas to their King;
   then 'Crucify!' is all their breath,
   and for his death they thirst and cry.

4. Why what hath my Lord done?
   What makes this rage and spite?
   He made the lame to run,
   he gave the blind their sight.
   Sweet injuries! Yet they at these
   themselves displease,
       and 'gainst him rise.

5. They rise, and needs will have
   my dear Lord made away;
   a murderer they save,
   the Prince of Life they slay.
   Yet cheerful he to suff'ring goes,
   that he his foes from thence might free.

6. Here might I stay and sing,
   no story so divine;
   never was love, dear King,
   never was grief like thine.
   This is my friend in whose sweet praise
   I all my days could gladly spend.

525 Timothy Dudley-Smith (b.1926)
      © *Timothy Dudley-Smith*

1. Name of all majesty, fathomless mystery,
   King of the ages by angels adored;
   power and authority, splendour and dignity,
   bow to his mastery, Jesus is Lord!

2. Child of our destiny, God from eternity,
   love of the Father on sinners outpoured;
   see now what God has done sending his
       only Son,
   Christ the belovèd One, Jesus is Lord!

3. Saviour of Calvary, costliest victory,
   darkness defeated and Eden restored;
   born as a man to die, nailed to a cross on
       high,
   cold in the grave to lie, Jesus is Lord!

4. Source of all sovereignty, light, immortality,
   life everlasting and heaven assured;
   so with the ransomed, we praise him
       eternally,
   Christ in his majesty, Jesus is Lord!

526 Sarah Flower Adams (1805-1848)

1. Nearer, my God, to thee,
   nearer to thee!
   E'en though it be a cross
   that raiseth me:
   still all my song would be,
   'Nearer, my God, to thee,
   nearer to thee.'

2. Though, like the wanderer,
   the sun gone down,
   darkness be over me,
   my rest like a stone;
   yet in my dreams I'd be
   nearer, my God, to thee,
   nearer to thee!

3. There let the way appear,
   steps unto heaven;
   all that thou sendest me
   in mercy given:
   angels to beckon me
   nearer, my God, to thee,
   nearer to thee!

4. Then, with my waking thoughts
   bright with thy praise,
   out of my stony griefs
   Bethel I'll raise;
   so by my woes to be
   nearer, my God, to thee,
   nearer to thee!

5. Or if on joyful wing
   cleaving the sky,
   sun, moon and stars forgot,
   upwards I fly,
   still all my song shall be,
   'Nearer, my God, to thee,
   nearer to thee.'

527
John Keble (1792-1866) based on Lamentations 3:23

1. New every morning is the love
   our wakening and uprising prove;
   through sleep and darkness safely
      brought,
   restored to life and power and thought.

2. New mercies, each returning day,
   hover around us while we pray;
   new perils past, new sins forgiven,
   new thoughts of God, new hopes of
      heav'n.

3. If on our daily course our mind
   be set to hallow all we find,
   new treasures still, of countless price,
   God will provide for sacrifice.

4. Old friends, old scenes, will lovelier be,
   as more of heav'n in each we see;
   some softening gleam of love and prayer
   shall dawn on every cross and care.

5. The trivial round, the common task,
   will furnish all we need to ask,
   room to deny ourselves, a road
   to bring us daily nearer God.

6. Only, O Lord, in thy dear love
   fit us for perfect rest above;
   and help us, this and every day,
   to live more nearly as we pray.

528
Christina Georgina Rossetti (1830-1894)

1. None other lamb, none other name,
   none other hope in heaven or earth or sea,
   none other hiding-place from guilt and
      shame,
   none beside thee!

2. My faith burns low, my hope burns low;
   only my heart's desire cries out in me,
   by the deep thunder of its want and woe,
   cries out to thee.

3. Lord, thou art life, though I be dead;
   love's fire thou art, however cold I be:
   nor heaven have I, nor place to lay my head,
   nor home, but thee.

529
Graham Kendrick (b. 1950)
© 1997 Ascent Music

1. No scenes of stately majesty
   for the King of kings.
   No nights aglow with candle flame
   for the King of love.
   No flags of empire hung in shame
   for Calvary.
   No flowers perfumed the lonely way
   that led him to
   a borrowed tomb for Easter Day.

2. No wreaths upon the ground were laid
   for the King of kings.
   Only a crown of thorns remained
   where he gave his love.
   A message scrawled in irony –
   King of the Jews –
   lay trampled where they turned away,
   and no one knew
   that it was the first Easter Day.

3. Yet nature's finest colours blaze
   for the King of kings.
   And stars in jewelled clusters say,
   'Worship heaven's King.'
   Two thousand springtimes more have
      bloomed –
   is that enough?
   Oh, how can I be satisfied
   until he hears
   the whole world sing of Easter love?

4. My prayers shall be a fragrance sweet
   for the King of kings.
   My love the flowers at his feet
   for the King of love.
   My vigil is to watch and pray
   until he comes.
   My highest tribute to obey
   and live to know
   the power of that first Easter Day.

5. I long for scenes of majesty
   for the risen King.
   For nights aglow with candle flame
   for the King of love.
   A nation hushed upon its knees
   at Calvary,
   where all our sins and griefs were nailed
   and hope was born
   of everlasting Easter Day.

530 George Bradford Caird (1917-1984)
© George Bradford Caird Memorial Trust

1. Not far beyond the sea nor high
   above the heavens, but very nigh
   thy voice, O God, is heard.
   For each new step of faith we take
   thou hast more truth and light to break
   forth from thy holy word.

2. The babes in Christ the Scriptures feed
   with milk sufficient for their need,
   the nurture of the Lord.
   Beneath life's burden and its heat
   the fully grown find stronger meat
   in thy unfailing word.

3. Rooted and grounded in thy love,
   with saints on earth and saints above
   we join in full accord,
   to grasp the breadth, length, depth and
      height,
   the crucified and risen might
   of Christ, the incarnate Word.

4. Help us to press toward that mark,
   and, though our vision now is dark,
   to live by what we see;
   so, when we see thee face to face,
   thy truth and light our dwelling-place
   for evermore shall be.

531 Timothy Dudley-Smith (b.1926) based on Psalm 115
© Timothy Dudley-Smith

1. Not to us be glory given but to him who
      reigns above:
   glory to the God of heaven for his
      faithfulness and love!
   What though unbelieving voices hear no
      word and see no sign,
   still in God my heart rejoices, working
      out his will divine.

2. Now what human fingers fashion, gold
      and silver, deaf and blind,
   dead to knowledge and compassion,
      having neither heart nor mind,
   lifeless gods, yet some adore them,
      nerveless hands and feet of clay;
   all become, who bow before them, lost
      indeed, and dead as they.

3. Not in them is hope of blessing, hope is
      in the living Lord:
   high and low, his name confessing, find
      in him their shield and sword.
   Hope of all whose hearts revere him,
      God of Israel, still the same!
   God of Aaron! Those who fear him, he
      remembers them by name.

4. Not the dead, but we the living, praise
      the Lord with all our powers;
   of his goodness freely giving, his is
      heaven; earth is ours.
   Not to us be glory given but to him who
      reigns above:
   glory to the God of heaven for his
      faithfulness and love!

532 Paulus Gerhardt (1607-1676)
Trans. Catherine Winkworth (1827-1878)

1. Now all the woods are sleeping,
   and night and stillness creeping
   o'er city, man and beast;
   but thou, my heart, awake thee,
   to prayer awhile betake thee,
   and praise thy Maker ere thou rest.

Continued overleaf

2. The last faint beam is going,
the golden stars are glowing
in yonder dark-blue deep;
and such the glory given
when called of God to heaven,
on earth no more we pine and weep.

3. Now thought and labour ceases,
for night the tired releases
and bids sweet rest begin:
my heart, there comes a morrow
shall set thee free from sorrow
and all the dreary toil of sin.

4. My Jesus, stay thou by me,
and let no foe come nigh me,
safe sheltered by thy wing;
but would the foe alarm me,
O let him never harm me,
but still thine angels round me sing.

5. My loved ones, rest securely,
from every peril surely
our God will guard your heads;
and happy slumbers send you,
and bid his hosts attend you,
and golden-armed watch o'er your beds.

533
Johann Andreas Rothe (1688-1758)
Trans. John Wesley (1703-1791)

1. Now I have found the ground wherein
sure my soul's anchor may remain –
the wounds of Jesus, for my sin
before the world's foundation slain;
whose mercy shall unshaken stay,
when heaven and earth are fled away.

2. Father, thine everlasting grace
our scanty thought surpasses far,
thy heart still melts with tenderness,
thy arms of love still open are
returning sinners to receive,
that mercy they may taste and live.

3, O Love, thou bottomless abyss,
my sins are swallowed up in thee!
Covered is my unrighteousness,
nor spot of guilt remains on me,
while Jesu's blood through earth and skies
'Mercy, free, boundless mercy!' cries.

4. With faith I plunge me in this sea,
here is my hope, my joy, my rest;
hither, when hell assails, I flee,
I look into my Saviour's breast;
away, sad doubt and anxious fear!
Mercy is all that's written there.

5. Though waves and storms go o'er my
head,
though strength, and health, and friends
be gone,
though joys be withered all and dead,
though every comfort be withdrawn,
on this my steadfast soul relies –
Father, thy mercy never dies!

6. Fixed on this ground will I remain,
though my heart fail and flesh decay;
this anchor shall my soul sustain,
when earth's foundations melt away;
mercy's full power I then shall prove,
loved with an everlasting love.

534
Fred Kaan (b. 1929)
© 1968 Stainer & Bell Ltd.

1. Now join we, to praise the Creator,
our voices in worship and song;
we stand to recall with thanksgiving
that to God all seasons belong.

2. We thank you, O Source of all goodness,
for the joy and abundance of crops,
for food that is stored in our larders,
for all we can buy in the shops.

3. But also of need and starvation
we sing with concern and despair,
of skills that are used for destruction,
of land that is burnt and laid bare.

4. We cry for the plight of the hungry
   while harvests are left on the field,
   for orchards neglected and wasting,
   for produce from markets withheld.

5. The song grows in depth and in
      wideness;
   the earth and its people are one.
   There can be no thanks without giving,
   no words without deeds that are done.

6. Then teach us, O God of the harvest,
   to be humble in all that we claim,
   to share what we have with the nations,
   to care for the world in your name.

535 Fred Kaan (b.1929)
    © 1968 Stainer & Bell Ltd.

1. Now let us from this table rise
   renewed in body, mind and soul;
   with Christ we die and rise again,
   his selfless love has made us whole.

2. With minds alert, upheld by grace,
   to spread the Word in speech and deed,
   we follow in the steps of Christ,
   at one with all in hope and need.

3. To fill each human house with love,
   it is the sacrament of care;
   the work that Christ began to do
   we humbly pledge ourselves to share.

4. Then grant us grace, Companion-God,
   to choose again the pilgrim way,
   and help us to accept with joy
   the challenge of tomorrow's day.

536 Benjamin Waugh (1839-1908)

1. Now let us see thy beauty, Lord,
   as we have seen before;
   and by thy beauty quicken us
   to love thee and adore.

2. 'Tis easy when with simple mind
   thy loveliness we see,
   to consecrate ourselves afresh
   to duty and to thee.

3. Our every feverish mood is cooled,
   and gone is every load,
   when we can lose the love of self,
   and find the love of God.

4. Lord, it is coming to ourselves
   when thus we come to thee;
   the bondage of thy loveliness
   is perfect liberty.

5. So now we come to ask again
   what thou hast often given,
   the vision of that loveliness
   which is the life of heaven.

537 Martin Rinkart (1586-1649)
    trans. Catherine Winkworth (1827-1878)

1. Now thank we all our God,
   with hearts and hands and voices,
   who wondrous things hath done,
   in whom his world rejoices;
   who from our mother's arms
   hath blessed us on our way
   with countless gifts of love,
   and still is ours today.

2. O may this bounteous God
   through all our life be near us,
   with ever joyful hearts
   and blessèd peace to cheer us;
   and keep us in his grace,
   and guide us when perplexed,
   and free us from all ills
   in this world and the next.

Continued overleaf

3. All praise and thanks to God
   the Father now be given,
   the Son and him who reigns
   with them in highest heaven,
   the one eternal God,
   whom earth and heaven adore;
   for thus it was, is now,
   and shall be evermore.

538 John Macleod Campbell Crum (1872-1958), alt.
© 1928 Oxford University Press

1. Now the green blade riseth
   from the buried grain,
   wheat that in the dark earth
   many days has lain;
   Love lives again,
   that with the dead has been:
   Love is come again,
   like wheat that springeth green.

2. In the grave they laid him,
   Love by hatred slain,
   thinking that never
   he would wake again,
   laid in the earth
   like grain that sleeps unseen:
   Love is come again,
   like wheat that springeth green.

3. Forth he came at Easter,
   like the risen grain,
   he that for three days
   in the grave had lain;
   quick from the dead,
   my risen Lord is seen:
   Love is come again,
   like wheat that springeth green.

4. When our hearts are wintry,
   grieving or in pain,
   thy touch can call us
   back to life again;
   fields of our hearts,
   that dead and bare have been:
   Love is come again,
   like wheat that springeth green.

539 Maintzisch Gesangbuch (1661)
Trans. Ray Palmer (1808-1887) alt.

1. O Bread to pilgrims given,
   O food that angels eat,
   O manna sent from heaven,
   for heav'n-born natures meet:
   give us, for thee long pining,
   to eat till richly filled;
   till, earth's delights resigning,
   our every wish is stilled.

2. O water, life-bestowing,
   forth from the Saviour's heart
   a fountain purely flowing,
   a fount of love thou art:
   O let us, freely tasting,
   our burning thirst assuage;
   thy sweetness, never wasting,
   avails from age to age.

3. Jesus, this feast receiving,
   we thee unseen adore;
   thy faithful word believing,
   we take, and doubt no more:
   give us, thou true and loving,
   on earth to live in thee;
   then, death the veil removing,
   thy glorious face to see.

540 Alfred Henry Vine (1845-1917)

1. O Breath of God, breathe on us now,
   and move within us while we pray;
   the spring of our new life art thou,
   the very light of our new day.

2. O strangely art thou with us, Lord,
   neither in height nor depth to seek:
   in nearness shall thy voice be heard;
   Spirit to spirit thou dost speak.

3. Christ is our Advocate on high;
   thou art our Advocate within:
   O plead the truth, and make reply
   to every argument of sin.

4. But ah, this faithless heart of mine!
   The way I know, I know my guide;
   forgive me, O my friend divine,
   that I so often turn aside.

5. Be with me when no other friend
   the mystery of my heart can share;
   and be thou known, when fears
      transcend,
   by thy best name of Comforter.

541

Elizabeth Ann Porter Head (1850-1936)
© *Copyright Control.*

1. O Breath of Life, come sweeping through
   us,
   revive your Church with life and power;
   O Breath of Life, come cleanse, renew us,
   and fit your Church to meet this hour.

2. O Breath of Love, come breathe within us,
   renewing thought and will and heart;
   come, love of Christ, afresh to win us,
   revive your Church in every part!

3. O Wind of God, come bend us, break us,
   till humbly we confess our need;
   then in your tenderness remake us,
   revive, restore – for this we plead.

4. Revive us, Lord; is zeal abating
   while harvest fields are vast and white?
   Revive us, Lord, the world is waiting –
   equip thy Church to spread the light.

542

Timothy Dudley-Smith (b.1926)
© *Timothy Dudley-Smith*

1. O changeless Christ, for ever new,
   who walked our earthly ways,
   still draw our hearts as once you drew
   the hearts of other days.

2. As once you spoke by plain and hill
   or taught by shore and sea,
   so be today our teacher still,
   O Christ of Galilee.

3. As wind and storm their master heard
   and his command fulfilled,
   may troubled hearts receive your word,
   the tempest-tossed be stilled.

4. And as of old to all who prayed
   your healing hand was shown,
   so be your touch upon us laid,
   unseen but not unknown.

5. In broken bread, in wine outpoured,
   your new and living way
   proclaim to us, O risen Lord,
   O Christ of this our day.

6. O changeless Christ, till life is past
   your blessing still be given;
   then bring us home, to taste at last
   the timeless joys of heaven.

543

Reginald Thomas Brooks (1918-1985)
© *1984 Hope Publishing*

1. O Christ the Lord, O Christ the King,
   who wide the gates of death didst fling,
   whose place upon creation's throne
   by Easter triumph was made known,
   rule now on earth from realms above,
   subdue the nations by thy love.

2. Lord, vindicate against our greed
   the weak, whose tears thy justice plead;
   thy pity, Lord, on those who lie
   oppressed by war and tyranny;
   show them the cross which thou didst
      bear,
   give them the power that conquered
      there.

3. Let those whose pride usurps thy throne
   acknowledge thou art Lord alone;
   cause those whose lust wracks
      humankind
   thy wrath to know, thy mercy find;
   make all the rebel world proclaim
   the almighty power of thy blest name.

Continued overleaf

4. So shall creation's bondage cease,
   its pangs of woe give birth to peace;
   and all the earth, redeemed by thee,
   shall know a glorious liberty:
   O haste the time, make short the days,
   till all our cries dissolve in praise!

544 Attributed to John Francis Wade (1711-1786)
trans. Frederick Oakeley (1802-1880)

1. O come, all ye faithful,
   joyful and triumphant,
   O come ye, O come ye to Bethlehem;
   come and behold him,
      born the king of angels:

   O come, let us adore him,
   O come let us adore him,
   O come, let us adore him,
   Christ the Lord.

2. God of God,
   Light of Light,
   lo, he abhors not the Virgin's womb;
   very God, begotten not created:

3. See how the shepherds,
   summoned to his cradle,
   leaving their flocks, draw nigh with lowly
      fear;
   we too will thither bend our joyful
      footsteps:

4. Lo, star-led chieftains,
   Magi, Christ adoring,
   offer him incense, gold and myrrh;
   we to the Christ-child bring our hearts'
      oblations:

5. Child, for us sinners
   poor and in the manger,
   fain we embrace thee, with love and awe;
   who would not love thee, loving us so
      dearly?

6. Sing, choirs of angels,
   sing in exultation,
   sing, all ye citizens of heaven above;
   glory to God in the highest:

7. Yea, Lord, we greet thee,
   born this happy morning,
   Jesu, to thee be glory given;
   Word of the Father, now in flesh
      appearing:

545 Charles Wesley (1707-1788)

1. O come and dwell in me,
   Spirit of power within,
   and bring the glorious liberty
   from sorrow, fear, and sin.

2. The seed of sin's disease,
   Spirit of health, remove,
   Spirit of finished holiness,
   Spirit of perfect love.

3. Hasten the joyful day
   which shall my sins consume,
   when old things shall be passed away,
   and all things new become.

4. I want the witness, Lord,
   that all I do is right,
   according to thy will and word,
   well-pleasing in thy sight.

5. I ask no higher state;
   indulge me but in this,
   and soon or later then translate
   to my eternal bliss.

546 from the 'Great O Antiphons' (12th - 13th century)
trans. John Mason Neale (1818-1866)

1. O come, O come, Emmanuel,
   and ransom captive Israel,
   that mourns in lonely exile here,
   until the Son of God appear.

Rejoice, rejoice!
Emmanuel shall come to thee,
O Israel.

2. O come, thou rod of Jesse, free
thine own from Satan's tyranny;
from depths of hell thy people save,
and give them victory o'er the grave.

3. O come, thou dayspring, come and
cheer
our spirits by thine advent here;
disperse the gloomy clouds of night,
and death's dark shadows put to flight.

4. O come, thou key of David, come
and open wide our heav'nly home;
make safe the way that leads on high,
and close the path to misery.

5. O come, O come, thou Lord of might,
who to thy tribes on Sinai's height
in ancient times didst give the Law,
in cloud and majesty and awe.

547 Henry Ernest Hardy
(Father Andrew S.D.C.) (1869-1946)
© Mowbray/Continuum International

1. O dearest Lord, thy sacred head
with thorns was pierced for me;
O pour thy blessing on my head
that I may think for thee.

2. O dearest Lord, thy sacred hands
with nails were pierced for me;
O shed thy blessing on my hands
that they may work for thee.

3. O dearest Lord, thy sacred feet
with nails were pierced for me;
O pour thy blessing on my feet
that they may follow thee.

4. O dearest Lord, thy sacred heart
with spear was pierced for me;
O pour thy Spirit in my heart
that I may live for thee.

548 Fred Pratt Green (1903-2000)
© 1979 Stainer & Bell Ltd.

1. Of all the Spirit's gifts to me,
I pray that I may never cease
to take and treasure most these three:
love, joy, and peace.

2. He shows me love is at the root
of every gift sent from above,
of every flower, of every fruit,
that God is love.

3. He shows me that if I possess
a love no evil can destroy,
however great is my distress,
then this is joy.

4. Though what's ahead is mystery,
and life itself is ours on lease,
each day the Spirit says to me:
'Go forth in peace!'

5. We go in peace – but made aware
that, in a needy world like this,
our clearest purpose is to share
love, joy, and peace.

549 William Cowper (1731-1800)

1. O for a closer walk with God,
a calm and heavenly frame;
a light to shine upon the road
that leads me to the Lamb.

2. What peaceful hours I once enjoyed,
how sweet their memory still!
But they have left an aching void
the world can never fill.

3. The dearest idol I have known,
whate'er that idol be,
help me to tear it from thy throne,
and worship only thee.

Continued overleaf

4. So shall my walk be close with God,
   calm and serene my frame;
   so purer light shall mark the road
   that leads me to the Lamb.

550 Charles Wesley (1707-1788)

1. O for a heart to praise my God,
   a heart from sin set free;
   a heart that's sprinkled with the blood
   so freely shed for me.

2. A heart resigned, submissive, meek,
   my great Redeemer's throne;
   where only Christ is heard to speak,
   where Jesus reigns alone.

3. A humble, lowly, contrite heart,
   believing, true and clean,
   which neither life nor death can part
   from him that dwells within.

4. A heart in every thought renewed,
   and full of love divine;
   perfect and right and pure and good –
   a copy, Lord, of thine.

5. Thy nature, gracious Lord, impart,
   come quickly from above;
   write thy new name upon my heart,
   thy new best name of love.

551 Charles Wesley (1707-1788)

When the tune 'Lyngham' is used

1. O for a thousand tongues to sing
   my dear Redeemer's praise,
   my dear Redeemer's praise,
   the glories of my God and King,
   the triumphs of his grace,
   the triumphs of his grace,
   the triumphs of his grace!

2. Jesus! the name that charms our fears,
   that bids our sorrows cease,
   that bids our sorrows cease;
   'tis music in the sinner's ears,
   'tis life and health and peace. *(x3)*

3. He breaks the pow'r of cancelled sin,
   he sets the pris'ner free,
   he sets the pris'ner free;
   his blood can make the foulest clean;
   his blood availed for me. *(x3)*

4. He speaks; and, list'ning to his voice,
   new life the dead receive,
   new life the dead receive,
   the mournful broken hearts rejoice,
   the humble poor believe. *(x3)*

5. Hear him, ye deaf; his praise, ye dumb,
   your loosened tongues employ,
   your loosened tongues employ;
   ye blind, behold your Saviour come;
   and leap, ye lame, for joy! *(x3)*

6. My gracious Master and my God,
   assist me to proclaim,
   assist me to proclaim
   and spread through all the earth abroad
   the honours of thy name. *(x3)*

When another tune is used

1. O for a thousand tongues to sing
   my dear Redeemer's praise,
   the glories of my God and King,
   the triumphs of his grace! *(x2)*

2. Jesus! the name that charms our fears,
   that bids our sorrows cease,
   'tis music in the sinner's ears,
   'tis life and health and peace. *(x2)*

3. He breaks the pow'r of cancelled sin,
   he sets the pris'ner free,
   his blood can make the foulest clean;
   his blood availed for me. *(x2)*

4. He speaks; and, list'ning to his voice,
   new life the dead receive,
   the mournful broken hearts rejoice,
   the humble poor believe. *(x2)*

5. Hear him, ye deaf; his praise, ye dumb,
   your loosened tongues employ,
   ye blind, behold your Saviour come;
   and leap, ye lame, for joy! *(x2)*

6. My gracious Master and my God,
   assist me to proclaim,
   and spread through all the earth abroad
   the honours of thy name. *(x2)*

552

Aurelius Clemens Prudentius (348-413)
Trans. John Mason Neale (1818-1866) alt.

1. Of the Father's love begotten,
   ere the worlds began to be,
   he is Alpha and Omega,
   he the source, the ending he,
   of the things that are, and have been,
   and that future years shall see,
   evermore and evermore.

2. At his word they were created;
   he commanded; it was done:
   heaven and earth and depths of ocean
   in their threefold order one;
   all that grows beneath the shining
   of the light of moon and sun,
   evermore and evermore.

3. O that birth for ever blessèd,
   when the Virgin, full of grace,
   by the Holy Ghost conceiving,
   bore the Saviour of our race,
   and the babe, the world's Redeemer,
   first revealed his sacred face,
   evermore and evermore.

4. O ye heights of heaven, adore him;
   angel hosts, his praises sing;
   powers, dominions, bow before him,
   and extol our God and King:
   let no tongue on earth be silent,
   every voice in concert ring,
   evermore and evermore.

5. This is he whom seers and sages
   sang of old with one accord;
   whom the writings of the prophets
   promised in their faithful word;
   now he shines, the long-expected;
   let our songs declare his worth,
   evermore and evermore.

6. Christ, to thee, with God the Father,
   and, O Holy Ghost, to thee,
   hymn and chant and high thanksgiving,
   and unwearied praises be;
   honour, glory, and dominion,
   and eternal victory,
   evermore and evermore.

553

Henry Kirke White (1785-1806) and others

1. Oft in danger, oft in woe,
   onward, Christians, onward go;
   bear the toil, endure the strife,
   strengthened with the bread of life.

2. Onward through the desert night,
   keeping faith and vision bright;
   face the challenge of the hour
   trusting in your Saviour's power.

3. Let not sorrow dim your eye,
   soon shall every tear be dry;
   let not fears your course impede,
   great your strength if great your need.

4. Let your drooping hearts be glad;
   march in faith and honour clad;
   march, nor think the journey long,
   march to hope's eternal song.

5. Onward, then, undaunted, move;
   more than faithful God will prove;
   though the raging waters flow,
   Christian pilgrims, onward go.

554
Michael Perry (1942-1996)
© Mrs B. Perry/Jubilee Hymns

1. O God beyond all praising,
   we worship you today,
   and sing the love amazing
   that songs cannot repay;
   for we can only wonder
   at every gift you send,
   at blessings without number
   and mercies without end:
   we lift our hearts before you
   and wait upon your word,
   we honour and adore you,
   our great and mighty Lord.

2. Then hear, O gracious Saviour,
   accept the love we bring,
   that we who know your favour
   may serve you as our King;
   and whether our tomorrows
   be filled with good or ill,
   we'll triumph through our sorrows
   and rise to bless you still:
   to marvel at your beauty
   and glory in your ways,
   and make a joyful duty
   our sacrifice of praise.

555
Michael Forster (b.1946)
© 2001 Kevin Mayhew Ltd.

1. O God of all creation, most holy One-in-
   Three,
   uniting perfect wholeness with rich
   diversity,
   beyond all human dogmas, above all class
   and race,
   pour out upon your people the riches of
   your grace:
   the love that dares to question, the
   courage to explore,
   the faith to tread where no one but
   Christ has gone before.

2. O God of liberation, who breaks the
   prison bars
   unchain our earthbound spirits to reach
   out for the stars.
   Release us from enslavement in
   narrowness of mind,
   from all that stops us searching for fear
   what we may find.
   Let faith join hands with knowledge, and
   wisdom set us free
   to celebrate with wonder the depths of
   mystery.

556
Charles Wesley (1707-1788)

1. O God of all grace,
   thy goodness we praise;
   thy Son thou hast given to die in our place.
   He came from above
   our curse to remove;
   he hath loved, he hath loved us, because
   he would love.

2. Loved moved him to die,
   and on this we rely;
   he hath loved, he hath loved us: we
   cannot tell why;
   but this we can tell,
   he hath loved us so well
   as to lay down his life to redeem us from
   hell.

3. He hath ransomed our race;
   O how shall we praise
   or worthily sing thy unspeakable grace?
   Nothing else will we know
   in our journey below,
   but singing thy grace to thy paradise go.

4. Nay, and when we remove
   to thy presence above,
   our heaven shall be still to sing of thy love.
   We all shall commend
   the love of our Friend,
   for ever beginning what never shall end.

557 Philip Doddridge (1702-1751) and John Logan (1748-1788) alt.

1. O God of Bethel, by whose hand
   thy people still are fed,
   who through this earthly pilgrimage
   has all our forebears led.

2. Our vows, our prayers, we now present
   before thy throne of grace;
   God of our forebears, be the God
   of their succeeding race.

3. Through each mysterious path of life
   be thou our constant guide;
   give us each day our daily bread,
   and raiment fit provide.

4. O spread thy covering wings around,
   till all our journeys cease,
   and at our Father's loved abode
   our souls arrive in peace.

558 William Vaughan Jenkins (1868-1920)

1. O God our Father, who dost make us one,
   heart bound to heart, in love of thy dear
      Son,
   now as we part and go our several ways,
   touch every lip, may every voice be praise.

2. Praise for the fellowship that here we
      find,
   the fellowship of heart and soul and mind,
   praise for the bonds of love and
      brotherhood,
   bonds wrought by thee, who makest all
      things good.

3. Lord, make us strong, for thou alone dost
      know
   how oft we turn our faces from the foe;
   how oft, when claimed by dark
      temptation's hour,
   we lose our hold on thee, and of thy
      power.

4. Go with us, Lord, from hence; we only ask
   that thou be sharer in our daily task;
   so, side by side with thee, shall each one
      know
   the blessedness of heaven begun below.

559 Isaac Watts (1674-1748) alt.

1. O God, our help in ages past,
   our hope for years to come,
   our shelter from the stormy blast,
   and our eternal home.

2. Beneath the shadow of thy throne,
   thy saints have dwelt secure;
   sufficient is thine arm alone,
   and our defence is sure.

3. Before the hills in order stood,
   or earth received her frame,
   from everlasting thou art God,
   to endless years the same.

4. A thousand ages in thy sight
   are like an evening gone;
   short as the watch that ends the night
   before the rising sun.

5. Time, like an ever-rolling stream,
   will bear us all away;
   we fade and vanish, as a dream
   dies at the op'ning day.

6. O God, our help in ages past,
   our hope for years to come,
   be thou our guard while troubles last,
   and our eternal home.

560 Joachim Lange (1670-1744). Trans. John Wesley (1703-1791)

1. O God, what offering shall I give
   to thee, the Lord of earth and skies?
   My spirit, soul, and flesh receive,
   a holy, living sacrifice:
   small as it is, 'tis all my store;
   more shouldst thou have, if I had more.

Continued overleaf

2. Now, O my God, thou hast my soul,
   no longer mine, but thine I am;
   guard thou thine own, possess it whole,
   cheer it with hope, with love inflame;
   thou hast my spirit, there display
   thy glory to the perfect day.

3. Thou hast my flesh, thy hallowed shrine,
   devoted solely to thy will;
   here let thy light for ever shine,
   this house still let thy presence fill;
   O source of life, live, dwell and move
   in me, till all my life be love!

4. Send down thy likeness from above,
   and let this my adorning be;
   clothe me with wisdom, patience, love,
   with lowliness and purity,
   than gold and pearls more precious far,
   and brighter than the morning star.

5. Lord, arm me with thy Spirit's might,
   since I am called by thy great name;
   in thee let all my thoughts unite,
   of all my works be thou the aim:
   thy love attend me all my days,
   and my sole business be thy praise.

561 John Mason Neale (1818-1866)
© v6:1996 Kevin Mayhew Ltd.

1. O happy band of pilgrims,
   if onward ye will tread,
   with Jesus as your fellow,
   to Jesus as your head.

2. The cross that Jesus carried
   he carried as your due:
   the crown that Jesus weareth
   he weareth it for you.

3. The faith by which ye see him,
   the hope in which ye yearn,
   the love that through all troubles
   to him alone will turn.

4. What are they but forerunners
   to lead you to his sight,
   the longed-for distant dawning
   of uncreated light?

5. The trials that beset you,
   the sorrows ye endure,
   are known to Christ your Saviour,
   whose perfect grace will cure.

6. O happy band of pilgrims,
   let fear not dim your eyes,
   remember, your afflictions
   shall lead to such a prize!

562 Philip Doddridge (1702-1751) alt.

1. O happy day! that fixed my choice
   on thee, my Saviour and my God!
   Well may this glowing heart rejoice,
   and tell its raptures all abroad.

2. 'Tis done, the work of grace is done!
   I am my Lord's, and he is mine!
   He drew me, and I followed on,
   glad to confess the voice divine.

3. Now rest, my long-divided heart,
   fixed on this blissful centre, rest;
   nor ever from thy Lord depart,
   with him of every good possessed.

4. High heaven, that heard the solemn vow,
   that vow renewed shall daily hear;
   till in life's latest hour I bow,
   and bless in death a bond so dear.

*When a tune with a Refrain is used this is
sung after each verse:*

*O happy day! O happy day!
When Jesus washed my sins away,
he taught me how to watch and pray,
and live rejoicing every day;
O happy day! O happy day!
When Jesus washed my sins away.*

563
Charles Wesley (1707-1788)

1. O heavenly King, look down from above;
   assist us to sing thy mercy and love:
   so sweetly o'erflowing, so plenteous the
   store,
   thou still art bestowing, and giving us
   more.

2. O God of our life, we hallow thy name;
   our business and strife is thee to
   proclaim.
   Accept our thanksgiving for creating
   grace;
   the living, the living shall show forth thy
   praise.

3. Our Father and Lord, almighty art thou;
   preserved by thy word, we worship thee
   now;
   the bountiful donor of all we enjoy,
   our tongues, to thine honour, and lives
   we employ.

4. But O above all thy kindness we praise,
   from sin and from thrall which saves the
   lost race;
   thy Son thou hast given the world to
   redeem,
   and bring us to heaven whose trust is in
   him.

5. Wherefore of thy love we sing and
   rejoice,
   with angels above we lift up our voice;
   thy love each believer shall gladly adore,
   for ever and ever, when time is no more.

564
Karl Johann Philipp Spitta (1801-1859)
Trans. Richard Massie (1800-1887)

1. O how blest the hour, Lord Jesus,
   when we can to thee draw near,
   promises so sweet and precious
   from thy gracious lips to hear.

2. Be with us this day to bless us,
   that we may not hear in vain;
   with the saving truths impress us
   which the word of life contain.

3. Open thou our minds, and lead us
   safely on our heavenward way;
   with the lamp of truth precede us,
   that we may not go astray.

4. Make us gentle, meek, and humble,
   and yet bold in doing right;
   scatter darkness, lest we stumble:
   safe our walking in the light.

5. Lord, endue thy word from heaven
   with such light, and love, and power,
   that in us its silent leaven
   may work on from hour to hour.

6. Give us grace to bear our witness
   to the truths we have embraced;
   and let others both their sweetness
   and their quickening virtue taste.

565
Johann Caspar Lavater (1741-1801)
Trans. Elizabeth Lee Smith (1817-1898)

1. O Jesus Christ, grow thou in me,
   and all things else recede;
   my heart be daily nearer thee,
   from sin be daily freed.

2. Each day let thy supporting might
   my weakness still embrace;
   my darkness vanish in thy light,
   thy life my death efface.

3. In thy bright beams which on me fall,
   fade every evil thought;
   that I am nothing, thou art all,
   I would be daily taught.

4. More of thy glory let me see,
   thou holy, wise, and true!
   I would thy living image be,
   in joy and sorrow too.

Continued overleaf

5. Fill me with gladness from above,
   hold me by strength divine!
   Lord, let the glow of thy great love
   through my whole being shine.

6. Make this poor self grow less and less,
   be thou my life and aim;
   O make me daily, through thy grace,
   more meet to bear thy name!

566 John Ernest Bode (1816-1874)

1. O Jesus, I have promised
   to serve thee to the end;
   be thou for ever near me,
   my Master and my friend:
   I shall not fear the battle
   if thou art by my side,
   nor wander from the pathway
   if thou wilt be my guide.

2. O let me feel thee near me:
   the world is ever near;
   I see the sights that dazzle,
   the tempting sounds I hear;
   my foes are ever near me,
   around me and within:
   but, Jesus, draw thou nearer,
   and shield my soul from sin.

3. O let me hear thee speaking
   in accents clear and still,
   above the storms of passion,
   the murmurs of self-will;
   O speak to reassure me,
   to hasten or control;
   O speak and make me listen,
   thou guardian of my soul.

4. O Jesus, thou hast promised,
   to all who follow thee,
   that where thou art in glory
   there shall thy servant be;
   and, Jesus, I have promised
   to serve thee to the end:
   O give me grace to follow,
   my Master and my friend.

5. O let me see thy foot-marks,
   and in them plant mine own;
   my hope to follow duly
   is in thy strength alone:
   O guide me, call me, draw me,
   uphold me to the end;
   and then in heaven receive me,
   my Saviour and my friend.

567 12th Century. Trans. Edward Caswall (1814-1878)

1. O Jesus, King most wonderful;
   thou conqueror renowned,
   thou sweetness most ineffable,
   in whom all joys are found!

2. When once thou visitest the heart,
   then truth begins to shine,
   then earthly vanities depart,
   then kindles love divine.

3. O Jesus, light of all below!
   Thou fount of living fire,
   surpassing all the joys we know,
   and all we can desire.

4. Jesus, may all confess thy name,
   thy wondrous love adore;
   and, seeking thee, themselves inflame
   to seek thee more and more.

5. Thee may our tongues for ever bless,
   thee may we love alone,
   and ever in our lives express
   the image of thine own.

6. Abide with us, and let thy light
   shine, Lord, on every heart;
   dispel the darkness of our night,
   and joy to all impart.

7. Jesus, our love and joy to thee,
   the Father's only Son,
   all might, and praise, and glory be,
   while endless ages run.

568

Michael Forster (b. 1946) based on the German
© 1996 Kevin Mayhew Ltd.

1. O Lamb of God, most holy,
   salvation's perfect sign,
   by your redeeming passion,
   we share the life divine.
   The cost of our deliverance
   in flowing blood is shown,
   and life in all its fullness
   is found in you alone.

2. Upon the cross you carried
   a universe of shame,
   your dying breath atoning
   for centuries of blame.
   So now accept your servant,
   who on your love relied,
   to rest in peace eternal
   redeemed and purified.

3. O draw us to your presence,
   beyond the sundered veil,
   to stand in silent wonder,
   where words and senses fail.
   In fellowship unbroken
   with all who went before,
   we join with saints and angels
   to worship and adore.

569

Philip Brooks (1835-1893) alt.

1. O little town of Bethlehem,
   how still we see thee lie!
   Above thy deep and dreamless sleep
   the silent stars go by.
   Yet in thy dark streets shineth
   the everlasting light;
   the hopes and fears of all the years
   are met in thee tonight.

2. O morning stars, together
   proclaim the holy birth,
   and praises sing to God the King,
   and peace to all the earth;
   for Christ is born of Mary;
   and, gathered all above,
   while mortals sleep, the angels keep
   their watch of wond'ring love;

3. How silently, how silently,
   the wondrous gift is giv'n!
   So God imparts to human hearts
   the blessings of his heav'n.
   No ear may hear his coming;
   but in this world of sin,
   where meek souls will receive him, still
   the dear Christ enters in.

4. O holy child of Bethlehem,
   descend to us, we pray;
   cast out our sin, and enter in,
   be born in us today.
   We hear the Christmas angels
   the great glad tidings tell:
   O come to us, abide with us,
   our Lord Emmanuel.

570

Patrick Appleford
© 1965 Josef Weinberger Ltd.

1. O Lord, all the world belongs to you,
   and you are always making all things new.
   What is wrong you forgive,
   and the new life you give
   is what's turning the world upside down.

2. The world's only loving to its friends,
   but you have brought us love that
        never ends;
   loving enemies too,
   and this loving with you
   is what's turning the world upside down.

Continued overleaf

3. This world lives divided and apart.
   You draw us all together and we start,
   in your body, to see
   that in a fellowship we
   can be turning the world upside down.

4. The world wants the wealth to live
      in state,
   but you show us a new way to be great:
   like a servant you came,
   and if we do the same,
   we'll be turning the world upside down.

5. O Lord, all the world belongs to you,
   and you are always making all things new.
   Send your Spirit on all
   in your Church, whom you call
   to be turning the world upside down.

571 John Greenleaf Whittier (1807-1892)

1. O Lord and Master of us all,
   whate'er our name or sign,
   we own thy sway, we hear thy call,
   we test our lives by thine.

2. Our thoughts lie open to thy sight;
   and, naked to thy glance,
   our secret sins are in the light
   of thy pure countenance.

3. Yet, weak and blinded though we be,
   thou dost our service own;
   we bring our varying gifts to thee,
   and thou rejectest none.

4. To thee our full humanity,
   its joys and pains, belong;
   the wrong of each to each on thee
   inflicts a deeper wrong.

5. Who hates, hates thee; who loves,
      becomes
   therein to thee allied;
   all sweet accords of hearts and homes
   in thee are multiplied.

6. Apart from thee all gain is loss,
   all labour vainly done;
   the solemn shadow of thy cross
   is better than the sun.

7. Our friend, our brother, and our Lord,
   what may thy service be?
   Nor name, nor form, nor ritual word,
   but simply following thee.

8. We faintly hear, we dimly see,
   in differing phrase we pray;
   but, dim or clear, we own in thee
   the Light, the Truth, the Way.

572
v.1: Nicolaus Ludwig von Zinzendorf (1700-1760)
vs.2-4: Johann Nitschmann (1712-1783)
v.5: Anna Nitschmann (1715-1760)
trans. John Wesley (1703-1791)

1. O Lord, enlarge our scanty thought
   to know the wonders thou hast wrought;
   unloose our stammering tongues, to tell
   thy love immense, unsearchable.

2. What are our works but sin and death,
   till thou thy quickening Spirit breathe?
   Thou giv'st the power thy grace to move:
   O wondrous grace! O boundless love!

3. How can it be, thou heavenly King,
   that thou shouldst us to glory bring;
   make slaves the partners of thy throne,
   decked with a never-fading crown?

4. Hence our hearts melt, our eyes o'erflow,
   our words are lost; nor will we know,
   nor will we think of aught beside,
   my Lord, my Love is crucified!

5. First-born of many brethren thou;
   to thee, lo! all our souls we bow;
   to thee our hearts and hands we give;
   thine may we die, thine may we live!

573 Taizé Community
© Ateliers et Presses de Taizé

O Lord, hear my prayer,
O Lord, hear my prayer:
when I call answer me.
O Lord, hear my prayer,
O Lord, hear my prayer.
Come and listen to me.

574 Karl Boberg (1859-1940)
trans. Stuart K. Hine (1899-1989)
© 1953 Stuart K. Hine
Published by Kingsway's Thankyou Music

1. O Lord, my God,
   when I in awesome wonder
   consider all the works
   thy hand has made,
   I see the stars,
   I hear the rolling thunder,
   thy pow'r throughout
   the universe displayed.

   Then sings my soul,
   my Saviour God, to thee:
   how great thou art, how great thou art.
   Then sings my soul,
   my Saviour God, to thee;
   how great thou art, how great thou art.

2. When through the woods
   and forest glades I wander
   and hear the birds sing
   sweetly in the trees;
   when I look down
   from lofty mountain grandeur,
   and hear the brook,
   and feel the gentle breeze.

3. And when I think that God,
   his Son not sparing,
   sent him to die,
   I scarce can take it in
   that on the cross,
   my burden gladly bearing,
   he bled and died
   to take away my sin.

4. When Christ shall come
   with shout of acclamation
   and take me home,
   what joy shall fill my heart;
   when I shall bow
   in humble adoration,
   and there proclaim:
   my God, how great thou art.

575 Robert Wilfrid Callin (1886-1951)
© The Trustees for Methodist Church Purposes.

1. O Lord of every lovely thing,
   the maker of them all,
   who from the winter's gloomy wing
   dost shed the splendours of the spring,
   on thy great name we call.

2. With flowers that through the valleys
      teach
   thy love and truth divine,
   with streams that sing, and hills that
      preach,
   with waves that laugh on every beach,
   we praise thee we are thine!

3. Not thine alone because from thee
   our life and breath we hold;
   but thine because in Christ we see
   the grace that sets our spirits free,
   and for the truth makes bold.

4. Count us amongst the radiant choir
   that sounds thy name abroad,
   set in our hands the heavenly lyre,
   with songs of love our hearts inspire,
   the mighty love of God.

5. Until with those who toiled and dreamed
      to build thy kingdom here,
   with those the world hath ne'er
      esteemed,
   with all the hosts of thy redeemed,
   we in thy home appear.

576
Christopher Wordsworth (1807-1885)

1. O Lord of heaven and earth and sea,
   to thee all praise and glory be;
   how shall we show our love to thee,
   who givest all?

2. The golden sunshine, vernal air,
   sweet flowers and fruits thy love declare;
   where harvests ripen, thou art there,
   who givest all.

3. For peaceful homes and healthful days,
   for all the blessings earth displays,
   we owe thee thankfulness and praise,
   who givest all.

4. Thou didst not spare thine only Son,
   but gav'st him for a world undone,
   and freely with that blessèd One
   thou givest all.

5. Thou giv'st the Spirit's blessèd dower,
   Spirit of life, and love, and power,
   and dost his sevenfold graces shower
   upon us all.

6. For souls redeemed, for sins forgiven,
   for means of grace and hopes of heaven,
   Father, all praise to thee be given,
   who givest all.

577
George MacDonald (1824-1905) alt.

1. O Lord of life, thy quickening voice
   awakes my morning song;
   In gladsome words I would rejoice
   that I to thee belong.

2. I see thy light, I feel thy wind;
   earth is thy uttered word;
   whatever wakes my heart and mind,
   thy presence is, my Lord.

3. Therefore I choose my highest part,
   and turn my face to thee;
   therefore I stir my inmost heart
   to worship fervently.

4. Within my heart speak, Lord, speak on,
   my heart alive to keep,
   till comes the night, and labour done,
   in thee I fall asleep.

578
Graham Kendrick (b. 1950)
© 1986 Kingsway's Thankyou Music

O Lord, your tenderness,
melting all my bitterness,
O Lord, I receive your love.
O Lord, your loveliness,
changing all my ugliness,
O Lord, I receive your love.
O Lord, I receive your love,
O Lord, I receive your love.

579
Charles Wesley (1707-1788) alt.

1. O Love divine, what hast thou done!
   The immortal God hath died for me!
   The Father's co-eternal Son
   bore all my sins upon the tree;
   the immortal God for me hath died!
   My Lord, my Love is crucified.

2. Is crucified for me and you,
   to bring us rebels back to God;
   believe, believe the record true,
   we all are bought with Jesu's blood,
   pardon for all flows from his side:
   my Lord, my Love is crucified.

3. Then let us stand beneath the cross,
   and feel his love a healing stream,
   all things for him account but loss,
   and give up all our hearts to him;
   of nothing think or speak beside:
   my Lord, my Love is crucified.

580

15th Century trans. Benjamin Webb (1819-1885)

1. O love, how deep, how broad, how high!
   It fills the heart with ecstasy,
   that God, the Son of God, should take
   our mortal form, for mortals' sake.

2. For us he was baptised, and bore
   his holy fast, and hungered sore;
   for us temptation sharp he knew,
   for us the tempter overthrew.

3. For us he prayed, for us he taught,
   for us his daily works he wrought:
   by words and signs and actions thus
   still seeking, not himself, but us.

4. For us to wicked men betrayed,
   scourged, mocked, in purple robe
       arrayed,
   he bore the shameful cross and death,
   for us at length gave up his breath.

5. For us he rose from death again;
   for us he went on high to reign;
   for us he sent his Spirit here
   to guide, to strengthen, and to cheer.

6. To him whose boundless love has won
   salvation for us through his Son,
   to God the Father, glory be,
   both now and through eternity.

581

Horatius Bonar (1808-1889)

1. O love of God, how strong and true,
   eternal and yet ever new;
   uncomprehended and unbought,
   beyond all knowledge and all thought!

2. O heavenly love, how precious still,
   in days of weariness and ill,
   in nights of pain and helplessness,
   to heal, to comfort, and to bless.

3. O wide-embracing, wondrous love,
   we read thee in the sky above;
   we read thee in the earth below,
   in seas that swell and streams that flow.

4. We read thee best in him who came
   to bear for us the cross of shame,
   sent by the Father from on high,
   our life to live, our death to die.

5. We read thy power to bless and save
   e'en in the darkness of the grave;
   still more in resurrection light
   we read the fullness of thy might.

6. O love of God, our shield and stay
   through all the perils of our way;
   eternal love, in thee we rest,
   for ever safe, for ever blest!

582

George Matheson (1842-1906)

1. O Love that wilt not let me go,
   I rest my weary soul in thee;
   I give thee back the life I owe,
   that in thine ocean depths its flow
   may richer, fuller be.

2. O Light that follow'st all my way,
   I yield my flick'ring torch to thee;
   my heart restores its borrowed ray,
   that in thy sunshine's blaze its day
   may brighter, fairer be.

3. O Joy that seekest me through pain,
   I cannot close my heart to thee;
   I trace the rainbow through the rain,
   and feel the promise is not vain
   that morn shall tearless be.

4. O Cross that liftest up my head,
   I dare not ask to fly from thee:
   I lay in dust life's glory dead,
   and from the ground there blossoms red
   life that shall endless be.

583 William Vaughan Jenkins (1868-1920)

1. O loving Lord, who art for ever seeking
   those of thy mind, intent to do thy will,
   strong in thy strength, thy power and
     grace bespeaking,
   faithful to thee, through good report and
     ill.

2. To thee we come, and humbly make
     confession,
   faithless so oft, in thought and word and
     deed,
   asking that we may have, in true
     possession,
   thy free forgiveness in the hour of need.

3. In duties small be thou our inspiration,
   in large affairs endue us with thy might;
   through faithful service cometh full
     salvation;
   so may we serve, thy will our chief
     delight.

4. Not disobedient to the heavenly vision,
   faithful in all things, seeking not reward;
   then, following thee, may we fulfil our
     mission,
   true to ourselves, our neighbours, and
     our Lord.

584 Washington Gladden (1836-1918)

1. O Master, let me walk with thee
   in lowly paths of service free;
   teach me thy secret; help me bear
   the strain of toil, the fret of care;
   help me the slow of heart to move
   by some clear winning word of love;
   teach me the wayward feet to stay,
   and guide them in the homeward way.

2. Teach me thy patience; still with thee
   in closer, dearer company,
   in work that keeps faith sweet and strong,
   in trust that triumphs over wrong,
   in hope that sends a shining ray
   far down the future's broadening way,
   in peace that only thou canst give,
   with thee, O Master, let me live!

585 Charles Wesley (1707-1788)

1. Omnipotent Redeemer,
   our ransomed souls adore thee;
   whate'er is done
   thy work we own,
   and give thee all the glory;
   with thankfulness acknowledge
   our time of visitation;
   thine hand confess,
   and gladly bless
   the God of our salvation.

2. Thou hast employed thy servants,
   and blessed their weak endeavours,
   and lo, in thee
   we myriads see
   of practical believers;
   the church of pardoned sinners,
   exulting in their Saviour,
   sing all day long
   the gospel song,
   and triumph in thy favour.

3. Thy wonders wrought already
   require our ceaseless praises;
   but show thy power,
   and myriads more
   endue with heavenly graces.
   But fill our earth with glory,
   and, known by every nation,
   God of all grace,
   receive the praise
   of all thy new creation.

George Bennard (1873-1958)
© The Rodeheaver Co./ Word Music Inc.
Administered by CopyCare

586

1. On a hill far away
stood an old rugged cross,
the emblem of suff'ring and shame;
and I loved that old cross
where the dearest and best
for a world of lost sinners was slain.

So I'll cherish the old rugged cross,
till my trophies at last I lay down;
I will cling to the old rugged cross
and exchange it some day for a crown.

2. O that old rugged cross,
so despised by the world,
has a wondrous attraction for me:
for the dear Lamb of God
left his glory above
to bear it to dark Calvary.

3. In the old rugged cross,
stained with blood so divine,
a wondrous beauty I see.
For 'twas on that old cross
Jesus suffered and died
to pardon and sanctify me.

4. To the old rugged cross
I will ever be true,
its shame and reproach gladly bear.
Then he'll call me some day
to my home far away;
there his glory for ever I'll share.

587

Henry More (1614-1687) alt. John Wesley
(1703-1791)

1. On all the earth thy Spirit shower;
the earth in righteousness renew;
thy kingdom come, and hell's o'erpower,
and to thy sceptre all subdue.

2. Like mighty winds, or torrents fierce,
let it opposers all o'errun;
and every law of sin reverse,
that faith and love may make all one.

3. Yea, let thy Spir't in every place
its richer energy declare;
while lovely tempers, fruits of grace,
the kingdom of thy Christ prepare.

4. Grant this, O holy God and true!
The ancient seers thou didst inspire;
to us perform the promise due;
descend, and crown us now with fire!

588

Cecil Frances Alexander (1818-1895) alt.
© This version 1996 Kevin Mayhew Ltd.

1. Once in royal David's city
stood a lowly cattle shed,
where a mother laid her baby
in a manger for his bed:
Mary was that mother mild,
Jesus Christ her little child.

2. He came down to earth from heaven,
who is God and Lord of all,
and his shelter was a stable,
and his cradle was a stall;
with the needy, poor and lowly,
lived on earth our Saviour holy.

3. For he is our childhood's pattern,
day by day like us he grew;
he was little, weak and helpless,
tears and smiles like us he knew;
and he feeleth for our sadness,
and he shareth in our gladness.

4. And our eyes at last shall see him
through his own redeeming love,
for that child so dear and gentle
is our Lord in heav'n above;
and he leads his children on
to the place where he is gone.

589

Traditional English carol, alt.

1. On Christmas night all Christians sing,
   to hear the news the angels bring,
   on Christmas night all Christians sing,
   to hear the news the angels bring,
   news of great joy, news of great mirth,
   news of our merciful King's birth.

2. Then why should we on earth be so sad,
   since our Redeemer made us glad,
   then why should we on earth be so sad,
   since our Redeemer made us glad,
   when from our sin he set us free,
   all for to gain our liberty?

3. When sin departs before his grace,
   then life and health come in its place,
   when sin departs before his grace,
   then life and health come in its place,
   angels and earth with joy may sing,
   all for to see the new-born King.

4. All out of darkness we have light,
   which made the angels sing this night:
   all out of darkness we have light,
   which made the angels sing this night:
   'Glory to God and peace to men,
   now and for evermore. Amen.'

590

Sydney Carter (b. 1915)
© 1971 Stainer & Bell Ltd.

1. One more step along the world I go,
   one more step along the world I go.
   From the old things to the new
   keep me travelling along with you.

   *And it's from the old
   I travel to the new,
   keep me travelling
   along with you.*

2. Round the corners of the world I turn,
   more and more about the world I learn.
   All the new things that I see
   you'll be looking at along with me.

3. As I travel through the bad and good,
   keep me travelling the way I should.
   Where I see no way to go,
   you'll be telling me the way, I know.

4. Give me courage when the world
       is rough,
   keep me loving though the world
       is tough.
   Leap and sing in all I do,
   keep me travelling along with you.

5. You are older than the world can be,
   you are younger than the life in me.
   Ever old and ever new,
   keep me travelling along with you.

591

John Newton (1725-1807)

1. One there is above all others
   well deserves the name of friend;
   his is love beyond a brother's,
   costly, free, and knows no end;
   they who once his kindness prove
   find it everlasting love.

2. Which of all our friends, to save us,
   could or would have shed his blood?
   But our Jesus died to have us
   reconciled in him to God;
   this was boundless love indeed;
   Jesus is a friend in need.

3. When he lived on earth abasèd,
   friend of sinners was his name;
   now, above all glory raisèd,
   he rejoices in the same;
   still he calls them brethren, friends,
   and to all their wants attends.

4. O for grace our hearts to soften!
   Teach us, Lord, at length to love;
   we, alas, forget too often
   what a friend we have above;
   but when home our souls are brought
   we shall love thee as we ought.

592 Narayan Vaman Tilak (1862-1919)
Trans. Nicol MacNicol (1870-1952)
© Helen MacNichol's Trust.

1. One who is all unfit to count
   as scholar in thy school,
   thou of thy love hast named a friend –
   O kindness wonderful!

2. So weak am I, O gracious Lord,
   so all unworthy thee,
   that e'en the dust upon thy feet
   outweighs me utterly.

3. Thou dwellest in unshadowed light,
   all sin and shame above –
   that thou shouldst bear our sin and
        shame,
   how can I tell such love?

4. Ah, did not he the heavenly throne
   a little thing esteem,
   and not unworthy for my sake
   a mortal body deem?

5. When in his flesh they drove the nails,
   did he not all endure?
   What name is there to fit a life
   so patient and so pure?

6. So, love itself in human form,
   for love of me he came;
   I cannot look upon his face
   for shame, for bitter shame.

7. If there is aught of worth in me,
   it comes from thee alone;
   then keep me safe, for so, O Lord,
   thou keepest but thine own.

593 Charles Coffin (1676-1749)
trans. John Chandler (1806-1876) alt.

1. On Jordan's bank the Baptist's cry
   announces that the Lord is nigh;
   awake, and hearken, for he brings
   glad tidings of the King of kings.

2. Then cleansed be ev'ry breast from sin;
   make straight the way for God within;
   prepare we in our hearts a home,
   where such a mighty guest may come.

3. For thou art our salvation, Lord,
   our refuge and our great reward;
   without thy grace we waste away,
   like flow'rs that wither and decay.

4. To heal the sick stretch out thine hand,
   and bid the fallen sinner stand;
   shine forth and let thy light restore
   earth's own true loveliness once more.

5. All praise, eternal Son, to thee
   whose advent doth thy people free,
   whom with the Father we adore
   and Holy Ghost for evermore.

594 Gerrit Gustafson
*© 1990 Integrity's Hosanna! Music/Kingsway's
Thankyou Music*

Only by grace can we enter,
only by grace can we stand;
not by our human endeavour,
but by the blood of the Lamb.
Into your presence you call us,
you call us to come.
Into your presence you draw us,
and now by your grace we come,
now by your grace we come.

Lord, if you mark our transgressions,
who would stand?
Thanks to your grace we are cleansed
by the blood of the Lamb.
(Repeat)

595

Geoff Baker
© 1998 Daybreak Music Ltd.

1. On the cross, on the cross,
   where the King of Glory died.
   Here is grace, here is love,
   flowing from that wounded side.
   Amazing mystery,
   that he should die for me,
   as a perfect sacrifice.
   On the cross, on the cross,
   love incarnate on the cross.

2. At the cross, at the cross,
   all my sin on Jesus laid.
   Mine the debt, his the cost,
   by his blood the price is paid.
   And through his suffering,
   that fragrant offering,
   arms of love are opened wide.
   At the cross, at the cross,
   there is healing at the cross.

3. To the cross, to the cross,
   Spirit lead me to the cross.
   Bowed in awe at his feet,
   richest gain I count as loss.
   Nothing compares with this,
   to share his righteousness,
   and be called a child of God.
   To the cross, to the cross,
   Spirit lead me to the cross.

596

Charles Wesley (1707-1788)

1. Open, Lord, my inward ear,
   and bid my heart rejoice;
   bid my quiet spirit hear
   thy comfortable voice;
   never in the whirlwind found,
   or where earthquakes rock the place,
   still and silent is the sound,
   the whisper of thy grace.

2. From the world of sin, and noise,
   and hurry I withdraw;
   for the small and inward voice
   I wait with humble awe;
   silent am I now and still,
   dare not in thy presence move;
   to my waiting soul reveal
   the secret of thy love.

3. Thou didst undertake for me,
   for me to death wast sold;
   wisdom in a mystery
   of bleeding love unfold;
   teach the lesson of thy cross:
   let me die, with thee to reign;
   all things let me count but loss,
   so I may thee regain.

4. Show me, as my soul can bear,
   the depth of inbred sin;
   all the unbelief declare,
   the pride that lurks within;
   take me, whom thyself hast brought,
   bring into captivity
   every high aspiring thought
   that would not stoop to thee.

5. Lord, my time is in thy hand,
   my soul to thee convert;
   thou canst make me understand,
   though I am slow of heart;
   thine in whom I live and move,
   thine the work, the praise is thine;
   thou art wisdom, power, and love,
   and all thou art is mine.

597

Robert Cull (b. 1949)
© 1976 Maranatha! Music/CopyCare

Open our eyes, Lord, we want to see Jesus,
to reach out and touch him
and say that we love him;
open our ears, Lord, and help us to listen;
O, open our eyes, Lord,
we want to see Jesus!

598

Dorothy Francis Gurney (1858-1932)
© Copyright control

1. O perfect love,
   all human thought transcending,
   lowly we kneel
   in prayer before thy throne,
   that theirs may be
   the love which knows no ending,
   whom thou for evermore
   dost join in one.

2. O perfect life,
   be thou their full assurance
   of tender charity
   and steadfast faith,
   of patient hope
   and quiet, brave endurance,
   with childlike trust that fears
   not pain nor death.

3. Grant them the joy
   which brightens earthly sorrow,
   grant them the peace
   which calms all earthly strife;
   and to life's day
   the glorious unknown morrow
   that dawns upon
   eternal love and life.

599

Psalm 150

1. O praise God in his holiness:
   praise him in the firmament of his power.

2. Praise him in his noble acts:
   praise him according to his excellent
   greatness.

3. Praise him in the sound of the trumpet:
   praise him upon the lute and harp.

4. Praise him in the cymbals and dances:
   praise him upon the strings and pipe.

5. Praise him upon the well-tuned cymbals:
   praise him upon the loud cymbals.

6. Let everything that hath breath
   praise the Lord!

   Glory be to the Father,
   and to the Son,
   and to the Holy Ghost;
   as it was in the beginning,
   is now, and ever shall be,
   world without end.
   Amen.

600

Henry Williams Baker (1821-1877)
based on Psalms 148 and 150, alt.

1. O praise ye the Lord!
   praise him in the height;
   rejoice in his word, ye angels of light;
   ye heavens, adore him,
   by whom ye were made,
   and worship before him,
   in brightness arrayed.

2. O praise ye the Lord!
   praise him upon earth,
   in tuneful accord, all you of new birth;
   praise him who hath brought you
   his grace from above,
   praise him who hath taught you
   to sing of his love.

3. O praise ye the Lord!
   all things that give sound;
   each jubilant chord re-echo around;
   loud organs his glory
   forth tell in deep tone,
   and, sweet harp, the story
   of what he hath done.

4. O praise ye the Lord!
   thanksgiving and song
   to him be outpoured all ages along:
   for love in creation,
   for heaven restored,
   for grace of salvation,
   O praise ye the Lord!

601

Paul Gerhardt (1607-1676), trans. James Waddell Alexander (1804-1859) and Rupert Eric Davies (1909-1994) © *Mrs Margaret Davies.*

1. O sacred head, sore wounded,
   with grief and pain weighed down,
   how scornfully surrounded
   with thorns, thine only crown!
   How pale art thou with anguish,
   with sore abuse and scorn!
   How does that visage languish
   which once was bright as morn!

2. O Lord of life and glory,
   what bliss till now was thine!
   I read the wondrous story,
   I joy to call thee mine.
   Thy grief and thy compassion
   were all for sinners' gain;
   mine, mine was the transgression,
   but thine the deadly pain.

3. What language shall I borrow
   to praise thee, dearest friend,
   for this thy dying sorrow,
   thy pity without end?
   Lord, make me thine for ever,
   nor let me faithless prove;
   O let me never, never
   abuse such dying love!

4. Be near me, Lord, when dying;
   O show thy cross to me,
   that I, for succour flying,
   my eyes may fix on thee;
   and then, thy grace receiving,
   let faith my fears dispel,
   for whoso dies believing
   in thee, dear Lord, dies well.

602

James Montgomery (1771-1854)

1. O Spirit of the living God,
   in all the fullness of your grace,
   wherever human feet have trod,
   descend upon our fallen race.

2. Give tongues of fire and hearts of love
   to preach the reconciling word;
   anoint with power from heaven above
   whenever gospel truth is heard.

3. Let darkness turn to radiant light,
   confusion vanish from your path;
   those who are weak inspire with might:
   let mercy triumph over wrath!

4. O Spirit of our God, prepare
   the whole wide world the Lord to meet;
   breathe out new life, like morning air,
   till hearts of stone begin to beat.

5. Baptise the nations; far and near
   the triumphs of the cross record;
   till Christ in glory shall appear
   and all the earth declare him Lord!
   Amen.

603

St Ambrose (c.340-c.397)
Trans. John Chandler (1806-1876) and others

1. O splendour of God's glory bright,
   who bringest forth the light from Light;
   O Light, of light the fountain-spring;
   O Day, our days illumining.

2. Come, very Sun of truth and love,
   come in thy radiance from above,
   and shed the Holy Spirit's ray
   on all we think or do today.

3. Teach us to work with all our might;
   put Satan's fierce assaults to flight;
   turn all to good that seems most ill;
   help us our calling to fulfil.

4. O joyful be the livelong day,
   our thoughts as pure as morning ray,
   our faith, like noonday's glowing height,
   our souls undimmed by shades of night.

5. O Christ, with each returning morn
   thine image to our hearts is borne;
   O may we ever clearly see
   our Saviour and our God in thee!

604
Theodore Monod (1836-1921)

1. O the bitter shame and sorrow,
   that a time could ever be
   when I let the Saviour's pity
   plead in vain, and proudly answered:
   All of self, and none of thee!

2. Yet he found me. I beheld him
   bleeding on the accursèd tree,
   heard him pray: Forgive them, Father!
   And my wistful heart said faintly:
   Some of self, and some of thee!

3. Day by day his tender mercy,
   healing, helping, full and free,
   sweet and strong, and, ah! so patient,
   brought me lower, while I whispered:
   Less of self, and more of thee!

4. Higher than the highest heaven,
   deeper than the deepest sea,
   Lord, thy love at last has conquered;
   grant me now my supplication:
   None of self, and all of thee!

605
Samuel Trevor Francis (1834-1925)

1. O the deep, deep love of Jesus!
   Vast, unmeasured, boundless, free;
   rolling as a mighty ocean
   in its fullness over me.
   Underneath me, all around me,
   is the current of thy love;
   leading onward, leading homeward,
   to my glorious rest above.

2. O the deep, deep love of Jesus!
   Spread his praise from shore to shore,
   how he loveth, ever loveth,
   changeth never, nevermore;
   how he watches o'er his loved ones,
   died to call them all his own;
   how for them he intercedeth,
   watcheth o'er them from the throne.

3. O the deep, deep love of Jesus!
   Love of ev'ry love the best;
   'tis an ocean vast of blessing,
   'tis a haven sweet of rest.
   O the deep, deep love of Jesus!
   'Tis a heav'n of heav'ns to me;
   and it lifts me up to glory,
   for its lifts me up to thee.

606
Francis Turner Palgrave (1824-1897)

1. O thou not made with hands,
   not throned above the skies,
   nor walled with shining walls,
   nor framed with stones of price,
   more bright than gold or gem,
   God's own Jerusalem!

2. Where'er the gentle heart
   finds courage from above,
   where'er the heart forsook
   warms with the breath of love,
   where faith bids fear depart,
   City of God, thou art.

3. Thou art where'er the proud
   in humbleness melts down;
   where self itself yields up;
   where martyrs win their crown;
   where faithful souls possess
   themselves in perfect peace.

4. Where in life's common ways
   with cheerful feet we go,
   where in his steps we tread
   who trod the way of woe,
   where he is in the heart,
   City of God, thou art.

5. Not throned above the skies,
   nor golden-walled afar,
   but where Christ's two or three
   in his name gathered are,
   lo, in the midst of them,
   God's own Jerusalem!

607

Charles Wesley (1707-1788) based on Leviticus 6:13

1. O thou who camest from above
   the fire celestial to impart,
   kindle a flame of sacred love
   on the mean altar of my heart.

2. There let it for thy glory burn
   with inextinguishable blaze,
   and trembling to its source return
   in humble prayer and fervent praise.

3. Jesus, confirm my heart's desire
   to work and speak and think for thee;
   still let me guard the holy fire
   and still stir up the gift in me.

4. Ready for all thy perfect will,
   my acts of faith and love repeat,
   till death thy endless mercies seal,
   and make the sacrifice complete.

608

Charles Wesley (1707-1788) based on John 5: 2-9

1. O thou, whom once they flocked to hear;
   thy words to hear, thy power to feel;
   suffer the sinners to draw near,
   and graciously receive us still.

2. They that be whole, thyself hast said,
   no need of a physician have;
   but I am sick, and want thine aid,
   and ask thine utmost power to save.

3. Thy power, and truth, and love divine,
   the same from age to age endure;
   a word, a gracious word of thine,
   the most inveterate plague can cure.

4. Helpless howe'er my spirit lies,
   and long hath languished at the pool,
   a word of thine shall make me rise,
   shall speak me in a moment whole.

5. Make this my Lord's accepted hour;
   come, O my soul's physician thou!
   Display thy justifying power,
   and show me thy salvation now.

609

Charles Wesley (1707-1788) alt.

1. O thou who this mysterious bread
   didst in Emmaus break,
   return, herewith our souls to feed,
   and to thy followers speak.

2. Unseal the volume of thy grace,
   apply the gospel word,
   open our eyes to see thy face,
   our hearts to know the Lord.

3. Of thee communing still, we mourn
   till thou the veil remove;
   talk with us, and our hearts shall burn
   with flames of fervent love.

4. Enkindle now the heavenly zeal,
   and make thy mercy known,
   and give our pardoned souls to feel
   that God and love are one.

610

Harriet Auber (1773-1862)

1. Our blest Redeemer, ere he breathed
   his tender last farewell,
   a Guide, a Comforter, bequeathed
   with us to dwell.

2. He came in tongues of living flame,
   to teach, convince, subdue;
   all-pow'rful as the wind he came,
   as viewless too.

3. He came sweet influence to impart,
   a gracious, willing guest,
   while he can find one humble heart
   wherein to rest.

4. And his that gentle voice we hear,
   soft as the breath of ev'n,
   that checks each fault, that calms each fear,
   and speaks of heav'n.

5. And ev'ry virtue we possess,
   and ev'ry vict'ry won,
   and ev'ry thought of holiness,
   are his alone.

6. Spirit of purity and grace,
   our weakness, pitying, see:
   O make our hearts thy dwelling-place,
   and worthier thee.

611 Traditional Caribbean, based on Matthew 6:9-13 and Luke 11:2-4

1. Our Father, who art in heaven,
   hallowèd be thy name.
   Thy kingdom come, thy will be done,
   hallowèd be thy name. (x2)

2. On earth as it is in heaven.
   hallowèd be thy name.
   Give us this day our daily bread,
   hallowèd be thy name. (x2)

3. Forgive us our trespasses,
   hallowèd be thy name.
   as we forgive those who trespass against us.
   hallowèd be thy name. (x2)

4. Lead us not into temptation,
   hallowèd be thy name.
   but deliver us from all that is evil.
   hallowèd be thy name. (x2)

5. For thine is the kingdom,
      the power, and the glory,
   hallowèd be thy name.
   for ever, and for ever and ever.
   hallowèd be thy name. (x2)

6. Amen, amen, it shall be so.
   hallowèd be thy name.
   Amen, amen, it shall be so.
   hallowèd be thy name. (x2)

612 Albert Frederick Bayly (1901-1984) © Oxford University Press

1. Our Father, whose creative love
   the gift of life bestows,
   each child of earthly union born
   thy heavenly likeness shows.

2. Grant those entrusted with the care
   of precious life from thee,
   thy grace, that worthy of the gift
   and faithful they may be.

3. Teach them to meet the growing needs
   of infant, child, and youth;
   to build the body, train the mind
   to know and love the truth;

4. And, highest task, to feed the soul
   with Christ, the living bread;
   that each unfolding life may grow
   strong in thy paths to tread.

5. These parents need thy wisdom's light,
   thy love within their heart;
   bless thou their home, and for their task
   thy Spirit's grace impart.

613 Charles Wesley (1707-1788) based on Psalm 24: 7-10

1. Our Lord is risen from the dead!
   Our Jesus is gone up on high!
   The powers of hell are captive led,
   dragged to the portals of the sky:
   Alleluia!

2. There his triumphal chariot waits,
   and angels chant the solemn lay:
   lift up your heads, ye heavenly gates;
   ye everlasting doors, give way:
   Alleluia!

3. Loose all your bars of massy light,
   and wide unfold the ethereal scene:
   he claims these mansions as his right;
   receive the King of Glory in!
   Alleluia!

4. Who is this King of Glory, who?
   The Lord, that all his foes o'ercame,
   the world, sin, death, and hell o'erthrew;
   and Jesus is the conqueror's name:
   Alleluia!

Continued overleaf

5. Lo! His triumphal chariot waits,
   and angels chant the solemn lay:
   lift up your heads, ye heavenly gates;
   ye everlasting doors, give way!
   Alleluia!

6. Who is this King of Glory, who?
   The Lord, of glorious power possessed;
   the King of saints, and angels too,
   God over all, for ever blest!
   Alleluia!

614
Martin Luther (1483-1546). Trans. Catherine
Winkworth (1827-1878) based on Psalm 130

1. Out of the depths I cry to thee,
   Lord God! O hear my prayer!
   Incline a gracious ear to me,
   and bid me not despair:
   if thou rememberest each misdeed,
   if each should have its rightful meed,
   Lord, who shall stand before thee?

2. 'Tis through thy love alone we gain
   the pardon of our sin;
   the strictest life is but in vain,
   our works can nothing win;
   that none should boast himself of aught,
   but own in fear thy grace hath wrought
   what in him seemeth righteous.

3. Wherefore my hope is in the Lord,
   my works I count but dust;
   I build not there, but on his word,
   and in his goodness trust.
   Up to his care myself I yield,
   he is my tower, my rock, my shield,
   and for his help I tarry.

4. And though it linger till the night,
   and round again till morn,
   my heart shall ne'er mistrust thy might,
   nor count itself forlorn.
   Do thus, O ye of Israel's seed,
   ye of the Spirit born indeed,
   wait for your God's appearing.

5. Though great our sins and sore our
      wounds,
   and deep and dark our fall,
   his helping mercy hath no bounds,
   his love surpasseth all:
   our trusty loving Shepherd, he
   who shall at last set Israel free
   from all their sin and sorrow.

615
Noel Richards
© 1994 Kingsway's Thankyou Music

1. Overwhelmed by love,
   deeper than oceans, high as the heavens.
   Ever-living God,
   your love has rescued me.

   No one could ever earn your love,
   your grace and mercy is free.
   Lord, these words are true,
   so is my love for you.

2. All my sin was laid
   on your dear Son, your precious One.
   All my debt he paid,
   great is your love for me.

616
Unknown, alt. the editors
© 2001 Kevin Mayhew Ltd.

O what a gift! What a wonderful gift!
Who can tell the wonders of the Lord?
Let us open our eyes, our ears and our
      hearts:
it is Christ the Lord, it is he.

1. In the stillness of the night,
   when the world was asleep,
   the almighty Word was made flesh.
   He came to Mary, he came to us.
   God-with-us in the land of Galilee.
   Christ our Saviour and King!

2. On the night before he died,
   it was Passover night,
   and he drew together his friends.
   He broke the bread, he poured out the
       wine,
   it became his own gift of love and life.
   Christ our Saviour and King!

3. On the hill of Calvary,
   all the world held its breath
   as, for all creation to see,
   God gave his Son, his very own Son,
   in a glory of love for you and me.
   Christ our Saviour and King!

4. In the early morning mist,
   when the guards were asleep,
   he arose in newness of life;
   he conquered death, he overcame sin,
   but the vict'ry he gave to you and me.
   Christ our Saviour and King!

5. At the end, with all his saints,
   we shall come before God,
   dance and sing in worship and praise,
   for in our midst, for all to behold,
   Christ will stand as our Saviour and
       King.
   Christ our Saviour and King!

617 Charles Wesley (1707-1788)

1. O what shall I do my Saviour to praise,
   so faithful and true, so plenteous in
       grace,
   so strong to deliver, so good to redeem
   the weakest believer that hangs upon
       him!

2. How happy the man whose heart is set
       free,
   the people that can be joyful in thee;
   their joy is to walk in the light of thy
       face,
   and still they are talking of Jesus's grace.

3. Their daily delight shall be in thy name;
   they shall as their right thy righteousness
       claim;
   thy righteousness wearing, and cleansed
   by thy blood,
   bold shall they appear in the presence of
       God.

4. For thou art their boast, their glory and
       power;
   and I also trust to see the glad hour,
   my soul's new creation, a life from the
       dead,
   the day of salvation, that lifts up my
       head.

618 William Walsham How (1823-1897)

1. O word of God incarnate,
   O wisdom from on high,
   O truth unchanged, unchanging,
   O light of our dark sky,
   we praise thee for the radiance
   that from the hallowed page,
   a lantern to our footsteps,
   shines on from age to age.

2. The Church from her dear Master
   received the gift divine,
   and still that light she lifteth,
   o'er all the earth to shine;
   it is the precious treasury
   where gems of truth are stored;
   it is the heaven-drawn picture
   of Christ, the living Word.

3. It floateth like a banner
   before God's host unfurled;
   it shineth like a beacon
   above the shadowed world;
   it is the chart and compass
   that, o'er life's surging sea,
   'mid mists, and rocks, and quicksands,
   still guides, O Christ, to thee.

Continued overleaf

4. O make thy Church, dear Saviour,
   a lamp of burnished gold,
   to bear before the nations
   thy true light, as of old;
   O teach thy wandering pilgrims
   by this their path to trace,
   till, clouds and darkness ended,
   they see thee face to face.

619 Robert Grant (1779-1838) based on Psalm 104

1. O worship the King
   all glorious above;
   O gratefully sing
   his pow'r and his love:
   our shield and defender,
   the Ancient of Days,
   pavilioned in splendour,
   and girded with praise.

2. O tell of his might,
   O sing of his grace,
   whose robe is the light,
   whose canopy space;
   his chariots of wrath
   the deep thunder-clouds form,
   and dark is his path
   on the wings of the storm.

3. This earth, with its store
   of wonders untold,
   almighty, thy pow'r
   hath founded of old:
   hath stablished it fast
   by a changeless decree,
   and round it hath cast,
   like a mantle, the sea.

4. Thy bountiful care
   what tongue can recite?
   It breathes in the air,
   it shines in the light;
   it streams from the hills,
   it descends to the plain,
   and sweetly distils
   in the dew and the rain.

5. Frail children of dust,
   and feeble as frail,
   in thee do we trust,
   nor find thee to fail;
   thy mercies how tender,
   how firm to the end!
   Our maker, defender,
   redeemer, and friend.

6. O measureless might,
   ineffable love,
   while angels delight
   to hymn thee above,
   thy humbler creation,
   though feeble their lays,
   with true adoration
   shall sing to thy praise.

620 John Samuel Bewley Monsell (1811-1875)

1. O worship the Lord in the beauty of
      holiness;
   bow down before him, his glory proclaim;
   with gold of obedience and incense of
      lowliness,
   kneel and adore him: the Lord is his
      name.

2. Low at his feet lay thy burden of
      carefulness,
   high on his heart he will bear it for thee,
   comfort thy sorrows, and answer thy
   prayerfulness,
   guiding thy steps as may best for thee be.

3. Fear not to enter his courts in the
      slenderness
   of the poor wealth thou wouldst reckon
      as thine;
   truth in its beauty, and love in its
      tenderness,
   these are the offerings to lay on his shrine.

4. These, though we bring them in
   trembling and fearfulness,
   he will accept for the name that is dear;
   mornings of joy give for evenings of
   tearfulness,
   trust for our trembling, and hope for our
   fear.

5. O worship the Lord in the beauty of
   holiness,
   bow down before him, his glory
   proclaim;
   with gold of obedience and incense of
   lowliness,
   kneel and adore him: the Lord is his
   name.

621
v 1-4: unknown
v 5: © 1999 Kevin Mayhew Ltd.

1. Peace is flowing like a river,
   flowing out through you and me,
   spreading out into the desert,
   setting all the captives free.

   (This refrain is not always sung.)

   Let it flow through me,
   let it flow through me,
   let the mighty peace of God
   flow out through me. (Repeat)

2. Love is flowing like a river,
   flowing out through you and me,
   spreading out into the desert,
   setting all the captives free.

3. Joy is flowing like a river,
   flowing out through you and me,
   spreading out into the desert,
   setting all the captives free.

4. Hope is flowing like a river,
   flowing out through you and me,
   spreading out into the desert,
   setting all the captives free.

5. Christ brings peace to all creation,
   flowing out through you and me,
   love, joy, hope and true salvation,
   setting all the captives free.

622
Kevin Mayhew (b. 1942)
© 1976 Kevin Mayhew Ltd.

1. Peace, perfect peace
   is the gift of Christ our Lord.
   Peace, perfect peace,
   is the gift of Christ our Lord.
   Thus says the Lord,
   will the world know my friends.
   Peace, perfect peace,
   is the gift of Christ our Lord.

2. Love, perfect love . . .

3. Faith, perfect faith . . .

4. Hope, perfect hope . . .

5. Joy, perfect joy . . .

623
Christopher Idle (b.1938)
© Christopher Idle/Jubilate Hymns

1. Powerful in making us wise to salvation,
   witness to faith in Christ Jesus the Word;
   breathed out for all by the life-giving
   Father –
   these are the Scriptures, and thus speaks
   the Lord.

2. Hammer for action and compass for
   travel,
   map in the desert and lamp in the dark;
   teaching, rebuking, correcting and
   training –
   these are the Scriptures, and this is their
   work.

Continued overleaf

3. Prophecy, history, song and
    commandment,
  gospel and letter and dream from on
    high;
  words of the wise who were steered by
    the Spirit –
  these are the Scriptures, on these we rely.

4. Gift for God's servants to fit them
    completely,
  fully equipping to walk in his ways;
  guide to good work and effective
    believing –
  these are the Scriptures, for these we give
    praise!

624 Albert F. Bayly (1901-1984) alt.
© 1988 Oxford University Press

1. Praise and thanksgiving, Father, we offer,
  for all things living you have made good;
  harvest of sown fields, fruits of the
    orchard,
  hay from the mown fields, blossom and
    wood.

2. Lord, bless the labour we bring to serve
    you,
  that with our neighbour we may be fed.
  Sowing or tilling, we would work with
    you;
  harvesting, milling, for daily bread.

3. Father, providing food for your children,
  your wisdom guiding teaches us share
  one with another, so that, rejoicing,
  sister and brother may know your care.

4. Then will your blessing reach ev'ry
    people;
  each one confessing your gracious hand:
  where you are reigning no one will
    hunger;
  your love sustaining fruitful the land.

625 Andy Piercy and Dave Clifton
© 1993 IQ Music Limited

Praise God from whom all blessings flow,
praise him, all creatures here below.
Praise him above, you heav'nly host,
praise Father, Son and Holy Ghost.

Give glory to the Father,
give glory to the Son,
give glory to the Spirit
while endless ages run.

'Worthy the Lamb,' all heaven cries,
'to be exalted thus.'
'Worthy the Lamb,' our hearts reply,
'for he was slain for us.'

626 Thomas Ken (1637-1710)

Praise God, from whom all
    blessings flow,
praise him, all creatures here below,
praise him above ye heav'nly host,
praise Father, Son and Holy Ghost.

627 Unknown

1. Praise him, praise him,
  praise him in the morning,
  praise him in the noontime.
  Praise him, praise him,
  praise him when the sun goes down.

2. Love him, love him, . . .

3. Trust him, trust him, . . .

4. Serve him, serve him, . . .

5. Jesus, Jesus, . . .

628

John Kennett, based on Psalm 150
© 1981 Kingsway's Thankyou Music

Praise him on the trumpet,
the psalt'ry and harp;
praise him on the timbrel and the dance;
praise him with stringed instruments too;
praise him on the loud cymbals,
praise him on the loud cymbals;
let ev'rything that has breath praise
   the Lord!

Hallelujah, praise the Lord;
hallelujah, praise the Lord:
let ev'rything that has breath
praise the Lord!
Hallelujah, praise the Lord;
hallelujah, praise the Lord:
let ev'rything that has breath
praise the Lord!

629

Henry Francis Lyte (1793-1847) based on Psalm 103

1. Praise, my soul, the King of heaven!
   To his feet thy tribute bring;
   ransomed, healed, restored, forgiven,
   who like me his praise should sing?
   Praise him! Praise him!
   Praise him! Praise him!
   Praise the everlasting King!

2. Praise him for his grace and favour
   to our fathers in distress;
   praise him still the same as ever,
   slow to chide and swift to bless.
   Praise him! Praise him!
   Praise him! Praise him!
   Glorious in his faithfulness!

3. Father-like, he tends and spares us;
   well our feeble frame he knows;
   in his hands he gently bears us,
   rescues us from all our foes.
   Praise him! Praise him!
   Praise him! Praise him!
   Widely as his mercy flows!

4. Angels, help us to adore him;
   ye behold him face to face;
   sun and moon, bow down before him,
   dwellers all in time and space.
   Praise him! Praise him!
   Praise him! Praise him!
   Praise with us the God of grace!

630

Henry Williams Baker (1821-1877)

1. Praise, O praise our God and King;
   hymns of adoration sing:

   *for his mercies still endure
   ever faithful, ever sure.*

2. Praise him that he made the sun
   day by day his course to run:

3. And the silver moon by night,
   shining with her gentle light:

4. Praise him that he gave the rain
   to mature the swelling grain:

5. And hath bid the fruitful field
   crops of precious increase yield:

6. Praise him for our harvest-store;
   he hath filled the garner-floor:

7. And for richer food than this,
   pledge of everlasting bliss:

8. Glory to our bounteous King;
   glory let creation sing:
   glory to the Father, Son
   and blest Spirit, Three in One.

631

Henry Francis Lyte (1793-1847)

1. Praise the Lord, his glories show,
   Alleluia!
   saints within his courts below,
   angels round his throne above,
   all that see and share his love.

Continued overleaf

2. Earth to heaven, and heaven to earth,
   tell his wonders, sing his worth;
   age to age and shore to shore,
   praise him, praise him evermore!

3. Praise the Lord, his mercies trace;
   praise his providence and grace,
   all that he for us has done,
   all he sends us through his Son.

4. Strings and voices, hands and hearts,
   in the concert play your parts;
   all that breathe, your Lord adore,
   praise him, praise him evermore!

632 Charles Wesley (1707-1788) based on Psalm 150

1. Praise the Lord who reigns above
   and keeps his court below;
   praise the holy God of love,
   and all his greatness show;
   praise him for his noble deeds,
   praise him for his matchless power:
   him from whom all good proceeds
   let earth and heaven adore.

2. Celebrate the eternal God
   with harp and psaltery,
   timbrels soft and cymbals loud
   in his high praise agree:
   praise him every tuneful string;
   all the reach of heavenly art,
   all the powers of music bring,
   the music of the heart.

3. Him, in whom they move and live,
   let every creature sing,
   glory to their Maker give,
   and homage to their King:
   hallowed be his name beneath,
   as in heaven on earth adored;
   praise the Lord in every breath,
   let all things praise the Lord.

633 vs. 1 and 2: from 'Foundling Hospital Collection' (1796) v. 3: Edward Osler (1798-1863)

1. Praise the Lord, ye heavens, adore him!
   Praise him, angels, in the height;
   sun and moon, rejoice before him,
   praise him, all ye stars and light.
   Praise the Lord, for he hath spoken;
   worlds his mighty voice obeyed:
   laws, which never shall be broken,
   for their guidance he hath made.

2. Praise the Lord, for he is glorious:
   never shall his promise fail.
   God hath made his saints victorious;
   sin and death shall not prevail.
   Praise the God of our salvation,
   hosts on high, his power proclaim;
   heaven and earth and all creation,
   laud and magnify his name!

3. Worship, honour, glory, blessing,
   Lord, we offer to thy name;
   young and old, thy praise expressing,
   join their Saviour to proclaim.
   As the saints in heaven adore thee,
   we would bow before thy throne;
   as thine angels serve before thee,
   so on earth thy will be done.

634 John Henry Newman (1801-1890)

1. Praise to the Holiest in the height,
   and in the depth be praise;
   in all his words most wonderful,
   most sure in all his ways.

2. O loving wisdom of our God!
   when all was sin and shame,
   a second Adam to the fight,
   and to the rescue came.

3. O wisest love! that flesh and blood,
   which did in Adam fail,
   should strive afresh against the foe,
   should strive and should prevail.

4. And that a higher gift than grace
   should flesh and blood refine,
   God's presence and his very self,
   and essence all divine.

5. And in the garden secretly,
   and on the cross on high,
   should teach his brethren, and inspire
   to suffer and to die.

6. Praise to the Holiest in the height,
   and in the depth be praise;
   in all his words most wonderful,
   most sure in all his ways.

635 Medieval Jewish Doxology. Trans. Max Landsberg (1945-1928) and Newton Mann (1836-1926)

1. Praise to the living God!
   All praisèd be his name,
   who was, and is, and is to be,
   for aye the same!
   The one eternal God
   ere aught that now appears:
   the First, the Last, beyond all thought
   his timeless years!

2. Formless, all lovely forms
   declare his loveliness;
   holy, no holiness of earth
   can his express.
   Lo, he is Lord of all!
   Creation speaks his praise,
   and everywhere, above, below,
   his will obeys.

3. His Spirit floweth free,
   high surging where it will:
   in prophet's word he spake of old,
   he speaketh still.
   Established is his law,
   and changeless it shall stand,
   deep writ upon the human heart,
   on sea, on land.

4. Eternal life hath he
   implanted in the soul;
   his love shall be our strength and stay,
   while ages roll.
   Praise to the living God!
   All praisèd be his name,
   who was, and is, and is to be,
   for aye the same.

636 Joachim Neander (1650-1680) trans. Catherine Winkworth (1827-1878)

1. Praise to the Lord,
   the Almighty, the King of creation!
   O my soul, praise him,
   for he is thy health and salvation.
   All ye who hear,
   now to his temple draw near;
   joining in glad adoration.

2. Praise to the Lord,
   who o'er all things so wondrously reigneth,
   shieldeth thee gently from harm,
   or when fainting sustaineth:
   hast thou not seen
   how thy heart's wishes have been
   granted in what he ordaineth?

3. Praise to the Lord,
   who doth prosper thy work and defend thee,
   surely his goodness and mercy
   shall daily attend thee:
   ponder anew
   what the Almighty can do,
   if to the end he befriend thee.

4. Praise to the Lord,
   O let all that is in us adore him!
   All that hath life and breath,
   come now with praises before him.
   Let the 'Amen'
   sound from his people again,
   gladly for ay we adore him.

637

Isaac Watts (1674-1748) based on Psalm 147

1. Praise ye the Lord! 'Tis good to raise
   our hearts and voices in his praise;
   his nature and his works invite
   to make this duty our delight.

2. He formed the stars, those heavenly
   flames,
   he counts their numbers, calls their
   names;
   his wisdom's vast, and knows no bound,
   a deep where all our thoughts are
   drowned.

3. Sing to the Lord! Exalt him high,
   who spreads his clouds along the sky;
   there he prepares the fruitful rain,
   nor lets the drops descend in vain.

4. He makes the grass the hills adorn,
   and clothes the smiling fields with corn;
   the beasts with food his hands supply,
   and the young ravens when they cry.

5. What is the creature's skill or force?
   The sprightly man, or warlike horse?
   The piercing wit, the active limb?
   All are too mean delights for him.

6. But saints are lovely in his sight,
   he views his children with delight;
   he sees their hope, he knows their fear,
   and looks, and loves his image there.

638

James Montgomery (1771-1854)

1. Prayer is the soul's sincere desire,
   uttered or unexpressed,
   the motion of a hidden fire
   that trembles in the breast.

2. Prayer is the burden of a sigh,
   the falling of a tear,
   the upward glancing of an eye
   when none but God is near.

3. Prayer is the simplest form of speech
   that infant lips can try;
   prayer the sublimest strains that reach
   the majesty on high.

4. Prayer is the contrite sinner's voice
   returning from his ways,
   while angels in their songs rejoice,
   and cry: 'Behold, he prays!'

5. Prayer is the Christian's vital breath,
   the Christian's native air,
   our watchword at the gates of death;
   we enter heaven with prayer.

6. O thou by whom we come to God,
   the Life, the Truth, the Way!
   The path of prayer thyself hast trod:
   Lord, teach us how to pray!

639

Brian Doerksen
© 1990 Mercy/Vineyard Publishing/CopyCare

1. Purify my heart,
   let me be as gold and precious silver.
   Purify my heart,
   let me be as gold, pure gold.

   Refiner's fire,
   my heart's one desire
   is to be holy,
   set apart for you, Lord.
   I choose to be holy,
   set apart for you, my master,
   ready to do your will.

2. Purify my heart,
   cleanse me from within and make me
   holy.
   Purify my heart,
   cleanse me from my sin, deep within.

640
Amos S. Cresswell based on a hymn by Georg Newmark (1621-1681)

1. Put all your faith in God's great goodness
   and hope in him for everyday;
   through all your anguish, pain and
        sadness
   his shadow guards along life's way:
   and if he leads you by the hand
   you never build on shifting sand.

2. When we are lonely and despairing,
   when visions fade and hopes are dim,
   he comes, our depths of sorrow sharing,
   invites our faith to turn to him;
   he never will forsake his child;
   his hold is firm though storms are wild.

3. Our Lord is present in our weakness,
   for this he left his heavenly throne.
   His power and strength lie in his
        meekness,
   'You will not agonise alone;
   I drank the bitter cup for you;
   my crucifixion proves this true.'

4. Sing, pray and tell the mighty story;
   God comes to us in vibrant Word.
   The wonder of the heavenly glory
   is seen by us in Christ, our Lord.
   Our God has never left in need
   a soul who trusted him indeed.

641
Fred Kaan (b. 1929)
© 1989 Stainer & Bell Ltd.

1. Put peace into each other's hands
   and like a treasure hold it,
   protect it like a candle-flame,
   with tenderness enfold it.

2. Put peace into each other's hands
   with loving expectation;
   be gentle in your words and ways,
   in touch with God's creation.

3. Put peace into each other's hands
   like bread we break for sharing;
   look people warmly in the eye:
   our life is meant for caring.

4. As at communion, shape your hands
   into a waiting cradle;
   the gift of Christ receive, revere,
   united round the table.

5. Put Christ into each other's hands,
   he is love's deepest measure;
   in love make peace, give peace a chance,
   and share it like a treasure.

642
Luke Connaughton (1917-1979)

1. Reap me the earth as a harvest to God,
   gather and bring it again,
   all that is his, to the Maker of all;
   lift it and offer it high:

   Bring bread, bring wine,
   give glory to the Lord;
   whose is the earth but God's,
   whose is the praise but his?

2. Go with your song and your music, with
        joy,
   go the the altar of God;
   carry your offerings, fruits of the earth,
   work of your labouring hands:

3. Gladness and pity and passion and pain,
   all that is ours and must die –
   lay all before him, return him his gift,
   God, to whom all shall go home:

643
Horatius Bonar (1808-1889)

1. Rejoice and be glad! The Redeemer
        hath come:
   go, look on his cradle, his cross, and
        his tomb:

Continued overleaf

Sound his praises, tell the story of him who
was slain,
sound his praises, tell with gladness he
liveth again.

2. Rejoice and be glad! For the Lamb that
was slain,
o'er death is triumphant, and liveth again:

3. Rejoice and be glad! Now the pardon
is free;
the just for the unjust hath died on
the tree:

4. Rejoice and be glad! For our King is
on high;
he pleadeth for us on his throne in
the sky:

5. Rejoice and be glad! For he cometh again;
he cometh in glory, the Lamb that
was slain:

644 Charles Wesley (1707-1788)

1. Rejoice the Lord is King!
Your Lord and King adore;
mortals, give thanks and sing,
and triumph evermore.

Lift up your heart, lift up your voice;
rejoice, again I say, rejoice.

2. Jesus the Saviour reigns,
the God of truth and love;
when he had purged our stains,
he took his seat above.

3. His kingdom cannot fail;
he rules o'er earth and heav'n;
the keys of death and hell
are to our Jesus giv'n.

4. He sits at God's right hand
till all his foes submit,
and bow to his command,
and fall beneath his feet.

645 Albert F. Bayly (1901-1984)
© Oxford University Press

1. Rejoice, the Lord of life ascends
in triumph from earth's battlefield:
his strife with human hatred ends,
as sin and death their conquests yield.

2. No more his mortal form we see;
he reigns invisible but near:
for in the midst of two or three
he makes his glorious presence clear.

3. He reigns, but with a love that shares
the troubles of our earthly life;
he takes upon his heart the cares,
the pain, and shame of human strife.

4. He reigns in heaven until the hour
when he, who once was crucified,
shall come in all love's glorious power
to rule the world for which he died.

646 Graham Kendrick (b. 1950) and Chris Rolinson
© 1981 Kingsway's Thankyou Music

1. Restore, O Lord,
the honour of your name,
in works of sov'reign power
come shake the earth again,
that all may see,
and come with rev'rent fear
to the living God,
whose kingdom shall outlast the years.

2. Restore, O Lord,
in all the earth your fame,
and in our time revive
the church that bears your name.
And in your anger,
Lord, remember mercy,
O living God,
whose mercy shall outlast the years.

3. Bend us, O Lord,
   where we are hard and cold,
   in your refiner's fire:
   come purify the gold.
   Though suff'ring comes
   and evil crouches near,
   still our living God
   is reigning, he is reigning here.

4. *As verse 1*

647 Albert Midlane (1825-1909)

1. Revive thy work, O Lord;
   thy mighty arm make bare;
   speak with the voice that wakes the dead,
   and make thy people hear:

   Revive thy work, O Lord,
   while here to thee we bow;
   descend, O gracious Lord, descend!
   O come and bless us now.

2. Revive thy work, O Lord;
   now let us thirst for thee;
   and hungering for the bread of life
   may all our spirits be:

3. Revive thy work, O Lord;
   exalt thy precious name;
   and, by the Holy Ghost, our love
   for thee and thine inflame:

4. Revive thy work, O Lord;
   give power unto thy word;
   grant that thy blessèd gospel may
   in living faith be heard:

5. Revive thy work, O Lord,
   and give refreshing showers;
   the glory shall be all thine own,
   the blessing, Lord, be ours:

648 William Williams (1717-1791) Trans. G.O. Williams (1913-1990)

1. Ride on, Jesus, all-victorious,
   bear thy sword upon thy side;
   none on earth can e'er withstand thee,
   nor yet hell, for all its pride:
   at thy mighty name tremendous
   every foe is forced to yield;
   hushed in awe, creation trembles:
   come then Jesus, take the field.

2. Rescue now our souls from bondage,
   in thy morn of victory,
   batter down the doors of Babel,
   break the bars and set us free:
   let thy rescued hosts, exulting,
   troop to freedom, wave on wave,
   like the surge of mighty waters:
   O come quickly, come and save!

3. Hark! I hear already, faintly,
   songs of vict'ry from afar,
   where the heirs of thy redemption
   hail thy triumph in the war.
   Clad in robes of shining glory,
   palms of conquest in each hand,
   joyful hosts, to freedom marching,
   enter now the promised land.

649 Henry Hart Milman (1791-1868) alt.

1. Ride on, ride on in majesty!
   Hark all the tribes hosanna cry;
   thy humble beast pursues his road
   with palms and scattered garments
      strowed.

2. Ride on, ride on in majesty!
   In lowly pomp ride on to die;
   O Christ, thy triumphs now begin
   o'er captive death and conquered sin.

Continued overleaf

3. Ride on, ride on in majesty!
   The wingèd squadrons of the sky
   look down with sad and wond'ring eyes
   to see th'approaching sacrifice.

4. Ride on, ride on in majesty!
   Thy last and fiercest strife is nigh;
   the Father, on his sapphire throne,
   awaits his own appointed Son.

5. Ride on, ride on in majesty!
   In lowly pomp ride on to die;
   bow thy meek head to mortal pain,
   then take, O God, thy pow'r, and reign.

650 Augustus Montague Toplady (1740-1778) alt.

1. Rock of ages, cleft for me,
   let me hide myself in thee;
   let the water and the blood,
   from thy riven side which flowed,
   be of sin the double cure:
   cleanse me from its guilt and pow'r.

2. Not the labours of my hands
   can fulfil thy law's demands;
   could my zeal no respite know,
   could my tears for ever flow,
   all for sin could not atone:
   thou must save, and thou alone.

3. Nothing in my hands I bring,
   simply to thy cross I cling;
   naked, come to thee for dress;
   helpless, look to thee for grace;
   tainted, to the fountain fly;
   wash me, Saviour, or I die.

4. While I draw this fleeting breath,
   when mine eyelids close in death,
   when I soar through tracts unknown,
   see thee on thy judgement throne;
   Rock of ages, cleft for me,
   let me hide myself in thee.

651 Adrian Howard and Pat Turner
© 1985 Restoration Music Ltd./Sovereign Music UK

1. Salvation belongs to our God,
   who sits on the throne,
   and to the Lamb.
   Praise and glory, wisdom and thanks,
   honour and power and strength.

   Be to our God for ever and ever,
   be to our God for ever and ever,
   be to our God for ever and ever. Amen.

2. And we, the redeemed, shall be strong
   in purpose and unity,
   declaring aloud,
   praise and glory, wisdom and thanks,
   honour and power and strength.

652 John Ellerton (1826-1893)

1. Saviour, again
   to thy dear name we raise
   with one accord
   our parting hymn of praise;
   we stand to bless thee
   ere our worship cease;
   then, lowly kneeling,
   wait thy word of peace.

2. Grant us thy peace
   upon our homeward way;
   with thee began,
   with thee shall end, the day:
   guard thou the lips from sin,
   the hearts from shame,
   that in this house
   have called upon thy name.

3. Grant us thy peace,
   Lord, through the coming night;
   turn thou for us
   its darkness into light;
   from harm and danger
   keep thy children free,
   for dark and light
   are both alike to thee.

4. Grant us thy peace
   throughout our earthly life,
   our balm in sorrow,
   and our stay in strife;
   then, when thy voice
   shall bid our conflict cease,
   call us, O Lord,
   to thine eternal peace.

653 Charles Wesley (1707-1788) alt.

1. Saviour, and can it be
   that thou shouldst dwell with me?
   From thy high and lofty throne,
   throne of everlasting bliss,
   will thy majesty stoop down
   to so mean a house as this?

2. I am not worthy, Lord,
   so wretched, self-abhorred,
   thee, my God, to entertain
   in this poor polluted heart:
   I so frail and full of sin
   all my nature cries: 'Depart!'

3. Yet come, thou heavenly guest,
   and purify my breast;
   come, thou great and glorious King,
   while before thy cross I bow;
   with thyself salvation bring,
   cleanse the house by entering now.

654 Godfrey Thring (1823-1903)

1. Saviour, blessèd Saviour,
   listen while we sing;
   hearts and voices raising
   praises to our King:
   all we have we offer,
   all we hope to be,
   body, soul, and spirit,
   all we yield to thee.

2. Nearer, ever nearer,
   Christ, we draw to thee,
   deep in adoration,
   bending low the knee.
   Thou, for our redemption,
   cam'st on earth to die;
   thou, that we might follow,
   hast gone up on high.

3. Clearer still, and clearer,
   dawns the light from heaven,
   in our sadness bringing
   news of sin forgiven;
   life has lost its shadows,
   pure the light within;
   thou hast shed thy radiance
   on a world of sin.

4. Onward, ever onward,
   journeying o'er the road
   worn by saints before us,
   journeying on to God;
   leaving all behind us,
   may we hasten on,
   never looking backward
   till the prize is won.

655 Charles Wesley (1707-1788)

1. Saviour from sin, I wait to prove
   that Jesus is thy healing name;
   to lose, when perfected in love,
   whate'er I have, or can, or am.
   I stay me on thy faithful word:
   the servant shall be as his Lord.

2. Answer that gracious end in me
   for which thy precious life was given;
   redeem from all iniquity,
   restore, and make me meet for heaven:
   unless thou purge my every stain,
   thy suffering and my faith are vain.

Continued overleaf

3. Didst thou not die that I might live
   no longer to myself, but thee,
   might body, soul, and spirit give
   to him who gave himself for me?
   Come then, my Master and my God,
   take the dear purchase of thy blood.

4. Thine own devoted servant claim
   for thine own truth and mercy's sake;
   hallow in me thy glorious name;
   me for thine own this moment take,
   and change, and throughly purify;
   thine only may I live and die.

656 Edward Caswall (1814-1878)

1. See, amid the winter's snow,
   born for us on earth below,
   see, the tender Lamb appears,
   promised from eternal years.

   Hail, thou ever-blessèd morn,
   hail, redemption's happy dawn!
   Sing through all Jerusalem,
   Christ is born in Bethlehem.

2. Lo, within a manger lies
   he who built the starry skies;
   he, who, throned in heights sublime,
   sits amid the cherubim.

3. Say, you holy shepherds, say,
   what your joyful news today?
   Wherefore have you left your sheep
   on the lonely mountain steep?

4. 'As we watched at dead of night,
   there appeared a wondrous light;
   angels, singing peace on earth,
   told us of the Saviour's birth.'

5. Sacred infant, all divine,
   what a tender love was thine,
   thus to come from highest bliss,
   down to such a world as this!

6. Virgin mother, Mary, blest,
   by the joys that fill thy breast,
   pray for us, that we may prove
   worthy of the Saviour's love.

657 Michael Perry (1942-1996)
© 1965 Mrs B. Perry/Jubilate Hymns

1. See him lying on a bed of straw;
   a draughty stable with an open door.
   Mary cradling the babe she bore:
   the Prince of Glory is his name.

   O now carry me to Bethlehem
   to see the Lord of love again:
   just as poor as was the stable then,
   the Prince of Glory when he came!

2. Star of silver, sweep across the skies,
   show where Jesus in the manger lies;
   shepherds, swiftly from your stupor rise
   to see the Saviour of the world!

3. Angels, sing again the song you sang,
   sing the glory of God's gracious plan;
   sing that Bethlehem's little baby can
   be the Saviour of us all.

4. Mine are riches, from your poverty;
   from your innocence, eternity;
   mine, forgiveness by your death for me,
   child of sorrow for my joy.

658 Charles Wesley (1707-1788)

1. See how great a flame aspires,
   kindled by a spark of grace!
   Jesu's love the nations fires,
   sets the kingdoms on a blaze.
   To bring fire on earth he came;
   kindled in some hearts it is:
   O that all might catch the flame,
   all partake the glorious bliss!

2. When he first the work begun,
   small and feeble was his day:
   now the word doth swiftly run,
   now it wins its widening way;
   more and more it spreads and grows
   ever mighty to prevail;
   sin's strongholds it now o'erthrows,
   shakes the trembling gates of hell.

3. Sons of God, your Saviour praise!
   He the door has opened wide;
   he has given the word of grace,
   Jesu's word is glorified;
   Jesus, mighty to redeem,
   he alone the work has wrought;
   worthy is the work of him,
   him who spake a world from nought.

4. Saw ye not the cloud arise,
   little as a human hand?
   Now it spreads along the skies,
   hangs o'er all the thirsty land:
   lo, the promise of a shower
   drops already from above;
   but the Lord will shortly pour
   all the Spirit of his love!

659 Philip Doddridge (1702-1751)

1. See Israel's gentle Shepherd stand
   with all-engaging charms;
   hark, how he calls the tender lambs,
   and folds them in his arms!

2. 'Permit them to approach,' he cries,
   'nor scorn their humble name;
   for 'twas to bless such souls as these
   the Lord of angels came.'

3. We bring them, Lord, in thankful hands,
   and yield them up to thee,
   joyful that we ourselves are thine;
   thine let our children be.

660 Charles Wesley (1707-1788)

1. See, Jesus, thy disciples see,
   the promised blessing give;
   met in thy name, we look to thee,
   expecting to receive.

2. Thee we expect, our faithful Lord,
   who in thy name are joined;
   we wait, according to thy word,
   thee in the midst to find.

3. With us thou art assembled here;
   but O thyself reveal!
   Son of the living God, appear!
   Let us thy presence feel.

4. Breathe on us, Lord, in this our day,
   and these dry bones shall live;
   speak peace into our hearts, and say:
   'The Holy Ghost receive!'

5. Whom now we seek, O may we meet!
   Jesus the crucified,
   show us thy bleeding hands and feet,
   thou who for us hast died.

6. Cause us the record to receive,
   speak, and the tokens show:
   'O be not faithless, but believe
   in me, who died for you!'

661 v. 1: Karen Lafferty (b. 1948), vs. 2 and 3: unknown, based on Matthew 6:33; 7:7
© 1972 Maranatha! Music/CopyCare

1. Seek ye first the kingdom of God,
   and his righteousness,
   and all these things shall be added unto you;
   allelu, alleluia.

   Alleluia, alleluia,
   alleluia, allelu, alleluia.

Continued overleaf

2. You shall not live by bread alone,
   but by ev'ry word
   that proceeds from the mouth of God;
   allelu, alleluia.

   Alleluia, alleluia,
   alleluia, allelu, alleluia.

3. Ask and it shall be given unto you,
   seek and ye shall find;
   knock, and it shall be opened unto you;
   allelu, alleluia.

662 Charles Wesley (1707-1788)

1. Servant of all, to toil for man
   thou didst not, Lord, refuse;
   thy majesty did not disdain
   to be employed for us.

2. Son of the carpenter, receive
   this humble work of mine;
   worth to my meanest labour give,
   by joining it to thine.

3. End of my every action thou,
   in all things thee I see;
   accept my hallowed labour now,
   I do it unto thee.

4. Whate'er the Father views as thine,
   he views with gracious eyes;
   Jesus, this mean oblation join
   to thy great sacrifice.

663 Elise S. Eslinger
© 1983 The Trustees for Methodist Church Purposes.

Shalom to you now, shalom, my friends.
May God's full mercies bless you, my
   friends.
In all your living and through your
   loving,
Christ be your shalom, Christ be your
   shalom.

664 Charles Wesley (1707-1788)
based on Genesis 32: 24-30

1. Shepherd divine, our wants relieve
   in this our evil day,
   to all thy tempted followers give
   the power to watch and pray.

2. Long as our fiery trials last,
   long as the cross we bear,
   O let our souls on thee be cast
   in never-ceasing prayer!

3. Thy Spirit's interceding grace
   give us in faith to claim;
   to wrestle till we see thy face
   and know thy hidden name.

4. Till thou thy perfect love impart,
   till thou thyself bestow,
   be this the cry of every heart:
   I will not let thee go –

5. I will not let thee go, unless
   thou tell thy name to me,
   with all thy great salvation bless,
   and make me all like thee.

6. Then let me on the mountain-top
   behold thine open face,
   where faith in sight is swallowed up,
   and prayer in endless praise.

665 John Ellerton (1826-1893) alt.

1. Shine thou upon us, Lord,
   the world's true light, today;
   and through the written word
   thy very self display;
   that so, from hearts which burn
   with gazing on thy face,
   the little ones may learn
   the wonders of thy grace.

2. Breathe thou upon us, Lord,
   thy Spirit's living flame,
   that so with one accord
   our lips may tell thy name;
   speak thou for us, O Lord,
   in all we say of thee;
   according to thy word
   let all our teaching be.

3. Live thou within us, Lord;
   thy mind and will be ours;
   be thou beloved, adored,
   and served, with all our powers;
   that so our lives may teach
   thy children what thou art,
   and plead, by more than speech,
   for thee with every heart.

666 Joseph Mohr (1792-1848)
trans. John Freeman Young (1820-1885)

1. Silent night, holy night,
   all is calm, all is bright,
   round yon virgin mother and child;
   holy infant, so tender and mild,
   sleep in heavenly peace,
   sleep in heavenly peace.

2. Silent night, holy night.
   Shepherds quake at the sight,
   glories stream from heaven afar,
   heav'nly hosts sing alleluia;
   Christ, the Saviour is born,
   Christ, the Saviour is born.

3. Silent night, holy night.
   Son of God, love's pure light,
   radiant beams from thy holy face,
   with the dawn of redeeming grace:
   Jesus, Lord, at thy birth,
   Jesus, Lord, at thy birth.

667 Michael Forster (b. 1946) based on the Gloria
© 1995, 1999 Kevin Mayhew Ltd.

1. Sing glory to God
   in the height of the heavens,
   salvation and peace to his people on earth;
   our King and our Saviour,
   our God and our Father,
   we worship and praise you
   and sing of your worth.

   Creation unites in the power of the Spirit,
   in praise of the Father,
   through Jesus, the Son.
   So complex, so simple, so clear, so mysterious,
   our God ever three yet eternally one.

2. Lord Jesus, the Christ,
   only Son of the Father,
   the Lamb who has carried our
   burden of shame,
   now seated on high
   in the glory of heaven,
   have mercy upon us who call
   on your name.

3. For you, only you,
   we acknowledge as holy,
   we name you alone as our
   Saviour and Lord;
   you only, O Christ,
   with the Spirit exalted,
   at one with the Father,
   for ever adored.

668 Sabine Baring-Gould (1834-1924)

1. Sing lullaby!
   Lullaby baby, now reclining,
   sing lullaby!
   Hush, do not wake the infant king.
   Angels are watching,
   stars are shining
   over the place where he is lying:
   sing lullaby!

Continued overleaf

2. Sing lullaby!
Lullaby baby, now a-sleeping,
sing lullaby!
Hush, do not wake the infant king.
Soon will come sorrow
with the morning,
soon will come bitter grief and weeping:
sing lullaby!

3. Sing lullaby!
Lullaby baby, now a-dozing,
sing lullaby!
Hush, do not wake the infant king.
Soon comes the cross,
the nails, the piercing,
then in the grave at last reposing:
sing lullaby!

4. Sing lullaby!
Lullaby! is the baby awaking?
Sing lullaby.
Hush, do not stir the infant king.
Dreaming of Easter,
gladsome morning,
conquering death, its bondage breaking:
sing lullaby!

669 Taizé Community, based on Scripture
© Ateliers et Presses de Taizé

Laudate Dominum,
laudate Dominum,
omnes gentes, alleluia. (Repeat)

or

Sing praise and bless the Lord,
sing praise and bless the Lord,
peoples, nations, alleluia. (Repeat)

1. Praise the Lord, all you nations,
praise God all you peoples.
Alleluia.
Strong is God's love and mercy,
always faithful for ever. Alleluia.

2. Alleluia, alleluia.
Let ev'rything living give praise to
the Lord.
Alleluia, alleluia.
Let ev'rything living give praise to
the Lord.

670 Johann Jakob Schütz (1640-1690) vs. 1, 3 and 4:
trans. Frances Elizabeth Cox (1812-1897);
v. 2: Honor Mary Twaites (1914-1993)
verse 2 © Mr Michael Thwaites.

1. Sing praise to God who reigns above,
the God of all creation,
the God of power, the God of love,
the God of our salvation;
with healing balm my soul he fills,
and every faithless murmur stills:
to God all praise and glory!

2. What God's almighty power has made
that will he ever cherish,
and will, unfailing, soon and late,
with loving-kindness nourish;
and where he rules in kingly might
there all is just and all is right:
to God all praise and glory!

3. The Lord is never far away,
but, through all grief distressing,
an ever-present help and stay,
our peace, and joy, and blessing;
as with a mother's tender hand,
he leads his own, his chosen band:
to God all praise and glory!

4. O ye who name Christ's holy name,
give God all praise and glory:
all ye who own his power, proclaim
aloud the wondrous story.
Cast each false idol from his throne,
the Lord is God, and he alone:
to God all praise and glory!

671

Charles Wesley (1707-1788)

1. Sing to the great Jehovah's praise;
   all praise to him belongs;
   who kindly lengthens out our days
   demands our choicest songs.

2. His providence has brought us through
   another various year;
   we all with vows and anthems new
   before our God appear.

3. Father, thy mercies past we own,
   thy still continued care;
   to thee presenting, through thy Son,
   whate'er we have or are.

4. Our lips and lives shall gladly show
   the wonders of thy love,
   while on in Jesus' steps we go
   to see thy face above.

5. Our residue of days or hours
   thine, wholly thine, shall be,
   and all our consecrated powers
   a sacrifice to thee.

672

Isaac Watts (1674-1748) based on Psalm 100

1. Sing to the Lord with joyful voice;
   let every land his name adore;
   the farthest isles shall send the noise
   across the ocean to the shore.

2. Nations, attend before his throne
   with solemn fear, with sacred joy;
   know that the Lord is God alone;
   he can create, and he destroy.

3. His sovereign power, without our aid,
   made us of clay, and formed us men;
   and when like wandering sheep we
   strayed,
   he brought us to his fold again.

4. We are his people, we his care,
   our souls and all our mortal frame;
   what lasting honours shall we rear,
   almighty Maker, to thy name?

5. We'll crowd thy gates with thankful
   songs,
   high as the heavens our voices raise;
   and earth with her ten thousand tongues
   shall fill thy courts with sounding praise.

6. Wide as the world is thy command,
   vast as eternity thy love;
   firm as a rock thy truth must stand
   when rolling years shall cease to move.

673

Charles Silvester Horne (1865-1914)

1. Sing we the King who is coming to reign;
   glory to Jesus, the Lamb that was slain!
   Life and salvation his empire shall bring,
   joy to the nations when Jesus is King:

   Come let us sing: praise to our King,
   Jesus our King: Jesus our King.
   This is our song, who to Jesus belong:
   glory to Jesus, to Jesus our King.

2. All shall be well in his kingdom of peace;
   freedom shall flourish and wisdom increase;
   justice and truth from his sceptre shall
   spring;
   wrong shall be ended when Jesus is King:

3. Souls shall be saved from the burden of sin;
   doubt shall not darken his witness within;
   hell has no terrors, and death has no sting;
   love is victorious when Jesus is King:

4. Kingdom of Christ, for thy coming we
   pray;
   hasten, O Father, the dawn of the day
   when this new song thy creation shall sing:
   Satan is vanquished, and Jesus is King:

674
Charles Wesley (1707-1788)
based on Ephesians 6:10-18

1. Soldiers of Christ, arise,
   and put your armour on,
   strong in the strength which God supplies
   through his eternal Son.

2. Strong in the Lord of hosts,
   and in his mighty pow'r;
   who in the strength of Jesus trusts
   is more than conqueror.

3. Stand then in his great might,
   with all his strength endued;
   and take, to arm you for the fight,
   the panoply of God.

4. To keep your armour bright,
   attend with constant care,
   still walking in your Captain's sight
   and watching unto prayer.

5. From strength to strength go on,
   wrestle and fight and pray;
   tread all the pow'rs of darkness down,
   and win the well-fought day.

6. That, having all things done,
   and all your conflicts past,
   ye may o'ercome, through Christ alone,
   and stand entire at last.

675
William Cowper (1731-1800)

1. Sometimes a light surprises
   the Christian while he sings
   it is the Lord who rises
   with healing in his wings:
   when comforts are declining,
   he grants the soul again
   a season of clear shining,
   to cheer it after rain.

2. In holy contemplation,
   we sweetly then pursue
   the theme of God's salvation,
   and find it ever new.
   Set free from present sorrow,
   we cheerfully can say,
   now let the unknown morrow
   bring with it what it may:

3. It can bring with it nothing
   but he will bear us through;
   who gives the lilies clothing
   will clothe his people too:
   beneath the spreading heavens
   no creature but is fed;
   and he who feeds the ravens
   will give his children bread.

4. Though vine nor fig-tree neither
   their wonted fruit should bear,
   though all the field should wither,
   nor flocks nor herds be there,
   yet, God the same abiding,
   his praise shall tune my voice;
   For, while in him confiding,
   I cannot but rejoice.

676
James Montgomery (1771-1854)

1. Songs of praise the angels sang,
   heaven with alleluias rang,
   when Jehovah's work begun,
   when he spake, and it was done.

2. Songs of praise awoke the morn
   when the Prince of Peace was born;
   songs of praise arose when he
   captive led captivity.

3. Heaven and earth must pass away,
   songs of praise shall crown that day;
   God will make new heavens, new earth,
   songs of praise shall hail their birth.

4. And shall earth alone be dumb
   till that glorious kingdom come?
   No! The church delights to raise
   psalms and hymns and songs of praise.

5. Saints below, with heart and voice,
   still in songs of praise rejoice,
   learning here, by faith and love,
   songs of praise to sing above.

6. Borne upon their latest breath,
   songs of praise shall conquer death;
   then, amidst eternal joy,
   songs of praise their powers employ.

677 Charles Wesley (1707-1788)

1. Son of God, if thy free grace
   again has raised me up,
   called me still to seek thy face,
   and given me back my hope:
   still thy timely help afford,
   and all thy loving-kindness show:
   keep me, keep me, gracious Lord,
   and never let me go!

2. By me, O my Saviour, stand
   in sore temptation's hour;
   save me with thine outstretched hand,
   and show forth all thy power;
   O be mindful of thy word,
   thy all-sufficient grace bestow:
   keep me, keep me, gracious Lord,
   and never let me go!

3. Give me, Lord, a holy fear,
   and fix it in my heart,
   that I may from evil near
   with timely care depart;
   sin be more than hell abhorred;
   till thou destroy the tyrant foe,
   keep me, keep me, gracious Lord,
   and never let me go!

4. Never let me leave thy breast,
   from thee, my Saviour, stray;
   thou art my support and rest,
   my true and living way;
   my exceeding great reward,
   in heav'n above and earth below:
   keep me, keep me, gracious Lord,
   and never let me go!

678 Andrew Reed (1787-1862)

1. Spirit divine, attend our prayers
   and make this house your home;
   descend with all your gracious powers:
   O come, great Spirit, come!

2. Come as the light: to us reveal
   our emptiness and woe,
   and lead us in those paths of life
   where all the righteous go.

3. Come as the fire; and purge our hearts
   like sacrificial flame;
   let our whole life an offering be
   to our Redeemer's name.

4. Come as the dove; and spread your
        wings,
   the wings of peaceful love;
   and let your church on earth become
   blest as the church above.

5. Come as the wind, with rushing sound
   and pentecostal grace,
   that all of woman born may see
   the glory of your face.

6. Spirit divine, attend our prayers;
   make this lost world your home;
   descend with all your gracious powers;
   O come, great Spirit, come!

679

Charles Wesley (1707-1788)

1. Spirit of faith, come down,
   reveal the things of God;
   and make to us the Godhead known,
   and witness with the blood:
   'tis thine the blood to apply,
   and give us eyes to see,
   who did for every sinner die,
   hath surely died for me.

2. No man can truly say
   that Jesus is the Lord,
   unless thou take the veil away,
   and breathe the living word;
   then, only then, we feel
   our interest in his blood,
   and cry, with joy unspeakable:
   'Thou art my Lord, my God!'

3. O that the world might know
   the all-atoning Lamb!
   Spirit of faith, descend, and show
   the virtue of his name;
   the grace which all may find,
   the saving power, impart,
   and testify to all mankind,
   and speak in every heart.

4. Inspire the living faith,
   which whosoe'er receives,
   the witness in himself he hath,
   and consciously believes;
   the faith that conquers all,
   and doth the mountain move,
   and saves whoe'er on Jesus call,
   and perfects them in love.

680

Timothy Dudley-Smith (b.1926)
© Timothy Dudley-Smith.

1. Spirit of God within me,
   possess my human frame;
   fan the dull embers of my heart,
   stir up the living flame.
   Strive till that image Adam lost,
   new minted and restored,
   in shining splendour brightly bears
   the likeness of the Lord.

2. Spirit of truth within me,
   possess my thought and mind;
   lighten anew the inward eye
   by Satan rendered blind;
   shine on the words that wisdom speaks,
   and grant me power to see
   the truth made known to all in Christ,
   and in that truth be free.

3. Spirit of love within me,
   possess my hands and heart;
   break through the bonds of self-concern
   that seeks to stand apart;
   grant me the love that suffers long,
   that hopes, believes and bears,
   the love fulfilled in sacrifice
   that cares as Jesus cares.

4. Spirit of life within me,
   possess this life of mine;
   come as the wind of heaven's breath,
   come as the fire divine!
   Spirit of Christ, the living Lord,
   reign in this house of clay,
   till from its dust with Christ I rise
   to everlasting day.

681

Daniel Iverson (1890-1972)
© 1963 Birdwing Music/EMI Christian Music
Publishing. Administered by CopyCare

1. Spirit of the living God, fall afresh on me.
   Spirit of the living God, fall afresh on me.
   Melt me, mould me, fill me, use me.
   Spirit of the living God, fall afresh on me.

2. Spirit of the living God, fall afresh on us.
   Spirit of the living God, fall afresh on us.
   Melt us, mould us, fill us, use us.
   Spirit of the living God, fall afresh on us.

*When appropriate a third verse may be
added, singing 'on them', for example, before
Confirmation, or at a service for the sick.*

682 Unknown

1. Spirit of wisdom, turn our eyes
   from earth and earthly vanities
   to heavenly truth and love;
   Spirit of understanding true,
   our souls with heavenly light endue
   to seek the things above.

2. Spirit of counsel, be our guide;
   teach us, by earthly struggle tried,
   our heavenly crown to win;
   Spirit of fortitude, thy power
   be with us in temptation's hour,
   to keep us pure from sin.

3. Spirit of knowledge, lead our feet
   in thine own paths, so safe and sweet,
   by angel footsteps trod;
   where thou our guardian true shalt be,
   Spirit of gentle piety,
   to keep us close to God.

4. Through all our life be ever near,
   Spirit of God's most holy fear,
   in our heart's inmost shrine;
   our souls with aweful reverence fill,
   to worship his most holy will,
   all-righteous and divine.

5. So lead us, Lord, through peace or strife,
   onward to everlasting life,
   to win our high reward:
   so may we fight our lifelong fight,
   strong in thine own unearthly might,
   and reign with Christ our Lord.

683 George Osborn Gregory (1881-1972)
© Copyright Control.

1. Spread the table of the Lord,
   break the bread and pour the wine;
   gathered at the sacred board,
   we would taste the feast divine.

2. Saints and martyrs of the faith
   to the cross have turned their eyes,
   sharing, in their life and death,
   that eternal sacrifice.

3. Humbly now our place we claim
   in that glorious company,
   proud confessors of the name,
   breaking bread, O Christ, with thee.

4. By the memory of thy love,
   to the glory of the Lord,
   here we raise thy cross above;
   gird us with thy Spirit's sword.

5. Guided by thy mighty hand,
   all thy mind we would fulfil,
   loyal to thy least command,
   serving thee with steadfast will.

684 James Montgomery (1771-1854)

1. Stand up and bless the Lord,
   ye people of his choice;
   stand up and bless the Lord your God
   with heart and soul and voice.

2. Though high above all praise,
   above all blessing high,
   who would not fear his holy name,
   and laud and magnify?

3. O for the living flame
   from his own altar brought,
   to touch our lips, our mind inspire,
   and wing to heav'n our thought.

4. God is our strength and song,
   and his salvation ours;
   then be his love in Christ proclaimed
   with all our ransomed pow'rs.

5. Stand up and bless the Lord,
   the Lord your God adore;
   stand up and bless his glorious name
   henceforth for evermore.

Cornelius F.A. Krummacher (1824-1884)
Trans. Amos S. Cresswell

1. Star whose light shines o'er me,
   Rock on whom I stand,
   Leader whom I follow,
   staff strong in my hand,
   Bread from whom I live,
   Fount from whom I flow,
   Goal of all my striving,
   all, my Lord, art thou!

2. Courage thou dost give me,
   thou dost strength supply,
   thou wilt lift my burden,
   no one else dare try.
   All my joys will vanish
   Lord, apart from thee
   all my faith will perish –
   Lord, remain near me!

3. So, my Lord, I'll wander
   on this earthly road
   till the trumpet soundeth
   and I'm home with God.
   Then with great rejoicing
   answer I the call
   'I, alone, am nothing;
   Jesus! – He is all'.

686 Samuel Greg (1804-1876)

1. Stay, Master, stay upon this heavenly hill;
   a little longer, let us linger still;
   with all the mighty ones of old beside,
   near to the aweful Presence still abide;
   before the throne of light we trembling
      stand,
   and catch a glimpse into the heav'nly land.

2. Stay, Master, stay! We breathe a purer air;
   this life is not the life that waits us there;
   thoughts, feelings, flashes, glimpses come
      and go;
   we cannot speak them – nay, we do not
      know;
   wrapt in this cloud of light we seem to be
   the thing we fain would grow – eternally.

3. No, saith the Lord, the hour is past, we go;
   our home, our life, our duties lie below.
   While here we kneel upon the mount of
      prayer,
   the plough lies waiting in the furrow there.
   Here we sought God that we might
      know his will;
   there we must do it, serve him, seek
      him still.

687 Spiritual

Steal away, steal away,
steal away to Jesus.
Steal away, steal away home.
I ain't got long to stay here.

1. My Lord, he calls me,
   he calls me by the thunder.
   The trumpet sounds within my soul;
   I ain't got long to stay here.

2. Green trees are bending,
   the sinner stands a-trembling.
   The trumpet sounds within my soul;
   I ain't got long to stay here.

3. My Lord, he calls me,
   he calls me by the lightning.
   The trumpet sounds within my soul;
   I ain't got long to stay here.

688 Charles Wesley (1707-1788) alt.

1. Stupendous height of heavenly love,
   of pitying tenderness divine;
   it brought the Saviour from above,
   it caused the springing day to shine;
   the Sun of Righteousness to appear,
   and gild our gloomy hemisphere.

2. God did in Christ himself reveal,
   to chase our darkness by his light,
   our sin and ignorance dispel,
   direct our wandering feet aright;
   and bring our souls, with pardon blest,
   to realms of everlasting rest.

3. Come then, O Lord, thy light impart,
   the faith that bids our terrors cease;
   into thy love direct my heart,
   into thy way of perfect peace;
   and cheer my soul, of death afraid,
   and guide me through the dreadful shade.

4. Answer thy mercy's whole design,
   my God incarnated for me;
   my spirit make thy radiant shrine,
   my light and full salvation be;
   and through the darkened vale unknown
   conduct me to thy dazzling throne.

689 Graham Kendrick (b. 1950)
© 1988 Make Way Music

1. Such love, pure as the whitest snow;
   such love weeps for the shame I know;
   such love, paying the debt I owe;
   O Jesus, such love.

2. Such love, stilling my restlessness;
   such love, filling my emptiness;
   such love, showing me holiness;
   O Jesus, such love.

3. Such love springs from eternity;
   such love, streaming through history;
   such love, fountain of life to me;
   O Jesus, such love.

690 William Walsham How (1823-1897)

1. Summer suns are glowing
   over land and sea,
   happy light is flowing
   bountiful and free;
   everything rejoices
   in the mellow rays,
   all earth's thousand voices
   swell the psalm of praise.

2. God's free mercy streameth
   over all the world,
   and his banner gleameth
   everywhere unfurled.
   Broad and deep and glorious
   as the heaven above,
   shines in might victorious
   his eternal love.

3. Lord, upon our blindness
   thy pure radiance pour;
   for thy loving-kindness
   make us love thee more;
   and when clouds are drifting
   dark across our sky,
   then, the veil uplifting,
   Father, be thou nigh.

4. We will never doubt thee,
   though thou veil thy light;
   life is dark without thee,
   death with thee is bright.
   Light of light, shine o'er us
   on our pilgrim way;
   go thou still before us
   to the endless day.

691 John Keble (1792-1866)

1. Sun of my soul, thou Saviour dear,
   it is not night if thou be near:
   O may no earth-born cloud arise
   to hide thee from thy servant's eyes.

Continued overleaf

2. When the soft dews of kindly sleep
   my wearied eyelids gently steep,
   be my last thought, how sweet to rest
   for ever on my Saviour's breast.

3. Abide with me from morn till eve,
   for without thee I cannot live;
   abide with me when night is nigh,
   for without thee I dare not die.

4. Watch by the sick; enrich the poor
   with blessings from thy boundless store;
   be ev'ry mourner's sleep tonight
   like infant's slumbers, pure and light.

692 Isaac Watts (1674-1748) based on Psalm 98

1. Sweet is the work, my God, my King,
   to praise your name, give thanks and
       sing;
   to show your love by morning light,
   and talk of all your truth at night.

2. Sweet is the day, the first and best,
   on which I share your sacred rest;
   so let my heart in tune be found,
   like David's harp of joyful sound.

3. My heart shall triumph in the Lord
   and bless his works, and bless his word:
   God's works of grace, how bright they
       shine –
   how deep his counsels, how divine!

4. Soon I shall see and hear and know
   all I desired on earth below
   and all my powers for God employ
   in that eternal world of joy.

693 Frances Ridley Havergal (1836-1879)

1. Take my life, and let it be
   consecrated, Lord, to thee;
   take my moments and my days,
   let them flow in ceaseless praise.

2. Take my hands, and let them move
   at the impulse of thy love;
   take my feet, and let them be
   swift and beautiful for thee.

3. Take my voice, and let me sing
   always, only, for my King;
   take my lips, and let them be
   filled with messages from thee.

4. Take my silver and my gold;
   not a mite would I withhold;
   take my intellect, and use
   ev'ry pow'r as thou shalt choose.

5. Take my will, and make it thine:
   it shall be no longer mine;
   take my heart: it is thine own;
   it shall be thy royal throne.

6. Take my love; my Lord, I pour
   at thy feet its treasure-store;
   take myself, and I will be
   ever, only, all for thee.

694 Charles Wesley (1707-1788) alt.

1. Talk with us, Lord, thyself reveal,
   while here o'er earth we rove;
   speak to our hearts, and let us feel
   the kindling of thy love.

2. With thee conversing, we forget
   all time, and toil, and care;
   labour is rest and pain is sweet,
   if thou, my God, art here.

3. Here then, my God, vouchsafe to stay,
   and bid my heart rejoice;
   my bounding heart shall own thy sway,
   and echo to thy voice.

4. Thou callest me to seek thy face;
   'tis all I wish to seek;
   to attend the whispers of thy grace,
   and hear thee inly speak.

5. Let this my every hour employ,
   till I thy glory see,
   enter into my Master's joy,
   and find my heaven in thee.

695 George Herbert (1593-1633)

1. Teach me, my God and King,
   in all things thee to see;
   and what I do in anything
   to do it as for thee.

2. A man that looks on glass,
   on it may stay his eye;
   or, if he pleaseth, through it pass,
   and then the heav'n espy.

3. All may of thee partake;
   nothing can be so mean
   which, with this tincture, 'For thy sake',
   will not grow bright and clean.

4. A servant with this clause
   makes drudgery divine;
   who sweeps a room, as for thy laws,
   makes that and the action fine.

5. This is the famous stone
   that turneth all to gold;
   for that which God doth touch and own
   cannot for less be told.

696 Graham Kendrick (b. 1950) and Steve Thompson
© 1993 Make Way Music

*Teach me to dance
to the beat of your heart,
teach me to move
in the pow'r of your Spirit,
teach me to walk
in the light of your presence,
teach me to dance
to the beat of your heart.*

*Teach me to love
with your heart of compassion,
teach me to trust
in the word of your promise,
teach me to hope
in the day of your coming,
teach me to dance
to the beat of your heart.*

1. You wrote the rhythm of life,
   created heaven and earth,
   in you is joy without measure.
   So, like a child in your sight,
   I dance to see your delight,
   for I was made for your pleasure, pleasure.

2. Let all my movements express
   a heart that loves to say 'yes',
   a will that leaps to obey you.
   Let all my energy blaze
   to see the joy in your face;
   let my whole being praise you,
   praise you.

697 Katherine Hankey (1834-1911)

1. Tell me the old, old story
   of unseen things above,
   of Jesus and his glory,
   of Jesus and his love.
   Tell me the story simply,
   as to a little child;
   for I am weak, and weary,
   and helpless, and defiled:

   *Tell me the old, old story,
   of Jesus and his love.*

2. Tell me the story slowly,
   that I may take it in –
   that wonderful redemption,
   God's remedy for sin.
   Tell me the story often,
   for I forget so soon;
   the early dew of morning
   has passed away at noon:

Continued overleaf

3. Tell me the story softly,
   with earnest tones and grave;
   remember, I'm the sinner
   whom Jesus came to save.
   Tell me the story always,
   if you would really be
   in any time of trouble
   a comforter to me:

   Tell me the old, old story,
   of Jesus and his love.

4. Tell me the same old story
   when you have cause to fear
   that this world's empty glory
   is costing me too dear.
   And when that next world's glory
   is dawning on my soul,
   tell me the old, old story –
   Christ Jesus makes thee whole!

698 W.H. Parker (1845-1929) alt; v. 6: Ruth Fagg (b.1920) verse 6 © *Copyright Control*

1. Tell me the stories of Jesus
   I love to hear;
   things I would ask him to tell me
   if he were here;
   scenes by the wayside,
   tales of the sea,
   stories of Jesus,
   tell them to me.

2. First let me hear how the children
   stood round his knee;
   and I shall fancy his blessing
   resting on me;
   words full of kindness,
   deeds full of grace,
   all in the love-light
   of Jesus' face.

3. Tell me, in accents of wonder,
   how rolled the sea,
   tossing the boat in a tempest
   on Galilee;
   and how the Master,
   ready and kind,
   chided the billows,
   and hushed the wind.

4. Into the city I'd follow
   the children's band,
   waving a branch of the palm-tree
   high in my hand;
   one of his heralds,
   yes, I would sing
   loudest hosannas,
   Jesus is King!

5. Show me that scene in the garden,
   of bitter pain;
   and of the cross where my Saviour
   for me was slain;
   and, through the sadness,
   help me to see
   how Jesus suffered
   for love of me.

6. Tell me with joy of his rising
   up from the grave;
   and how he still lives triumphant,
   ready to save.
   Wonderful story,
   Jesus my friend,
   living and loving
   right to the end.

699 Timothy Dudley-Smith (b. 1926) based on Luke 1:46-55 © *1961 Timothy Dudley-Smith From 'Enlarged Songs of Praise'. Used by permission*

1. Tell out, my soul, the greatness of the Lord:
   unnumbered blessings, give my
        spirit voice;
   tender to me the promise of his word;
   in God my Saviour shall my heart rejoice.

2. Tell out, my soul, the greatness of
    his name:
  make known his might, the deeds his
      arm has done;
  his mercy sure, from age to age the same;
  his holy name, the Lord, the mighty one.

3. Tell out, my soul, the greatness of
    his might:
  pow'rs and dominions lay their glory by;
  proud hearts and stubborn wills are put
      to flight,
  the hungry fed, the humble lifted high.

4. Tell out, my soul, the glories of his word:
  firm is his promise, and his mercy sure.
  Tell out, my soul, the greatness of
      the Lord
  to children's children and for evermore.

700 Jean Holloway (b. 1939)
© 1994 Kevin Mayhew Ltd.

Thanks for the fellowship found at this meal,
thanks for a day refreshed;
thanks to the Lord for his presence we feel,
thanks for the food he blessed.
Joyfully sing praise to the Lord,
praise to the risen Son,
alleluia, ever adored,
pray that his will be done.
As he was known in the breaking of bread,
now is he known again,
and by his hand have the hungry been fed,
thanks be to Christ. Amen!

701 Reginald Thomas Brooks (1918-1985)
© 1954, renewal 1982 Hope Publishing

1. Thanks to God whose word was spoken
  in the deed that made the earth.
  His the voice that called a nation,
  his the fires that tried her worth.
  God has spoken:
  praise him for his open word.

2. Thanks to God whose word incarnate
  human flesh has glorified,
  who by life and death and rising
  grace abundant has supplied.
  God has spoken:
  praise him for his open word.

3. Thanks to God whose word was written
  in the Bible's sacred page,
  record of the revelation
  showing God to every age.
  God has spoken:
  praise him for his open word.

4. Thanks to God whose word is published
  in the tongues of every race.
  See its glory undiminished
  by the change of time or place.
  God has spoken:
  praise him for his open word.

5. Thanks to God whose word is answered
  by the Spirit's voice within.
  Here we drink of joy unmeasured,
  life redeemed from death and sin.
  God is speaking:
  praise him for his open word.

702 Sabine Baring-Gould (1843-1924),
based on 'Birjina gaztettobat zegoen

1. The angel Gabriel from heaven came,
  his wings as drifted snow, his eyes
      as flame.
  'All hail,' said he,
  'thou lowly maiden, Mary,
  most highly favoured lady.' Gloria!

2. 'For known a blessèd Mother thou
      shalt be.
  All generations laud and honour thee.
  Thy Son shall be Emmanuel,
  by seers foretold,
  most highly favoured lady.' Gloria!

Continued overleaf

3. Then gentle Mary meekly bowed her head.
'To me be as it pleaseth God,' she said.
'My soul shall laud and magnify
his holy name.'
Most highly favoured lady! Gloria!

4. Of her, Emmanuel, the Christ, was born
in Bethlehem, all on a Christmas morn;
and Christian folk throughout
the world will ever say:
'Most highly favoured lady.' Gloria!

703 Fred Pratt Green (1903-2000)
© 1971 Stainer & Bell Ltd.

1. The Church of Christ, in every age
beset by change but Spirit-led,
must claim and test its heritage
and keep on rising from the dead.

2. Across the world, across the street,
the victims of injustice cry
for shelter and for bread to eat,
and never live until they die.

3. Then let the servant Christ arise,
a caring Church that longs to be
a partner in Christ's sacrifice,
and clothed in Christ's humanity.

4. For he alone, whose blood was shed,
can cure the fever in our blood,
and teach us how to share our bread
and feed the starving multitude.

5. We have no mission but to serve
in full obedience to our Lord:
to care for all, without reserve,
and spread his liberating Word.

704 Samuel John Stone (1839-1900)

1. The Church's one foundation
is Jesus Christ, her Lord;
she is his new creation,
by water and the word;
from heav'n he came and sought her
to be his holy bride,
with his own blood he bought her,
and for her life he died.

2. Elect from ev'ry nation,
yet one o'er all the earth,
her charter of salvation,
one Lord, one faith, one birth;
one holy name she blesses,
partakes one holy food,
and to one hope she presses,
with ev'ry grace endued.

3. 'Mid toil and tribulation,
and tumult of her war,
she waits the consummation
of peace for evermore;
till with the vision glorious
her longing eyes are blest,
and the great Church victorious
shall be the Church at rest.

4. Yet she on earth hath union
with God the Three in One,
and mystic sweet communion
with those whose rest is won:
O happy ones and holy! Lord,
give us grace that we
like them, the meek and lowly,
on high may dwell with thee.

705 St John of Damascus (c. 750)
trans. John Mason Neale (1818-1866)

1. The day of resurrection!
Earth, tell it out abroad;
the passover of gladness,
the passover of God!
From death to life eternal,
from earth unto the sky,
our Christ hath brought us over
with hymns of victory.

2. Our hearts be pure from evil,
that we may see aright
the Lord in rays eternal
of resurrection-light;
and list'ning to his accents,
may hear so calm and plain
his own 'All hail' and, hearing,
may raise the victor strain.

3. Now let the heav'ns be joyful,
and earth her song begin,
the round world keep high triumph,
and all that is therein;
let all things, seen and unseen,
their notes of gladness blend,
for Christ the Lord hath risen,
our joy that hath no end.

706 John Ellerton (1826-1893)

1. The day thou gavest, Lord, is ended:
the darkness falls at thy behest;
to thee our morning hymns ascended;
thy praise shall sanctify our rest.

2. We thank thee that thy Church unsleeping,
while earth rolls onward into light,
through all the world her watch
   is keeping,
and rests not now by day or night.

3. As o'er each continent and island
the dawn leads on another day,
the voice of prayer is never silent,
nor dies the strain of praise away.

4. The sun that bids us rest is waking
our brethren 'neath the western sky,
and hour by hour fresh lips are making
thy woundrous doings heard on high.

5. So be it, Lord; thy throne shall never,
like earth's proud empires, pass away;
thy kingdom stands, and grows for ever,
till all thy creatures own thy sway.

707 Robert Bridges (1844-1930) alt. Based on Paul Gerhardt (1607-1676)

1. The duteous day now closes,
each flower and tree reposes,
shade creeps o'er wild and wood:
let us, as night is falling,
on God our maker calling,
give thanks to him, the giver good.

2. Now all the heavenly splendour
breaks forth in starlight tender
from myriad worlds unknown;
and we, the marvel seeing,
forget our selfish being,
for joy of beauty not our own.

3. Awhile our mortal blindness
may miss God's loving-kindness,
and grope in faithless strife;
but when life's day is over
shall death's fair night discover
the fields of everlasting life.

708 From William Sandys' 'Christmas Carols, Ancient and Modern' (1833) alt.

1. The first Nowell the angel did say
was to certain poor shepherds in fields as
   they lay:
in fields where they lay keeping their sheep,
on a cold winter's night that was so deep.

Nowell, Nowell, Nowell, Nowell,
born is the King of Israel!

2. They lookèd up and saw a star,
shining in the east, beyond them far,
and to the earth it gave great light,
and so it continued both day and night.

3. And by the light of that same star,
three wise men came from country far;
to seek for a king was their intent,
and to follow the star wherever it went.

4. This star drew nigh to the north-west,
o'er Bethlehem it took its rest,
and there it did both stop and stay
right over the place where Jesus lay.

5. Then entered in those wise men three,
full rev'rently upon their knee,
and offered there in his presence,
their gold and myrrh and frankincense.

Continued overleaf

6. Then let us all with one accord
sing praises to our heav'nly Lord,
who with the Father we adore
and Spirit blest for evermore.

709

Thomas Olivers (1725-1799)
based on the Hebrew Yigdal, alt.

1. The God of Abraham praise,
who reigns enthroned above,
Ancient of everlasting Days,
and God of love:
Jehovah, great I Am,
by earth and heav'n confessed;
we bow and bless the sacred name,
for ever blest.

2. The God of Abraham praise,
at whose supreme command
from earth we rise, and seek the joys
at his right hand:
we all on earth forsake,
its wisdom, fame and pow'r;
and him our only portion make,
our shield and tow'r.

3. The God of Abraham praise,
whose all-sufficient grace
shall guide us all our happy days,
in all our ways:
he is our faithful friend;
he is our gracious God;
and he will save us to the end,
through Jesus' blood.

4. He by himself has sworn –
we on his oath depend –
we shall, on eagles' wings upborne,
to heav'n ascend:
we shall behold his face,
we shall his pow'r adore,
and sing the wonders of his grace
for evermore.

5. The whole triumphant host
give thanks to God on high:
'Hail, Father, Son and Holy Ghost!'
they ever cry:
Hail, Abraham's God and ours!
We join the heav'nly throng,
and celebrate with all our pow'rs
in endless song.

710

George Herbert (1593-1633) based on Psalm 23

1. The God of love my shepherd is,
and he that doth me feed;
while he is mine and I am his,
what can I want or need?

2. He leads me to the tender grass,
where I both feed and rest;
then to the streams that gently pass:
in both I have the best.

3. Or if I stray, he doth convert,
and bring my mind in frame,
and all this not for my desert,
but for his holy name.

4. Yea, in death's shady black abode
well may I walk, nor fear;
for thou art with me, and thy rod
to guide, thy staff to bear.

5. Surely thy sweet and wondrous love
shall measure all my days;
and, as it never shall remove,
so neither shall my praise.

711

Fred Pratt Green (1903-2000), based on 1 Peter 3: 7
© 1970 Stainer & Bell Ltd.

1. The grace of life is theirs
who on this wedding day
delight to make their vows,
and for each other pray.
May they, O Lord, together prove
the lasting joy of Christian love.

2. Where love is, God abides;
   and God shall surely bless
   a home where trust and care
   give birth to happiness.
   May they, O Lord, together prove
   the lasting joy of such a love.

3. How slow to take offence
   love is! How quick to heal!
   How ready in distress
   to know how others feel!
   May they, O Lord, together prove
   the lasting joy of such a love.

4. And when time lays its hand
   on all we hold most dear,
   and life, by life consumed,
   fulfils its purpose here,
   may we, O Lord, together prove
   the lasting joy of Christian love.

712 Daniel T. Niles (1908-1970)
© *D. Preman Niles, Council for World Mission*

1. The great love of God
   is revealed in the Son,
   who came to this earth
   to redeem everyone.

2. That love, like a stream
   flowing clear to the sea,
   makes clean every heart
   that from sin would be free.

3. It binds the whole world,
   every barrier it breaks,
   the hills it lays low,
   and the mountains it shakes.

4. It's yours, it is ours,
   O how lavishly given!
   The pearl of great price,
   and the treasure of heaven.

713 Thomas Kelly (1769-1855)

1. The head that once was crowned
     with thorns
   is crowned with glory now:
   a royal diadem adorns
   the mighty victor's brow.

2. The highest place that heav'n affords
   is his, is his by right.
   The King of kings and Lord of lords,
   and heav'ns eternal light.

3. The joy of all who dwell above,
   the joy of all below,
   to whom he manifests his love,
   and grants his name to know.

4. To them the cross, with all its shame,
   with all its grace is giv'n;
   their name an everlasting name,
   their joy the joy of heav'n.

5. They suffer with their Lord below,
   they reign with him above,
   their profit and their joy to know
   the myst'ry of his love.

6. The cross he bore is life and health,
   though shame and death to him;
   his people's hope, his people's wealth,
   their everlasting theme.

714 Isaac Watts (1674-1748)

1. The heavens declare thy glory, Lord,
   in every star thy wisdom shines;
   but when our eyes behold thy word,
   we read thy name in fairer lines.

2. The rolling sun, the changing light,
   and night and day, thy power confess;
   but the blest volume thou hast writ
   reveals thy justice and thy grace.

Continued overleaf

3. Sun, moon, and stars convey thy praise
   round this whole earth, and never stand;
   so when thy truth began its race,
   it touched and glanced on every land.

4. Nor shall thy spreading gospel rest
   till through the world thy truth has run;
   till Christ has all the nations blest,
   that see the light or feel the sun.

5. Great Sun of Righteousness, arise,
   bless our dark world with heavenly light:
   thy gospel makes the simple wise;
   thy laws are pure, thy judgements right.

6. Thy noblest wonders here we view,
   in souls renewed, and sins forgiven;
   Lord, cleanse my sins, my soul renew,
   and make thy word my guide to heaven.

715
Emily Chisholm (1910-1991)
© 1972 Stainer & Bell Ltd.

1. The holly and the ivy
   are dancing in a ring,
   round the berry-bright red candles
   and the white and shining King.

2. Oh, one is for God's people
   in every age and day.
   We are watching for his coming.
   We believe and we obey.

3. And two is for the prophets
   and for the light they bring.
   They are candles in the darkness,
   all alight for Christ the King.

4. And three for John the Baptist.
   He calls on us to sing:
   'O prepare the way for Jesus Christ,
   he is coming, Christ the King.'

5. And four for mother Mary.
   'I cannot see the way,
   but you promise me a baby.
   I believe you. I obey.'

6. And Christ is in the centre,
   for this is his birthday,
   with the shining lights of Christmas
   singing: 'He has come today!'

716
Bryn A. Rees (1911-1983)
© Mr. Alexander Scott. Used by permission

1. The kingdom of God
   is justice and joy,
   for Jesus restores
   what sin would destroy;
   God's power and glory
   in Jesus we know,
   and here and hereafter
   the kingdom shall grow.

2. The kingdom of God
   is mercy and grace,
   the captives are freed,
   the sinners find place,
   the outcast are welcomed
   God's banquet to share,
   and hope is awakened
   in place of despair.

3. The kingdom of God
   is challenge and choice,
   believe the good news,
   repent and rejoice!
   His love for us sinners
   brought Christ to his cross,
   our crisis of judgement
   for gain or for loss.

4. God's kingdom is come,
   the gift and the goal,
   in Jesus begun,
   in heaven made whole;
   the heirs of the kingdom
   shall answer his call,
   and all things cry 'Glory!'
   to God all in all.

717

Henry Williams Baker (1821-1877) based on Psalm 23

1. The King of love my shepherd is,
   whose goodness faileth never;
   I nothing lack if I am his
   and he is mine for ever.

2. Where streams of living water flow
   my ransomed soul he leadeth,
   and where the verdant pastures grow
   with food celestial feedeth.

3. Perverse and foolish oft I strayed,
   but yet in love he sought me,
   and on his shoulder gently laid,
   and home, rejoicing, brought me.

4. In death's dark vale I fear no ill
   with thee, dear Lord, beside me;
   thy rod and staff my comfort still,
   thy cross before to guide me.

5. Thou spread'st a table in my sight,
   thy unction grace bestoweth:
   and O what transport of delight
   from thy pure chalice floweth!

6. And so through all the length of days
   thy goodness faileth never;
   good Shepherd, may I sing thy praise
   within thy house for ever.

718

Isaac Watts (1674-1748)

1. The Lord Jehovah reigns;
   his throne is built on high,
   the garments he assumes
   are light and majesty:
   his glories shine with beams so bright,
   no mortal eye can bear the sight.

2. The thunders of his hand
   keep the wide world in awe;
   his wrath and justice stand
   to guard his holy law;
   and where his love resolves to bless,
   his truth confirms and seals the grace.

3. Through all his mighty works
   amazing wisdom shines,
   confounds the powers of hell,
   and breaks their dark designs;
   strong is his arm, and shall fulfil
   his great decrees and sovereign will.

4. And will this sovereign King
   of Glory condescend?
   And will he write his name
   my Father and my Friend?
   I love his name, I love his word –
   join all my powers to praise the Lord.

719

Psalm 23 from 'The Scottish Psalter' (1650)

1. The Lord's my shepherd, I'll not want.
   He makes me down to lie
   in pastures green.
   He leadeth me the quiet waters by.

2. My soul he doth restore again,
   and me to walk doth make
   within the paths of righteousness,
   e'en for his own name's sake.

3. Yea, though I walk in death's dark vale,
   yet will I fear no ill.
   For thou art with me, and thy rod
   and staff me comfort still.

4. My table thou hast furnishèd
   in presence of my foes,
   my head thou dost with oil anoint,
   and my cup overflows.

5. Goodness and mercy all my life
   shall surely follow me.
   And in God's house for evermore
   my dwelling-place shall be.

720
John Milton (1608-1674)
based on Psalms 82, 85 and 86, alt.

1. The Lord will come and not be slow,
his footsteps cannot err;
before him righteousness shall go,
his royal harbinger.

2. Truth from the earth, like to a flow'r,
shall bud and blossom free;
and justice, from her heav'nly bow'r,
bless all humanity.

3. The nations all whom thou hast made
shall come, and all shall frame
to bow them low before thee, Lord,
and glorify thy name.

4. For great thou art, and wonders great
by thy strong hand are done:
thou in thy everlasting seat
remainest God alone.

721
Laurence Housman (1865-1959) alt.
© Oxford University Press.

1. The maker of the sun and moon,
the maker of our earth,
lo! late in time, a fairer boon,
himself is brought to birth.

2. How blest was all creation then,
when God so gave increase;
and Christ, to heal the hearts of men,
brought righteousness and peace.

3. No star in all the heights of heaven
but burned to see him go;
yet unto earth alone was given
his human form to know.

4. His human form, by us denied,
took death for human sin:
his endless love, through faith descried,
still lives the world to win.

5. O perfect Love, outpassing sight,
O Light of every heart,
come down through all the world tonight,
and healing grace impart!

722
John Morrison (1750-1798) based on Isaiah 9:2-7

1. The race that long in darkness pined
has seen a glorious light:
the people dwell in day,
who dwelt in death's surrounding night.

2. To hail thy rise, thou better sun,
the gath'ring nations come,
joyous as when the reapers bear
the harvest treasures home.

3. To us a child of hope is born,
to us a Son is giv'n;
him shall the tribes of earth obey,
him all the hosts of heav'n.

4. His name shall be the Prince of Peace
for evermore adored,
the Wonderful, the Counsellor,
the great and mighty Lord.

5. His pow'r increasing still shall spread,
his reign no end shall know;
justice shall guard his throne above,
and peace abound below.

723
Cecil Frances Alexander (1818-1895) alt.

1. There is a green hill far away,
outside a city wall,
where the dear Lord was crucified
who died to save us all.

2. We may not know, we cannot tell
what pains he had to bear,
but we believe it was for us
he hung and suffered there.

3. He died that we might be forgiv'n,
he died to make us good;
that we might go at last to heav'n,
saved by his precious blood.

4. There was no other good enough
to pay the price of sin;
he only could unlock the gate
of heav'n, and let us in.

5. O, dearly, dearly has he loved,
   and we must love him too,
   and trust in his redeeming blood,
   and try his works to do.

724 Frederick Whitfield (1829-1904)

1. There is a name I love to hear,
   I love to speak its worth;
   its sounds like music in my ear,
   the sweetest name on earth.

   O how I love the Saviour's name,
   O how I love the Saviour's name,
   O how I love the Saviour's name,
   the sweetest name on earth.

2. It tells me of a Saviour's love,
   who died to set me free;
   it tells me of his precious blood,
   the sinner's perfect plea.

3. It tells of one whose loving heart
   can feel my deepest woe;
   who in my sorrow bears a part
   that none can bear below.

4. It bids my trembling heart rejoice,
   it dries each rising tear;
   it tells me in a still, small voice
   to trust and never fear.

725 Melody Green, based on Scripture
© 1982 Birdwing Music/BMG Songs Inc/
Ears to hear music/EMI Christian Music
Publishing/CopyCare Ltd.

1. There is a Redeemer,
   Jesus, God's own Son,
   precious Lamb of God, Messiah,
   Holy One.

   Thank you, O my Father,
   for giving us your Son,
   and leaving your Spirit
   till the work on earth is done.

2. Jesus, my Redeemer,
   Name above all names,
   precious Lamb of God, Messiah,
   O for sinners slain.

3. When I stand in glory,
   I will see his face,
   and there I'll serve my King for ever,
   in that holy place.

726 Brian Foley (b.1919) based on Psalm 139
© 1971 Faber Music Ltd.

1. There is no moment of my life,
   no place where I may go,
   no action which God does not see,
   no thought he does not know.

2. Before I speak, my words are known,
   and all that I decide,
   to come or go: God knows my choice,
   and makes himself my guide.

3. If I should close my eyes to him,
   he comes to give me sight;
   if I should go where all is dark,
   he makes my darkness light.

4. He knew my days before all days,
   before I came to be;
   he keeps me, loves me, in my ways –
   no lover such as he.

727 Henry Burton (1840-1930)

1. There's a light upon the mountains, and
   the day is at the spring,
   when our eyes shall see the beauty and
   the glory of the King;
   weary was our heart with waiting, and
   the night-watch seemed so long;
   but his triumph-day is breaking, and we
   hail it with a song.

Continued overleaf

2. There's a hush of expectation, and a quiet
   in the air;
   and the breath of God is moving in the
   fervent breath of prayer:
   for the suffering, dying Jesus is the Christ
   upon the throne,
   and the travail of our spirit is the travail
   of his own.

3. He is breaking down the barriers, he is
   casting up the way;
   he is calling for his angels to build up the
   gates of day:
   but his angels here are human, not the
   shining hosts above;
   for the drum-beats of his army are the
   heart-beats of our love.

4. Hark! We hear a distant music, and it
   comes with fuller swell;
   'tis the triumph-song of Jesus, of our
   King, Immanuel:
   Zion, go ye forth to meet him; and, my
   soul, be swift to bring
   all thy finest and thy noblest for the
   triumph of our King!

728 Brian A. Wren (b.1936)
© 1969, 1995 Stainer & Bell Ltd.

1. There's a spirit in the air,
   telling Christians everywhere:
   praise the love that Christ revealed,
   living, working, in our world!

2. Lose your shyness, find your tongue;
   tell the world what God has done:
   God in Christ has come to stay;
   live tomorrow's life today!

3. When believers break the bread,
   when a hungry child is fed,
   praise the love that Christ revealed,
   living, working, in our world.

4. Still his Spirit gives us light,
   seeing wrong and setting right:
   God in Christ has come to stay;
   live tomorrow's life today!

5. When a stranger's not alone,
   where the homeless find a home,
   praise the love that Christ revealed,
   living, working, in our world.

6. May the Spirit fill our praise,
   guide our thoughts and change our ways:
   God in Christ has come to stay;
   live tomorrow's life today!

7. There's a spirit in the air,
   calling people everywhere:
   praise the love that Christ revealed,
   living, working, in our world.

729 Frederick William Faber (1814-1863) alt.

1. There's a wideness in God's mercy
   like the wideness of the sea;
   there's a kindness in his justice
   which is more than liberty.

2. There is plentiful redemption
   in the blood that has been shed;
   there is joy for all the members
   in the sorrows of the Head.

3. There is grace enough for thousands
   of new worlds as great as this;
   there is room for fresh creations
   in our God's eternal bliss.

4. For the love of God is broader
   than the measures of our mind;
   and the heart of the Eternal
   is most wonderfully kind.

5. But we make his love too narrow
   by false limits of our own;
   and we magnify his strictness
   with a zeal he will not own.

6. If our love were but more simple
we should take him at his word;
and our lives would be illumined
by the presence of our Lord.

Elizabeth Cecilia Clephane (1830-1869)
adapted by Michael Forster (b.1946)
© 2001 Kevin Mayhew Ltd.

730

1. There were ninety and nine that
safely lay
in the shelter of the fold;
but one was out on the hills away,
far off from the gates of gold.
Away on the mountains wild and bare,
away from the tender shepherd's care.

2. 'Thou hast, Lord, in thy care, thy
ninety-nine,
are they not enough for thee?'
The Shepherd answered, 'This sheep
of mine
has wandered away from me.
By roads that are rocky, rough and steep,
I'll search 'til I find and save my sheep.'

3. Yet not one of the ransomed ever knew
what deep waters had been crossed,
how dark a night had the Lord
passed through
that none of the sheep be lost,
'til out in the wilds he heard its cry,
exhausted and sick, about to die.

4. What, O Lord, is the blood along
the way,
marking out the mountain's track?
It flowed for sheep who had gone astray,
it ransomed and brought them back.
Lord, whence are thy hands so rent
and torn?
They suffer the wounds of nail and
thorn.

5. Over mountainous ranges, thunder-riv'n;
out of valleys dark and deep,
there rose a cry to the gate of heav'n,
'Rejoice I have found my sheep.'
Then echoed the angels round
the throne:
'Rejoice, for the Lord brings back
his own.'

731

Venantius Fortunatus (c. 530-609) trans. Rupert E.
Davies (1909-1994) © Copyright control

1. The royal banners forward go,
the myst'ry of the cross to show,
when he in flesh, all flesh who made,
is on the tree of death displayed.

2. For us he bore those pains severe,
the cruel wounds, the soldier's spear;
by blood and water from his side
our souls from sin are purified.

3. Fulfilled is now what David told
in faithful prophet's song of old,
inviting all the world to see:
our God has suffered on the tree!

4. O tree, most beautiful, most glad,
O tree in royal purple clad,
chosen from noble stock to bear
the holy limbs that suffer there!

5. O tree, on whose blest arms is laid
the price that has the balance swayed,
our souls from slav'ry to regain,
and rescue us from hell's domain!

6. To thee, eternal Three in One,
let homage due by all be done;
whom by the cross thou dost restore,
preserve and govern evermore.

732
Tai Jun Park (b.1900)
Trans. William Scott and Yung Oon Kim.
© World Student Christian Federation.

1. The Saviour's precious blood
   has made all nations one.
   United let us praise this deed
   the Father's love has done.

2. In this vast world of men,
   a world so full of sin,
   no other theme can be our prayer
   than this: your kingdom come!

3. In this sad world of war
   can peace be ever found?
   Unless the love of Christ prevail,
   true peace will not abound.

4. The Master's new command
   was: love each other well!
   O brothers, let us all unite
   to do his holy will.

733 Joseph Addison (1672-1719)

1. The spacious firmament on high,
   with all the blue ethereal sky,
   and spangled heavens, a shining frame,
   their great Original proclaim.
   The unwearied sun, from day to day,
   does his Creator's power display;
   and publishes to every land
   the work of an almighty hand.

2. Soon as the evening shades prevail,
   the moon takes up the wondrous tale,
   and nightly to the listening earth
   repeats the story of her birth:
   while all the stars that round her burn,
   and all the planets in their turn,
   confirm the tidings as they roll,
   and spread the truth from pole to pole.

3. What though in solemn silence all
   move round this dark terrestrial ball;
   what though no real voice nor sound
   amid their radiant orbs be found:
   in reason's ear they all rejoice,
   and utter forth a glorious voice,
   for ever singing as they shine:
   'The hand that made us is divine!'

734
Martin E. Leckebusch (b.1962)
© 2000 Kevin Mayhew Ltd.

1. The Spirit came at Pentecost
   in unexpected ways
   and loosed believing hearts and tongues
   in floods of prayer and praise.

2. Discernment, healing, prophecy –
   so many gifts he brought,
   but all to make the Church mature
   in deed and word and thought.

3. He showed them love and joy and peace
   to kindle their desire
   for lives producing godly fruit
   and purified by fire.

4. With grace and tenderness he came,
   as gently as a dove,
   and whispered, 'Children, you belong
   within your Father's love.'

5. A faithful witness to the truth,
   as Advocate he came;
   he stirred the saints to rise and go,
   the Gospel to proclaim.

6. To blow the breath of life upon
   the dying and the lost,
   to bring them to a second birth,
   he came at Pentecost.

7. We need your Holy Spirit, Lord,
   today as much as then –
   so send him to us now, we pray,
   to fill our hearts again!

735
Damian Lundy (1944-1997)
© 1978, 1993 Kevin Mayhew Ltd.

1. The Spirit lives to set us free,
   walk, walk in the light.
   He binds us all in unity,
   walk, walk in the light.

   Walk in the light (x3)
   walk in the light of the Lord.

2. Jesus promised life to all,
   walk, walk in the light.
   The dead were wakened by his call,
   walk, walk in the light.

3. He died in pain on Calvary,
   walk, walk in the light.
   To save the lost like you and me,
   walk, walk in the light.

4. We know his death was not the end,
   walk, walk in the light.
   He gave his Spirit to be our friend,
   walk, walk in the light.

5. By Jesus' love our wounds are healed,
   walk, walk in the light.
   The Father's kindness is revealed,
   walk, walk in the light.

6. The Spirit lives in you and me,
   walk, walk in the light.
   His light will shine for all to see,
   walk, walk in the light.

736
Latin hymn (17th century)
trans. Francis Pott (1832-1909)

1. The strife is o'er, the battle done;
   now is the Victor's triumph won;
   O let the song of praise be sung:
   Alleluia.

2. Death's mightiest pow'rs have done
       their worst,
   and Jesus hath his foes dispersed;
   let shouts of praise and joy outburst:
   Alleluia.

3. On the third morn he rose again
   glorious in majesty to reign;
   O let us swell the joyful strain:
   Alleluia.

4. Lord, by the stripes which wounded thee
   from death's dread sting thy servants free,
   that we may live, and sing to thee:
   Alleluia.

737
Traditional West Indian

1. The Virgin Mary had a baby boy,
   the Virgin Mary had a baby boy,
   the Virgin Mary had a baby boy,
   and they said that his name was Jesus.

   He came from the glory,
   he came from the glorious kingdom.
   He came from the glory,
   he came from the glorious kingdom.
   O yes, believer. O yes, believer.
   He came from the glory,
   he came from the glorious kingdom.

2. The angels sang when the baby
       was born, *(x3)*
   and proclaimed him the Saviour Jesus.

3. The wise men saw where the baby
       was born, *(x3)*
   and they saw that his name was Jesus.

738
Edward Hayes Plumptre (1821-1891) alt.

1. Thine arm, O Lord, in days of old
   was strong to heal and save;
   it triumphed o'er disease and death,
   o'er darkness and the grave:
   to thee they went, the blind, the dumb,
   the palsied and the lame,
   the outcasts with their grievances,
   the sick with fevered frame.

Continued overleaf

2. And lo, thy touch brought life and
      health,
   gave speech and strength and sight;
   and youth renewed and frenzy calmed
   owned thee, the Lord of light:
   and now, O Lord, be near to bless,
   almighty as before,
   in crowded street, by restless couch,
   as by that ancient shore.

3. Be thou our great deliv'rer still,
   thou Lord of life and death;
   restore and quicken, soothe and bless,
   with thine almighty breath:
   to hands that work, and eyes that see,
   give wisdom's heav'nly lore,
   that whole and sick, and weak
      and strong,
   may praise thee evermore.

739   'A toi la gloire' Edmond Louis Budry (1854-1932)
trans. Richard Birch Hoyle (1875-1939)
© Copyright Control

1. Thine be the glory,
   risen, conqu'ring Son,
   endless is the vict'ry
   thou o'er death hast won;
   angels in bright raiment
   rolled the stone away,
   kept the folded grave-clothes
   where thy body lay.

   Thine be the glory,
     risen, conqu'ring Son,
   endless is the vict'ry
     thou o'er death has won.

2. Lo! Jesus meets us,
   risen from the tomb;
   lovingly he greets us,
   scatters fear and gloom.
   Let the Church with gladness
   hymns of triumph sing,
   for her Lord now liveth;
   death hath lost its sting.

3. No more we doubt thee,
   glorious Prince of Life!
   Life is naught without thee:
   aid us in our strife.
   Make us more than conqu'rors
   through thy deathless love.
   Bring us safe through Jordan
   to thy home above.

740   Reuben Morgan
© 1995 Reuben Morgan/Hillsongs Australia/Kingsway's
Thankyou Music

This is my desire, to honour you.
Lord, with all my heart,
I worship you.
All I have within me I give you praise.
All that I adore is in you.

Lord, I give you my heart,
I give you my soul;
I live for you alone.
Every breath that I take,
every moment I'm awake,
Lord, have your way in me.

741   Les Garrett (b. 1944)
© 1967 Scripture in Song/Integrity Music/
Kingsway's Thankyou Music

1. This is the day, this is the day
   that the Lord has made,
   that the Lord has made;
   we will rejoice, we will rejoice
   and be glad in it, and be glad in it.
   This is the day that the Lord has made;
   we will rejoice and be glad in it.
   This is the day, this is the day
   that the Lord has made.

2. This is the day, this is the day
   when he rose again,
   when he rose again;
   we will rejoice, we will rejoice
   and be glad in it, and be glad in it.
   This is the day when he rose again;
   we will rejoice and be glad in it.
   This is the day, this is the day
   when he rose again.

3. This is the day, this is the day
   when the Spirit came,
   when the Spirit came;
   we will rejoice, we will rejoice
   and be glad in it, and be glad in it.
   This is the day when the Spirit came;
   we will rejoice and be glad in it.
   This is the day, this is the day
   when the Spirit came.

742 Bob Fitts

This is the day that the Lord has made;
I will rejoice and celebrate.
This is the day that the Lord has made;
I will rejoice, I will rejoice and celebrate.
(Repeat)

He goes before me (he goes before me),
he walks beside me (he walks beside me),
he lives within me,
he's the lover of my soul.
He's my defender (he's my defender),
he's my provider (he's my provider),
his overflowing mercies
are brand new every day.

743 George Ratcliffe Woodward (1848-1934)

1. This joyful Eastertide,
   away with sin and sorrow.
   My love, the Crucified,
   hath sprung to life this morrow.

   Had Christ, that once was slain,
   ne'er burst his three-day prison,
   our faith had been in vain:
   but now hath Christ arisen,
   arisen, arisen, arisen.

2. My flesh in hope shall rest,
   and for a season slumber;
   till trump from east to west
   shall wake the dead in number.

3. Death's flood hath lost its chill,
   since Jesus crossed the river:
   lover of souls, from ill
   my passing soul deliver.

744 Joseph Hart (1712-1768)

1. This, this is the God we adore,
   our faithful, unchangeable friend,
   whose love is as great as his power,
   and neither knows measure nor end.

2. 'Tis Jesus, the first and the last,
   whose Spirit shall guide us safe home;
   we'll praise him for all that is past,
   and trust him for all that's to come.

745 George Washington Doane (1799-1859)
based on John 14

1. Thou art the Way: by thee alone
   from sin and death we flee;
   and all who would the Father seek
   must seek him, Lord, by thee.

2. Thou art the Truth: thy word alone
   true wisdom can impart;
   thou only canst inform the mind
   and purify the heart.

3. Thou art the Life: the rending tomb
   proclaims thy conqu'ring arm;
   and those who put their trust in thee
   nor death nor hell shall harm.

4. Thou art the Way, the Truth, the Life:
   grant us that Way to know,
   that Truth to keep, that Life to win,
   whose joys eternal flow.

746

Emily Elizabeth Steele Elliott (1836-1897)
based on Luke 2:7
adapted by Michael Forster (b. 1946)
© This version copyright 1996 Kevin Mayhew Ltd.

1. Thou didst leave thy throne
   and thy kingly crown
   when thou camest to earth for me,
   but in Bethlehem's home
   was there found no room
   for thy holy nativity.

   O come to my heart, Lord Jesus,
   there is room in my heart for thee.

2. Heaven's arches rang
   when the angels sang
   and proclaimed thee of royal degree,
   but in lowliest birth
   didst thou come to earth
   and in deepest humility.

3. Though the fox found rest,
   and the bird its nest
   in the shade of the cedar tree,
   yet the world found no bed
   for the Saviour's head
   in the desert of Galilee.

4. Though thou camest, Lord,
   with the living word
   that should set all thy people free,
   yet with treachery,
   scorn and a crown of thorn
   did they bear thee to Calvary.

5. When the heav'ns shall ring
   and the angels sing
   at thy coming to victory,
   let thy voice call me home,
   saying 'Heav'n has room,
   there is room at my side for thee.'

747

Charles Wesley (1707-1788)

1. Thou God of truth and love,
   we seek thy perfect way,
   ready thy choice to approve,
   thy providence to obey;
   enter into thy wise design,
   and sweetly lose our will in thine.

2. Why hast thou cast our lot
   in the same age and place,
   and why together brought
   to see each other's face,
   to join with loving sympathy,
   and mix our friendly souls in thee?

3. Didst thou not make us one,
   that we might one remain,
   together travel on,
   and bear each other's pain,
   till all thy utmost goodness prove,
   and rise renewed in perfect love?

4. Then let us ever bear
   the blessèd end in view,
   and join, with mutual care,
   to fight our passage through;
   and kindly help each other on,
   till all receive the starry crown.

5. O may thy Spirit seal
   our souls unto that day,
   with all thy fullness fill,
   and then transport away:
   away to our eternal rest,
   away to our Redeemer's breast.

748

Gerhard Tersteegen (1697-1769)
Trans. John Wesley (1703-1791)

1. Thou hidden love of God, whose height,
   whose depth unfathomed, no-one knows,
   I see from far thy beauteous light,
   I sign within for thy repose;
   my heart is pained, nor can it be
   at rest, till it finds rest in thee.

2. Thy secret voice invites me still
   the sweetness of thy yoke to prove;
   and fain I would, but though my will
   seems fixed, yet wide my passions rove;
   yet hindrances strew all the way;
   I aim at thee, yet from thee stray.

3. 'Tis mercy all, that thou hast brought
   my mind to seek her peace in thee;
   yet, while I seek but find thee not,
   no peace my wandering soul shall see;
   O when shall all my wanderings end,
   and all my steps toward thee tend?

4. Each moment draw from earth away
   my heart, that lowly waits thy call;
   speak to my inmost soul, and say,
   'I am thy Love, thy God, thy All!'
   To feel thy power, to hear thy voice,
   to know thy love, be all my choice.

749 Charles Wesley (1707-1788)

1. Thou hidden source of calm repose,
   thou all-sufficient love divine,
   my help and refuge from my foes,
   secure I am, if thou art mine:
   and lo, from sin, and grief, and shame,
   I hide me, Jesus, in thy name.

2. Thy mighty name salvation is,
   and keeps my happy soul above;
   comfort it brings, and power, and peace,
   and joy, and everlasting love:
   to me, with thy dear name, are given
   pardon, and holiness, and heaven.

3. Jesus, my all in all thou art:
   my rest in toil, my ease in pain,
   the med'cine of my broken heart,
   in war my peace, in loss my gain,
   my smile beneath the tyrant's frown,
   in shame my glory and my crown.

4. In want my plentiful supply,
   in weakness my almighty power,
   in bonds my perfect liberty,
   my light in Satan's darkest hour,
   in grief my joy unspeakable,
   my life in death, my heaven in hell.

750 Charles Wesley (1707-1788)

1. Thou Shepherd of Israel, and mine,
   the joy and desire of my heart,
   for closer communion I pine,
   I long to reside where thou art;
   the pasture I languish to find
   where all, who their Shepherd obey,
   are fed, on thy bosom reclined,
   and screened from the heat of the day.

2. Ah, show me that happiest place,
   the place of thy people's abode,
   where saints in an ecstasy gaze,
   and hang on a crucified God;
   thy love for a sinner declare,
   thy passion and death on a tree;
   my spirit to Calvary bear,
   to suffer and triumph with thee.

3. 'Tis there, with the lambs of thy flock,
   there only, I covet to rest,
   to lie at the foot of the rock,
   or rise to be hid in thy breast;
   'tis there I would always abide,
   and never a moment depart,
   concealed in the cleft of thy side,
   eternally held in thy heart.

751 John Marriott (1780-1825) alt.

1. Thou, whose almighty word
   chaos and darkness heard,
   and took their flight;
   hear us, we humbly pray,
   and where the gospel day
   sheds not its glorious ray,
   let there be light.

Continued overleaf

2. Thou, who didst come to bring
   on thy redeeming wing,
   healing and sight,
   health to the sick in mind,
   sight to the inly blind,
   O now to humankind
   let there be light.

3. Spirit of truth and love,
   life-giving, holy Dove,
   speed forth thy flight;
   move on the water's face,
   bearing the lamp of grace,
   and in earth's darkest place
   let there be light.

4. Holy and blessèd Three,
   glorious Trinity,
   Wisdom, Love, Might;
   boundless as ocean's tide
   rolling in fullest pride,
   through the earth far and wide
   let there be light.

752 Psalm 34 in 'New Version' (Tate and Brady, 1696)

1. Through all the changing scenes of life,
   in trouble and in joy,
   the praises of my God shall still
   my heart and tongue employ.

2. O magnify the Lord with me,
   with me exalt his name;
   when in distress to him I called,
   he to my rescue came.

3. The hosts of God encamp around
   the dwellings of the just;
   deliv'rance he affords to all
   who on his succour trust.

4. O make but trial of his love:
   experience will decide
   how blest are they, and only they,
   who in his truth confide.

5. Fear him, ye saints, and you will then
   have nothing else to fear;
   make you his service your delight,
   your wants shall be his care.

6. To Father, Son and Holy Ghost,
   the God whom we adore,
   be glory as it was, is now,
   and shall be evermore.

753 Bernhardt Severin Ingemann (1789-1862) trans. Sabine Baring-Gould (1834-1924) alt.

1. Through the night of doubt and sorrow
   onward goes the pilgrim band,
   singing songs of expectation,
   marching to the promised land.

2. Clear before us, through the darkness,
   gleams and burns the guiding light;
   so we march in hope united,
   stepping fearless through the night.

3. One the light of God's own presence
   o'er his ransomed people shed,
   chasing far the gloom and terror,
   bright'ning all the path we tread.

4. One the object of our journey,
   one the faith which never tires,
   one the earnest looking forward,
   one the hope our God inspires.

5. One the strain that lips of thousands
   lift as from the heart of one:
   one the conflict, one the peril,
   one the march in God begun.

6. One the gladness of rejoicing
   on the far eternal shore,
   where the one almighty Father
   reigns in love for evermore.

7. Onward, therefore, fellow pilgrims,
   onward with the Cross our aid;
   bear its shame and fight its battle,
   till we rest beneath its shade.

8. Soon shall come the great awaking,
   soon the rending of the tomb;
   then the scatt'ring of all shadows,
   and the end of toil and gloom.

754 Charles Wesley (1707-1788)

1. Thy ceaseless, unexhausted love,
   unmerited and free,
   delights our evil to remove,
   and help our misery.

2. Thou waitest to be gracious still;
   thou dost with sinners bear,
   that, saved, we may thy goodness feel,
   and all thy grace declare.

3. Thy goodness and thy truth to me,
   to ev'ry soul, abound,
   a vast, unfathomable sea,
   where all our thoughts are drowned.

4. Its streams the whole creation reach,
   so plenteous is the store,
   enough for all, enough for each,
   enough for evermore.

5. Faithful, O Lord, thy mercies are,
   a rock that cannot move;
   a thousand promises declare
   thy constancy of love.

6. Throughout the universe it reigns,
   unalterably sure;
   and while the truth of God remains
   the goodness must endure.

755 Charles Wesley (1707-1788)

1. Thy faithfulness, Lord, each moment
      we find,
   so true to thy word, so loving and kind;
   thy mercy so tender to all the lost race,
   the vilest offender may turn and find
      grace.

2. O let me commend my Saviour to you,
   I set to my seal that Jesus is true;
   you all may find favour who come at
      his call;
   O come to my Saviour! His grace is
      for all.

3. To save what was lost, from heaven he came;
   come, sinners, and trust in Jesus's name;
   he offers you pardon, he bids you be free:
   'If sin be your burden, O come unto me!'

4. Then let us submit his grace to receive,
   fall down at his feet and gladly believe;
   we all are forgiven for Jesus's sake;
   our title to heaven his merits we take.

756 Edward Hayes Plumptre (1821-1891) alt.

1. Thy hand, O God, has guided
   thy flock, from age to age;
   the wondrous tale is written,
   full clear, on ev'ry page;
   our forebears owned thy goodness,
   and we their deeds record;
   and both of this bear witness:
   one Church, one Faith, one Lord.

2. Thy heralds brought glad tidings
   to greatest, as to least;
   they bade them rise, and hasten
   to share the great King's feast;
   and this was all their teaching,
   in ev'ry deed and word,
   to all alike proclaiming:
   one Church, one Faith, one Lord.

3. Through many a day of darkness,
   through many a scene of strife,
   the faithful few fought bravely
   to guard the nation's life.
   Their gospel of redemption,
   sin pardoned, hope restored,
   was all in this enfolded:
   one Church, one Faith, one Lord.

Continued overleaf

4. And we, shall we be faithless?
   Shall hearts fail, hands hang down?
   Shall we evade the conflict,
   and cast away our crown?
   Not so: in God's deep counsels
   some better thing is stored:
   we will maintain, unflinching,
   one Church, one Faith, one Lord.

5. Thy mercy will not fail us,
   nor leave thy work undone;
   with thy right hand to help us,
   the vict'ry shall be won;
   and then by all creation,
   thy name shall be adored.
   And this shall be their anthem:
   One Church, one Faith, one Lord.

757 Lewis Hensley (1824-1905) alt.

1. Thy kingdom come, O God,
   thy rule, O Christ, begin;
   break with thine iron rod
   the tyrannies of sin.

2. Where is thy reign of peace
   and purity and love?
   When shall all hatred cease,
   as in the realms above?

3. When comes the promised time
   that war shall be no more,
   and lust, oppression, crime
   shall flee thy face before?

4. We pray thee, Lord, arise,
   and come in thy great might;
   revive our longing eyes,
   which languish for thy sight.

5. Some scorn thy sacred name,
   and wolves devour thy fold;
   by many deeds of shame
   we learn that love grows cold.

6. O'er lands both near and far
   thick darkness broodeth yet:
   arise, O morning star,
   arise, and never set.

758 Caroline Bonnett, Sue Rinaldi & Steve Bassett
© 1998 Kingsway's Thankyou Music

Time and again I come back to you
like it was the first time.
Time and again
you restore my soul like dew in the
      morning,
so gracious and kind and slow to anger,
you're the welcome of home when I am a
      stranger;
time and again, time and again.

759 Timothy Dudley-Smith (b.1926) based on Psalm 89
© Timothy Dudley-Smith.

1. Timeless love! We sing the story,
   praise his wonders, tell his worth;
   love more fair then heaven's glory,
   love more firm than ancient earth!
   Tell his faithfulness abroad:
   who is like him? Praise the Lord!

2. By his faithfulness surrounded,
   north and south his hand proclaim;
   earth and heaven formed and founded,
   skies and seas, declare his name!
   Wind and storm obey his word:
   who is like him? Praise the Lord.

3. Truth and righteousness enthrone him,
   just and equal are his ways;
   more than happy, those who own him,
   more than joy, their songs of praise!
   Sun and shield and great reward:
   who is like him? Praise the Lord!

760

Noel Richards
© 1991 Kingsway's Thankyou Music

1. To be in your presence,
   to sit at your feet,
   where your love surrounds me
   and makes me complete.

   This is my desire, O Lord, this is my desire,
   this is my desire, O Lord, this is my desire.

2. To rest in your presence,
   not rushing away,
   to cherish each moment,
   here I would stay.

761

Frances Jane van Alstyne
(Fanny J. Crosby) (1820-1915)

1. To God be the glory!
   great things he hath done;
   so loved he the world
   that he gave us his Son;
   who yielded his life
   an atonement for sin,
   and opened the life-gate
   that all may go in.

   Praise the Lord, praise the Lord!
   let the earth hear his voice;
   praise the Lord, praise the Lord!
   let the people rejoice:
   O come to the Father,
   through Jesus the Son,
   and give him the glory;
   great things he hath done!

2. O perfect redemption,
   the purchase of blood!
   to ev'ry believer
   the promise of God;
   the vilest offender
   who truly believes,
   that moment from Jesus
   a pardon receives.

3. Great things he hath taught us,
   great things he hath done,
   and great our rejoicing
   through Jesus the Son;
   but purer, and higher,
   and greater will be
   our wonder, our rapture,
   when Jesus we see.

762

William Chatterton Dix (1837-1898) alt.

1. To thee, O Lord, our hearts we raise
   in hymns of adoration,
   to thee bring sacrifice of praise
   with shouts of exultation;
   bright robes of gold the fields adorn,
   the hills with joy are ringing,
   the valleys stand so thick with corn
   that even they are singing.

2. And now, on this our festal day,
   thy bounteous hand confessing,
   before thee thankfully we lay
   the first-fruits of thy blessing.
   By thee thy children's souls are fed
   with gifts of grace supernal;
   thou who dost give us earthly bread,
   give us the bread eternal.

3. We bear the burden of the day,
   and often toil seems dreary;
   but labour ends with sunset ray,
   and rest comes from the weary:
   may we, the angel-reaping o'er,
   stand at the last accepted,
   Christ's golden sheaves for evermore
   to garners bright elected.

4. O blessèd is that land of God
   where saints abide for ever,
   where golden fields spread far and broad,
   where flows the crystal river.
   The strains of all its holy throng
   with ours today are blending;
   thrice blessèd is that harvest song
   which never has an ending.

763

Unknown (15th Century)
Trans. John Mason Neale (1818-1866), and others

1. To the Name of our salvation,
   laud and honour let us pay,
   which for many a generation
   hid in God's foreknowledge lay,
   but with holy exultation
   we may sing aloud today.

2. Jesus is the Name we treasure,
   Name beyond what words can tell;
   Name of gladness, Name of pleasure,
   ear and heart delighting well;
   Name of sweetness passing measure,
   saving us from sin and hell.

3. 'Tis the Name that whoso preacheth
   speaks like music to the ear;
   who in prayer this Name beseecheth
   sweetest comfort findeth near;
   who its perfect wisdom reacheth,
   heavenly joy possesseth here.

4. Jesus is the Name exalted
   over every other name;
   in this Name, whene'er assaulted,
   we can put our foes to shame:
   strength to them who else had halted,
   eyes to blind, and feet to lame.

5. Therefore we in love adoring,
   this most blessèd Name revere,
   holy Jesu, thee imploring
   so to write it in us here
   that, hereafter heavenward soaring,
   we may sing with angels there.

764

Helen H. Lemmel
© 1992 Singspiration MusicCorp. Administered by
Bucks Music Ltd.

Turn your eyes upon Jesus,
look full in his wonderful face,
and the things of earth
will grow strangely dim
in the light of his glory and grace.

765

'Puer nobis nascitur'
15th century trans. Percy Dearmer (1867-1936) alt.
© Oxford University Press

1. Unto us a boy is born!
   King of all creation;
   came he to a world forlorn,
   the Lord of ev'ry nation,
   the Lord of ev'ry nation.

2. Cradled in a stall was he,
   watched by cows and asses;
   but the very beasts could see
   that he the world surpasses,
   that he the world surpasses.

3. Then the fearful Herod cried,
   'Pow'r is mine in Jewry!'
   So the blameless children died
   the victims of his fury,
   the victims of his fury.

4. Now may Mary's Son, who came
   long ago to love us,
   lead us all with hearts aflame
   unto the joys above us,
   unto the joys above us.

5. Omega and Alpha he!
   Let the organ thunder,
   while the choir with peals of glee
   shall rend the air asunder,
   shall rend the air asunder.

766

Charles Wesley (1707-1788)

1. Victim divine, thy grace we claim,
   while thus thy precious death we show;
   once offered up, a spotless Lamb,
   in thy great temple here below,
   thou didst for all mankind atone,
   and standest now before the throne.

2. Thou standest in the holiest place,
   as now for guilty sinners slain;
   thy blood of sprinkling speaks, and prays,
   all-prevalent for helpless man;
   thy blood is still our ransom found,
   and spreads salvation all around.

3. We need not now go up to heaven,
   to bring the long-sought Saviour down;
   thou art to all already given,
   thou dost ev'n now thy banquet crown:
   to every faithful soul appear,
   and show thy real presence here!

767
Bernard Barton (1784-1849)

1. Walk in the light: so shalt thou know
   that fellowship of love
   his Spirit only can bestow,
   who reigns in light above.

2. Walk in the light: and thou shalt find
   thy heart made truly his
   who dwells in cloudless light enshrined,
   in whom no darkness is.

3. Walk in the light: and thou shalt own
   thy darkness passed away,
   because that Light has on thee shone
   in which is perfect day.

4. Walk in the light: and e'en the tomb
   no fearful shade shall wear;
   glory shall chase away its gloom,
   for Christ has conquered there.

5. Walk in the light: and thine shall be
   no thornless path, but bright;
   for God, by grace, shall dwell in thee,
   and God himself is Light.

768
Martin E. Leckebusch (b.1962)
© 1999 Kevin Mayhew Ltd.

1. We are called to stand together
   with the saints of ages past,
   with the patriarchs and prophets
   in the faith they once held fast;
   promises and hopes they treasured
   now we find fulfilled at last!

2. Those whom Jesus called apostles
   journeyed with him side by side,
   heard his teaching, felt his power,
   saw the way he lived and died;
   then the news of resurrection
   they delivered far and wide.

3. Through the intervening ages
   round the world the gospel spread:
   faithful heralds took the message,
   guided where the Spirit led;
   so the body grew in stature,
   serving Christ, its living Head.

4. Now in many tongues and cultures
   songs of celebration ring;
   millions who confess our Saviour
   honour him as Lord and King
   and, for courage, grace and guidance
   every day their prayers they bring.

5. To each coming generation
   tell the truth, persuade, explain,
   till the time when time is ended,
   till the Saviour comes again –
   till the saints are all united
   under Christ's eternal reign!

769
Traditional South African
v.1: trans. Anders Nyberg vs. 2 & 3 trans. Andrew Maries
© v.1 1990 Wild Goose Publications
vs 2 & 3: Sovereign Music UK

1. We are marching in the light of God. *(x4)*

   We are marching,
   Oo-ooh! We are marching in the light
   of God. *(Repeat)*

2. We are living in the love of God . . .

3. We are moving in the pow'r of God . . .

770

Viola Grafstrom
© Copyright 1996 Kingsway's Thankyou Music

We bow down and confess
you are Lord in this place.
We bow down and confess
you are Lord in this place.
You are all I need;
it's your face I seek.
In the presence of your light
we bow down, we bow down.

771

Thomas Hornblower Gill (1819-1906)

1. We come unto our fathers' God;
   their Rock is our salvation;
   the eternal arms, their dear abode,
   we make our habitation;
   we bring thee, Lord, the praise they
       brought;
   we seek thee as thy saints have sought
   in every generation.

2. The fire divine their steps that led
   still goeth bright before us;
   the heavenly shield around them spread
   is still high holden o'er us;
   the grace those sinners that subdued,
   the strength those weaklings that renewed,
   doth vanquish, doth restore us.

3. The cleaving sins that brought them low
   are still our souls oppressing;
   the tears that from their eyes did flow
   fall fast, our shame confessing;
   as with thee, Lord, prevailed their cry,
   so our strong prayer ascends on high
   and bringeth down thy blessing.

4. Their joy unto their Lord we bring;
   their song to us descendeth;
   the Spirit who in them did sing
   to us his music lendeth;
   his song in them, in us, is one;
   we raise it high, we send it on,
   the song that never endeth.

5. Ye saints to come, take up the strain,
   the same sweet theme endeavour;
   unbroken be the golden chain;
   keep on the song for ever;
   safe in the same dear dwelling-place,
   rich with the same eternal grace,
   bless the same boundless giver.

772

Isaac Watts (1674-1748)

1. We give immortal praise
   to God the Father's love
   for all our comforts here
   and better hopes above:
   he sent his own
   eternal Son,
   to die for sins
   that we had done.

2. To God the Son belongs
   immortal glory too,
   who bought us with his blood
   from everlasting woe:
   and now he lives,
   and now he reigns,
   and sees the fruit
   of all his pains.

3. To God the Spirit's name
   immortal worship give,
   whose new-creating pow'r
   makes the dead sinner live:
   his work completes
   the great design,
   and fills the soul
   with joy divine.

4. To God the Trinity
   be endless honours done,
   the undivided Three,
   and the mysterious One:
   where reason falls
   with all her pow'rs,
   there faith prevails,
   and love adores.

773

Michael Forster (b. 1946)
based on the speech by Martin Luther King Jr.
© 1997 Kevin Mayhew Ltd.

1. We have a dream:
   this nation will arise,
   and truly live
   according to its creed,
   that all are equal
   in their maker's eyes,
   and none shall suffer
   through another's greed.

2. We have a dream
   that one day we shall see
   a world of justice,
   truth and equity,
   where sons of slaves
   and daughters of the free
   will share the banquet
   of community.

3. We have a dream
   of deserts brought to flow'r,
   once made infertile
   by oppression's heat,
   when love and truth
   shall end oppressive pow'r,
   and streams of righteousness
   and justice meet.

4. We have a dream:
   our children shall be free
   from judgements based on
   colour or on race;
   free to become
   whatever they may be,
   of their own choosing
   in the light of grace.

5. We have a dream
   that truth will overcome
   the fear and anger
   of our present day;
   that black and white
   will share a common home,
   and hand in hand
   will walk the pilgrim way.

6. We have a dream:
   each valley will be raised,
   and ev'ry mountain,
   ev'ry hill brought down;
   then shall creation
   echo perfect praise,
   and share God's glory
   under freedom's crown!

774

Edward Joseph Burns (b. 1938)
© The Revd. Edward J. Burns
Reproduced by kind permission

1. We have a gospel to proclaim,
   good news for all throughout the earth;
   the gospel of a Saviour's name:
   we sing his glory, tell his worth.

2. Tell of his birth at Bethlehem,
   not in a royal house or hall,
   but in a stable dark and dim,
   the Word made flesh, a light for all.

3. Tell of his death at Calvary,
   hated by those he came to save;
   in lonely suff'ring on the cross:
   for all he loved, his life he gave.

4. Tell of that glorious Easter morn,
   empty the tomb, for he was free;
   he broke the pow'r of death and hell
   that we might share his victory.

5. Tell of his reign at God's right hand,
   by all creation glorified.
   He sends his Spirit on his Church
   to live for him, the Lamb who died.

6. Now we rejoice to name him King:
   Jesus is Lord of all the earth.
   This gospel-message we proclaim:
   we sing his glory, tell his worth.

775
William Bullock (1798-1874) and
Henry Williams Baker (1821-1877)

1. We love the place, O God,
   wherein thy honour dwells;
   the joy of thine abode
   all earthly joy excels.

2. It is the house of prayer,
   wherein thy servants meet;
   and thou, O Lord, art there
   thy chosen flock to greet.

3. We love the sacred font;
   for there the holy Dove
   to pour is ever wont
   his blessing from above.

4. We love thine altar, Lord;
   O what on earth so dear?
   For there, in faith adored,
   we find thy presence near.

5. We love the word of life,
   the word that tells of peace,
   of comfort in the strife,
   and joys that never cease.

6. We love to sing below
   for mercies freely giv'n;
   but O, we long to know
   the triumph-song of heav'n.

7. Lord Jesus, give us grace
   on earth to love thee more,
   in heav'n to see thy face,
   and with thy saints adore.

776
Matthias Claudius (1740-1815)
trans. Jane Montgomery Campbell (1817-1878) alt.

1. We plough the fields and scatter
   the good seed on the land,
   but it is fed and watered
   by God's almighty hand:
   he sends the snow in winter,
   the warmth to swell the grain,
   the breezes and the sunshine,
   and soft, refreshing rain.

*All good gifts around us
are sent from heav'n above;
then thank the Lord, O thank the Lord,
for all his love.*

2. He only is the maker
   of all things near and far;
   he paints the wayside flower,
   he lights the evening star;
   he fills the earth with beauty,
   by him the birds are fed;
   much more to us, his children,
   he gives our daily bread.

3. We thank thee then, O Father,
   for all things bright and good:
   the seed-time and the harvest,
   our life, our health, our food.
   Accept the gifts we offer
   for all thy love imparts,
   and, what thou most desirest,
   our humble, thankful hearts.

777
Alan Gaunt (b.1935)
© 1991 Stainer & Bell Ltd.

1. We pray for peace,
   but not the easy peace
   built on complacency
   and not the truth of God;
   we pray for real peace,
   the peace God's love alone can seal.

2. We pray for peace,
   but not the cruel peace
   leaving God's poor bereft
   and dying in distress;
   we pray for real peace,
   enriching all humanity.

3. We pray for peace,
   and not the evil peace
   defending unjust laws
   and nursing prejudice,
   but for the real peace
   of justice, truth and brotherhood.

4. We pray for peace:
   holy communion
   with Christ our risen Lord
   and every living thing;
   God's will fulfilled on earth,
   and all creation reconciled.

5. We pray for peace,
   and, for the sake of peace,
   look to the risen Christ,
   who gives the grace we need
   to serve the cause of peace
   and make our own self-sacrifice.

6. God, give us peace;
   if you withdraw your love
   there is no peace for us,
   nor any hope of it.
   With you to lead us on,
   through death or tumult, peace will come.

778 Spiritual, alt.

1. Were you there
   when they crucified my Lord? *(Repeat)*
   O, sometimes it causes me to
   tremble, tremble, tremble.
   Were you there
   when they crucified my Lord?

2. Were you there
   when they nailed him to a tree? . . .

3. Were you there
   when they pierced him in the side? . . .

4. Were you there
   when they laid him in the tomb? . . .

5. Were you there
   when he rose to glorious life? . . .

779 Thomas Kelly (1769-1855) alt.

1. We sing the praise of him who died,
   of him who died upon the cross;
   the sinner's hope, though all deride,
   will turn to gain this bitter loss.

2. Inscribed upon the cross we see
   in shining letters, 'God is love';
   he bears our sins upon the tree;
   he brings us mercy from above.

3. The cross! it takes our guilt away:
   it holds the fainting spirit up;
   it cheers with hope the gloomy day,
   and sweetens ev'ry bitter cup.

4. It makes the coward spirit brave
   to face the darkness of the night;
   it takes the terror from the grave,
   and gilds the bed of death with light.

5. The balm of life, the cure of woe,
   the measure and the pledge of love,
   the sinner's refuge here below,
   the angels' theme in heav'n above.

780 George Edward Lynch Cotton (1813-1866)

1. We thank thee, Lord, for this fair earth,
   the glittering sky, the silver sea;
   for all their beauty, all their worth,
   their light and glory, come from thee.

2. Thanks for the flowers that clothe the
      ground,
   the trees that wave their arms above,
   the hills that gird our dwellings round,
   as thou dost gird thine own with love.

3. Yet teach us still how far more fair,
   more glorious, Father, in thy sight,
   is one pure deed, one holy prayer,
   one heart that owns thy Spirit's might.

4. So, while we gaze with thoughtful eye
   on all the gifts thy love has given,
   help us in thee to live and die,
   by thine to rise from earth to heaven.

781

John Henry Hopkins (1820-1891) alt.

1. We three kings of Orient are;
   bearing gifts we traverse afar;
   field and fountain, moor and mountain,
   following yonder star.

   O star of wonder, star of night,
   star with royal beauty bright,
   westward leading still proceeding,
   guide us to thy perfect light.

2. Born a King on Bethlehem plain,
   gold I bring, to crown him again,
   King for ever, ceasing never,
   over us all to reign.

3. Frankincense to offer have I,
   incense owns a Deity nigh,
   prayer and praising, gladly raising,
   worship him, God most high.

4. Myrrh is mine, its bitter perfume
   breathes a life of gathering gloom;
   sorrowing, sighing, bleeding, dying,
   sealed in the stone-cold tomb.

5. Glorious now behold him arise,
   King and God and sacrifice;
   alleluia, alleluia,
   earth to heav'n replies.

782

Fred Kaan (b.1929)
© 1967, 1991, 1997 Stainer & Bell Ltd.

1. We turn to you, O God of every nation,
   giver of good and origin of life;
   your love is at the heart of all creation,
   your hurt is people's pain in war and
      death.

2. We turn to you, that we may be forgiven
   for crucifying Christ on earth again;
   we know that we have never wholly
      striven,
   to share with all the promise of your
      reign.

3. Free every heart from haughty self-
      reliance;
   our ways of thought inspire with simple
      grace;
   break down among us barriers of defiance;
   speak to the soul of all the human race.

4. On all who fight on earth for right
      relations,
   we pray the light of love from hour to
      hour.
   Grant wisdom to the leaders of the
      nations,
   the gift of carefulness to those in power.

5. Teach us, good Lord, to serve the need of
      others;
   help us to give and not to count the cost;
   unite us all, to live as sisters, brothers,
   defeat our Babel with your Pentecost.

783

Doug Horley
© 1993 Kingsway's Thankyou Music

We want to see Jesus lifted high,
a banner that flies across this land,
that all men might see the truth
and know he is the way to heaven.
(Repeat)

We want to see, we want to see,
we want to see Jesus lifted high.
We want to see, we want to see,
we want to see Jesus lifted high.

Step by step we're moving forward,
little by little taking ground,
every prayer a powerful weapon,
strongholds come tumbling down,
and down, and down, and down.

784

Martin Smith
© 1996 Curious? Music/UK Administered by
Kingsway's Thankyou Music.

1. What a friend I've found,
   closer than a brother;
   I have felt your touch,
   more intimate than lovers.

Jesus, Jesus, Jesus,
friend for ever.

2. What a hope I've found,
more faithful than a mother;
it would break my heart
to ever lose each other.

785 Joseph Medlicott Scriven (1819-1886)

1. What a friend we have in Jesus,
all our sins and griefs to bear!
What a privilege to carry
ev'rything to him in prayer!
O what peace we often forfeit,
O what needless pain we bear,
all because we do not carry
ev'rything to God in prayer!

2. Have we trials and temptations?
Is there trouble anywhere?
We should never be discouraged:
take it to the Lord in prayer!
Can we find a friend so faithful,
who will all our sorrows share?
Jesus knows our ev'ry weakness –
take it to the Lord in prayer!

3. Are we weak and heavy-laden,
cumbered with a load of care?
Jesus only is our refuge,
take it to the Lord in prayer!
Do thy friends despise, forsake thee?
Take it to the Lord in prayer!
In his arms he'll take and shield thee,
thou wilt find a solace there.

786 David Mowbray (b.1938)
© David Mowbray/Jubilate Hymns

1. What if the One who shapes the stars
and puts the planets in their place
should set all majesty aside
and move amongst the human race?
What if the One who engineers
the eye, the ear, the heart, the brain,
should make his home here as a child
at Mary's breast in Bethlehem?

2. What if the One who spoke the word
when all was dark, 'Let there be light!'
should enter this disordered world
to make our fading hopes more bright?
What if the God who waits outside
should all at once be found within,
and Mary's child be given the strength
to overturn the power of sin?

3. What if the One who always was,
creation's hidden energy,
should – for love's sake – inhabit time,
God's living Word for all to see?
Yes, true it is: Christ's gospel truth,
the truth on which we all may build!
So let this be the truth for us
as now we welcome Mary's child.

787 Charles Wesley (1707-1788)

1. What is our calling's glorious hope
but inward holiness?
For this to Jesus I look up,
I calmly wait for this.

2. I wait, till he shall touch me clean,
shall life and power impart,
give me the faith that casts out sin
and purifies the heart.

3. This is the dear redeeming grace,
for every sinner free;
surely it shall on me take place,
the chief of sinners, me.

4. From all iniquity, from all,
he shall my soul redeem;
in Jesus I believe, and shall
believe myself to him.

5. When Jesus makes my heart his home,
my sin shall all depart;
and lo, he saith: 'I quickly come,
to fill and rule thy heart.'

Continued overleaf

6. Be it according to thy word!
   Redeem me from all sin;
   my heart would now receive thee, Lord,
   come in, my Lord, come in!

788 Graham Kendrick (b. 1950)
© 1994 Make Way Music

1. What kind of greatness can this be,
   that chose to be made small?
   Exchanging untold majesty
   for a world so pitiful.
   That God should come as one of us,
   I'll never understand.
   The more I hear the story told,
   the more amazed I am.

   O what else can I do
   but kneel and worship you,
   and come just as I am,
   my whole life an offering.

2. The One in whom we live and move
   in swaddling cloths lies bound.
   The voice that cried, 'Let there be light',
   asleep without a sound.
   The One who strode among the stars,
   and called each one by name,
   lies helpless in a mother's arms
   and must learn to walk again.

3. What greater love could he have shown
   to shamed humanity,
   yet human pride hates to believe
   in such deep humility.
   But nations now may see his grace
   and know that he is near,
   when his meek heart, his words, his
       works
   are incarnate in us.

789 Charles Wesley (1707-1788)

1. What shall I do my God to love,
   my loving God to praise?
   The length, and breadth, and height
       to prove,
   and depth of sovereign grace?

2. Thy sovereign grace to all extends,
   immense and unconfined;
   from age to age it never ends;
   it reaches all mankind.

3,. Throughout the world its breadth is
       known,
   wide as infinity;
   so wide it never passed by one,
   or it had passed by me.

4. My trespass was grown up to heaven;
   but, far above the skies,
   in Christ abundantly forgiven,
   I see thy mercies rise.

5. The depth of all-redeeming love
   what angel tongue can tell?
   O may I to the utmost prove
   the gift unspeakable!

6. Come quickly, gracious Lord, and take
   possession of thine own;
   my longing heart vouchsafe to make
   thine everlasting throne.

790 Charles Wesley (1707-1788)

1. What shall I do my God to love,
   my Saviour, and the world's, to praise?
   Whose tenderest compassions move
   to me and all the fallen race,
   whose mercy is divinely free
   for all the fallen race, and me!

2. I long to know, and to make known,
the heights and depths of love divine,
the kindness thou to me hast shown,
whose every sin was counted thine:
my God for me resigned his breath;
he died to save my soul from death.

3. How shall I thank thee for the grace
on me and all mankind bestowed?
O that my every breath were praise!
O that my heart were filled with God!
My heart would then with love o'erflow,
and all my life thy glory show.

791 Charles Wesley (1707-1788)

1. What shall I render to my God
for all his mercy's store?
I'll take the gifts he hath bestowed,
and humbly ask for more.

2. The sacred cup of saving grace
I will with thanks receive,
and all his promises embrace,
and to his glory live.

3. My vows I will to his great name
before his people pay,
and all I have, and all I am,
upon his altar lay.

4. Thy lawful servant, Lord, I owe
to thee whate'er is mine,
born in thy family below,
and by redemption thine.

5. Thy hands created me, thy hands
from sin have set me free,
the mercy that hath loosed my bands
hath bound me fast to thee.

6. The God of all-redeeming grace
my God I will proclaim,
offer the sacrifice of praise,
and call upon his name.

7. Praise him, ye saints, the God of love,
who hath my sins forgiven,
till, gathered to the church above,
we sing the songs of heaven.

792 Fred Pratt Green (1903-2000) © 1975 Stainer & Bell Ltd.

1. What shall our greeting be:
sign of our unity?
'Jesus is Lord!'
May we no more defend
barriers he died to end:
give me your hand, my friend –
one Church, one Lord!

2. What is our mission here?
He makes his purpose clear:
one world, one Lord!
Spirit of truth, descend;
all our confusions end:
give me your hand, my friend –
'Jesus is Lord!'

3. He comes to save us now:
to serve him is to know
life's true reward.
May he our lives amend,
all our betrayals end:
give me your hand, my friend –
'Jesus is Lord!'

793 August Gottlieb Spangenberg (1704-1792). Trans. John Wesley (1703-1791)

1. What shall we offer our good Lord,
poor nothings, for his boundless grace?
Fain would we his great name record
and worthily set forth his praise.

2. Great object of our growing love,
to whom our more than all we owe,
open the fountain from above,
and let it our full souls o'erflow.

Continued overleaf

3. Open a door which earth and hell
   may strive to shut, but strive in vain;
   let thy word richly in us dwell,
   and let our gracious fruit remain.

4. O multiply the sower's seed!
   And fruit we every hour shall bear,
   throughout the world thy gospel spread,
   thy everlasting truth declare.

5. So shall our lives thy power proclaim,
   thy grace for every sinner free;
   till all mankind shall learn thy name,
   shall all stretch out their hands to thee.

794 Joseph Addison (1672-1719) alt.

1. When all thy mercies, O my God,
   my rising soul surveys,
   transported with the view, I'm lost
   in wonder, love and praise.

2. Unnumbered comforts to my soul
   thy tender care bestowed,
   before my infant heart conceived
   from whom those comforts flowed.

3. When in such slipp'ry paths I ran
   in childhood's careless days,
   thine arm unseen conveyed me safe,
   to walk in adult ways.

4. When worn with sickness oft hast thou
   with health renewed my face;
   and when in sins and sorrows sunk,
   revived my soul with grace.

5. Ten thousand thousand precious gifts
   my daily thanks employ,
   and not the least a cheerful heart
   which tastes those gifts with joy.

6. Through ev'ry period of my life
   thy goodness I'll pursue,
   and after death in distant worlds
   the glorious theme renew.

7. Through all eternity to thee
   a joyful song I'll raise;
   for O! eternity's too short
   to utter all thy praise.

795 W.H. Hamilton (1886-1958)

1. When Easter to the dark world came,
   fair flowers glowed like scarlet flame:

   At Eastertide, at Eastertide,
   O glad was the world at Eastertide.

2. When Mary in the garden walked,
   and with her risen Master talked:

3. When John and Peter in their gloom
   met angels at the empty tomb:

4. When Thomas' heart with grief was black,
   then Jesus like a king came back:

5. And friend to friend in wonder said:
   'The Lord is risen from the dead!'

6. This Eastertide with joyful voice
   we'll sing: 'The Lord is King! Rejoice!'

   At Eastertide, at Eastertide,
   O sing, all the world, for Eastertide.

796 Keri Jones and David Matthew

When I feel the touch
of your hand upon my life,
it causes me to sing a song
that I love you, Lord.
So from deep within
my spirit singeth unto thee,
you are my King,
you are my God,
and I love you, Lord.

797
Wayne and Cathy Perrin
© 1980 Integrity's Hosanna! Music/Kingsway's Thankyou Music

When I look into your holiness,
when I gaze into your loveliness,
when all things that surround
become shadows in the light of you;
when I've found the joy
of reaching your heart,
when my will becomes
enthrall'd in your love,
when all things that surround
become shadows in the light of you:
I worship you, I worship you,
the reason I live is to worship you,
I worship you, I worship you,
the reason I live is to worship you.

798
Sydney Carter (b. 1915)
© 1965 Stainer & Bell Ltd.

1. When I needed a neighbour,
   were you there, were you there?
   When I needed a neighbour,
   were you there?

   *And the creed and the colour
   and the name won't matter,
   were you there?*

2. I was hungry and thirsty,
   were you there, were you there?
   I was hungry and thirsty,
   were you there?

3. I was cold, I was naked,
   were you there, were you there?
   I was cold, I was naked,
   were you there?

4. When I needed a shelter,
   were you there, were you there?
   When I needed a shelter,
   were you there?

5. When I needed a healer,
   were you there, were you there?
   When I needed a healer,
   were you there?

6. Wherever you travel,
   I'll be there, I'll be there,
   wherever you travel,
   I'll be there.

799 Isaac Watts (1674-1748)

1. When I survey the wondrous cross
   on which the Prince of Glory died,
   my richest gain I count but loss,
   and pour contempt on all my pride.

2. Forbid it, Lord, that I should boast,
   save in the death of Christ, my God:
   all the vain things that charm me most,
   I sacrifice them to his blood.

3. See from his head, his hands, his feet,
   sorrow and love flow mingling down:
   did e'er such love and sorrow meet,
   or thorns compose so rich a crown?

4. Were the whole realm of nature mine,
   that were an off'ring far too small;
   love so amazing, so divine,
   demands my soul, my life, my all.

800
Fred Pratt Green (1903-2000)
© 1980 Stainer & Bell Ltd.

1. When Jesus came to Jordan
   to be baptised by John,
   he did not come for pardon,
   but as his Father's Son.
   He came to share repentance
   with all who mourn their sins,
   to speak the vital sentence
   with which good news begins.

Continued overleaf

2. He came to share temptation,
   our utmost woe and loss,
   for us and our salvation
   to die upon the cross.
   So when the Dove descended
   on him, the Son of Man,
   the hidden years had ended,
   the age of grace began.

3. Come, Holy, Spirit, aid us
   to keep the vows we make;
   this very day invade us,
   and every bondage break.
   Come, give our lives direction,
   the gift we covet most:
   to share the resurrection
   that leads to Pentecost.

801 German (19th century)
trans. Edward Caswall (1814-1878)

1. When morning gilds the skies,
   my heart awaking cries,
   may Jesus Christ be praised.
   Alike at work and prayer
   to Jesus I repair;
   may Jesus Christ be praised.

2. The night becomes as day,
   when from the heart we say:
   may Jesus Christ be praised.
   The pow'rs of darkness fear,
   when this sweet chant they hear:
   may Jesus Christ be praised.

3. In heav'n's eternal bliss
   the loveliest strain is this:
   may Jesus Christ be praised.
   Let air, and sea, and sky
   from depth to height reply:
   may Jesus Christ be praised.

4. Be this, while life is mine,
   my canticle divine:
   may Jesus Christ be praised.
   Be this th'eternal song
   through all the ages on:
   may Jesus Christ be praised.

802 John Reynell Wreford (1800-1881) alt.

1. When my love to Christ grows weak,
   when for deeper faith I seek,
   then in thought I go to thee,
   Garden of Gethsemane

2. There I walk amid the shades,
   while the lingering twilight fades,
   see that suffering, friendless One,
   weeping, praying there alone.

3. When my love for man grows weak,
   when for stronger faith I seek,
   hill of Calvary, I go
   to thy scenes of fear and woe.

4. There behold his agony,
   suffered on the bitter tree;
   see his anguish, see his faith,
   love triumphant still in death.

5. Then to life I turn again,
   learning all the worth of pain,
   learning all the might that lies
   in a full self-sacrifice.

6. And I praise with firmer faith
   Christ who vanquished pain and death;
   and to Christ enthroned above
   raise my song of selfless love.

803 Horatio G. Spafford (1828-1888)

1. When peace like a river
   attendeth my way,
   when sorrows like sea-billows roll,
   whatever my lot,
   thou hast taught me to know,
   it is well, it is well with my soul.

   It is well (it is well)
   with my soul (with my soul),
   it is well, it is well with my soul.

2. Though Satan should buffet,
   though trials should come,
   let this blest assurance control,
   that Christ hath regarded
   my helpless estate,
   and hath shed his own blood for my
      soul.

3. For me be it Christ,
   be it Christ, hence to live!
   If Jordan above me shall roll,
   no pang shall be mine,
   for in death as in life,
   thou wilt whisper thy peace to my soul.

4. But, Lord, 'tis for thee,
   for thy coming we wait,
   the sky, not the grave, is our goal;
   oh, trump of the angel!
   O voice of the Lord!
   Blessed hope! blessed rest of my soul!

804 Fred Pratt Green (1903–2000)
© 1969 Stainer & Bell Ltd.

1. When the Church of Jesus
   shuts its outer door,
   lest the roar of traffic
   drown the voice of prayer:
   may our prayers, Lord,
   make us ten times more aware
   that the world we banish
   is our Christian care.

2. If our hearts are lifted
   where devoted soars
   high above this hungry,
   suffering world of ours:
   lest our hymns should drug us
   to forget its needs,
   forge our Christian worship
   into Christian deeds.

3. Lest the gifts we offer,
   money, talents, time,
   serve to salve our conscience,
   to our secret shame:
   Lord, reprove,
   inspire us by the way you give;
   teach us, dying Saviour,
   how true Christians live.

805 Matt Redman
© 1997 Kingsway's Thankyou Music

1. When the music fades,
   all is stripped away,
   and I simply come.
   Longing just to bring
   something that's of worth,
   that will bless your heart.

   I'll bring you more than a song,
   for a song in itself
   is not what you have required.
   You search much deeper within,
   through the way things appear;
   you're looking into my heart.

   I'm coming back to the heart of worship,
   and it's all about you,
   all about you, Jesus.
   I'm sorry, Lord,
   for the thing I've made it,
   when it's all about you,
   all about you, Jesus.

2. King of endless worth,
   no one could express
   how much you deserve.
   Though I'm weak and poor,
   all I have is yours,
   every single breath.

   I'll bring you . . .

806
John Henry Sammis (1846-1919)

1. When we walk with the Lord
in the light of his word,
what a glory he sheds on our way!
While we do his good will,
he abides with us still,
and with all who will trust and obey.

Trust and obey,
for there's no other way
to be happy in Jesus,
but to trust and obey.

2. Not a burden we bear,
not a sorrow we share,
but our toil he doth richly repay;
not a grief nor a loss,
not a frown nor a cross,
but is blest if we trust and obey.

3. But we never can prove
the delights of his love
until all on the altar we lay;
for the favour he shows,
and the joy he bestows,
are for them who will trust and obey.

4. Then in fellowship sweet
we will sit at his feet,
or we'll walk by his side in the way.
What he says he will do,
where he sends we will go,
never fear, only trust and obey.

807
Frank Mason North (1850-1935) alt.
© *Copyright Control.*

1. Where cross the crowded ways of life,
where sound the cries of race and clan,
above the noise of selfish strife,
we hear thy voice, O Son of Man.

2. In haunts of wretchedness and need,
on shadowed thresholds dark with fears,
from paths here hide the lures of greed,
we catch the vision of thy tears.

3. The cup of water given for thee
still holds the freshness of thy grace;
yet long these multitudes to see
the strong compassion of thy face.

4. O Master, from the mountain-side
make haste to heal these hearts of pain;
among these restless throngs abide,
O tread the city's streets again:

5. Till humankind shall learn thy love,
and follow where thy feet have trod;
till glorious from thy heaven above
shall come the city of our God.

808
Charles Wesley (1707-1788)

1. Where shall my wondering soul begin?
How shall I all to heaven aspire?
A slave redeemed from death and sin,
a brand plucked from eternal fire,
how shall I equal triumphs raise,
or sing my great deliverer's praise?

2. O how shall I the goodness tell,
Father, which thou to me hast showed?
That I, a child of wrath and hell,
I should be called a child of God,
should know, should feel my sins
forgiven,
blest with this antepast of heaven!

3. And shall I slight my Father's love?
Or basely fear his gifts to own?
Unmindful of his favours prove?
Shall I, the hallowed cross to shun,
refuse his righteousness to impart,
by hiding it within my heart?

4. Outcasts of men, to you I call,
   harlots, and publicans, and thieves!
   He spreads his arms to embrace you all;
   sinners alone his grace receives:
   no need of him the righteous have;
   he came the lost to seek and save.

5. Come, O my guilty brethren, come,
   groaning beneath your load of sin!
   His bleeding heart shall make you room,
   his open side shall take you in;
   he calls you now, invites you home:
   come, O my guilty brethren, come!

809 Nahum Tate (1652-1715)

1. While shepherds watched their flocks
      by night,
   all seated on the ground,
   the angel of the Lord came down,
   and glory shone around.

2. 'Fear not,' said he, (for mighty dread
   had seized their troubled mind)
   'glad tidings of great joy I bring
   to you and all mankind.

3. To you in David's town this day
   is born of David's line
   a Saviour, who is Christ the Lord;
   and this shall be the sign:

4. The heav'nly babe you there shall find
   to human view displayed,
   all meanly wrapped in swathing bands,
   and in a manger laid.'

5. Thus spake the seraph, and forthwith
   appeared a shining throng
   of angels praising God, who thus
   addressed their joyful song:

6. 'All glory be to God on high,
   and on the earth be peace,
   goodwill henceforth from heav'n to all
   begin and never cease.'

810 Graham Kendrick (b. 1950)
© 1988 Make Way Music

1. Who can sound the depths of sorrow
   in the Father heart of God,
   for the children we've rejected,
   for the lives so deeply scarred?
   And each light that we've extinguished
   has brought darkness to our land:
   upon our nation, upon our nation
   have mercy, Lord.

2. We have scorned the truth you gave us,
   we have bowed to other lords.
   We have sacrificed the children
   on the altar of our gods.
   O let truth again shine on us,
   let your holy fear descend:
   upon our nation, upon our nation
   have mercy, Lord.

(Men)

3. Who can stand before your anger?
   Who can face your piercing eyes?
   For you love the weak and helpless,
   and you hear the victims' cries.

(All)

   Yes, you are a God of justice,
   and your judgement surely comes:
   upon our nation, upon our nation
   have mercy, Lord.

(Women)

4. Who will stand against the violence?
   Who will comfort those who mourn?
   In an age of cruel rejection,
   who will build for love a home?

Continued overleaf

(All)

Come and shake us into action,
come and melt our hearts of stone:
upon your people, upon your people
have mercy, Lord.

5. Who can sound the depths of mercy
in the Father heart of God?
For there is a Man of sorrows
who for sinners shed his blood.
He can heal the wounds of nations,
he can wash the guilty clean:
because of Jesus, because of Jesus
have mercy, Lord.

811 John Greenleaf Whittier (1807-1892)

1. Who fathoms the eternal thought?
Who talks of scheme and plan?
The Lord is God! He needeth not
the poor device of man.

2. I see the wrong that round me lies,
I feel the guilt within;
I hear, with groan and travail-cries,
the world confess its sin.

3. Yet, in the maddening maze of things,
and tossed by storm and flood,
to one fixed stake my spirit clings;
I know that God is good!

4. And if my heart and flesh are weak
to bear an untried pain,
the bruisèd reed he will not break,
but strengthen and sustain.

5. I know not what the future hath
of marvel or surprise,
assured alone that life and death
his mercy underlies.

812 Frances Ridley Havergal (1836-1879)

1. Who is on the Lord's side?
Who will serve the King?
Who will be his helpers
others lives to bring?
Who will leave the world's side?
Who will face the foe?
Who is on the Lord's side?
Who for him will go?
By thy call of mercy,
by thy grace divine,
we are on the Lord's side;
Saviour, we are thine.

2. Jesus, thou hast bought us,
not with gold or gem,
but with thine own life-blood,
for thy diadem.
With thy blessing filling
each who comes to thee,
thou hast made us willing,
thou hast made us free.
By thy great redemption,
by thy grace divine,
we are on the Lord's side;
Saviour, we are thine.

3. Fierce may be the conflict,
strong may be the foe;
but the King's own army
none can overthrow.
Round his standard ranging,
victory is secure;
for his truth unchanging
makes the triumph sure.
Joyfully enlisting,
by thy grace divine,
we are on the Lord's side;
Saviour, we are thine.

4. Chosen to be soldiers
   in an alien land,
   chosen, called, and faithful,
   for our Captain's band,
   in the service royal
   let us not grow cold;
   let us be right loyal,
   noble, true, and bold.
   Master, thou wilt keep us,
   by thy grace divine,
   always on the Lord's side,
   Saviour, always thine.

814

C. Austin Miles
© The Rodeheaver Co./Word Music Inc./CopyCare Ltd.

Wide, wide as the ocean,
high as the heavens above;
deep, deep as the deepest sea
is my Saviour's love.
I, though so unworthy,
still am a child of his care,
for his word teaches me that
his love reaches me ev'rywhere.

813

John Bunyan (1628-1688)

1. Who would true valour see,
   let him come hither;
   one here will constant be,
   come wind, come weather;
   there's no discouragement
   shall make him once relent
   his first avowed intent
   to be a pilgrim.

2. Whoso beset him round
   with dismal stories
   do but themselves confound;
   his strength the more is.
   No lion can him fright;
   he'll with a giant fight;
   but he will have a right
   to be a pilgrim.

3. Hobgoblin nor foul fiend
   can daunt his spirit;
   he knows he at the end
   shall life inherit.
   Then fancies fly away,
   he'll fear not what men say;
   he'll labour night and day
   to be a pilgrim.

815

John L. Bell (b. 1949) and Graham Maule (b. 1958)
© 1987 WGRG, Iona Community

1. Will you come and follow me
   if I but call your name?
   Will you go where you don't know,
   and never be the same?
   Will you let my love be shown,
   will you let my name be known,
   will you let my life be grown
   in you, and you in me?

2. Will you leave yourself behind
   if I but call your name?
   Will you care for cruel and kind,
   and never be the same?
   Will you risk the hostile stare
   should your life attract or scare,
   will you let me answer prayer
   in you, and you in me?

3. Will you let the blinded see
   if I but call your name?
   Will you set the pris'ners free,
   and never be the same?
   Will you kiss the leper clean
   and do such as this unseen,
   and admit to what I mean
   in you, and you in me?

4. Will you love the 'you' you hide
   if I but call your name?
   Will you quell the fear inside,
   and never be the same?
   Will you use the faith you've found
   to reshape the world around
   through my sight and touch and sound
   in you, and you in me?

5. Lord, your summons echoes true
   when you but call my name.
   Let me turn and follow you,
   and never be the same.
   In your company I'll go
   where your love and footsteps show.
   Thus I'll move and live and grow
   in you, and you in me.

816 Priscilla Jane Owens (1829-1899)

1. Will your anchor hold
   in the storms of life,
   when the clouds unfold
   their wings of strife?
   When the strong tides lift,
   and the cables strain,
   will your anchor drift,
   or firm remain?

   We have an anchor
   that keeps the soul
   steadfast and sure
   while the billows roll;
   fastened to the rock
   which cannot move,
   grounded firm and deep
   in the Saviour's love!

2. Will your anchor hold
   in the straits of fear,
   when the breakers roar
   and the reef is near?
   While the surges rage,
   and the wild winds blow,
   shall the angry waves
   then your bark o'erflow?

3. Will your anchor hold
   in the floods of death,
   when the waters cold
   chill your latest breath?
   On the rising tide
   you can never fail,
   while your anchor holds
   within the veil.

4. Will your eyes behold
   through the morning light,
   the city of gold
   and the harbour bright?
   Will you anchor safe
   by the heav'nly shore,
   when life's storms are past
   for evermore?

817 Michael Saward (b.1932)
© Michael Saward/Jubilate Hymns

1. Wind of God, dynamic Spirit,
   breathe upon our hearts today;
   that we may your power inherit
   hear us, Spirit, as we pray:
   fill the vacuum that enslaves us –
   emptiness of heart and soul;
   and, through Jesus Christ who saves us,
   give us life and make us whole.

2. Voice of God, prophetic Spirit,
   speak to every heart today
   to encourage or prohibit,
   urging action or delay:
   clear the vagueness which impedes us –
   come, enlighten mind and soul;
   and, through Jesus Christ who leads us,
   teach the truth that makes us whole.

3. Fire of God, volcanic Spirit,
   burn within our hearts today;
   cleanse our sin – may we exhibit
   holiness in every way:
   purge the squalidness that shames us,
   soils the body, taints the soul;
   and, through Jesus Christ who claims us,
   purify us, make us whole.

818

James Thomas East (1860-1937)
© The Trustees for Methodist Church Purposes

1. Wise men, seeking Jesus,
   travelled from afar,
   guided on their journey
   by a beauteous star.

2. But if we desire him,
   he is close at hand;
   for our native country
   is our Holy Land.

3 Prayerful souls may find him
   by our quiet lakes,
   meet him on our hillsides
   when the morning breaks.

4. In our fertile cornfields
   while the sheaves are bound,
   in our busy markets,
   Jesus may be found.

5. Fishermen talk with him
   by the great North Sea,
   as the first disciples
   did in Galilee.

6. Every town and village
   in our land might be
   made by Jesus' presence
   like sweet Bethany.

7. He is more than near us,
   if we love him well;
   for he seeketh ever
   in our hearts to dwell.

819

George Rawson (1807-1889)

1. With gladness we worship, rejoice as
      we sing,
   free hearts and free voices how blessèd
      to bring;
   the old, thankful story shall scale thine
      abode,
   thou King of all glory, most bountiful God.

2. Thy right would we give thee – true
      homage thy due,
   and honour eternal, the universe
      through,
   with all thy creation, earth, heaven
      and sea,
   in one acclamation we celebrate thee.

3. Renewed by thy Spirit, redeemed by
      thy Son,
   thy children revere thee for all thou
      hast done.
   O Father! Returning to love and to light,
   thy children are yearning to praise
      thee aright.

4. We join with the angels, and so there
      is given
   from earth 'Alleluia', in answer to heaven.
   Amen! Be thou glorious below and
      above,
   redeeming, victorious, and infinite Love!

820

Charles Wesley (1707-1788)

1. With glorious clouds encompassed
      round,
   whom angels dimly see,
   will the Unsearchable be found,
   or God appear to me?

2. Will he forsake his throne above,
   himself to me impart?
   Answer, thou Man of grief and love,
   and speak it to my heart!

3. In manifested love explain
   thy wonderful design;
   what meant the suffering Son of Man,
   the streaming blood divine?

4. Didst thou not in our flesh appear,
   and live and die below,
   that I may now perceive thee near,
   and my Redeemer know?

Continued overleaf

5. Come then, and to my soul reveal
the heights and depths of grace,
the wounds which all my sorrows heal,
that dear disfigured face.

6. I view the Lamb in his own light,
whom angels dimly see,
and gaze, transported at the sight,
through all eternity.

821
Isaac Watts (1674-1748) based on Hebrews 4:14-16 and Isaiah 42:3

1. With joy we meditate the grace
of our High Priest above;
his heart is made of tenderness,
and overflows with love.

2. Touched with a sympathy within,
he knows our feeble frame;
he knows what sore temptations mean,
for he has felt the same.

3. But spotless, innocent, and pure
the great Redeemer stood,
while Satan's fiery darts he bore,
and did resist to blood.

4. He, in the days of feeble flesh,
poured out his cries and tears;
and in his measure feels afresh
what every member bears.

5. He'll never quench the smoking flax,
but raise it to a flame;
the bruisèd reed he never breaks,
nor scorns the meanest name.

6. Then let our humble faith address
his mercy and his power;
we shall obtain delivering grace
in each distressing hour.

822
Geoff Baker
© 1994 Sovereign Music UK

1. With this bread we will remember him,
Son of God, broken and suffering;
for our guilt – innocent offering.
As we eat, remember him.

2. With this wine we will remember him,
on the cross, paying the price for sin –
blood of Christ cleansing us deep within.
As we drink, remember him.

823
Charles Wesley (1707-1788)

1. Worship, and thanks, and blessing,
and strength ascribe to Jesus!
Jesus alone
defends his own,
when earth and hell oppress us.
Jesus with joy we witness
almighty to deliver;
our seals set to,
that God is true,
and reigns a King for ever.

2. Omnipotent Redeemer,
our ransomed souls adore thee:
our Saviour thou,
we find it now,
and give thee all the glory.
We sing thine arm unshortened,
brought through our sore temptation;
with heart and voice
in thee rejoice,
the God of our salvation.

3. Thine arm has safely brought us
a way no more expected,
than when thy sheep
passed through the deep,
by crystal walls protected.
Thy glory was our rearward,
thine hand our lives did cover,
and we, ev'n we,
have walked the sea,
and marched triumphant over.

4. The world and Satan's malice
   thou, Jesus, hast confounded;
   and, by thy grace,
   with songs of praise
   our happy souls resounded.
   Accepting our deliverance,
   we triumph in thy favour,
   and for the love
   which now we prove
   shall praise thy name for ever.

824 Charles Wesley (1707-1788)

1. Would Jesus have the sinner die?
   Why hangs he then on yonder tree?
   What means that strange expiring cry?
   Sinners, he prays for you and me:
   Forgive them, Father, O forgive!
   They know not that by me they live.

2. Thou loving, all-atoning Lamb,
   thee – by thy painful agony,
   thy sweat of blood, thy grief and shame,
   thy cross and passion on the tree,
   thy precious death and life – I pray:
   take all, take all my sins away!

3. O let me kiss thy bleeding feet,
   and bathe and wash them with my tears;
   the story of thy love repeat
   in every drooping sinner's ears;
   that all may hear the quickening sound,
   since even I have mercy found.

4. O let thy love my heart control,
   thy love for every sinner free,
   that every fallen human soul
   may taste the grace that found out me;
   that all mankind with me may prove
   thy sovereign, everlasting love!

825 Richard Baxter (1615-1691) and John Hampden Gurney (1802-1862)

1. Ye holy angels bright,
   who wait at God's right hand,
   or through the realms of light
   fly at your Lord's command,
   assist our song,
   for else the theme
   too high doth seem
   for mortal tongue.

2. Ye blessèd souls at rest,
   who ran this earthly race,
   and now, from sin released,
   behold the Saviour's face,
   God's praises sound,
   as in his sight
   with sweet delight
   ye do abound.

3. Ye saints, who toil below,
   adore your heav'nly King,
   and onward as ye go
   some joyful anthem sing;
   take what he gives
   and praise him still,
   through good or ill,
   who ever lives.

4. My soul, bear thou thy part,
   triumph in God above:
   and with a well-tuned heart
   sing thou the songs of love;
   let all thy days
   till life shall end,
   whate'er he send,
   be filled with praise.

826 Charles Wesley (1707-1788)

1. Ye servants of God, your Master proclaim,
   and publish abroad his wonderful name;
   the name all-victorious of Jesus extol;
   his kingdom is glorious, and rules over all.

Continued overleaf

2. God ruleth on high, almighty to save;
   and still he is nigh, his presence we have;
   the great congregation his triumph
      shall sing,
   ascribing salvation to Jesus our King.

3. 'Salvation to God who sits on the
      throne!'
   Let all cry aloud, and honour the Son;
   the praises of Jesus the angels proclaim,
   fall down on their faces, and worship
      the Lamb.

4. Then let us adore, and give him his right;
   all glory and power, all wisdom and
      might,
   all honour and blessing, with angels
      above,
   and thanks never-ceasing, and infinite
      love.

827 Philip Doddridge (1702-1751) alt.

1. Ye servants of the Lord,
   each for his coming wait,
   observant of his heav'nly word,
   and watchful at his gate.

2. Let all your lamps be bright,
   and trim the golden flame;
   gird up your loins as in his sight,
   for awesome is his name.

3. Watch! 'tis your Lord's command,
   and while we speak, he's near;
   mark the first signal of his hand,
   and ready all appear.

4. O happy servants they,
   in such a posture found,
   who share their Saviour's triumph day,
   with joy and honour crowned.

5. Christ shall the banquet spread
   with his own royal hand,
   and raise each faithful servant's head
   amid th'angelic band.

828 John Hampden Gurney (1802-1862)

1. Yes, God is good – in earth and sky,
   from ocean-depths and spreading wood,
   ten thousand voices seem to cry:
   'God made us all, and God is good.'

2. The sun that keeps his trackless way
   and downward pours his golden flood,
   night's sparkling hosts, all seem to say
   in accents clear that God is good.

3. The merry birds prolong the strain,
   their song with every spring renewed;
   and balmy air and falling rain,
   each softly whispers: 'God is good.'

4. We hear it in the rushing breeze;
   the hills that have for ages stood,
   the echoing sky and roaring seas,
   all swell the chorus: 'God is good.'

5. For all thy gifts we bless thee, Lord,
   but chiefly for our heavenly food,
   thy pardoning grace, thy quickening
      word,
   these prompt our song, that God is good.

829 Mavis Ford

You are the King of Glory,
you are the Prince of Peace,
you are the Lord of heav'n and earth,
you're the Son of righteousness.
Angels bow down before you,
worship and adore, for
you have the words of eternal life,
you are Jesus Christ the Lord.
Hosanna to the Son of David!
Hosanna to the King of kings!
Glory in the highest heaven,
for Jesus the Messiah reigns.

830
Noel Richards
© 1985 Kingsway's Thankyou Music

You laid aside your majesty,
gave up everything for me,
suffered at the hands of those you had
     created.
You took all my guilt and shame,
when you died and rose again;
now today you reign,
in heav'n and earth exalted.

I really want to worship you, my Lord,
you have won my heart and I am yours
for ever and ever;
I will love you.
You are the only one who died for me,
gave your life to set me free,
so I lift my voice to you in adoration.

831
Freda Head (b.1914)

1. Your will for us and others, Lord,
   is perfect health and wholeness,
   and we must seek for nothing less
   than life in all its fullness.

2. As Jesus dealt with human ills,
   your purposes revealing,
   so may your servants in this day
   be channels of your healing.

3. For suffering bodies, minds and souls
   that long for restoration,
   accept our prayers of faith and love,
   and grant us all salvation.

4. So we would claim your promised grace,
   your presence and protection;
   and, tasting now eternal life,
   press on toward perfection.

832
George Currie Martin (1865-1937) alt.
© Copyright Control

1. Your words to me are life and health;
   they fortify my soul,
   enable, guide and teach my heart
   to reach its perfect goal.

2. Your words to me are light and truth;
   from day to day they show
   their wisdom, passing earthly lore,
   as in their truth I grow.

3. Your words to me are full of joy,
   of beauty, peace and grace;
   from them I learn your blessèd will,
   through them I see your face.

4. Your words are perfected in One,
   yourself, the living Word;
   within my heart your image print
   in clearest lines, O Lord.

833
Steffi Geiser Rubin and Stuart Dauermann
© 1975 Lillenas Publishing Co./CopyCare

You shall go out with joy
and be led forth with peace,
and the mountains and the hills
shall break forth before you.
There'll be shouts of joy
and the trees of the field shall clap,
shall clap their hands.
And the trees of the field
shall clap their hands,
and the trees of the field
shall clap their hands,
and the trees of the field
shall clap their hands,
and you'll go out with joy.

CHILDREN'S HYMNS AND SONGS

834 Traditional

1. All in an Easter garden,
   before the break of day,
   an angel came from heaven
   and rolled the stone away.
   When Jesus' friends came seeking,
   with myrrh and spices rare,
   they found the angels at the door,
   but Jesus was not there.

2. All in an Easter garden,
   where water lilies bloom,
   the angels gave their message
   beside an empty tomb:
   'The Lord is here no longer,
   come, see where once he lay;
   the Lord of life is ris'n indeed,
   for this is Easter day.'

835 Doug Marks-Smirchirch
© Right on the Mark Music/Copyright control

All of my heart, all of my soul,
all of my mind, all of my strength.

(Repeat)

With everything within me
I want to praise you, Lord.
I want to love you with all that I am,
and bring joy to your heart.

Last time:

Let me bring joy to your heart all of
my life.

836 Michael Forster (b. 1946)
© 1993 Kevin Mayhew Ltd.

1. All of the creatures God had made
   came to the ark, a big parade,
   walked up the gangplank, two by two,
   'Coo!' said the doves, 'it's a floating zoo!'

2. Ev'rything seemed to come in pairs,
   camels and dogs and big brown bears;
   Noah said to God, 'It's rather rough;
   one of the fleas would be quite enough.'

3. All huddled up in one small space,
   one of the dogs said, 'What a place!
   I haven't room to swing a cat!'
   'Well,' said the cat, 'thank the Lord for
       that!'

4. People are often like that, too,
   living in boxes, two by two.
   We have to learn to get along,
   just like the animals in this song.

837 18th century

1. As Jacob with travel
   was weary one day,
   at night on a stone
   for a pillow he lay;
   he saw in a vision
   a ladder so high
   that its foot was on earth
   and its top in the sky:

   Alleluia to Jesus who died on the tree,
   and has raised up a ladder of mercy for me,
   and has raised up a ladder of mercy for me.

2. This ladder is long,
   it is strong and well-made,
   has stood hundreds of years
   and is not yet decayed;
   many millions have climbed it
   and reached Zion's hill,
   and thousands by faith
   are climbing it still:

3. Come let us ascend!
   all may climb it who will;
   for the angels of Jacob
   are guarding it still:
   and remember, each step
   that by faith we pass o'er,
   some prophet or martyr
   has trod it before:

4. And when we arrive
   at the haven of rest
   we shall hear the glad words,
   'Come up hither, ye blest,
   here are regions of light,
   here are mansions of bliss.'
   O who would not climb
   such a ladder as this?

838 Original text: William James Kirkpatrick (1838-1921)
Alternative text, vs. 2 & 3: Michael Forster (b. 1946)
© *Alternative verses 2 and 3 1996 Kevin Mayhew Ltd.*

1. Away in a manger,
   no crib for a bed,
   the little Lord Jesus
   laid down his sweet head.
   The stars in the bright sky
   looked down where he lay,
   the little Lord Jesus,
   asleep on the hay.

2. The cattle are lowing,
   the baby awakes,
   but little Lord Jesus
   no crying he makes.
   I love thee, Lord Jesus!
   Look down from the sky,
   and stay by my side
   until morning is nigh.

3. Be near me, Lord Jesus;
   I ask thee to stay
   close by me for ever,
   and love me, I pray.
   Bless all the dear children
   in thy tender care,
   and fit us for heaven,
   to live with thee there.

An alternative version

1. Away in a manger,
   no crib for a bed,
   the little Lord Jesus
   laid down his sweet head.
   The stars in the bright sky
   looked down where he lay,
   the little Lord Jesus,
   asleep on the hay.

2. The cattle are lowing,
   they also adore
   the little Lord Jesus
   who lies in the straw.
   I love you, Lord Jesus,
   I know you are near
   to love and protect me
   till morning is here.

3. Be near me, Lord Jesus;
   I ask you to stay
   close by me for ever,
   and love me, I pray.
   Bless all the dear children
   in your tender care,
   prepare us for heaven,
   to live with you there.

839 Susan Sayers (b. 1946)
© *1986 Kevin Mayhew Ltd.*

1. Caterpillar, caterpillar,
   munching, munching,
   ate through a leaf or two,
   for caterpillar, caterpillar,
   munching, munching,
   didn't have a lot to do.
   But the leaves were very tasty,
   and there seemed a lot to spare,
   so caterpillar, caterpillar, went on
   munching, munching ev'rywhere.

Continued overleaf

2. Caterpillar, caterpillar,
   feeling sleepy,
   fixed up a silken bed.
   Then caterpillar, caterpillar
   climbed inside
   and covered up his sleepy head.
   In the dark he slept and rested
   as the days and nights went by,
   till on a sunny morning when the
   silk bed burst, he was a butterfly!

3. Butterfly, oh butterfly,
   a flitt'ring, flutt'ring;
   oh what a sight so see.
   And as the lovely butterfly
   was flutt'ring by,
   I heard him sing a song to me:
   'Oh I never knew God could do
   such a wondrous thing for me;
   for he took me as a caterpillar
   and he made a butterfly of me.'

841 John Henley (1800-1842)

1. Children of Jerusalem
   sang the praise of Jesus' name;
   children, too, of modern days,
   join to sing the Saviour's praise:

   *Hark! Hark! Hark! While children's voices
   sing. (x2)
   loud hosannas, loud hosannas, loud
   hosannas to our King.*

2. We are taught to love the Lord,
   we are taught to read his word,
   we are taught the way to heaven;
   praise for all to God be given:

3. Parents, teachers, old and young,
   all unite to swell the song;
   higher and yet higher rise,
   till hosannas reach the skies:

840 Estelle White (b. 1925)
© 1977 Kevin Mayhew Ltd.

1. 'Cheep!' said the sparrow
   on the chimney top,
   'All my feathers are known to God.'
   'Caw!' said the rook in a tree so tall,
   'I know that God gladly made us all.'

2. 'Coo!' said the gentle one,
   the grey-blue dove,
   'I can tell you that God is love.'
   High up above sang the lark in flight,
   'I know the Lord is my heart's delight.'

3. 'Chirp!' said the robin
   with his breast so red,
   'I don't want to work at all, yet I'm fed.'
   'Whoo!' called the owl in a leafy wood,
   'our God is wonderful, wise and good.'

842 Unknown

1. Come and praise the Lord our King,
   alleluia,
   come and praise the Lord our King,
   alleluia!

2 Christ was born in Bethlehem,
   Son of God and Son of Man.

3. He grew up an earthly child,
   in the world, but undefiled.

4. He who died at Calvary,
   rose again triumphantly.

5. He will cleanse us from our sin,
   if we live by faith in him.

843

Katherine K. Davis, Henry V. Onorati and Harry Simeone
© 1958 EMI Mills Music Inc./Delaware Music Corp

1. Come, they told me,
   pah-rum-pum-pum-pum!
   our new-born King to see,
   pah-rum-pum-pum-pum!
   Our finest gifts we bring,
   pah-rum-pum-pum-pum!
   to lay before the King,
   pah-rum-pum-pum-pum!
   Rum-pum-pum-pum!
   Rum-pum-pum-pum!
   So, to honour him,
   pah-rum-pum-pum-pum!
   when we come.

2. Baby Jesus,
   pah-rum-pum-pum-pum!
   I am a poor child too,
   pah-rum-pum-pum-pum!
   I have no gift to bring,
   pah-rum-pum-pum-pum!
   that's fit to give a King,
   pah-rum-pum-pum-pum!
   Rum-pum-pum-pum!
   Rum-pum-pum-pum!
   Shall I play for you,
   pah-rum-pum-pum-pum!
   on my drum?

3. Mary nodded,
   pah-rum-pum-pum-pum!
   The ox and lamb kept time,
   pah-rum-pum-pum-pum!
   I played my drum for him,
   pah-rum-pum-pum-pum!
   I played my best for him,
   pah-rum-pum-pum-pum!
   Rum-pum-pum-pum!
   Rum-pum-pum-pum!
   Then he smiled at me,
   pah-rum-pum-pum-pum!
   me and my drum.

844

Unknown

Dear child divine, sweet brother mine,
be with me all the day,
and when the light has turned to night
be with me still, I pray.
Where'er I be, come down to me
and never go away.

845

Michael Forster (b. 1946)
© 1997 Kevin Mayhew Ltd.

1. Do you ever wish you could fly like a bird,
   or burrow like a worm? Well, how absurd!
   Think of all the things that you can do
   and just be glad God made you 'you'!

2. Do you ever wish you could swim
      like a duck?
   Unless your feet are webbed you're
      out of luck!
   Think of all the things that you can do
   and just be glad God made you 'you'!

3. Do you ever wish you could run
      like a hare?
   Well, wishing it won't get you anywhere!
   Think of all the things that you can do
   and just be glad God made you 'you'!

4. Do you ever wish you could hang
      like a bat?
   There's really not a lot of fun in that!
   Think of all the things that you can do
   and just be glad God made you 'you'!

5. Do you ever wish – well, that's
      really enough!
   To wish away your life is silly stuff!
   Think of all the things that you can do
   and just be glad God made you 'you'!

846

Michael Forster (b. 1946)
© 1997 Kevin Mayhew Ltd.

Each of us is a living stone,
no one needs to stand alone,
joined to other living stones,
we're building the temple of God.

1. We're building, we're building
   the temple of God on earth,
   but it needs no walls or steeple,
   for we're making a house of greater worth,
   we're building it with people!

2. The stone that, the stone that
   the builders once cast aside
   has been made the firm foundation,
   and the carpenter who was crucified
   now offers us salvation.

847

Peter Watcyn-Jones
© 1978 Kevin Mayhew Ltd.

1. Ev'ry bird, ev'ry tree
   helps me know, helps me see,
   helps me feel
   God is love and love's around.
   From each river painted blue
   to the early morning dew
   this is love, God is love, love's around.

2. Ev'ry prayer, ev'ry song
   makes me feel I belong
   to a world filled
   with love that's all around.
   From each daybreak to each night,
   out of darkness comes the light,
   this is love, God is love, love's around.

3. Ev'ry mountain, ev'ry stream,
   ev'ry flower, ev'ry dream
   comes from God,
   God is love and love's around.
   From the ever-changing sky
   to a new-born baby's cry,
   this is love, God is love, love's around.

848

Michael Forster (b. 1946)
© 1997 Kevin Mayhew Ltd.

1. God sends a rainbow after the rain,
   colours of hope gleaming through pain;
   bright arcs of red and indigo light,
   making creation hopeful and bright.

Colours of hope dance in the sun,
while it yet rains the hope has begun;
colours of hope shine through the rain,
colours of love, nothing is vain.

2. When we are lonely, when we're afraid,
   though it seems dark, rainbows are made;
   even when life itself has to end,
   God is our rainbow, God is our friend.

3. Where people suffer pain or despair,
   God can be seen in those who care;
   even where war and hatred abound,
   rainbows of hope are still to be found.

4. People themselves like rainbows are made,
   colours of hope in us displayed;
   old ones and young ones, women
      and men,
   all can be part of love's great 'Amen'!

849

Michael Forster (b. 1946)
© 1993 Kevin Mayhew Ltd.

1. Goliath was big and Goliath was strong,
   his sword was sharp and his spear
      was long;
   he bragged and boasted but he was wrong:
   biggest isn't always best!

Biggest isn't always best!
Biggest isn't always best!
God told David, 'Don't be afraid,
biggest isn't always best!'

2. A shepherd boy had a stone and sling;
   he won the battle and pleased the King!
   Then all the people began to sing:
   'Biggest isn't always best!'

3. So creatures made in a smaller size,
   like tiny sparrows and butterflies,
   are greater than we may realise:
   biggest isn't always best!

850 Unknown

Hallulu, hallelu, hallelu, hallelujah;
we'll praise the Lord! *(Repeat)*
We'll praise the Lord, hallelujah! *(x3)*
We'll praise the Lord!

851 Christian Strover
© *Christian Strover/Jubilate Hymns*

1. Have you heard the raindrops
   drumming on the rooftops?
   Have you heard the raindrops
   dripping on the ground?
   Have you heard the raindrops
   splashing in the streams
   and running to the rivers all around?

   There's water, water of life,
   Jesus gives us the water of life;
   there's water, water of life,
   Jesus gives us the water of life.

2. There's a busy worker
   digging in the desert,
   digging with a spade that
   flashes in the sun;
   soon there will be water
   rising in the well-shaft,
   spilling from the bucket as it comes.

3. Nobody can live
   who hasn't any water,
   when the land is dry,
   then nothing much grows;
   Jesus gives us life if we drink
   the living water,
   sing it so that everybody knows.

852 Michael Forster (b.1946)
© *1997 Kevin Mayhew Ltd.*

Hee haw! Hee haw!
Doesn't anybody care?
There's a baby in my dinner
and it's just not fair!

1. Jesus in the manger,
   lying in the hay,
   far too young to realise he's getting in the
      way!
   I don't blame the baby,
   not his fault at all,
   but his parents should respect a donkey's
   feeding stall!

2. After all that journey,
   with my heavy load,
   did I ever once complain about the
      dreadful road?
   I can cope with backache,
   and these swollen feet.
   All I ask is some respect, and one square
      meal to eat.

3. 'Be prepared,' I told them,
   'better book ahead.'
   Joseph said, 'Don't be an ass,' and took a
      chance instead.
   Now they've pinched my bedroom,
   people are so rude!
   I can cope with that, but not a baby in
      my food!

853 Traditional

1. He's got the whole world in his hand. *(x4)*

2. He's got you and me, brother . . .

3. He's got you and me, sister . . .

4. He's got the little tiny baby . . .

5. He's got ev'rybody here . . .

854

Michael Forster (b.1946)
© 1993 Kevin Mayhew Ltd.

1. He was born in the winter in a draughty
     shed,
   and his cradle was a feeding trough where
     cattle fed.
   And the only kind of heating was the
     cattle's heavy breathing
   when they got too close for comfort to
     the baby's bed.

2. He was trained as a carpenter, his father's
     trade,
   but there's no one who remembers
     anything he made,
   for he left his friends and neighbours and
     his profitable labours,
   and he went to be a preacher who was
     never paid!

3. He was friends with the guilty, and he
     helped the poor,
   and he told them all that heaven has an
     open door,
   but the government said, 'Never! Better
     silence him for ever,
   just in case he starts a riot or a civil war.'

4. He was whipped by the soldiers at the
     city hall,
   and they nailed him to a wooden cross
     outside the wall.
   They ignored the people crying as they
     stood and watched him dying,
   then they took him down and buried
     him and said, 'That's all!'

5. He was back three days later, and his
     word is clear:
   that he means to live for ever and be
     always here.
   And the promise that he's giving is the
     joy of simply living
   in a world of truth and freedom where
     there's no more fear.

855

Hugh Mitchell
© 1973 Zondervan Corporation/Brentwood-Benson
Music Publishing

How did Moses cross the Red Sea?
How did Moses cross the Red Sea?
How did Moses cross the Red Sea?
How did he get across?
Did he swim? No! No!
Did he row? No! No!
Did he jump? No! No! No! No!
Did he drive? No! No!
Did he fly? No! No!
How did he get across?
God blew with his wind, puff, puff,
   puff, puff,
he blew just enough, 'nough, 'nough,
   'nough, 'nough,
and through the sea he made a path,
that's how he got across.

856

Brian Howard
© 1975 Mission Hills Music. Administered by CopyCare

1. If I were a butterfly,
   I'd thank you, Lord, for giving me wings,
   and if I were a robin in a tree,
   I'd thank you, Lord, that I could sing,
   and if I were a fish in the sea,
   I'd wiggle my tail and I'd giggle with glee,
   but I just thank you, Father,
       for making me 'me'.

   For you gave me a heart,
   and you gave me a smile,
   you gave me Jesus
   and you made me your child,
   and I just thank you, Father,
   for making me 'me'.

2. If I were an elephant,
   I'd thank you, Lord, by raising my trunk,
   and if I were a kangaroo,
   you know I'd hop right up to you,
   and if I were an octopus,
   I'd thank you, Lord, for my fine looks,
   but I just thank you, Father,
       for making me 'me'.

3. If I were a wiggly worm,
   I'd thank you, Lord, that I could squirm,
   and if I were a billy goat,
   I'd thank you, Lord, for my
       strong throat,
   and if I were a fuzzy wuzzy bear,
   I'd thank you, Lord, for my fuzzy
       wuzzy hair,
   but I just thank you, Father,
       for making me 'me'.

857 Michael Forster (b. 1946)
© 1993 Kevin Mayhew Ltd.

1. I'm black, I'm white, I'm short, I'm tall,
   I'm all the human race.
   I'm young, I'm old, I'm large, I'm small,
   and Jesus knows my face.

   The love of God is free to ev'ryone,
   free to ev'ryone, free to ev'ryone.
   The love of God is free, oh yes!
   That's what the gospel says.

2. I'm rich, I'm poor, I'm pleased, I'm sad,
   I'm ev'ryone you see.
   I'm quick, I'm slow, I'm good, I'm bad,
   I know that God loves me.

3. So tall and thin, and short and wide,
   and any shade of face,
   I'm one of those for whom Christ died,
   part of the human race.

858 Alan J. Price
© 1992 Daybreak Music Ltd.

Isn't it good to be together,
being with friends old and new?
Isn't it good?
The Bible tells us Jesus our Lord is here too!
Isn't it good to be together,
being with friends old and new?
Isn't it good?
The Bible tells us Jesus our Lord is here too!

He's here!
By his Spirit he's with us. He's here!
His promise is true. He's here!
Though we can't see him, he's here
for me and you. *(Repeat)*

859 Spiritual

It's me, it's me, it's me, O Lord,
standing in the need of prayer. (Repeat)

1. Not my brother or my sister,
   but it's me, O Lord,
   standing in the need of prayer. *(Repeat)*

2. Not my mother or my father . . .

3. Not the stranger or my neighbour . . .

860 Ian Smale
© 1989 Kingsway's Thankyou Music

I will click my fingers, clap my hands,
stamp my feet and shout hallelujah!
Then I'll whistle as loud as I can.
(Whistle)
I'm happy I'm a child of the Lord.

861 Susan Warner (1819-1885)

1. Jesus bids us shine
   with a pure, clear light,
   like a little candle
   burning in the night.
   In this world is darkness:
   so we must shine,
   you in your small corner,
   and I in mine.

2. Jesus bids us shine,
   first of all for him;
   well he sees and knows it,
   if our light grows dim.
   He looks down from heaven
   to see us shine,
   you in your small corner,
   and I in mine.

Continued overleaf

3. Jesus bids us shine,
   then, for all around,
   many kinds of darkness
   in the world abound:
   sin, and want and sorrow;
   so we must shine,
   you in your small corner,
   and I in mine.

862 Walter John Mathams (1853-1931)
© Oxford University Press

1. Jesus, friend of little children,
   be a friend to me;
   take my hand, and ever keep me
   close to thee.

2. Teach me how to grow in goodness
   daily as I grow;
   thou hast been a child, and surely
   thou dost know.

3. Never leave me nor forsake me,
   ever be my friend;
   for I need thee from life's dawning
   to its end.

863 Michael Forster (b. 1946)
© 1993 Kevin Mayhew Ltd.

Jesus had all kinds of friends,
so the gospel stories say.
Jesus had all kinds of friends,
and there's room for us today.

1. Some were happy, some were sad,
   some were good and some were bad,
   some were short and some were tall,
   Jesus said he loved them all.

2. Some were humble, some were proud,
   some were quiet, some were loud,
   some were fit and some were lame,
   Jesus loved them all the same.

3. Some were healthy, some were sick,
   some were slow, and some were quick,
   some were clever, some were not,
   Jesus said he loved the lot!

864 Margaret Cropper (1886-1980)
© Stainer & Bell Ltd.

1. Jesus' hands were kind hands, doing
      good to all,
   healing pain and sickness, blessing
      children small,
   washing tired feet and saving those who
      fall;
   Jesus' hands were kind hands, doing
      good to all.

2. Take my hands, Lord Jesus, let them
      work for you;
   make them strong and gentle, kind in all
      I do;
   let me watch you, Jesus, till I'm gentle
      too,
   till my hands are kind hands, quick to
      work for you.

865 Graham Kendrick (b. 1950)
© 1986 Kingsway's Thankyou Music

1. Jesus put this song into our hearts, *(x2)*
   it's a song of joy no one can take away.
   Jesus put this song into our hearts.

2. Jesus taught us how to live in
      harmony, *(x2)*
   diff'rent faces, diff'rent races, he made
      us one.
   Jesus taught us how to live in harmony.

3. Jesus turned our sorrow into dancing, *(x2)*
   changed our tears of sadness into rivers
      of joy.
   Jesus turned our sorrow into a dance.

866 Spiritual

1. Kum ba yah, my Lord, kum ba yah. *(x3)*
   O Lord, kum ba yah.

2. Someone's crying, Lord,
      kum ba yah, *(x3)*
   O Lord, kum ba yah.

3. Someone's singing, Lord,
      kum ba yah, *(x3)*
   O Lord, kum ba yah.

4. Someone's praying, Lord,
      kum ba yah, *(x3)*
   O Lord, kum ba yah.

867
Eric Boswell. *© 1959 Chapell Music Ltd.*

1. Little donkey, little donkey,
   on the dusty road,
   got to keep on plodding onwards
   with your precious load.
   Been a long time, little donkey,
   through the winter's night;
   don't give up now, little donkey,
   Bethlehem's in sight.

   Ring out those bells tonight,
   Bethlehem, Bethlehem,
   follow that star tonight,
   Bethlehem, Bethlehem.
   Little donkey, little donkey,
   had a heavy day,
   little donkey, carry Mary safely on her way.

2. Little donkey, little donkey,
   on the dusty road,
   there are wise men, waiting for a
   sign to bring them here.
   Do not falter, little donkey,
   there's a star ahead;
   it will guide you, little donkey,
   to a cattle shed.

868
Christopher Massey (b. 1956)
© 1999 Kevin Mayhew Ltd.

1. Little Jesus, sleep away, in the hay,
   while we worship, watch and pray.
   We will gather at the manger,
   worship this amazing stranger:
   little Jesus born on earth,
   sign of grace and human worth.

2. Little Jesus, sleep away, while you may;
   pain is for another day.
   While you sleep, we will not wake you,
   when you cry we'll not forsake you.
   Little Jesus, sleep away,
   we will worship you today.

869
Traditional Czech carol
trans. Percy Dearmer (1867-1936)
© Oxford University Press. Used by permission

1. Little Jesus, sweetly sleep, do not stir;
   we will lend a coat of fur;
   we will rock you, rock you, rock you,
   we will rock you, rock you, rock you;
   see the fur to keep you warm,
   snugly round your tiny form.

2. Mary's little baby sleep, sweetly sleep,
   sleep in comfort, slumber deep;
   we will rock you, rock you, rock you,
   we will rock you, rock you, rock you;
   we will serve you all we can,
   darling, darling little man.

870
Unknown

Our God is so great,
so strong and so mighty,
there's nothing that he cannot do.
(Repeat)

1. The rivers are his,
   the mountains are his,
   the stars are his handiwork too.

2. He's called you to live for him
   ev'ry day
   in all that you say and you do.

871
Traditional

1. O when the saints go marching in,
   O when the saints go marching in,
   I want to be in that number
   when the saints go marching in.

Continued overleaf

2. O when they crown him Lord of all . . .

3. O when all knees bow at his name . . .

4. O when they sing the Saviour's praise . . .

5. O when the saints go marching in . . .

872 Unknown, based on Acts 3

Peter and John went to pray,
they met a lame man on the way.
He asked for alms
and held out his palms
and this is what Peter did say:
'Silver and gold have I none,
but such as I have I give thee,
in the name of Jesus Christ of Nazareth,
rise up and walk!'
He went walking and leaping
and praising God,
walking and leaping and praising God.
'In the name of Jesus Christ of Nazareth,
rise up and walk.'

873
Percy Dearmer (1867-1936)
based on Carey Bonner (1859-1938)
© *Oxford University Press. Used by permission*

1. Praise him, praise him,
   all his children praise him!
   He is love, he is love.
   Praise him, praise him,
   all his children praise him!
   He is love, he is love.

2. Thank him, thank him,
   all his children thank him!
   He is love, he is love.
   Thank him, thank him,
   all his children thank him!
   He is love, he is love.

3. Love him, love him,
   all his children love him!
   He is love, he is love.
   Love him, love him,
   all his children love him!
   He is love, he is love.

4. Crown him, crown him,
   all his children crown him!
   He is love, he is love.
   Crown him, crown him,
   all his children crown him!
   He is love, he is love.

874 Unknown, based on Genesis 6:4

Rise and shine,
and give God his glory, glory, (x3)
children of the Lord.

1. The Lord said to Noah,
   'There's gonna be a floody, floody.'
   Lord said to Noah,
   'There's gonna be a floody, floody,'
   Get those children out of the muddy,
     muddy,
   children of the Lord.'

2. So Noah, he built him,
   he built him an arky, arky,
   Noah, he built him,
   he built him an arky, arky,
   built it out of hickory barky, barky,
   children of the Lord.

3. The animals, they came on,
   they came on, by twosies, twosies,
   animals, they came on, they came on,
   by twosies, twosies,
   elephants and kangaroosies, roosies,
   children of the Lord.

4. It rained and poured
   for forty daysies, daysies,
   rained and poured
   for forty daysies, daysies,
   nearly drove those animals
     crazies, crazies,
   children of the Lord.

5. The sun came out
   and dried up the landy, landy,
   sun came out
   and dried up the landy, landy,
   ev'rything was fine and dandy, dandy,
   children of the Lord.

6. If you get to heaven
   before I do-sies, do-sies,
   you get to heaven
   before I do-sies, do-sies,
   tell those angels I'm coming
      too-sies, too-sies,
   children of the Lord.

875
Diane Davis Andrew
adapted by Geoffrey Marshall-Taylor
© 1971 Celebration/Kingsway's Thankyou Music

1. Thank you, Lord, for this new day, *(x3)*
   right where we are.

   Alleluia, praise the Lord, (x3)
   right where we are.

2. Thank you, Lord, for food to eat, *(x3)*
   right where we are.

3. Thank you, Lord, for clothes to wear, *(x3)*
   right where we are.

4. Thank you, Lord, for all your gifts, *(x3)*
   right where we are.

876
David Arkin
© 1970 Earl Robinson and David Arkin
Templeton Publishing Co.

1. The ink is black, the page is white,
   together we learn to read and write,
   to read and write;
   and now a child can understand
   this is the law of all the land,
   all the land;
   the ink is black, the page is white,
   together we learn to read and write,
   to read and write.

2. The slate is black, the chalk is white,
   the words stand out so clear and bright,
   so clear and bright;
   and now at last we plainly see
   the alphabet of liberty,
   liberty;
   the slate is black, the chalk is white,
   together we learn to read and write,
   to read and write.

3. A child is black, a child is white,
   the whole world looks upon the sight,
   upon the sight;
   for very well the whole world knows,
   this is the way that freedom grows,
   freedom grows;
   a child is black, a child is white,
   together we learn to read and write,
   to read and write.

4. The world is black, the world is white,
   it turns by day and then by night,
   and then by night;
   it turns so each and ev'ry one
   can take his station in the sun,
   in the sun;
   the world is black, the world is white,
   together we learn to read and write,
   to read and write.

877 Unknown

1. The wise man built his house
   upon the rock, *(x3)*
   and the rain came tumbling down.
   And the rain came down
   and the floods came up,
   the rain came down
   and the floods came up, *(x2)*
   and the house on the rock stood firm.

Continued overleaf

2. The foolish man built his house
   upon the sand, *(x3)*
   and the rain came tumbling down.
   And the rain came down
   and the floods came up,
   the rain came down
   and the floods came up, *(x2)*
   and the house on the sand fell flat.

878
Michael Forster (b. 1946)
© 1997 Kevin Mayhew Ltd.

The world is full of smelly feet,
weary from the dusty street.
The world is full of smelly feet,
we'll wash them for each other.

1. Jesus said to his disciples,
   'Wash those weary toes!
   Do it in a cheerful fashion,
   never hold your nose!'

2. People on a dusty journey
   need a place to rest;
   Jesus says, 'You say you love me,
   this will be the test!'

3. We're his friends, we recognise him
   in the folk we meet;
   smart or scruffy, we'll still love him,
   wash his smelly feet!

879
Doreen Newport
© 1969 Stainer & Bell Ltd.

1. Think of a world without any flowers,
   think of a world without any trees,
   think of a sky without any sunshine,
   think of the air without any breeze.
   We thank you, Lord, for flow'rs and trees
       and sunshine,
   we thank you, Lord, and praise your
       holy name.

2. Think of a world without any animals,
   think of a field without any herd,
   think of a stream without any fishes,
   think of a dawn without any bird.
   We thank you, Lord, for all your living
       creatures,
   we thank you, Lord, and praise your
       holy name.

3. Think of a world without any people,
   think of a street with no one living there,
   think of a town without any houses,
   no one to love and nobody to care.
   We thank you, Lord, for families and
       friendships,
   we thank you, Lord, and praise your
       holy name.

880
Traditional

This little light of mine,
I'm gonna let it shine, (x3)
let it shine, let it shine, let it shine.

1. The light that shines is the light of love,
   lights the darkness from above,
   it shines on me and it shines on you,
   and shows what the power of love can do.
   I'm gonna shine my light both far
       and near,
   I'm gonna shine my light both bright
       and clear.
   Where there's a dark corner in this land,
   I'm gonna let my little light shine.

2. On Monday he gave me the gift of love,
   Tuesday peace came from above.
   On Wednesday he told me to have
       more faith,
   on Thursday he gave me a little
       more grace.
   On Friday he told me to watch and pray,
   on Saturday he told me just what to say,
   on Sunday he gave me the pow'r divine
   to let my little light shine.

881

Eric Reid (1936-1970)
© Copyright 1969 Stainer & Bell Ltd.

1. Trotting, trotting through Jerusalem,
   Jesus, sitting on a donkey's back,
   children waving branches, singing:
   'Happy is he that comes in the name of
      the Lord!'

2. Many people in Jerusalem
   thought he should have come on a
      mighty horse
   leading all the Jews to battle:
   'Happy is he that comes in the name of
      the Lord!'

3. Many people in Jerusalem
   were amazed to see such a quiet man
   trotting, trotting on a donkey:
   'Happy is he that comes in the name of
      the Lord!'

4. Trotting, trotting through Jerusalem,
   Jesus, sitting on a donkey's back;
   let us join the children singing:
   'Happy is he that comes in the name of
      the Lord!'

882

Paul Booth
© 1977 Stainer & Bell Ltd.

1. When God made the garden of creation,
   he filled it full of his love;
   when God made the garden of creation,
   he saw that it was good.
   There's room for you, and room for me,
   and room for ev'ryone:
   for God is a Father who loves
      his children
   and gives them a place in the sun.
   When God made the garden of creation,
   he filled it full of his love.

2. When God made the hamper of
      creation,
   he filled it full of his love;
   when God made the hamper of creation,
   he saw that it was good.
   There's food for you, and food for me,
   and food enough for all,
   but often we're greedy, and waste
      God's bounty,
   so some don't get any at all.
   When God made the hamper of creation,
   he filled it full of his love.

3. When God made the fam'ly of creation,
   he filled it full of his love;
   when God made the fam'ly of creation,
   he saw that it was good.
   There's love for you, and love for me,
   and love for ev'ryone:
   but sometimes we're selfish, ignore
      our neighbours,
   and seek our own place in the sun.
   When God made the fam'ly of creation,
   he made it out of his love.

4. When God made us stewards of creation,
   he gave us his vision to share;
   when God made us stewards of creation,
   our burdens he wanted to bear.
   He cares for you, he cares for me,
   he cares for all in need:
   for God is a Father who loves his children,
   no matter what colour or creed.
   When God made us stewards of creation,
   he gave us his vision to share.

883

Peter Smith (b.1938)
© 1978, 1979 Stainer & Bell Ltd. and the Trustees for
Methodist Church Purposes.

1. When Jesus the healer passed through
      Galilee,
   heal us, heal us today!
   The deaf came to hear and the blind
      came to see.
   Heal us, Lord Jesus!

Continued overleaf

2. A paralysed man was let down through a
    roof,
  heal us, heal us today!
  His sins were forgiven; his walking
    the proof.
  Heal us, Lord Jesus!

3. The death of his daughter caused Jairus
    to weep,
  heal us, heal us today!
  The Lord took her hand and he raised
    her from sleep.
  Heal us, Lord Jesus!

4. When blind Bartimaeus cried out to the
    Lord,
  heal us, heal us today!
  His faith made him whole and his sight
    was restored.
  Heal us, Lord Jesus!

5. The twelve were commissioned and set
    out by twos,
  heal us, heal us today!
  To make the sick whole and to spread the
    good news.
  Heal us, Lord Jesus!

6. The lepers were healed and the demons
    cast out;
  heal us, heal us today!
  Now lame leap for joy and the dumb
    laugh and shout;
  heal us, Lord Jesus!

7. There's still so much sickness and
    suffering today;
  heal us, heal us today!
  We gather together for healing,
    and pray:
  heal us, Lord Jesus!

884 Paul Booth
© Paul Booth/CopyCare

1. Who put the colours in the rainbow?
  Who put the salt into the sea?
  Who put the cold into the snowflake?
  Who made you and me?
  Who put the hump upon the camel?
  Who put the neck on the giraffe?
  Who put the tail upon the monkey?
  Who made hyenas laugh?
  Who made whales and snails and quails?
  Who made hogs and dogs and frogs?
  Who made bats and cats and rats?
  Who made ev'rything?

2. Who put the gold into the sunshine?
  Who put the sparkle in the stars?
  Who put the silver in the moonlight?
  Who made Earth and Mars?
  Who put the scent into the roses?
  Who taught the honey-bee to dance?
  Who put the tree inside the acorn?
  It surely can't be chance!
  Who made seas and leaves and trees?
  Who made snow and winds that blow?
  Who made streams and rivers flow?
  God made all of these!

885 Unknown

Zacchaeus was a very little man,
and a very little man was he.
He climbed up into a sycamore tree,
for the Saviour he wanted to see.
And when the Saviour passed that way,
he looked into the tree and said,
'Now Zacchaeus, you come down,
for I'm coming to your house for tea.'

886

Sue McClellan, John Paculabo and Keith Ryecroft
© 1972 Kingsway's Thankyou Music

Zip bam boo, zama lama la boo,
there's freedom in Jesus Christ. (Repeat)
Though we hung him on a cross
till he died in pain,
three days later he's alive again.
Zip bam boo, zama lama la boo,
there's freedom in Jesus Christ.

1. This Jesus was a working man
   who shouted 'Yes' to life,
   but didn't choose to settle down,
   or take himself a wife.
   To live for God he made his task,
   'Who is this man?' the people ask.
   Zip bam boo, zama lama la boo,
   there's freedom in Jesus Christ.

2. He'd come to share good news from God
   and show that he is Lord.
   He made folk whole who trusted him
   and took him at his word.
   He fought oppression, loved the poor,
   gave the people hope once more.
   Zip bam boo, zama lama la boo,
   there's freedom in Jesus Christ.

3. 'He's mad! He claims to be God's Son
   and give new life to men!
   Let's kill this Christ, once and for all,
   no trouble from him then!'
   'It's death then, Jesus, the cross for you!'
   Said, 'Man, that's what I came to do!'
   Zip bam boo, zama lama la boo,
   there's freedom in Jesus Christ.

INDEXES

INDEXES

Index of Authors, Translators and Sources of Text

Scriptural Index

ACTS

GALATIANS

EPHESIANS

Index of Uses

Hope and Assurance

Intercession and Petition

Joy and Thanksgiving

Index of Hymns for the Revised Common Lectionary

Index of First Lines

ACKNOWLEDGEMENTS

The publishers wish to express their gratitude to the following for permission to include copyright material in this publication. Details of copyright owners are given above each individual hymn.

The Executors of J. Arlott, The Old Presbytery, Alderney, Guernsey, GY9 3TF.

Ascent Music, PO Box 263, Croydon, Surrey, CR9 5AP. International copyright secured. All rights reserved.

Ateliers et Presses de Taizé, F-71250 Taizé Communauté, France.

Bucks Music, Onward House, London, W8 7TQ.

Revd E. Burns, Christ Church Vicarage, 19 Vicarage Close, Fulwood, Preston, PR2 8EG.

Executors of the late G. B. Caird, Mansfield College, Oxford, OX13 3TF.

The Church Pension Fund, 445 Fifth Avenue, New York, NY 10016, USA.

Continuum Publishing, Wellington House, 125 Strand, London, WC2R 0BB.

Council for World Mission, Ipalo House, 32-34 Great Peter Street, London, SW1 2DB.

CopyCare Ltd, PO Box 77, Hailsham, East Sussex, BN27 3EF, on behalf of Hope Publishing; Birdwing Music/EMI Christian Music Publishing; Birdwing Music/BMG Songs Inc./Ears to Hear Music/EMI Christian Music Publishing; Paul Booth; Bud John Songs/EMI Christian Music Publishing; The Rodeheaver Co.; Deep Fryed Music/Word Music Inc./Maranatha! Music; HarperCollins Religious; Lillenas Publishing Co.; Maranatha! Music; Mercy/Vineyard Publishing; Mission Hills Music; PDI Worship; Straightway/Mountain Spring/EMI Christian Music Publishing; Word Music/Maranatha! Music; Word of God Music; Word's Spirit of Praise Music.

Elizabeth Cosnett, 34 Meadway, Wavertree, Liverpool, L15 7LZ.

The Revd Amos Cresswell, 2 Sage Park Road, Braunton, Devon, EX33 1HH.

Mrs M. Cross, Honeybee House, Brigsteer, Kendal, Cumbria, LA8 8AP.

J. Curwen & Sons, 8/9 Frith Street, London, W1V 5TZ.

Margaret Davies, 23 Round Barrow Close, Colerne, Chippenham, Wilts, SN14 8EF.

Daybreak Music Ltd, Silverdale Road, Eastbourne, East Sussex, BN20 7AB. All rights reserved. International copyright secured.

Dr E. F. Downs, 26 Dinmore Road, Selkirk, New York, NY 12158, USA.

The Rt Revd Timothy Dudley-Smith, 9 Ashlands, Ford, Salisbury, Wilts, SP4 6DY.

Mr Desmond Dunkerley, 23 Haslemere Road, Southsea, Hants, PO4 8BB.

Durham Music Ltd, 11 Uxbridge Street, London, W8 7TQ.

Faber Music Ltd, 3 Queens Square, London, WC1N 3AU.

GIA Publications Inc, 7404 S. Mason Avenue, Chicago, IL 60638, USA.

Revd M. J. Hancock, 55 Huntspill Road, London, SW17 0AA.

Mrs Freda Head, 2 St Wilfrid's Court, St Wilfrid's Green, Hailsham, East Sussex, BN27 1BW.

David Higham Associates Ltd, 5-8 Lower John Street, Golden Square, London, W1F 9HA.

The Estate of D. W. Hughes, 10 Tan-y-Gaer, Abersoch, Gwynedd, LL53 7LY.

Hymns Ancient & Modern, Canterbury Press, St Mary's Works, St Mary's Plain, Norwich, NR3 3BH.

IMP Ltd, Griffin House, 161 Hammersmith Road, London, W6 8BS.

IQ Music Ltd, Orchard House, Broad Street, Tylers Green, Cuckfield, West Sussex, RH17 5DZ.

Dr Ivor H. Jones, 1 Greestone Terrace, Lincoln, LN2 1PR.

Revd Richard Jones, 35 Davies Road, West Bridgford, Nottingham, NG2 5JE.

Jubilate Hymns, Southwick House, 4 Thorne Park Road, Chelston, Torquay, TQ2 6RX.

Kingsway's Thankyou Music, PO Box 75, Eastbourne, East Sussex, BN23 6NW, on behalf of Kingsway's Thankyou Music; Peter West/Integrity's Hosanna! Music; Darlene Zschech/Hillsong Publishing (for UK and Europe); Integrity's Praise! Music (for UK only); Scripture in Song (for UK only); Integrity's Hosanna! Music (for UK only); Celebration (for Europe and British Commonwealth); Tanya Riches/Hillsong Publishing (for UK and Europe); Stuart K. Hine/SK Hine Trust (excluding North and South America); Reuben Morgan/Hillsong Publishing (for UK and Europe); Curious? Music UK (excluding USA).

Leosong Copyright Service Ltd, 13 Berners Street, London, W1T 3LH.

Helen MacNicol's Trust, 133 Lauriston Place, Edinburgh, EH3 9JN.

Make Way Music, PO Box 263, Croydon, Surrey, CR9 5AP. International copyright secured. All rights reserved.

McCrimmon Publishing Co. Ltd, 10-12 High Street, Gt Wakering, Southend-on-Sea, Essex, SS3 0EQ.

Methodist Publishing House, 20 Ivatt Way, Peterborough, PE3 7PG.

Caryl Micklem, Wells House, 11 Chapmangate, Pocklington, York, YO42 2AY.

Novello & Co, 8/9 Frith Street, London, W1V 5TZ.

OCP Publications, 5536 NE Hassalo, Portland, OR 97213, USA.

Mr Herbert O'Driscoll, 1000 Jasmine Avenue, Victoria, BC Canada, V8Z ZP4.

Oxford University Press, Great Clarendon Street, Oxford, OX2 6DP.

Mrs E. V. Pilcher, 94 Willingdon Blvd, Toronto, Canada, M8X 2H7.

Restoration Music Ltd, PO Box 356, Leighton Buzzard, Beds, LU7 8WP.

Mr Alexander Scott, 4 Anthony Close, Colchester, Essex, CO4 4LD.

Sovereign Lifestyle Music Ltd, PO Box 356, Leighton Buzzard, Beds, LU7 8WP.

Sovereign Music UK, PO Box 356, Leighton Buzzard, Beds, LU7 8WP.

SPCK, Holy Trinity Church, Marylebone Road, London, NW1 4DU.

Stainer & Bell Ltd, PO Box 110, Victoria House, 23 Gruneisen Road, London, N3 1DZ.

Mr Michael Thwaites, 49 Cobby Street, Campbell, ACT 2612, Australia.

Josef Weinberger Ltd, 12-14 Mortimer Street, London, W1N 7RD.

Wild Goose Resource Group, Iona Community, 840 Govan Road, Glasgow, G51 3UU.

World Student Christian Federation, 5 Route des Morillons, 1218 Grand-Saconnex, Geneva, Switzerland.